Competitiveness in the Real Economy

Competitiveness in the Real Economy

Value Aggregation, Economics and Management in the Provision of Goods and Services

RUI VINHAS DA SILVA
ISCTE Business School, Portugal

Routledge
Taylor & Francis Group

LONDON AND NEW YORK

First published in paperback 2024

First published 2013 by Gower Publishing

Published 2016 by Routledge
4 Park Square, Milton Park, Abingdon, Oxon OX14 4RN

and by Routledge
605 Third Avenue, New York, NY 10158

Routledge is an imprint of the Taylor & Francis Group, an informa business

Gower Applied Business Research
Our programme provides leaders, practitioners, scholars and researchers with thought provoking, cutting edge books that combine conceptual insights, interdisciplinary rigour and practical relevance in key areas of business and management.

British Library Cataloguing in Publication Data
A catalogue record for this book is available from the British Library.

The Library of Congress has cataloged the printed edition as follows:
Silva, Rui Vinhas da.
    Competitiveness in the real economy : value aggregation, economics and management in the provision of goods and services / by Rui Vinhas da Silva.
        pages cm
    Includes bibliographical references and index.
    ISBN 978-1-4094-6122-7 (hardback) – ISBN 978-1-4094-6123-4 (ebook) – ISBN 978-1-4094-6124-1 (epub)
    1. Competition. 2. Leadership. 3. Entrepreneurship. I. Title.

    HD41.S549 2013
    338.6048 – dc23

                                                                    2013020031

ISBN: 978-1-4094-6122-7 (hbk)
ISBN: 978-1-03-283747-5 (pbk)
ISBN: 978-1-315-57316-8 (ebk)

DOI: 10.4324/9781315573168

Contents

List of Figures

List of Tables

About the Author

Rui Vinhas da Silva has honours degrees in Business Administration and Economics from York University in Toronto, Canada, an MBA from Aston Business School and a PhD and Post-Doctorate from Manchester Business School. Before joining ISCTE in April 2010, he was an Associate Professor at Manchester Business School having joined as a member of faculty in 1998. He has held visiting professorial appointments at the University of São Paulo and ISCTE Business School in Lisbon throughout this period, and has taught regularly and supervised research on MBA, Executive and Doctoral programs at MBS and other institutions.

Vinhas da Silva has since 1998 been actively involved in senior executive training and consultancy, through Manchester Business School. These included regular appointments as lecturer on senior executive training programs in blue-chip organizations, including PWC in New Jersey, KPMG, Lukoil, British senior military officers (AMAC), senior executives from the former Soviet Union (TACIS) and senior government officials in Malaysia.

Vinhas da Silva has research interests in the areas of national competitiveness and economics, country branding, corporate reputation and country of origin effects on the competitiveness of nations having published books and journal articles in these and other areas.

Preface

September 11, 2009

On this day an email was circulated to faculty members at Manchester Business School, calling their attention to an article published the week before in *The New York Times* by Nobel Laureate, Paul Krugman. His article is reproduced below:

> ### Mistaking Mathematical Beauty for Economic Truth
> *Few economists saw our current crisis coming, but this predictive failure was the least of the field's problems. More important was the profession's blindness to the very possibility of catastrophic failures in a market economy ... the economics profession went astray because economists, as a group, mistook beauty, clad in impressive-looking mathematics, for truth ... economists fell back in love with the old, idealized vision of an economy in which rational individuals interact in perfect markets, this time gussied up with fancy equations ... Unfortunately, this romanticized and sanitized vision of the economy led most economists to ignore all the things that can go wrong. They turned a blind eye to the limitations of human rationality that often lead to bubbles and busts; to the problems of institutions that run amok; to the imperfections of markets – especially financial markets – that can cause the economy's operating system to undergo sudden, unpredictable crashes; and to the dangers created when regulators don't believe in regulation ... When it comes to the all-too-human problem of recessions and depressions, economists need to abandon the neat but wrong solution of assuming that everyone is rational and markets work perfectly.*
>
> The New York Times, September 2, 2009,
> Paul Krugman, Nobel Laureate

1

Is It Only about Working Harder? ... or the Other Side of GDP

Gross domestic product (GDP) is the universal metric for the measurement of the wealth of a nation. It is a widely accepted measure, and despite certain ideas that periodically emerge on the need to think about alternative methods for measuring economic growth, GDP continues to be a barometer accepted by everyone. Some proponents of alternative, more inclusive measures, that would possibly constitute better indicators of the true level of national economic welfare, suggest that GDP is a crude and simplistic measure, that fails to take into account such fundamental notions as the equitable redistribution of wealth, widespread access to education and healthcare, the ability to provide minimum cover for the disenfranchised, or more radically its failure in incorporating more subjective criteria, including metrics on social solidarity or even happiness.

The World Economic Forum (WEF) produces its Global Competitiveness Report annually. National competitiveness is a good indicator of an economy's potential for wealth creation, and an excellent barometer of its ability to provide decent standards of living and adequate levels of human and social development for national citizens. The 2012/2013 ranking of the most competitive nations globally indicates the following reality:

Table 1.1   The Global Competitiveness Index of the WEF (2012/13)

Ranking	Country
1st	Switzerland
2nd	Singapore
3rd	Finland
4th	Sweden

Table 1.1   The Global Competitiveness Index of the WEF (2012/13) *continued*

Ranking	Country
5th	Netherlands
6th	Germany
7th	USA
8th	United Kingdom
9th	Hong Kong SAR
10th	Japan
11th	Qatar
12th	Denmark
13th	Taiwan, China
14th	Canada
15th	Norway
16th	Austria
17th	Belgium
18th	Saudi Arabia
19th	Korea, Rep.
20th	Australia

Source: World Economic Forum (2012)

The competitiveness of the UK economy has shown slight variations over a period of little more than a decade, ranking consistently in the top 15 most competitive economies in the world, and often in the top ten in the global rankings. The UK has been progressively improving its global competitive position over the last four years.

Table 1.2   UK global competitiveness trends 2000–2012

Year	Ranking
2000	8th
2001	7th
2002	11th
2003	15th
2004	11th
2005	9th
2006	10th

2007	9th
2008	12th
2009	13th
2010	12th
2011	10th
2012	8th

Source: World Economic Forum (2000–2012)

What is interesting about the analysis of the Global Competitiveness Report of the WEF is that it shows a clear link between national competitiveness, exports and the attraction of foreign direct investment (FDI) rankings. This means that, in broad terms, the nations that rank highest in the competitiveness tables are also the nations that export more, and the ones that attract more FDI into their economies. Crucially these are also the nations that show better levels of social and human development, measured by such key indicators as low infant mortality rates and better levels and standards of education and healthcare. If this is the case, it then follows that in identifying the simultaneous drivers of national economic competitiveness, of value aggregation to exports, and of the attraction of FDI into an economy, national governments and policy-makers may be acting in the only way possible to guarantee the sustainability of models of national competitiveness and the viability of the livelihoods of these societies to the levels that they have become accustomed to.

If the countries that excel in competitive performance, export value and ability to attract FDI tend to be the same, then it stands to reason that the identification of a typology of behaviour crossing a variety of characteristics that intersect those nations will provide an excellent roadmap for the definition of a model of economic competitiveness that stands a chance of success in a ever more complex and dynamic global competitive environment. That said it is crucial that any archetype of national competitiveness is adjusted to the idiosyncrasies of the country in question, its history, traditions, level of industrial development, culture and economy.

GDP is calculated at factor costs as the sum of the remuneration of factors of production, labour, capital and land or at market prices through the formula of C+I+G+X-M (consumption + investment + government spending + exports – imports). It is worth retaining this formula for the discussion that ensues on productivity and its impact on the competitiveness of nations. GDP is also the universally accepted measure for the wealth of a nation.

Despite recurrent calls for alternative metrics, GDP continues to be the universal barometer for national wealth creation measured over a period of a year. Proponents of complementary metrics to GDP suggest the need for more inclusive measures that are better reflections of the state of development of nations and in particular are able to reveal great inequalities in income distribution. Some believe GDP to be a crude and simplistic measure that fails to take into account the equitable redistribution of wealth, widespread access and the level and standards of education and the universal provision of healthcare to members of society.

GDP is a universal barometer of the material well-being of a nation. For good or for worse, GDP is the measure of wealth of a nation, and the terms economic growth or recession refer to positive or negative variations in GDP over a period of time. Two consecutive quarters of negative economic growth equate to a technical recession. The component of exports in the GDP formula and the aggregation of value to exported goods and services are given emphasis in this chapter. The million dollar question is then why have some countries become so good at playing the value aggregation game whilst others are still busy competing on price for just about every product in every sector of economic activity? A little story perhaps illustrates the difference between these two types of countries.

This is the story of two pairs of shoes, both made in a little town in the north of Portugal. The reason why the shoes are distinguished for the purposes of this story is not because they are in any significant way different. In fact technically they are exactly the same pair of shoes. In effect there is nothing to tell them apart. Both pairs of shoes share identical trajectories until just before they reach the consumer, the very same path from production to consumption, with one crucial exception. One pair of shoes is exported directly from Portugal to the UK, where it finds its way into a high street footwear retailer in London, Manchester or Glasgow. The other identical pair of shoes goes through a last but crucial stage. The manufacturing company in Portugal, very aware of the importance attributed to the origin of branded shoes by consumers in key export markets, and in particular in the British market, decides to do something about the origin of the Portuguese pair of shoes.

Shrewd manufacturers, only too knowledgeable of the fact that consumers in more affluent and discriminatory markets, believe that it is better for branded foreign shoes to enter the British market with a more resounding label, claiming perhaps an Italian origin, and will do everything to ensure that the shoe is branded with a name and logo that are Italian, or at least sound and look Italian. It is desirable that the consumer in the country of destination of the pair of shoes in question perceives a more noble origin to the shoe. To refer to countries as more or less noble may be inappropriate and even derogatory, and may indeed in this context have negative connotations and biases associated with it, but it corresponds to the harsh reality of preconceived notions and country stereotyping that prevails in contemporary economies.

This was certainly the case with Portuguese shoe manufacturing up until recently, but there has been a remarkable turnaround in the business over the last five years or so. The industry has begun to understand the value chain of the global branded shoe sector and has decided to progress downstream in it placing key players that create high-quality manufacturers' brands that incorporate exceptional design, changing the landscape with respect to the perceptions and stereotypes held by foreign constituencies of their best branded shoes. What is still missing is a strong retail presence, key for establishing brand notoriety and goodwill and for the management and control of the most valuable links in value chains in the global shoe business.

The story however, up until not too long ago, was that Portuguese origin was not a good cue for shoes or most other products with perhaps the exception of port wine. This had nothing to do with the low intrinsic quality of Portuguese products, quite the contrary. Shoes and many other Portuguese exports have traditionally been of very high quality indeed. The tragedy is that only very seldom does the consumer know about the origin of most products, which would otherwise enable for the making of associations between consumption experiences and the country of origin of the product in question. This was true with shoes, but it was also true with wine up until recently. The wine sector is also beginning to improve its reputation abroad.

Continuing with our little story, irrespective of the fact that Portuguese firms manufacture shoes of the highest calibre, our organization had to ship its shoes over to a small manufacturing facility, somewhere in the north of Italy, where an Italian logo would be stuck on the pair of shoes. In reality, it is extremely important for the consumer in key export markets, and particularly in the more affluent and sophisticated markets, but not only, to believe that the pair of shoes is indeed Italian or has a brand name that at least has an Italian phonetic ring to it. In effect the only task performed on the shoe that has any remote connection with Italy is a label of an Italian brand that is juxtaposed on the shoe. Two pairs of shoes, one Italian, the other one Portuguese, both made in Portugal, the same number of man hours put on both, same leather and design, summing all of this up, the very same shoe. Or is it?

The Portuguese shoe is sold at a certain price. The other Portuguese shoe, claiming Italian origin with a well-recognized brand originating from this country, and sometimes not even that, retails at prices that are three, four times and even higher than what discerning consumers are willing to pay for the unbranded Portuguese shoe on the high street of any major British city.

There is therefore something in the formation or creation of value that goes beyond the functional content that has been built into a product. It somehow means that individuals in a consumerist society, in a market economy, where there is disposable income, will buy as a function of the intangibles in products, and are more than willing to pay more for goods that they perceive to provide them with what, in economics jargon, is known as higher utility. These motivations for purchase often have little to do with the more obvious physical expressions of products and their more tangible cues, and instead relate to other dimensions of supply, including the country of origin and reputational capital built into the good or service in question.

In the light of a globally competitive landscape, typified by the dominance of low-cost production, the difficulty of incumbent players in the more developed economies in maintaining sustainable competitive advantages in labour-intensive sectors of economic activity, and their inability in aggregating value to exported goods and services is, along with sovereign debt, perhaps the most poignant of problems afflicting national economies today.

This means that sectors of these economies that are unable to achieve distinction and high perceived value in the minds of discerning and sophisticated consumers in key target export markets will find it difficult to withstand the test of a very competitive global environment for labour-intensive economic activities. As a result, these sectors of the economy will have to shift ever more towards a knowledge-based, capital-intensive economic paradigm, as well as work on shrewd brand-building strategies, which presupposes understanding their target markets well, and developing a cosmopolitan view of the world that encompasses a plethora of aesthetic expressions, as many as there are cultures, and cultures within cultures, and how all of these are reflected in heterogeneous consumption decision-making.

Firms in developed economies, that do not yet benefit from a positive reputational capital of goodwill, find it very difficult to create next to their more affluent foreign constituencies the psychological willingness to pay a premium for unbranded products which, in terms of sheer technical performance, are often at the level of equivalent branded German or Japanese products. Many of these products do not lose in comparison to Italian or French products on design and style too.

The problem with these products is that they are not German or Japanese and therefore cannot claim the technological reputation and clout of products with these origins. They are also not French or Italian and are therefore not perceived in the same class when it comes to aesthetics, image or design. This theme will be further developed when analysing country of origin stereotypes and their effects on external consumer perceptions held about products that emanate from them, irrespective of whether these products are in any way related or not. Country of origin effects are also approached here in the context of labour productivity issues and their impact on the global competitiveness of nations.

The difference between a group of nations with indistinctive country brands, and the likes of Germany, the UK, or France resides in the reputational capital that the latter have accumulated next to worldly consumers, built over decades of positive experiences with exceptional branded goods. Crucially this reputational capital is not restricted to a single product or even a group of products in a particular sector, but it instead traduces a collection of competencies and know-how that transfers over to products that are often unrelated to the goods and services that the exporting nation has acquired a reputation for.

Critically, consumers in foreign markets make these associations and reflect them onto their structure of preferences and finally into their willingness to pay price premiums for products that they perceive as offering higher utilities. The mechanism is one where high-quality products, with exquisite design and aesthetics that coincide with those of targeted foreign consumers, act as conduits for the establishment of a strong tradition of technical virtuosity or style, a priceless heritage, that is then carried over to other totally separate and unrelated products, both technologically but also functionally, in terms of design, or by way of any other possible comparison.

A good example of this would be the purchase of a lawnmower or indeed any other product for which technical content, albeit a tangible feature of the good in question, does not constitute a major criterion in the buying decision-making process. For most buyers anywhere in the world faced with the option of buying a local brand, or indeed a brand claiming any other less reputable origin, or a German equivalent instead, the buying decision under conditions of high disposable income and low price sensitivity will most probably err on the side of the German brand.

The reason is a simple one, and has nothing to do with lawnmowers. It has to do with the fact that for consumers worldwide, the high quality and performance of German products, as well as their excellent engineering, has been consolidated and is ever-present in their subconscious minds and is naturally reflected on their preferences, irrespective of whether it is lawnmowers or automobiles that they are buying.

Country of origin stereotypes supersede mere image effects and of course need to be mounted on decades of excellence and consistent delivery of exceptionally high-quality products and services. Underpinning country reputation and favourable stereotyping there needs to be a sustained delivery of well-engineered automobiles, electronics goods or any other products that can act as metaphors for the industrial prowess and technocratic competencies of those engaged in their manufacturing.

This means that virtually anything that incorporates technology and advanced know-how acts as a conduit for the development of a favourable reputation for the country in question, positive cues that are then transferred over to every other product category emanating from that country, and that which end up benefitting from this aura of technological sophistication, without them ever having done anything to deserve this distinction. All of this is then neatly packaged under the banner of great consumer brand names such as Mercedes or Porsche, or other household industrial and retail brands like Sony or Mitsubishi.

Finally, and faced with the weight of evidence, the global consumer ends up buying a German lawnmower in the comfort that its reliability and technical superiority will not disappoint him. Of course none of this was even supposed to have mattered as technology was not an important product characteristic and a buying differentiator to begin with. In the end however it makes all the difference. The same goes for Italian or French products in relation to design, fashion or gastronomy and Japanese miniaturization and electronics. Beyond the hard criteria that configure and shape buying decision-making processes, so-called country of origin effects and their effective management have become critical to countries' export strategies.

Going back to the shoe analogy, the pair of shoes found their way into an Italian factory where a label was stuck on it. In reality nothing happened to the shoe, none of its significant features were altered. Its design had remained unchanged. But its appeal had changed next to consumers who could tell the difference. There was no addition of technology or any meaningful change in the aesthetic characterization of the product, yet the value aggregated to it by a logo claiming a valuable origin had perhaps become its most significant asset.

This is critical in that any value augmentation here refers in its entirety to perception and not to any noticeable addition to the product and its tangible features. It is in the end all about consumer perceptions, the generalized views that consumers in the country of destination of exported goods have of products emanating from a certain country as a function of their origin, which acts as a cue for the purchase of other unrelated products claiming the same origin.

Value aggregation to goods and services is unbelievably important to the balance of trade of modern nations, yet it receives such minute attention by economists and policy-makers alike, and by many who have responsibilities on worker productivity issues, people who are decisive in the shaping of the decisive debate on national competitiveness and productivity and how to improve on both. In essence, value aggregation is detected only in the willingness of consumers to pay more for a product as a result of higher perceived value.

This higher utility may be totally unrelated to intrinsic or functional value and just derive in its entirety from reputational goodwill towards a product, corporate or country brand. In these harsh times, where many developed nations are undergoing severe economic difficulties, and in the light of cut-throat low-cost global competition, this reputational capital constitutes a crucial and much sought after dimension of national competitiveness.

Lower cost structures favour the delocalization of production to low-wage economies stimulated by generous schemes and widespread fiscal incentives. Municipalities and national governments often support companies who want to settle locally and develop their activities in limited geographic regions, in an attempt to attract foreign investment and stimulate the generation of local employment. Extraordinary conditions are granted to companies who set up operations locally.

Many of these multinational organizations often take advantage of these favourable conditions, setting up shop when fiscal incentives and subsidies exist, only to leave the country as soon as they find other governments who provide them with even better conditions. Much of this is often justified under the umbrella of cost rationalization and the permanent search for lower labour cost structures that lead to the production of cheap goods and services.

The strategic approach of these organizations has often coincided with the internationalization agenda of the wealthy economies where they overwhelmingly originate from. The delocalization of many of these economic activities away from the more developed economies into the less developed nations would occur independently of lower wage structures in the latter, as they correspond to activities that for every reason have not been tolerated within the boundaries of the wealthier nations for some time.

Economic sectors of activity that are less palatable to contemporary societies and their concerns, namely those with unacceptable negative externalities in the more developed economies, are often farmed out to the less fortunate nations, befitting of a definition nothing short of industrial dumping. These less developed nations in turn accept these industries with open arms, strapped as they are of any form of foreign investment and in dire need of employment creation.

The fallout of these economic activities would not be acceptable by the standards and low tolerance thresholds of modern, environmentally-sensitive, educated and conscious societies. Many of these industrial activities would fail to meet the stringent legal and regulatory criteria of the more developed economies. Legislation in the latter nations is indeed much stricter than the more relaxed regulatory environment in the all too welcoming countries of destination of undesirable industrial manufacturing activities.

There is of course an inherent cynicism to all of this. When things go drastically wrong, as was the case of the industrial disaster in Bhopal in India in the 1980s, this is unequivocally construed as an appalling tragedy, but nevertheless one that happened in India, not in the backyard of one of the developed economies, in the US, the UK or in any other European Union

(EU) country. There is a subtle yet significant difference and, albeit politically incorrect and cynical, it is nevertheless true as an argument for delocalization of less politically and environmentally palatable industrial activities that simply would not be allowed or tolerated back home.

Country of origin effects are stereotypes, positive or negative, held by external constituencies and namely foreign consumers about certain countries that get transferred over to the products that emanate from those countries. These stereotypes constitute an aura about the country in question that descends upon its products in the form of positive or negative impressions held by foreign consumers often based on very little or untrue bits and pieces of disconnected information.

The reverse of this suggests that by being exposed consistently to branded experiences that can be traced back to a particular country, the consumer will form an opinion, positive or negative, about that country. The combined collective perceptions of external stakeholders will constitute that nation's reputation. This reputational halo, when positive, has been proved to be a phenomenal asset to national competitiveness, through the propensity of consumers to prefer brands claiming a reputable origin to the detriment of others whose origin is unknown, or over which hang negative stereotypes and bad feelings. When these preconceived notions about a country are negative they often render the intrinsic qualities of products emanating from those nations as little more than useless.

Product intangibles are then the unique set of characteristics that surround a core product function. These traits or characteristics have no physical expression but they are probably the most important clues to what the product can really do for the consumer and are decisive contributors to the shaping of buying decision-making processes in contemporary consumer societies. Above all, country of origin effects, when positive, allow the manufacturer and then the retailer to benefit from subsidiary value over and above the basic core functionality of the manufactured product without needing to objectively add anything tangible to it.

A country's good or bad reputation, the way in which products benefit or are severely hampered by positive or negative connotations of national origin constitute the intangible elements that are more difficult to build, but they are also potentially the most important source of relevant differentiation for a country's economy. Those nations that have refined country reputation management to an art form have seen its positive results in terms of aggregated value to exported goods and services and its impact manifested on increased and sustainable national competitiveness.

The word sustainable is appropriate here as these intangible cues, although difficult to build at first, when attained are subsequently impossible to copy, layered as they are on very deep cultural and idiosyncratic foundations, anchored on political maturity, industrial tradition and other societal traits that cannot be replicated. If foreign consumers are more than willing to pay price premiums for a slice of that, then that is the fulfilment of the holy grail of national branding.

The productivity of a sector of economic activity is a ratio, and has both a numerator and a denominator. As an example, when it is said that a southern European worker is less productive than the average worker in the EU, what is implied is that, given an identical allocation of production resources (capital and labour), the southern European worker generates less output than his northern European counterpart. However, and this is key, what the southern European worker generates is not necessarily less output, or even output of a lesser quality, what he fails to do is to generate for the same quantity of output, the same value as his northern European counterpart.

The failure to aggregate value to output may in itself have nothing to do with the southern European worker, his work ethic or even the organization of labour in southern European work contexts. It may relate to lower worker competencies, but it may also have to do with the failure of entrepreneurs in these economies to position goods and services in the minds of foreign consumers as being more valuable than their functional content suggests, or more likely a combination of the two effects, low labour skills and insular entrepreneurs with no strategic vision and commercial acumen.

No value added to goods and services may also result from the absence of a positive country halo upstream that impedes products from benefiting downstream at consumer level from positive perceptions held about a country and the goods that emanate from it. This makes it very difficult to guarantee the aggregation of value to goods and services irrespective of their quality and other tangible characteristics associated with them. The absence of a positive country reputation, and even negative country of origin stereotypes, will withdraw perceived value from a country's offer.

Conversely, a government policy myopia, as well as a collective failure of the institutions and of the entrepreneurial class in acknowledging the critical role of marketing and reputation functions in building notorious and valuable country, corporate and product brands, traduce an absence of a strategic roadmap for nations and organizations and their competitiveness in the world stage and a lowering of the standards of living of individuals in society. In cut-throat globally competitive environments for just about every sector of economic activity, positive country of origin cues make all the difference.

The productivity of any national economy is defined as the ratio at market prices of the output value resulting from economic activity in that nation over the inputs that have been incurred in generating that output value measured by the remuneration of the factors of production utilized in the creation of that output value. With this as background, let us once again go back to the scenario described earlier of the Portuguese shoe industry, which is paradigmatic of much of what goes on in any industry anywhere that has not been able to establish a clear, distinct and valuable reputation.

In the Portuguese shoe story, António makes shoes in a medium-sized factory outside the small-town surroundings of São João da Madeira. This is not far from Oporto, where the world renowned vineyards used for the making of exceptional port wine cut through a breath-taking landscape of rare beauty. What for many decades could best be termed as an insipid cottage footwear industry has flourished into a dynamic export niche in the leather and shoe sector, with a plethora of undifferentiated players struggling to keep up with demand for their good-quality products. This was indeed the case for decades but things began to change a while ago.

It is about time that we introduce another character into the story – John, the British retailer. He sold António's shoes in London or Manchester at prices that were five or six times higher than those he paid António for the same pair of shoes. If both John's and António's activities were comparable, it would be possible to contrast their productivities. However they operate at different stages of the footwear value chain, their activities are distinct and therefore their productivities cannot be compared.

When this thinking is extrapolated to the realities of northern European industry, what is observable is that these economies have for more than a century now been subcontracting manufacturing activities that are located upstream in supply chains to southern European economies, including Portugal.

These activities generate comparatively little value and the more developed economies have no interest in them.

The story however is not yet completed. Giuseppe, an Italian known for his exquisite taste, refined aesthetics and genuine style, knowing of António's reputation for making exceptional quality shoes, decided some time ago to work with him and indeed is known for making regular orders of shoes from the Portuguese footwear manufacturer. António is delighted with the work he keeps getting from his exquisite Italian buyer. This is regular stuff and it keeps the small manufacturing facility up north going, providing employment to António, his entire family and ten other people, as well as earning him a reasonable upkeep which he could never hope to attain by doing anything else within the São João da Madeira vicinity.

Things are not what they used to be and in reality life has never been easy in this neck of the woods, but it is particularly bad now with the economic crisis and cut-throat global competition. António has no qualms or hesitations. He exports everything that he produces to whoever is willing to pay for his high-quality shoes made by artisans that have learnt their trade over decades, building a tradition of exceptional quality shoe manufacturing that has been passed on from generation to generation.

Giuseppe however has other ideas for the shoes that he has imported from Portugal. Being a well-established name in the shoe business, a reputation that he acquired from the times when his grandfather was a shoe artisan, he decides to do something about the shoes that he buys from António, adding a final yet crucial stage to the whole process. Giuseppe decides to add his brand name to the shoes purchased from Portugal. He has a factory, or more aptly named, a labelling infrastructure up in Lombardy which he uses just for that very purpose. He is now ready to export what by now are high-quality Italian shoes to the best household names all over the world, in London, Paris or New York. In London Giuseppe's shoes retail at a price seven to ten times higher than what he originally disbursed.

At this point it is worth reminding those with a lower attention span and less propensity for recalling details that António's and Giuseppe's shoes are the very same pair of shoes. The only difference, albeit a significant one for the purpose and outcome of the story, is that Giuseppe's shoes have his initials engraved on them on a well-designed and very refined logo. This is a logo that tells a story. In everything else the shoes are exactly the same. The same leather was used in the manufacturing process, the same number of worker hours were required in making the shoes. The shoes were manufactured by the same workers too. They have the same design. In effect it would be virtually impossible to tell one pair of shoes apart from the other, were it not for Giuseppe's shining logo.

It could be argued that this story ends with everyone happy ever after. António is able to shift all of his production through the system. His excellent-quality products find their way into the very top retail shops in Europe and North America. Current times are harsh and to be able to have regular work from top houses such as Giuseppe's is a tall order. Many footwear manufacturers around António have failed miserably, having gone bankrupt, as their customary clients began looking for new suppliers in other countries. These suppliers, typically from the Far East, were able to outcompete European suppliers on price with products whose quality, although not comparable, had improved significantly in recent years.

In these emerging economies footwear manufacturers were able to operate at substantially lower costs of labour and did not need to abide by the stringent rules and regulations of European labour law. This naturally trimmed down their cost structure, making them incomparably more competitive in terms of the prices at which they were able to supply their footwear products to key target markets. These are national economies that, from António's perspective, present a serious threat to the survival of the incumbents in the footwear business markets, where he has operated for decades. These thriving emerging players adopt what António characterizes as unfair competitive practices that make life for local manufacturers very hard indeed.

António believes that these low-cost manufacturers that have come out of emerging economies at breath-taking speed over the last 20 years need not comply with the strict practices and legislation at a level of rigour akin to anything that exists in Europe regarding labour practices and law. António in turn has to abide by stringent labour rules and regulations. Pan-European legislation is incomparably more rigorous on the enforcement of such ethical matters as child labour and the rights of workers than anything these companies in emerging economies have to comply with, and António perceives this to be an unfair advantage for these economies who have their work cut out when it comes to being competitive on price in the global markets.

These players originating from the emerging economies in the Far East operate in António's economic space and seek the same consumers in key markets, which he had for years taken for granted. The UK was one such market. He now needs to cope with cut-throat competition from these new players who have unlimited access to cheap labour. As a corporate citizen of the EU he has to adhere to and strictly comply with rigorous legislation and regulations on just about everything that relates to the labour process. Of course it is also a moral imperative for him to do so, particularly when it comes to issues of the calibre of child labour, but António fails to see how morality may concede him a sustainable competitive advantage in the global market.

The way he sees it, these emerging economies and the obscure characters that populate them could not care less about child labour, the rights of workers, the rights of women in the workplace or the environment. In any event, even if they were to claim to care and to pay careful attention to all of that, there would be no way of objectively monitoring any of it would there? How can anyone possibly scrutinize with any degree of plausibility labour practices in such far away manufacturing hubs as China or India? António feels that this is very unfair indeed.

These countries also engage in what is a de facto dumping of manufactured goods into European markets, trading products at prices that, although not below their costs of production as production costs are indeed low in these economies, are well below those of equivalent and competing products in the markets which they are destined for. For António this is a good definition of an unfair advantage and unacceptable competition.

António spent his late teens in Leeds, reading for an undergraduate university degree in Textile Engineering, sent by his father who, utterly convinced of the merits of British higher education, decided to ship the lad over to learn about state-of-the-art of textile engineering and production. In Leeds he learnt everything there was to know about technology and the optimization of production processes, worker efficiencies and productivity, and was indoctrinated into the idea of the constant pursuit of quality in manufacturing, which he was to subsequently adapt to the footwear business. He became aware of the latest technologies in his field and was trained to always be on the lookout for better processes and methodologies and generally identifying cheaper ways of doing things. António learnt the production side of the business inside out. This is why he is a very happy character in this story as the orders keep flowing in from the retail buyers. He has never known any other world.

Now, if António is happy, then Giuseppe is laughing all the way to the bank. In times that he never knew, in his great grandfather's generation, people around his hometown built a reputation for manufacturing very high-quality fashion clothing and footwear. The local market began to be too small for Giuseppe's forefathers, and orders began to come in from England and the USA, where Giuseppe's great grandfather's name had acquired a bit of a reputation due to the magnificent quality of the products that he manufactured, along with his other Italian artisan friends in the Lombardy region. As he came to the realization that he was unable to satisfactorily deal with so many orders alone, he decided to subcontract some of the activities entailed in shoe manufacturing to local artisans who were also more than happy to lay their hands on any work that came their way. When the business eventually came into Giuseppe's hands, shoe manufacturing had for many years been a distant concern for the family and a far cry from its core business activity. All production had been farmed out to emerging economies where workers were paid much lower wages, whilst some specialist activities continued to be subcontracted locally to very skilled artisans.

Giuseppe's family was adamant however on retaining a crucial asset, what undoubtedly was to become the most important asset in the value chain of the shoe business, the company's brand name associated with footwear. The family name had over the years become synonymous with high quality and the reputation of the brand had crossed borders, having established itself, in the minds of affluent and avid consumers worldwide, who were only too keen to dispose of unreasonable sums of money to pay for the goodwill and reputation that Giuseppe's shoes carried next to affluent consumers all over the world.

Giuseppe's greatest concern now was to be alert to every possible danger to the integrity of his company's reputation. He had to envisage every possible way in which his brand could potentially be damaged. In so doing he had to monitor his suppliers carefully for quality, ensuring a zero defect policy, and preferably this had to be done at source next to the supplier. Quality control mechanisms were installed and exercised at source with manufacturers who worked in strict compliance with the Italian brand's stringent requirements.

Giuseppe would later progress to a situation where over and beyond the scrutiny and monitoring of all aspects of product quality and the definition and compliance with concrete specifications, he would also exercise strict control over such critical features as innovation and design ideas. In addition he would ensure that compliance with delivery schedules and responsiveness to requests was kept by the supplier, by working closely with him and developing close personal relationships with that particular person, and later with his son or daughter which he had seen growing up. More than business partners, these were friends.

From Giuseppe's viewpoint the role of the manufacturer would virtually be rendered as just that of a provider of goods, with no autonomy on any of the key dimensions of whatever it was that made consumers eventually prefer Giuseppe's branded shoes. Everything was stipulated in minute detail, and it was up to the producer to manufacture products according to strict retail buyer specifications.

This was a way of distancing the manufacturer from the end consumer, a shrewd and clever move as in this and many other sectors of economic activity, it was to be he who would end up controlling the brand that would stand to dictate the terms of engagement in this business and control the links of the supply chain that effectively generated more value. Not only could Giuseppe generate more value by controlling links in the value chain downstream next to the consumer, the control over those links also meant that the competitive position of incumbent players was more sustainable than upstream in the same value chain where incumbents were easily dislodged by virtue of imitation of whatever sustained their competitive angle.

The manufacturer again had no autonomy on critical issues of product design or innovation content in the production process. It also wasn't his prerogative to question or interpret the ideas that emanated from the market. In the textile and garment sector there was an acronym for this. It was called CMT, meaning cut, make and trim. The manufacturer was limited to cutting, making and trimming in a deliberate attempt to emptying his activities of any remote possibility of economic value augmentation.

Our friend Giuseppe is by now a very happy man indeed, as he has built a name for himself and his company over many years, anchored on the heritage of his forefathers, to the point where the family name is today synonymous with value and high quality in the retailing of shoes and leather products. It is that name that allows Giuseppe to charge whatever prices he wishes for shoes carrying the family brand name.

As for John, the British retailer, any recollection of manufacturing, or of a thriving textile and clothing sector, was by now a mere memory, from the times of the industrial revolution in England, and now not more than a stereotype held by foreigners of British contemporary life. In effect, by the middle and towards the end of the last century, there were already few manufacturing sites or textile mills in operation around the Manchester or Leeds areas at least in comparison to the once thriving burst of industrial activity in the area.

From a very early stage it became abundantly clear that these activities had to be farmed out to countries that were more than capable of manufacturing these straightforward products with recourse to labour-intensive means at substantially lower costs. This was the economically rational and logical thing to do as these emerging economies offered much lower labour cost structures to manufacturing processes that were essentially labour-intensive. They enjoyed endless supplies of cheap labour, and it was explicit from early economic theory that economies should specialize in sectors of economic activity where they held comparative advantages. Their passage from agrarian into basic industrial economies was for these nations a much more recent phenomenon too.

John was required, as an astute and experienced retailer, to find great products emanating from anywhere around the world to cater to the affluent and discerning British consumer, who could choose from a plethora of alternatives for every kind of product available and functional benefit sought, to satisfy just about every real or latent need imaginable. With the emergence of a consumerist society, sufficient numbers of people began to have disposable income that allowed them choice, but they also had little time, and so it became all the more important that organizations would be able to create clear and distinct imprints in peoples' minds with their market offers. This is where branding and brands came in.

The globalization of sources of supply meant that the opportunity presented itself for the consumer to discern between alternative offers in the market. This had never happened before. The incumbent retail model, which essentially consisted of putting product out to the market hoping that people would purchase it, had its days well and truly numbered. Reputed and well-established retail organizations, carrying prestigious household names, including C&A and Woolworths who had been around for decades, ended up vanishing from the British retail scene. The department store model of doing business that had been pursued for decades, where fashion was sold like toasters, was to be their downfall.

The incumbent paradigm in the fashion business was replaced by the quick response models introduced by then newcomers Spanish Zara, Italian Diesel or Swedish H&M. Their angle was that of cheap fashion, but it was also fashion with a short time-span, in accordance with the erratic and volatile times and contemporary societal values, where change is the only constant.

These recent arrivals into the British retail scene had the advantage of understanding the nature and characteristics of demand better, and used the latest mechanisms and technology to refine the scrutiny of customer demand to a fine art. By introducing the concept of fast-fashion, these retailers were also forced to develop the art of manipulating consumer persuasion to new heights, and at times, as was the case with Zara, they did not have to spend much on advertising to do it. The story went that about a decade ago the average punter would walk into a Zara store in London 17 times a year. The industry average was four times.

By setting new trends and copying what celebrities were wearing and bringing that to the masses at affordable prices, these new retail formats were able to shift the incumbent retail paradigm towards the induction of a consumer, fast-fashion frenzy downstream at retail store level, with a corresponding imperative of quick response in manufacturing upstream. Emerging fashion retailers learnt to set the trends themselves, and that was a departure from the established way.

John is of course also a happy man. Having incurred the risks that are inherent to dealing with changing consumer preferences and aesthetics, he is nevertheless the only one privileged enough to have direct contact and access to the consumer. He is in a much better position than anyone else of hearing the truth from the horse's mouth, the consumer, who is really the only one whose opinion truly matters in this most complex of games. In reality, John is, of all those occupying valuable links in this supply chain, the only one who is able to monitor in a more capable and systematic way what people want at all times.

Having concluded that all characters in this short story are happy in the end, some of them are indeed happier than others. John is a happy man because he controls hand and foot a crucial and valuable part of the business. He is close to the consumer. Profit margins are also much higher at John's end of the value chain. António is happy because in adverse economic times, felt by all, he manages not only to survive, but to do much better than that, he maintains a regular flow of orders from retail buyers in traditional export markets. Not everyone around São João da Madeira can claim to do that.

Giuseppe has managed to fine-tune his business to minimize production or retail risk. He runs a sophisticated intermediary operation and all that he needs to worry about is to ensure that the status quo is kept on a family brand that has a history, an established tradition and a rock solid reputation. He needs to focus on nurturing the brand and enhancing its image next to its most important constituencies, suppliers and customers, ensuring that none of his stakeholders, both internal and external, denigrates the brand or causes it any harm. This is why he is very careful with his choice of suppliers, preferring to maintain close and longstanding relationships with them even when they are not the cheapest source.

Damage to the corporate brand's reputation can occur in a variety of ways. Problems could arise with the quality of products brought into the market and hence the need to monitor manufacturing processes closely. Quality control therefore needs to be exercised at source, next to suppliers and inside production processes. There potentially exist a series of threats to the reputation of Giuseppe's corporate brand that could emanate, for example, from the use of celebrities, endorsing the brand as part of the company's communications strategy. He is very aware of all of that as in his early years his father had sent him over to Manchester but in his case to read management. He ended up studying for an MBA at Manchester Business School, where it rained every day. He never knowingly crossed paths with António who was around the same time enduring the cold across the Pennines.

Giuseppe knows of course that it is crucial that the brand values are constantly fed downward to the retail client through a constant flow of exceptional products, and the consistent provision of memorable experiences. He does sell shoes, but the stories that they tell need to be nurtured and kept contemporary. There is always the chance that the core values by which the organization and its brands are recognized become dated and lose relevance, but in the end Giuseppe's concerns fade by comparison to those of António.

António does not know it yet but he is in a very uncomfortable situation. He survives in a very competitive environment, where he has to constantly come up with reasons for ensuring retail buyer preference for his products to the detriment of those that emanate from the myriad of other suppliers of identical products that crowd the sector. This cut-throat competitive environment forces

António to be in constant search of competitive advantages, seeking the best production methods around, that lead to the best-quality products, and he needs to do all of this whilst acknowledging the importance of maintaining exceptional relationships with his business clientele. These business-to-business relationships are elusive and loyal customers can pretty much cancel orders and switch suppliers at short notice. They can buy from other suppliers in Portugal, or more likely from other emergent nations such as China or India, where prices of comparable goods are such that António simply cannot afford to compete. Even Giuseppe can in the end cancel his orders from António if he fails to be competitive on price.

In reality, there is nothing about the nature of António's work that may stop anyone from entering the market and replicate both products and processes, particularly in what concerns the more labour-intensive stages of manufacturing. There is nothing unique about these processes and, within reasonable parameters of quality, anyone can imitate the work and do it whilst incurring substantially lower labour costs and consequently lower total costs of production. There aren't any technological or knowledge barriers that cannot be overcome with a modicum of persistence and patience. António's competitors in China certainly have that. As the retail client provides the design ideas and stipulates product specifications, the manufacturer is limited to complying with those. António's position is in this sense precarious.

The tale above may be best summed up as follows: The characters in this short story are John, António and Giuseppe. They are all fictional yet they are all absolutely real as metaphors for explaining the dynamics of modern national competitiveness in contemporary economies. The delocalization of economic activities that are less valuable within an economic sector to regions of the world that are in dire need of foreign investment and that witness strong pressures on local employment creation is not a recent phenomenon.

These less developed economies are sought for their relatively low labour cost structures and because there is of course an incomparably more relaxed legislative environment regulating the more controversial aspects of economic activity, including environmentally-sensitive sectors and investments made in them. These economic sectors are usually frowned upon by the more educated echelons in the affluent societies who do not want to have controversial economic activities in their own backyard and within sight.

These environmentally-sensitive sectors of the economy embody industrial manufacturing activities and processes whose outcome potentially jeopardizes the fine balance of local environments. Whilst being politically sensitive, and consequently needing to be farmed out to nations who are only now witnessing the emergence of some rudimentary form of industrial activity, these activities are also typically less regulated in new environments that are tolerant of everything under the sun.

What indeed does go on is a kind of subcontracting of economic activity to less developed countries who struggle to survive. These countries do not appear favourably in any competitiveness table of national economies and their best brands will not show up on the Interbrand top 100 rank of the best global brands. These are countries that, from the viewpoint of sophisticated and savvy consumers, do not possess the power to appeal, or attract custom to their more sophisticated products, when there are any, precisely due to their dubious or unknown origin. Consumers would not recognize them.

These are also countries whose citizens struggle to survive, never mind have the financial clout, to distinguish between alternative brands of products performing identical functions. However these are also countries whose societal make-up configures acute social asymmetries, with the aspirational upper echelons possessing both the disposable income and the desire to buy reputable brand names, signifying an opportunity for the notorious and valuable brands of the developed economies. The poor and the disenfranchised on the other hand find it difficult to survive with a modicum of dignity, but this is not first and foremost in the concerns of the capitalist system and the market economy.

These countries are not known for anything, good or bad, and tragically from a country branding perspective they are non-entities, which means that when bringing their products into the global market they have at best a positioning that is neutral next to their most important constituencies, affluent consumers in developed economies. These elites in economically developed countries are willing to pay price premiums that are totally independent of the total costs of production of these goods, in the quest for the satisfaction of sought benefits, in line with the value system of the affluent lifestyles in which they live.

Different facets of lifestyle shape consumer preferences and correspond to different manifestations of consumption. Successful organizations are the ones that are able to tap effectively into the determinants of consumer behaviour in these markets. They achieve that by developing corporate and product brands that pop up as top of mind names in consumer buying decision-making processes across a range of products and areas of consumption. More often than not, these brands originate from countries with well-established reputations, whose image is surrounded by an aura of elitism that transfers over to the products that emanate from them. These are countries with brands. They are also branded countries.

The emergence of economies such as China, India, Pakistan, Turkey and others, which by virtue of their quick learning, very flexible legal frameworks on labour issues, including dubious and less, if at all, scrutinized child labour practices, has meant that these nations have been able to develop an offer of manufactured quality products and place them in the more developed and sophisticated markets at very competitive prices.

This has meant a tremendous headache for the incumbent players, in what remains of the more labour-intensive sectors in the developed economies in Europe, that have simply been unable to compete on the basis of price. Key players originating from these emerging nations arrived on the global scene anchored on a competitive paradigm whose pillars reside on incomparably low labour cost structures, whilst consistently delivering functionally equivalent products, albeit with debateable levels of quality. They are however quickly catching up.

In addition, products that have been brought into the more affluent and sophisticated European markets over the last couple of decades or so are consistently competitively priced, rendering untenable the competitive position of European low-cost manufacturers. In particular, those less resourceful or imaginative producers, who have not been able to build successful networks with key retail buyers in desirable target markets, that have been relaxed on matters related to the development of close ties with their retail customer base, and whose competitive angle has traditionally been based on price, suffer more than anyone. European labour-intensive manufacturing sectors, and in particular those who were left stuck in the middle between a position of low-cost leadership, which is untenable, and relevant differentiation, which is based on excellent marketing and branding and virtually non-existent in these cases, will find it impossible to survive.

Differentiation here is less about technological superiority or ephemeral advantages on tangible product features, but more related to the promotion of a special kind of emotional difference, anchored on strong and valuable brands, that in turn command price premiums for products perceived as superior at some significant level by sophisticated, discerning and affluent consumers, who are willing to pay extra for the societal values and the metaphors that these products embody and represent. This capital of emotional difference and goodwill is thus impossible to replicate by the low-cost economies when attempting to enter capital-intensive, knowledge-based sectors of economic activity. They also constitute a formidable source of competitive advantage in modern economies.

Many European firms were also outright averse to risk-taking and not ready for this kind of aggressive competitive environment. The technological complexity inherent to many sectors of economic activity was not enough to dissuade Indian, Pakistani or Chinese corporations from entering the more sophisticated markets. Where technology constituted a significant obstacle, the emerging economies were able to work patiently on catching up and reaching, if not state-of-the-art of technology and know-how in specific sectors of economic activity, at least a level of manufacturing prowess that would enable them to target the lower ends of these markets satisfactorily.

These entrepreneurs, or more aptly put, factory owners from India and China would send their children over to the UK and the USA to acquire formal education in the engineering and business management disciplines. Engineers, many of whom had formally trained in elite bastions of education in the UK and the USA would frequent industry fairs in Germany. There they would acquire the latest technology available, thus guaranteeing the basic competitive conditions for entering export markets with a modicum of success. Subsequent adaptation to market requirements and constant fine-tuning would do the rest. These entrepreneurs avidly began to pay careful attention to market trends. They were also quick learners.

The rest is a well-known story. Chinese and Indian companies were able to go back home and began to imitate trendy products emanating from the more developed economies and subsequently supply often well-established brands in western Europe and North America with their low-cost products. The particular susceptibility to imitation that characterizes the less knowledge-based labour-intensive manufacturing sectors, and in particular those of the low-tech variety, was augmented by the virtually non-existent barriers to entry in these sectors. In the cases where these barriers do exist, they are by no means insurmountable.

Low-tech sectors are characterized by low capital requirements and are therefore not inaccessible even to cottage-like operations. Economies of scale, albeit important drivers of cost effectiveness in manufacturing, are not critical to the emergence of these cottage-type industries, in that these are low-scale operations that are often able to thrive just by carving out niches in restricted market segments and serving these specialist niches efficiently.

Technological complexity and technical know-how are also not a problem at the lower ends and for low-quality thresholds in the less demanding markets. The progressive development and fine-tuning of these competencies leads to the creation of sustainable long-term competitive advantages that, anchored on a seemingly endless supply of cheap labour, provides emerging economies with formidable advantages.

Where shortage of know-how, technology, or business and commercial acumen would have the potential to be barriers to success in a particular industrial sector, these never really constituted insurmountable obstacles, as exceptional Indian and Pakistani scholars and students and others from the less developed nations began to crowd the top institutions of higher learning in the UK and the USA in search of specialist knowledge which they subsequently brought back home.

Upon graduating they would return back to their home countries, equipped with state-of-the-art competencies in the technical and business disciplines. They brought along with them another all important asset – an informed intuition as to the local culture and its value systems, beliefs, explicit and implicit codes, subtleties and idiosyncrasies. This would come in handy in understanding the particular brand of cosmopolitism and cultural identity and specificities of each culture and market. This has not yet allowed these emerging nations to go the full monty and create their own corporate and product brands, but this is precisely the kind of skill base that is complementary of knowledge and technology as competencies that are required in a world of globalized competition, and in the light of modern consumption profiles and behaviours.

This is valuable stuff for these would-be entrepreneurs, as it configures the much needed market knowledge which they would need to tap into later when at the helm of their home country organizations if they were to be successful in the more affluent export markets. In manufacturing sectors, as in others, there has always been nothing intrinsically unique and specific to a particular business or sector of activity that would impede someone from quickly attaining a good grasp of its rudiments and a readiness to at least be able to cater to the low-ends of consumer markets. By adapting and learning, improving processes and techniques and adjusting to local realities, the average Indian, Pakistani or Chinese entrepreneur was able to operate and compete on less demanding and unsophisticated market niches.

Whilst acquiring basic competencies, manufacturers in these emerging nations quickly became competitive in the global market, exporting to the lower ends of sophisticated economies as well as supplying the world with low-priced equivalents for just about everything. Technological backwardness has never been an insurmountable obstacle, at least in the medium term, and one only needs to look at the history of manufacturing in southern Europe, where the proliferation of many small firms in relatively concentrated geographies has meant that technological barriers have not been an issue to the emergence of new firms at different stages of the nineteenth and twentieth centuries.

In such sectors as textiles, clothing and footwear, technology was never a significant deterrent for the propagation of the thousands of cottage-like operations that at one time existed in the backwaters of northern Portugal and Spain. Technological superiority was also not a worthy explanation for the enormous success enjoyed by these sectors. Thousands of small units of production operated successfully for decades on end, often out of garages and home basements. Many of them had no more than five or six people working in them and were typically small family-owned artisan operations.

There were, in conclusion, not too many barriers to the entry of new firms from emerging economies operating in key manufacturing sectors. Specific know-how was of course important in maintaining a privileged position in the industry, but the absence of an essential requirement for technological complexity in production processes, or of any degree of exceptional knowledge incorporated into basic products, made it obvious that the only relevant and sustainable differentiation that would be needed was going to be one of compliance with other more subtle, yet crucially more important criteria, and those were the soft skills entailed in the market offer. It would be those who were fastest to acknowledge this reality and effectively manoeuvre around it that would come out as winners in this complex global competitiveness game.

Low-tech manufacturing sectors did not favour a differentiation strategy based on the pursuit of innovation, at least to the point where competition would be rendered obsolete through the constant introduction of technology into ever more sophisticated production processes and end products. If the end consumer did not perceive there to be a worthwhile and valuable difference then why bother? Thus competitors from countries with a less sophisticated industrial base were able to compete mainly on price.

In low-tech manufacturing, and by contrast with other sectors of economic activity that incorporate more complex technologies, resultant output is straightforward and easily imitable by new entrants in cut-throat competitive markets. Quality is thus a fundamental criterion in the buyer decision-making process, but that which constitutes quality, the way in which quality parameters are complied with in what concerns technological content, are in low-tech manufacturing easily imitable by willing and perseverant contenders.

These low-tech manufacturing sectors, many of them based in southern Europe, needed to understand the harsh realities of world trade and competitiveness in a cut-throat global environment. The truth of the matter is that manufacturing sectors in these economies were not able to inscribe into their output what should have been perceived as significant and valuable difference next to discerning consumers in sophisticated markets.

In not being able to inscribe notorious and valuable differences into their market offer, they failed to develop sustainable competitive advantages in relation to their strong emerging contenders, who were able to flat out beat them on price. On the contrary, low-tech manufacturing in Europe had clear labour cost disadvantages in labour-intensive sectors. They were also not capable of commanding relevant and sustainable differentiation, and critically emotional difference, anchored on recognizable and highly valued branded identities associated with manufactured goods.

In globalized markets, where there are many suppliers of what are often undifferentiated products, it would have been critical for these European manufacturers to have downplayed relative cost disadvantages, and have compensated them not only with emotional differentiation expressed in great retail and product brands, but also with the building of solid and long-term relationships with key retail organizations and their buyers. By developing an understanding of buyers' needs and requirements, anticipating and exceeding them, they would be better capable of catering to these needs, and to thus make better use of a God-given geographical proximity to key export markets.

In many cases this geographical advantage had become diluted, as manufacturers had failed miserably on the compliance with key determinants of successful buyer–supplier relationships, including the failure to abide by delivery schedules, to respond to requests efficiently and expeditiously, and to provide after-sales service. In addition to all of this, these suppliers did not have their own design ideas, and were also stereotyped as rating low on innovation capabilities and level of industrial development, much of it factually untrue, but this was the perception next to key retail markets and organizational buyers in the more developed northern European economies.

European manufacturers, and in particular those of southern European nations who should have stood to benefit tremendously had they gone downstream in their respective supply chains with the overriding objective of building corporate and product brands, did not, in the comfort that they were sourced regularly for business. Instead they were complacent and in the end most of them were rendered meaningless and unknown in the minds of the affluent and savvy cosmopolitan consumers of key target markets. Some, very few, went downstream in key supply chains, as is evident in the success of the Inditex group and its stable of brands, including its flagship operation Zara, but also Massimo Dutti, Stradivarius, Bershka and others. However, this and other examples were tragically the exception rather than the norm, as there are literally hundreds of thousands of isolated manufacturing units scattered across southern Europe. They could not all have followed the route of going downstream and opening up their own retail stores or creating corporate or product brands, but more of them should have done that or perhaps have created clusters of inter-related economic activities with a modicum of international expression.

Credit restrictions, along with a false sense of security that came with ad hoc currency devaluations, and the comparative disadvantages in the financing of small and medium-sized firms in these economies which placed them at a relative disadvantage when competing with other firms with much lower costs of financing and that aimed for the same key export markets, reflected a collective myopia that has come to characterize the typology of competitiveness in the manufacturing sector in southern Europe, with immeasurable detrimental economic and sociological consequences that are only now beginning to surface.

Comparatively higher costs of production in southern European manufacturing could have perhaps been mitigated or even offset by the capital of goodwill and confidence that came from knowledge of the needs and idiosyncrasies of retail buyers in the more affluent economies. This would have certainly restrained retail buyers, deterring them from quickly switching suppliers as soon as they became uncompetitive on cost. When buyer–supplier relationships were not properly cultivated and nurtured, there remained few tangible, or indeed psychological, barriers impeding their switch to lower-cost alternatives.

Quality criteria and parameters were replicated in the short term and with ease by manufacturing sectors in the emerging economies of such recent powerhouses as China and India. European low-cost manufacturing sectors, clearly unprepared for this, were unable to respond with any degree of success to sudden changes in the dynamics of world trade or even the progressive elimination of trade barriers. Many attribute the main cause for the dramatic fall of the low-tech manufacturing sector, particularly in southern Europe, to the dumping of Chinese products into European markets, but in reality it was to the failure of these economies in envisaging what was heading towards them and in adequately preparing for impending competitive threats by insulating their respective offers that blame should be apportioned.

In the aforementioned case of fashion retail, subsequent alternative business models were introduced into the market that were to eventually revolutionize and substitute the incumbent paradigm that had dominated the world of fashion retailing for decades. These new models were based on flexibility of supply, shorter lead times, and the constant search for alternative supply sources that were closer to home, which meant cutting dramatically on delivery times of four to six months that were the norm when buying from the traditional sources in the Far East. Fast-fashion offered ample opportunity for subcontracting activities locally. Good examples of this are what the region of Galicia represented for the likes of Zara, or the Italian artisans for the top Italian brands.

In reality, a new retail paradigm in fashion demanded quick response models and an agility and flexibility in the management of the supply chain, allowing for an organization to respond to more sophisticated and stringent demands at a much faster pace, configuring a totally different rhythm and agility in bringing product to market. The scrutiny and monitoring of new trends was something totally alien to old school manufacturers, and the antiquated department store retail formats no longer reflected consumer wants and needs.

There are many examples of this concerning well-established household names, including the likes of Marks & Spencer and C&A, but in general the traditional department store formats were to go through very tough times in the early 1990s, to the point where eminent players ended up filing for bankruptcy at that time, incapable as they were of adjusting to the new retail formats and realities. This happened in the case of Woolworths as well as other long-established corporate brands in the British retail scene, including the household name C&A. Marks & Spencer went through a very rough patch for a good part of a decade, and it never really recovered its position of prominence in British fashion, at least in comparison to its market dominance of the British retail scene in years gone by. The times had simply changed and some retail organizations were better than others at adapting to changing conditions and crucially in pre-empting change themselves.

The imperative of value aggregation as a crucial determinant of global competitiveness was to be the demise of much that related to manufacturing in southern European countries. Production activities in labour-intensive sectors failed miserably as, for the most part, suppliers lacked the strategic acumen to envisage what was coming. Proximity to the consumer through astute branding and the creation of relevant emotional difference would have been very important in establishing a strategic platform for value aggregation to goods that people wanted, but it was not done. This would have meant that the outcome on the very viability of entire sectors of economic activity would have been different, particularly in economies and in sectors that were not so dependent on endless supplies of cheap labour. This was certainly the case with the more sophisticated segments of the textiles, clothing and footwear sectors, where many firms simply vanished overnight.

The social repercussions deriving from tens of thousands of bankruptcies in geographically limited areas are tremendous. On the one hand it is often the case with low-tech manufacturing that the structure of property in these sectors tends to be extremely fragmented, with hundreds of thousands of cottage-type firms of varying sizes, but mostly small operators, coexisting in a relatively limited geography. On the other hand, the structure and nature of employment tends to be concentrated here, with entire families working in the same manufacturing unit from working age, and sometimes earlier, until they retire. The potential for reconversion of formally uneducated individuals and their reintegration back into the job market is minimal, and this produces severe adverse consequences to stretching social security platforms and welfare benefit schemes.

In a context of unfavourable demographic trends, the sustainability of social systems, including those of health and education, has to be seriously questioned. This is due to various factors, but an ageing population and the gradual lowering of the ratio of people in employment as a percentage of the total population are important explanatory variables as to why this state of affairs cannot go on for much longer, particularly in the light of a very generous pan-European social welfare system. The rate of effort required from those who are lucky enough to find employment, has been stretched to breaking point.

It stands to reason, therefore, that the inability of sectors of economic activity or whole economies in aggregating value to their best goods and services, means that no matter how hard workers work, how productive and efficient they are in lending their knowledge and competencies to production processes, all of this is immaterial and inconsequential for the overriding objective of increasing national productivity levels, if ingenious, creative and pro-active entrepreneurship simply fails to show up and contribute to the numerator of output value in the productivity ratio.

In optimizing the relationship between worker skills and capabilities with other inputs in the production process, including technology and infrastructure, labour is limited to offering its knowledge and technical acumen. It cannot look for new markets or tap into the wealthier segments of existing ones. Enhancing productivity in a firm, a sector of economic activity or a nation is then about every stakeholder that directly or indirectly engages in this systemic process in doing their part of the deal. Apart from the blame game and the apportioning of mutual accusations that comes from a dichotomous view of the world, polarized between labour and capital, which finds ample expression in party political side-taking, tragically national productivity and economic competitiveness on the global stage is correlated with indicators of human and economic development and the sustainability of these over time.

Reality Check...

Fred Smith, FedEx and Out-of-the-Box Thinking

Fred Smith returned from the war in Vietnam. As he ran out of ideas as to what to do next in life, and vividly traumatized by the experience in Southeast Asia, Fred understood early on that he had to turn around the massive odds mounted against him as, without any special academic qualifications, the future looked bleak for the war veteran. He detected a business opportunity in the idea of delivering packages anywhere in the US within 24 hours. From this simple idea, and the confidence that investors deposited in him at the time, Federal Express was born. Today FedEx aircraft can be found taking-off and landing at airports, large and small, across the world.

The brand was immortalized a few years ago in cinema in the Hollywood movie, *Castaway*, a production that achieved relative success in the European market. Tom Hanks, an overzealous FedEx employee, is the only survivor of a plane crash, ending up in a lost island in the middle of the Pacific Ocean. He survives for many years, having as sole company a Wilson basketball (another well-conceived publicity stunt), and manages, with recourse to an unbreakable spirit and sheer willpower, never to give up and escape the island, later to be rescued by a cargo ship.

Upon coming back to his former life and after successive trials and tribulations in adjusting to a personal reality that had changed in the meantime, the Tom Hanks character ends the movie, restarting his love life. He does that by delivering a FedEx package that had lived with him on the island for years and which he made it a point never to open as was his duty and obligation. In true FedEx fashion the package is finally delivered to its ultimate destination, thus redeeming the FedEx promise (another wonderful publicity stunt). He delivered the package a few years late, but delivered the package was. Fred Smith believed firmly where others dared not even begin to dream. He found opportunity where others found obstacle.

Imagine what it would be like today for someone like Fred Smith to walk into a bank, meet with a commercial credit manager and ask for financial backing for his business idea. He would have certainly been asked to produce a detailed strategic plan for his intended project. Even in less agitated economic times when the credit crunch was but a foreign notion, and unheard of in pre-subprime corporate America, Fred Smith would have found it difficult to obtain funding for his business project.

This was a simple concept, to deliver packages initially anywhere in the US in 24 hours. The obvious scrutiny that any worthy commercial credit manager would pose, in protecting the interests of the financial institution that he represented, would be to pass judgement on the future of the business as a viable and going concern. In ascertaining the financial viability of the business, the competitive macro-environment would have to be scrutinized. This would help to establish a degree of probability of success of the proposed business concept and consequently of the safety of the project funding.

In this context, the obvious question that a loans manager would ask would be something along the lines of what is the purpose of the US Mail, if not to deliver packages the next day anywhere in the USA? This would certainly be a key question in establishing the viability of FedEx in the light of the business environment where it operated. The truth of the matter is that by creating FedEx in 1971, Fred Smith started a billion dollar company following on the footsteps of UPS and DHL. These two companies, UPS founded in 1907 and DHL in 1969, also generate billions of dollars in revenue, and the sector employs directly or indirectly, tens if not hundreds of thousands of individuals the world over.

Even with significant change in the macro-environment on dimensions that are crucial to the raison d'être of the business, including the breath-taking pace of evolution in communications and in information technology as well as fast-paced change in the more mundane operational aspects of logistics, and the potential for the overtaking of the organization by others that are more competent and expeditious at dealing with these changes, the reality has shown that FedEx has survived, grown and is today a successful company operating in a cut-throat global environment.

Back when it began, the company had to deal with such important drawbacks as the oil crisis. Often the most important quality for an entrepreneur is that of perseverance. Fred Smith was persistent precisely where and when others were convinced that his ideas would not be viable, that the competitive environment was way too crowded, and the business difficult to break into, due to the large economies of scale implied.

If there is a business trait or quality that transverses sectors of economic activity, a characteristic of top CEOs and visionary founders of great organizations, it is that of an obstinate persistence and a firm belief in core principles and values when others have ceased to believe that it can be done. It is a safe bet to say that European nations are in dire need of a few Fred Smiths to set the course for the coming decades.

2

Productivity, Value Aggregation and National Competitiveness

Value aggregation to goods and services has to be about more than the occasional improvement of manufacturing processes and products. It needs to be a philosophical orientation within organizations, an obsession with the search for ways in which to achieve constant enhancements to the tangible and intangible features in output.

This search needs to include a systematic scrutiny of best practices both within but also outside the sector for which they are intended, with a view to the betterment of processes and products, raising quality parameters, as well as improving constantly on other functional criteria within the supply package. This however does not suffice, and careful attention needs to be apportioned to the intangible cues, namely the branding and reputational aspects of corporations and products. Aggregation of value to goods and services implies doing all of the above in a way that is reflective of the values and aspirations of the firm's key constituencies and in particular its prospective customer base.

Organizations that do this well are better equipped than others to command higher prices next to discriminating and discerning consumers in sophisticated and affluent markets. This is one of the most potent ways of improving national productivity, in that by increasing the numerator of output value over the input costs that have been incurred to generate that level of wealth in an economy, productivity gains are obtained in a way that is sustainable. This is true in the light of global dynamics of labour markets and the non-viability of a competitive model anchored on low costs of labour on the one hand and the nature of competition in cosmopolitan and sophisticated economies with discretionary income that makes compulsory the search for creative differentiation and branding on the other.

A focus on the numerator of output value in the productivity ratio is important, in that upstream in the value chain in manufacturing, a specific allocation of productive resources, independently of a more or less efficient combination of these inputs, may translate into disparate output values for essentially identical products downstream, often in the same physical or geographic market, depending on how the soft dimensions of supply are treated, including the excellence of the branding of goods and services. The reasons why this should be the case may be marketing-related or not, but crucially they are often unrelated to traditional concepts and notions about the productivity of labour and its efficiency, or ideas that prevail about the suboptimal combination of productive resources in an economy.

Attaining production efficiencies is of course the Holy Grail of manufacturing, but in the end if there are no markets and willing customers with discretionary income in them, irrespective of how efficiently products are manufactured, the whole exercise is simply pointless. Even when there are markets out there, the question is then what makes consumers, and in particular those in foreign constituencies, pay price premiums for products that are otherwise virtually the same.

By increasing the value of exports, with the same input factor base, and under comparable conditions of optimality in the combination of these, GDP in an economy goes up. This happens of course in economies or in sectors of economic activity that have been able to build strong reputational capital for their product, corporate and national brands next to affluent constituencies in key destination markets. In doing this, these economies have created the reputational goodwill for them and the goods and services that they supply to sophisticated markets, which allows organizations to command premium prices for their exports to these more affluent and consumerist markets. The topic of value aggregation, its links with productivity and its critical role for the building of national competitiveness is thus crucial for modern economies.

A true story is told of a man who worked in the marketing department at Heathrow airport back in the early 1990s. Amongst other tasks he was responsible for managing the airport parking lot. As he looked into its profitability, he realized that there was potential to do much better. He decided to split the parking lot into two distinct and clearly identifiable zones. One, closest to the terminal, was destined for company executives, a segment for whom, time was critical and money not a concern. These people needed to get to and from the terminal as quickly as possible. The other group of people didn't much care for time. They were occasional travellers and time wasn't really, within reasonable limits of patience, much of a concern to them. These people were allocated a more distant parking spot and of course they did not have to pay as much as the executives who had the privilege of parking nearer to the terminal building.

Proximity to the terminal and consequent easiness and speed of access to the parking lot meant that those executives had to incur an extra cost for this privilege, which they didn't really mind as often it wasn't them but instead the organization that they worked for that paid for this. For these people, time literally meant money too, so in effect it also made economic sense for them to pay extra money to be nearer to the airport terminal. For them it meant savings and not a superfluous expense or luxury.

Clearly, the marketing guy was able to identify a profit opportunity out of apparently nothing. Initially he was given, what to the untrained eye looked to be, an indistinctive service – parking space at London Heathrow. He recognized that this otherwise undifferentiated service could in effect attract different typologies of demand, meaning that essentially the same service could be broken down into distinct benefit offerings that could be ascribed different utilities by groups of people with dissimilar needs, and for which therefore punters would be willing to disburse of their money accordingly.

The key was to realize that what our marketing guy was selling was not parking space but instead time, or even the economic value that time savings permit. With that in mind, the next step would be to identify groups of users for whom time had different ascriptions of meaning and more to the point a different value. In economics lingo this means that there were distinct groups of consumers with different price-demand sensitivities, which in the end implied that he was able to improve the overall profitability of the parking lot. The key point here is that the identification of these typologies of demand was achieved in a context where this was not immediately visible or at least intuitive to most.

The Heathrow airport parking facility was divided according to the needs of distinct groups of people who had different degrees of economic freedom to exercise their choice, and this in the end is what happens in most markets for most products. Our marketing person then decided to opt for the simple idea of splitting the parking lot into two, with recourse to a rudimentary solution that simply meant that the most expensive parking slots were nearer to the terminal, whilst parking places further away from the terminal were cheaper. As a consequence of this, the net profitability of the parking lot went up by 60 per cent.

This is an infrastructure few envisaged as susceptible of economic value enhancement. Others did not even think of the airport parking lot as anything other than a necessary airport infrastructure, a cost centre and definitely not a profit opportunity. All it took was to split the parking lot in half and a few signs put in to identify parking slots conveniently, and the trick was done. Outside-the-box thinking is not immediate and for everyone, but this is a good metaphor for what should be the philosophical orientation of organizations and people in them in the contemporary global economy.

Up until the fast-fashion revolution revoked the pillar of seasonality in the fashion business, replacing it with immediate fashion, and well before the time of department stores, if someone wanted to buy a suit he would look for a tailor. The prospective customer would walk into a tailor's shop, a shopping assistant would proceed to obtain all the necessary body measurements and, a few weeks later and after a number of in-between visits to the tailor's for second and third proofs just to be on the safe side, a suit would be custom-made for the individual in question, and for nobody else but that person.

The breath-taking diffusion of technology has allowed for the term customization to acquire an entirely different meaning in bringing product to the market. The suit is tailored to the needs and requirements of that individual, but it is now produced en masse, still custom-made for a particular person, but now catering to as many consumers as wish to buy the product. The basic idea here is the satisfaction of the individual needs of vast amounts of consumers in the market.

Splitting markets into distinct groups of buyers who share similar characteristics in terms of their consumption patterns and behaviours requires different manipulations of the market offer considered in its entirety, and that consists of what in business terminology is termed as the marketing mix of price, product, promotion and place. The aim of this is to cater to the requirements of different groups of prospective consumers, and its ultimate expression can be found in the concept of mass customization, the interpretation of each individual's needs as different and valuable, and the finding of tailored responses to everyone's needs.

The dynamics of consumption in contemporary markets illustrates this point well. The purchase of a car is a good example of this phenomenon. The extras or added options to the basic product often make up for 40 to 50 per cent of the total price of a car. The mass customization concept forces the organization to develop an offer that is totally in accordance with the buyer's stringent requirements. In doing this, the organization's market offer becomes more insulated from competition and imitation, as it caters to well-defined needs and wants of individuals whose specificity cannot be replicated easily.

In reality, just about every market is susceptible to segmentation. From drinks, to credit cards, to pharmaceutical products, just about everything can be differentiated effectively, to the point of catering to the needs and wants of distinct groups of buyers as long as they have disposable income and are willing to buy the difference that is built into an otherwise undifferentiated good or service.

A bottle of Johnnie Walker Honour whisky retails at a price that is ten times higher than that of an equivalent bottle of Johnnie Walker Red. There are of course tangible differences entailed in both experiences and these are justified by the fact that in reality they are different products, with different maturations, in a product category where time is a critical dimension of quality augmentation. Time is also money and the storage of whisky for decades in warehouses increases production costs for whisky manufacturers. The total costs of production of both goods are also different, but the question is whether the differential in production costs justifies a difference in retail prices of this magnitude.

What is truly important here is that there exist distinct groups of consumers, with varying degrees of disposable income that are willing and able to acquire both types of products. Nobody buys a Rolex because he or she wants an instrument that tells the time. A Rolex is an object whose primary function is arguably that of timekeeping. In all probability, a Rolex is instead a great metaphor for the fulfilment of social status and aspirational needs.

The aforementioned brands are but a few amongst a plethora of corporate and product brands whose true worth resides in the intangible peripheral circles of value that surround its functional inner core. The ultimate expression of value that is inherent to these products is of course embodied in brand image and the reputational goodwill that they carry next to key stakeholder constituencies who know about them and what they do.

The importance of functionality as a buying criterion ends where the intangible dimensions in the product offer begin. In a spectrum that goes from tangibility to intangibility, consumers may just take functionality and intrinsic quality for granted and look for intangible cues as the true differentiators in buying decision-making processes. These intangible cues may cover dimensions of aspirational social status and relative position in social hierarchies in societies as well as criteria whose materialization in products act as conduits for social distinction. Intangible cues may also be linked to feelings of belonging, as the membership of cult brands, including the following of football clubs, suggests.

As long as these intangible cues are reflective of the cosmopolitan lifestyle ideals and societal values that are subscribed by groups of prospective buyers that share similar characteristics and that have acquisitive power, then it stands to reason that organizations should segment markets and serve them adequately. Effective market segmentation leads to higher profitability levels through increased customer satisfaction, as well as to the improvement of organizational capabilities in the detection of opportunities for economic growth.

Market segmentation also allows for a sharper focus of the firm's communications strategy enhancing the propensity for customers to remain loyal to the organization as well as acting as a stimulus for in-house innovation cultures and practices. Organizations stand to benefit from market segmentation because prospective consumers have different price-demand sensitivities and they also have different aesthetic values and preferences, expressed in complex consumption decisions that discriminate between functionally identical products and that lead to the choice of those goods and services that offer higher comparative utilities.

In a capitalist system, in market economies where there is disposable income, organizations have felt there to be unlimited possibilities when it comes to the splitting of markets into distinct groups of buyers that share approximate needs. Consumers in the same target group are expected to respond in similar and expectable ways to manipulations of the marketing mix of communications, product, price and distribution.

The marketing literature has for years offered a conceptual notion of product that can be expressed visually in a series of concentric circles, at the nucleus of which lies the core product, its function, what it is and what it really does. The nucleus of the product consists of its problem-solving capabilities, the benefits that customers effectively look for when buying the product. When a woman buys lipstick, she is in fact buying much more than lip colour. Charles Revson of cosmetics giant Revlon evidenced this thinking clearly when he made the statement: 'In the factory we make cosmetics, but in the store we sell hope.'

Competitiveness is intense in just about every market. In many markets, the winners are those who are able to aggregate the most valuable intangible dimensions to core product functionality and add to the basic elements at the nucleus of a product notion that is much more than function. It encompasses packaging, service, delivery, installation and whatever other tangible or intangible dimensions of the market offer that are perceived by prospective consumers to augment value to the initial functional core in products, and whose ultimate expression is brand image and reputation and the goodwill that it carries.

All of this only makes sense if consumers see it that way, that is if they perceive these outer layers in a product notion, defined as a set of concentric circles, as true aggregators of value and not superfluous additions that they can do without, and more to the point that they are not willing to pay for. It is consumers that will ultimately decide in the end what is valuable and when. If consumers are willing to pay for these outer layers of our product concept then corporations stand to benefit immensely, as on the one hand it is much more difficult for competitors to imitate whatever competitive advantages are conferred by these intangible outer layers, and on the other, profit margins for branded goods are of course incomparably higher than for unbranded and undifferentiated products.

Organizations feel that they need to effectively differentiate their market offer in order to achieve above average profitability in highly competitive market settings. They need to create sustainable bases for distinction in markets where often the objective differences between products are irrelevant or minor at best. Over and beyond the critical issues of the financing of small and medium-sized enterprises that have surfaced with the credit crunch and the astonishing burden of sovereign debt, finding sustainable differentiation in cut-throat competitive markets is indeed the greatest challenge facing organizations today.

The bases for differentiation of market offers are perhaps the same as they have always been. The criteria are demographic, psychographic, lifestyle and others, but the ways in which to achieve relevant difference in contemporary markets are now a much more intricate and complex problematic, not least because of the critical role of technology and information diffusion and its widespread availability, but also because societal differences entail such subjective notions as heterogeneous value systems, cosmopolitism and aesthetics, and the nuances as well as the explicit and implicit codes that are conduits for the expression of all of the above across widely varying cultural landscapes.

The understanding of what constitutes value in a consumerist society, blessed with disposable income, has rendered product functionality as secondary in the pecking order of why people choose certain goods and services to the detriment of others. The use of products (brands) as embodiments of values, to which sufficient numbers of economically empowered individuals adhere to, is something that exceptional corporate and nation brands make good use of. This is what Nike or Mercedes are all about. This is also what is meant by country of origin effects and the positive cues that derive from the acknowledgement of a brand emanating from Italy or Germany on such dimensions as design and engineering for example. It is not really about where the product was made, it is instead about where the brand originates from.

For those who have great reservations in thinking about countries as brands, or to make analogies that somehow demean the integrity of nations by comparing them with corporate and product brands, this statement attempts to be no more than a reflection of contemporary consumer societies and a widespread collective tendency to infer complex knowledge from very little information, and then to generalize from that to stereotyping about nations and their people. One can ill-afford to not be part of this global competitive game, as in modern economies, due to their complex, systemic and integrated nature, interconnectivity and interdependence, cultural heterogeneity and global networks and relationships are increasingly the norm. In this context, the fluidity of capital, ideas, goods, services and people constitute a historically unprecedented challenge to national economies, and therefore any idea hinging on both technocratic, but more crucially market and commercial insularity, is counterintuitive and destined for failure.

Nobody wrote the roadmap for this brave new world and it is very likely that this was not what Aldous Huxley had in mind when he wrote the title of the same name. To think of a nation as an embodiment of values, to which consumers adhere unreservedly and give their undivided preference, is not something that is acceptable to many whose idea of a nation is based on territorial and cultural notions and consequently not susceptible to commercialization as if it were a product.

This is however precisely the thinking that, in the case of countries that excel in nurturing and living their brand values and portraying them effectively, represents the genesis of competitive economies. This is achieved either by recourse to institutional means through communications campaigns that portray the relative merits of the country in question, in what is called in the literature the branded house model, or, alternatively, through exceptional and consistent experiences with branded goods that emanate from a particular country, in what is designated as the house of brands model, or even a combination of both. A house of brands strategy is in all probability much more effective in that it benefits from the legitimacy of unhindered consumer judgments being passed on the relative merits of brands that happen to emanate from a particular country. The branded house model on the other hand is always tainted by the notion that we are in the presence of institutional paid advertising and may therefore be less credible.

Crucially, these branded products originate in various sectors of economic activity and they correspond to the satisfaction of different consumption needs. The way it works is that if from morning to evening, from cradle to coffin, if one's quotidian is filled with experiences with branded consumption experiences embodied in products that can be traced back to a specific origin, and if these experiences have been positive to the point where the brands that embody them constitute comfort zones or safe harbours for consumers, then the latter can literally be sold on anything remotely claiming origin to that country, whether it is or not in any way related to the original product that gave the country its reputation.

Building an excellent country reputation from scratch is obviously not easy. Countries are entities with a political history, a culture and a collective identity, often accommodating in the same geography a myriad of subcultures that are at times irreconcilable. Cultural diversity is not necessarily an obstacle to country brand-building – on the contrary, a solid reputation builds on the idiosyncrasies of the culture, and desirably on the ones that are construed to be positive by foreign constituencies.

The branded house model and the house of brands paradigms of thinking about country brand-building are distinct. There is much debate about the merits and shortcomings of both models. The house of brands model whose key protagonists are countries like Japan or Germany deserves perhaps a sharper focus due to the industrial post-war success of these economies, and the plethora of consumer brands that have emanated from these nations over decades of exceptional branded experiences that can be traced back to organizations in these and other economies.

Also important to the value equation is how organizations grow and expand internationally. Firms begin by operating locally in their domestic markets only to subsequently expand abroad, typically to one or two foreign markets at first, according to criteria of geographical or cultural proximity. Organizations then go on to extend their coverage to other more distant markets, both geographically and culturally. Cultural proximity mitigates physical distance as criteria for business expansion due to a perception of reduced business risk, as cultural connectedness and language proximity are important cues for understanding other peoples and markets. More than physical distance, what is important is that societal codes of conduct, both explicit and implicit, are clearly understood and embedded in the modus operandi of the organization abroad.

The internationalization strategies of companies like Zara are examples of forms of progressive expansion according to geographic criteria first, and the perception of control that this entails, but also according to cultural proximity. In the case of the Inditex Group and of the expansion of the Zara retail brand, cultural and geographic proximity get mixed up because the Group has its headquarters in La Coruña, Galicia in north-western Spain, not far from the Portuguese border, but crucially where there is a cultural continuum rather than a clear identity split between Portugal and Spain as happens in other borders. For a group of companies from Galicia, it made sense that initial steps towards the internationalization of retail operations would be given in the biggest city in the north of Portugal, Oporto.

When Zara began to subcontract operations to the Minho region in the northwest of Portugal, and subsequently opened its first retail store in Oporto, for Ortega and Inditex operating out of Galicia it would not have been very different from opening a retail store in Barcelona. At least from the viewpoint of cultural proximity, the north of Portugal is probably closer to the Galician collective spirit and attitude. This makes a lot of sense because in the context of the internationalization of the activities of the organization there were risks that needed to be mitigated by reducing cultural gaps between the domestic and destination markets. It is evident that geographic but also cultural proximity allow for aesthetic references to be retained and for comfort zones to emerge.

Low labour productivities are associated with less than desirable performances of economies on national competitiveness rankings when less competent workers are unable to aggregate value to goods and services, to the point where they are not easily susceptible to imitation by competitors in cut-throat markets. It can also be argued however that there is a corresponding negative impact of an economy that consistently ranks low on national competitiveness and on low productivity ratios in the economy, as negative or neutral country reputations act as deterrents to the choice of national products by foreign consumers who also simply refuse to pay price premiums for them. Again, if productivity is a ratio of output over inputs in an economy, it stands to reason that this will not be good for the numerator in this ratio.

Negative country stereotyping thus acts as a deterrent, not only to preference as a function of country of origin, but also on how much people are willing to pay for brands that are perceived to claim that particular origin. In other words, negative country of origin effects act to impose price thresholds on products emanating from a certain country. Analogous to this, a negative country aura impedes consumers from perceiving higher utilities in products that emanate from the country in question.

The failure of organizations and economies in aggregating value to goods and services in key export markets receives very little attention in the context of the national productivity debate. The usual approach to productivity emphasizes the notion that by devising an optimal combination of inputs and working tirelessly on improving the relationship between labour and technology in production processes, these become more efficient allowing for higher quantities of output of a higher quality. Thus labour productivity increases.

Although all of this is conceptually irrefutable, the truth of the matter is that most market environments are characterized by intense competition and one can expect to find a multitude of players out there looking to compete with our products for the same destination markets. These competitors will have different degrees of efficiency in combining input resources in production processes that are often the same and that lead to products that perform the same function, products that are sometimes identical. What they cannot replicate however is the brand and in particular what the brand stands for.

Some of these market players will be more efficient than others in optimizing production processes, but crucially they will have different degrees of ability in convincing foreign consumer markets of the intrinsic merits of their respective offers. This means that some goods may derive from very efficient production processes, where labour productivity is high when measured in output quantities, as workers keep churning out large quantities of output for a given allocation of input resources, but still no one will buy them, simply because consumers do not know the brand and what it stands for, if it does stand for anything at all.

At times consumers may also refuse to buy the product in the knowledge that it comes from a part of the world about which, for whatever reason, they hold negative stereotypes. Some consumers may still want to buy the brand but are certainly not willing to pay premium prices for it as the only thing they are buying is its core functionality. This means that the numerator of output in the productivity ratio may be independent of the optimal or suboptimal combination of inputs in production processes and therefore also independent of how hard and how well workers work, if this is measured by the quantity of output generated per a specific allocation of production inputs mixed optimally in production processes. If consumers don't know about it, they won't buy it.

It is a fact that well-trained, competent labour will transfer its knowledge set of skills to manufacturing processes and products, thus enhancing the quality and value of output, but high productivity levels are also very much a function of the ability of dynamic entrepreneurs in convincing discerning consumers in affluent markets of the superiority of their products. The onus of responsibility here lies therefore more on the entrepreneur and his ability to read and interpret what heterogeneous markets want, than with workers in the shop floor.

This being the case, it stands to reason that in aiming for success, an economy's export strategy and model of competitiveness needs to be based on the constant pursuit of organizational and human competencies that lead it to systematically outcompete its main rivals in cluttered markets. This of course includes the all-important entrepreneurial qualities of pro-activity, dynamism and cosmopolitism, as well as an interest in understanding other people and their aspirations. In particular, ambitious firms need to outdo incumbents on product dimensions considered key by discerning consumers when making decisions to choose between competing offers of identical products. In a word they have to convince consumers to switch and this is not easy.

If an organization, a sector of the economy, or key stakeholders in an entire economy judge what are called wrongly the soft elements in the market offer to be superfluous or immaterial then, and in the absence of an unusual provision of natural resources in that economy, resources that the rest of the world uses and values, the organization, economic sector or entire economy are destined for disaster. Consumers will simply prefer the brands that they recognize and have learnt to love, to the detriment of unbranded goods that they have never heard of. Being competitive on price is thus rendered irrelevant. In fact, in sophisticated cosmopolitan retail markets of high disposable income, price is not the most important buying decision-making attribute in many product categories. In fact, for almost every product category there will always be market segments where price is irrelevant. This is not only applicable to the elite higher ends of consumer goods markets, as criteria other than cost matter in business-to-business (B2B), as well as in business-to-consumer (B2C) markets, including the development of buyer–supplier relationships in B2B and branding in B2C markets.

Consumer preferences will dictate who is to succeed and who is to quickly fade away. This will always be the case, irrespective of how efficient production processes in our own turf turn out to be. If we cannot find markets for our best products, it doesn't matter how efficient the production processes that lead to their making are. Our most cherished products will simply fail to even be acknowledged by key target groups. If foreign consumers, on the other hand, prefer our products to those of our competitors, and are willing to pay premium prices for them, this will crucially lead to improved output–input ratios of productivity in the economy through the aggregation of value to the numerator of output. In other words national productivity levels increase.

What is not mentioned often enough today is that what it takes for organizations and economies to be competitive in contemporary sophisticated and cosmopolitan foreign markets is somewhat different from the determinants of competitiveness of yesteryear, as economies fight it out in the global arena for notoriety and positions of prominence next to ever more selective consumers, who are increasingly able to choose from a wide variety of solutions, for just about every need and want, real or latent. Being competitive in today's markets is about aggregating value to our products, so that highly discerning consumers with disposable income in sophisticated markets prefer them to those of competitors.

If organizations, sectors of economic activity and even entire national economies are able to do this systematically, they stand to improve their labour, sectorial and national productivities. In so doing, the balance of trade in an economy also improves, as exports increase in value. GDP per capita increases too. By adding value to the same quantity of exported output, and for an identical combination of inputs, irrespective of the efficiency levels of production processes or the comparative productivities of labour, organizations are thus capable of commanding higher market prices for their products. These organizations are therefore contributing to the betterment of the wealth of their economy by augmenting GDP – in the domestic market by increasing consumption and in foreign markets by having a positive impact on the exports variable of GDP. National productivity levels also go up via the improvement of the numerator of output value and its impact on the output–input ratio of productivity.

The aggregation of value to products as a function of perceived improvements in levels and standards of quality, the betterment of the image and reputation of products, organizations and countries, and what this implies on the enabling of firms for commanding higher prices for their products downstream next to consumers, translates into higher productivity levels for an economy when output is measured at market prices and not in quantities. This means that upstream a specific allocation of productive resources, independently of a more or less efficient combination of these inputs in production processes, may translate into different market values for the same products downstream, depending upon factors that may be totally unrelated to labour productivity, and may traduce instead a lack of entrepreneurial spirit and an absence of dynamic pro-activity in searching for new markets and consumers. This, along with a lesser focus on marketing and branding issues, as well as the crucial work that requires doing on country of origin effects and stereotyping, may account for low levels of economic productivity, often more so than the idiosyncrasies of workers and their stereotyping as lazy and conformist.

The fact that we are dealing with output market value and not output quantities implies that what is critical here is the higher or lower propensity for consumers to buy our products to the detriment of someone else's offer, and crucially to pay premium prices for them. In sectors of economic activity that have been able to build a solid and valuable capital of reputational goodwill for their best firms and branded goods in traditional and up-and-coming destination markets, organizations are better able to translate this accumulated goodwill into premium retail prices for their best products.

Productivity is a ratio, whose numerator of output has to be calculated at market prices to reflect value rather than quantities, whilst the denominator indicates the total costs of factors of production incurred in the generation of that specific output value. The numerator of output value is both attainable and is the responsibility of dynamic entrepreneurs who are able to aggregate value to goods and services by permanently being on the lookout for markets, and prospective consumers for them, and to do this whilst working on the intangible aspects of supply, thus making market offers more appealing to sophisticated foreign constituencies. The numerator of output value is also the responsibility of competent and skilled labour, who equipped with adequate training and specialist knowledge, make better and higher-quality products, thus rendering the task of the entrepreneur in bringing product to the market easier. The product sells itself in other words.

In the case of the denominator of the productivity ratio, the same thing happens. Entrepreneurs, managers and workers all have an onus of responsibility in improving the denominator in the productivity ratio by finding the most efficient combinations of input resources with a view to optimizing production processes. Workers need to be skilled and educated and therefore more competent and efficient, and entrepreneurs, as well as senior management, or the technostructure (as Galbraith, the notable Canadian economist called this new stakeholder in contemporary economies) in multinational corporations need to acknowledge that workers require adequate training, as well as state-of-the-art technology, in order to perform at high levels of efficiency and thus be capable of aggregating value to goods and services.

In open economies where goods, services and technology are exchanged freely, and consumers have disposable income, the imperative of the consumer as a dictator of choice stands, and any viable concept of labour productivity cannot be dissociated from the effective wealth that is generated in the context of a real economy of production of goods and services, and not from a paper economy of speculative action and intent. A concept of labour productivity that focuses on output value does not in any way minimize the responsibility of workers, or in any way take the onus away from the labour force as now, more than ever before, and in the light of intense competition from everywhere, workers are required to be efficient, competent, skilled and constantly looking to improve for their own good.

However, workers have little intervention in establishing market prices for the products that they manufacture in foreign and indeed in domestic markets.

Despite the fact that they are the ones who directly manufacture these products, workers often have very little to do with the persuasion of foreign consumers to buy the products that they manufacture and consequently with the effective value that these goods can command in those markets. This is particularly true in external markets as workers may not know about the particular idiosyncrasies and specificities of demand in foreign markets. Of particular gravity is when entrepreneurs are also not knowledgeable of the finer aspects of the nature and characterization of demand and peculiarities of consumption in the same foreign markets.

The stigmatization of the worker, often cast-typed as less productive, can, under a fresh perspective that offers a stronger focus on the aggregation of value to the numerator of output, be demystified. A concept of labour productivity that strictly emphasizes factor costs and not market prices, that looks at the denominator and not at the numerator of the national productivity ratio is an inadequate portrayal of most contemporary realities, at least in developed economic systems.

A product that claims its origin in a country with higher labour costs is also a product that, by virtue of its sophisticated or elitist origins and the way in which it is rated very highly on key dimensions by prospective consumers, can be valued very highly by them. It can in this way command substantially higher prices than other equivalent products that cost much less to manufacture in contexts where workers are paid lower wages.

Productivity is much more than searching for an optimal combination of productive inputs in manufacturing processes with the objective of maximizing output quantities. In an open system of interdependent economic relationships, productivity is a ratio of the value at market prices of output over the costs incurred in obtaining and combining factors of production that are used in the generation of that output value. The problem is that, depending on which side of the ideological fence one sits on, the numerator or the denominator in this ratio are often conveniently forgotten or alternatively exploited by either camp. To put it simply, if the intention is to stigmatize workers and blame them for low productivities, the numerator remains unspoken and the focus is on labour inefficiency in the production process. If, on the other hand, the intention is to apportion blame for low productivity in an economy to the absence of a dynamic and pro-active entrepreneurial class, then the emphasis will be on the numerator of the productivity ratio that indicates just how hopeless entrepreneurs are in failing to aggregate value to goods and services.

The link between productivity and competitiveness is often unduly used as an argument against workers the world over, and a justification for the lowering of wages. The logic is a simplistic one. There is an idea of efficiency that is associated with keeping costs of production low. It is particularly important that labour costs are kept low as a proxy to higher levels of productivity and this is particularly true in the labour-intensive sectors. Yet the most competitive national economies that consistently show up at the very top on credible productivity rankings are often precisely those where the costs of labour tend to be the highest. This is true of Switzerland, Singapore and the USA and less true of the Scandinavian economies and Germany.

Table 2.1   Pay/productivity relationship (Top 20 ranking of the most competitive nations plus EU countries that have been intervened by the IMF, the European Commission and European Central Bank)

Country	Pay Strongly Related to Worker Productivity				
	2008	2009	2010	2011	2012
Switzerland	5th	5th	5th	5th	4th
Singapore	2nd	1st	1st	1st	2nd
Finland	60th	69th	69th	47th	72nd
Sweden	59th	71st	83rd	79th	46th
Netherlands	90th	84th	74th	66th	67th
Germany	51st	54th	43rd	38th	41st
USA	7th	8th	9th	8th	12th
UK	32nd	24th	25th	21st	13th
Hong Kong SAR	1st	2nd	2nd	2nd	1st
Japan	12th	13th	12th	11th	21st
Qatar	19th	4th	7th	20th	6th
Denmark	24th	23rd	27th	52nd	53rd
Taiwan, China	4th	3rd	3rd	3rd	5th
Canada	31st	26th	30th	32nd	24th
Norway	74th	70th	65th	70th	77th
Austria	83rd	76th	75th	65th	62nd
Belgium	96th	87th	88th	92nd	90th
Saudi Arabia	40th	31st	14th	6th	15th
Korea, Rep.	14th	28th	24th	15th	9th
Australia	26th	33rd	53rd	40th	80th

Table 2.1   Pay/productivity relationship *continued*

Country	Pay Strongly Related to Worker Productivity				
	2008	2009	2010	2011	2012
Ireland	76th	77th	56th	25th	32nd
Greece	103rd	120th	118th	122nd	132nd
Portugal	44th	72nd	106th	112nd	120th
Spain	84th	91st	109th	126th	133rd

Source: World Economic Forum (2008–2012)

In capital-intensive economies, a competent and skilled workforce needs to be adequately compensated. Although low costs of production are key in gaining competitive advantages in labour-intensive economic sectors that compete in cut-throat markets, the idea that low labour costs equate to higher productivity levels and higher levels of competitiveness, albeit correct in a stritu sense, never work that way in reality as one needs to look at comparative productivities and not at the productivity of an economy in isolation in ascertaining its relative global competitive position.

The reason why labour costs are not a good proxy for the competitiveness of a nation is threefold. On the one hand there is the issue of the sustainability of a cost–leadership strategy and the likelihood of competitor retaliation leading to the erosion of a competitive advantage based on cost. As in the goods and services markets, competitors do not stay put when one of the players decides unilaterally to lower prices. Competitors simply begin to retaliate. In the case of the labour market, wage cuts will be met by competitors with endless supplies of cheap labour. In a context of limitless supplies of virtually free labour that characterizes the labour markets of the less developed nations competing in labour-intensive economic sectors, it doesn't take much to guess who will end up on the losing side of a worldwide wage war.

This in labour markets is again analogous to what happens in the goods and services markets, and perhaps a good illustration would be an average neighbourhood corner store competing head to head against a large food retailer benefitting from huge economies of scale. The grocery shop next door decides to enter a price war with the hypermarket. Who will last longer? There are few doubts that the small retail operation would simply not last long. The same goes for the labour markets in labour-intensive sectors in the more developed economies as, if there can only be one cost leader, it stands to reason that it will be those economies that have plentiful and cheap labour resources that will be best equipped to sustain a model of this type for longer. What this means is that there will always be someone out there capable of undermining one's low labour cost strategy no matter how virtuous it may turn out to be.

The second reason why low costs of labour do not necessarily lead to improvements in productivity and national competitiveness is that if the economic environment is characterized as largely labour-intensive, then most likely competition in the market will be price-led, and lower-cost manufacturers will have the leeway to outcompete incumbents on price too. The third reason why low labour costs on the one hand and productivity and competitiveness on the other do not always go together is a marketing and branding one, and goes something along the lines of the idea that even by slashing labour costs, which allows you to sell cheaper, you've still not addressed the fundamental reasons why people should buy your products and not those of your low-cost competitors, as their prices, remember, are lower and price is typically a dominating criterion in buyer decision-making in labour-intensive sectors of the economy.

This would be of course different in capital-intensive, knowledge-based sectors of economic activity, as labour-endowed economies would not be able to respond effectively to wage cuts, in that their specific brand of labour is indistinct and does not hold any special skills or competencies. The problem here is that if you were to lower wages of highly skilled workers enough they would go somewhere else to exercise their trade, and that would have to be another capital-intensive competitor economy.

The other notion that is prevalent in today's economy is that lower labour cost structures impact favourably on the lowering of total costs of production and this has to be good news. This again is of course irrefutable. However, low labour costs are more a symptom of something pernicious and deeply wrong than a good thing. More than anything they signal a concentration of the productive effort in labour-intensive sectors that aggregate little value to output, rather than being a sign of high productivity and efficiency levels in the economy.

When exporting these basic, low value-added goods to sophisticated markets, where consumers are able to discern between competing offers and have the economic power to do so, these consumers will vote with their wallets. They will refuse to pay premium prices for products that in their minds have little intangible value, albeit with acknowledged tangible benefits. This is of course not a good sign when it comes to the more sophisticated export markets, those that demand products with higher technological content, higher knowledge requirements or fundamentally products that benefit from a higher reputational capital, and the anchored value that comes with a strong image and brand goodwill.

That said it is a fact of life that under the current economic climate, and for that matter under any economic climate, it would not be a good idea to increase salaries arbitrarily. This is a crass mistake, adding misery to grief in already debilitated economies. Salaries should of course always reflect worker productivities, measured by the scarce competencies and skills that are needed in production processes for the aggregation of value to goods and services under conditions of intense competition, where pretty much everyone else can potentially do the same. A concept of competitiveness anchored on low labour costs is also paradoxically the last thing a developed nation should want as it is not sustainable in the light of contemporary global economic dynamics.

The sociological ramifications of the thinking behind low salaries in economies are easy to fathom, but the economic rationale for the lowering of wages appears to be more difficult to counter as short-sighted entrepreneurs justify the prevalence of low wages in an economy as a pre-requisite for economic competitiveness of an economic sector or an entire economy. Low comparative salaries that prevail in some European economies, when contrasted with the average wages that are practised in other more developed European nations, are still much higher than the wage bills of competitors emanating from emerging economies that seek to be present in and that compete for the same export markets.

European organizations will never be able, nor should they desire to, compete with the emerging economies on low costs of labour. What needs to happen instead, in the cases of the less developed economies in Europe that have suffered significant erosions of their competitive positions, is a focus on higher economic order activities. These allow for the aggregation of value to goods and services founded on complex state-of-the-art knowledge and technological sophistication, applied to complex production processes, and translated into products that people want and buy, thus building reputational capital next to a key stakeholder constituency, that of consumers both domestically and abroad.

Organizations do not have any qualms or reservations in easily shutting down shop in one place only to open up the very next day somewhere completely different. In the majority of cases, delocalization allows organizations to add to low labour cost advantages that are inherent to newly found cheap labour markets, very generous (from the viewpoint of the organization) legal frameworks that regulate labour relations and practices in those economies, and which are much more favourable than those in their countries of origin, or those that are prevalent in countries where they are delocalizing from.

Organizations only delocalize their economic activity, however, if they understand the decision of leaving as purely one of rationally opting for lower total cost structures obtained by way of lower labour costs in labour-intensive sectors. Companies also tend to leave when and if the labour force they require is characterized as indistinct and undifferentiated and can easily be obtained anywhere in the world. However, if it is not that easy to find a qualified workforce that in addition to solid academic qualifications is also capable of drawing from a deep knowledge base and can easily cater to the specific requirements and modus operandi of the organization in question or the sector of economic activity in which it operates, then a decision to delocalize into cheaper labour markets is not straightforward by any means. In this context there will necessarily be other variables that will need to be brought into the equation, namely the costs of training a new workforce, or staffing the delocalized organization with specialist imported knowledge and identifying a resource pool of rare and valuable skills and competencies that are simply not available locally. If that is not achieved successfully the loss in output quality and competitive position of the organization is unquestionably what follows.

A workforce whose knowledge base is not only restricted to the technical and commercial issues that hinge on the particular economic sector in which it labours but whose skills and competencies easily cross over to other related and unrelated sectors, that is capable of understanding technology but also different ways of doing business, will certainly contribute to the economic competitiveness of a nation in ways that cannot be achieved by a pool of undifferentiated and unskilled labour. A workforce which is capable of demonstrating a well-rounded knowledge of upstream and downstream activities that are important links in the value chains of which the organization is a key player, whose knowledge competencies directly and objectively impact on business performance cannot easily be found elsewhere, making the decision to delocalize a more complex one than a mere comparison of wage structures would suggest.

An economy blessed with a highly knowledgeable and commercially versed workforce will create obstacles to organizations leaving its shores.

These in turn will think twice before delocalizing their activities on the grounds of having identified the next cheap labour hub somewhere in the world, as they may not find it that easy or even advantageous to move around searching relentlessly for the next lowest labour cost paradise. Many of them would be much more reluctant to abandon a country simply because labour costs are marginally lower somewhere else. They would have to sit down and consider other dimensions of the decision to leave and set up shop somewhere else, other perhaps more important variables that stand to play an important role on organizational success down the line, namely general levels and standards of knowledge of the workforce and its quality, measured by how easy it is to find equivalent substitutes in the countries where organizations delocalize to.

Without a highly qualified workforce, characterized by stringent knowledge requirements and excellent academic and professional credentials, it is impossible for organizations in an economy to acquire the expertise that is necessary to face contemporary challenges in the highly competitive global economy. Excellence in teaching and research in academic institutions and their corresponding output measured in a qualified workforce offer an added dimension to the competitiveness of firms in an economy, and need to be considered when an organization is making a decision to delocalize its business activities.

Academically rigorous training and the intellectual preparedness that comes with it allows for a more capable workforce, providing fertile ground for a typology of labour that is much more in tune with contemporary challenges and threats, as well as being more adept at detecting opportunities and interpreting reality better for every possible reason. Without the benefit of a knowledgeable workforce all that is left is an undifferentiated mass that can easily be replaced by almost anyone irrespective of origin. If this is the case multinational corporations are free to go anywhere they wish, the only relevant criterion for delocalization being the geography of costs of labour.

If the nature of labour is undifferentiated, in labour-intensive sectors where the only requirement is that of a basic workforce with rudimentary skills, in arriving at a decision to stay or leave, decision-makers do not even have to incorporate any sunk costs that have been incurred in training human resources in the countries from where they are leaving or to where they are migrating, as there are none. It is simply not an issue as labour is unskilled and undifferentiated. In this context, companies respond with a purist economic rationality of the kind that immediately suggests that the thing to do is to delocalize, searching for lower labour cost structures in less developed economies, without pondering these decisions in a more careful way. They do not need to. It is relatively straightforward.

Costs however are only the tip of the iceberg and, apart from workforce qualifications, there are a myriad of other dimensions that should matter, including the existence or not of adequate infrastructure, its calibre and widespread availability, the efficiency of the bureaucratic machine, the judicial system, and its capacity for arbitrating labour-related conflicts and the degree of enforcement of the law, amongst many other variables, that in the end may turn out to be the make or break of success when delocalizing to a new geography. When one or more of these fails, it may just be the case that the new found labour cost advantages are totally offset by the added costs incurred in unexpected bureaucracy or a judicial–justice system that simply does not work.

In protecting national interests, it is always difficult to find an optimum equilibrium between the mechanisms that are put in place to attract FDI into a country and the penalties that necessarily need to be stipulated to prevent premature abandonment of the economy by organizations that are often the beneficiaries of very privileged fiscal conditions, and other incentives that presuppose consistency of purpose and an idea of permanence.

In other words, the idea is not to dissuade these multinational corporations and other investors from coming in in the first place. On the contrary, the intention is to create the incentives for organizations to come into a country but it is also important to ensure that it is not easy for them to leave. Much of this however has little to do with legislation and perhaps a lot more with the reason why they came in the first place. If the reason why they came in was that of low labour costs, when a new cheaper source becomes available these organizations will just migrate there, but if the reason why they came in was a highly educated and skilled labour force, then they have no reason to leave.

The only reason why companies do not leave in the long run is because they believe it does not make economic sense for them to leave. That of course needs to be a function of perceived labour quality and scarcity of critical skills, how difficult and costly it would be to replicate labour of this calibre in the short run elsewhere in the event of a delocalization of activity into a lower labour cost economy. Again in capital-intensive economies this should not be a problem, as the high calibre of labour simply makes it extremely difficult to find widespread equivalent skills and competencies just around the corner.

The scrutiny of multinational corporations is strictly about the economic rationale of competing alternatives and its evaluation. Can both scenarios of staying or leaving be quantified? Multinational corporations move from country to country according to economic criteria, searching for an elusive equilibrium between rationalizing labour cost structures and searching for a skilled, competent and knowledgeable workforce.

There is historical precedent for the phenomenon of delocalization, and the North American Free Trade Agreement (NAFTA) between Canada, the USA and Mexico at the end of the 1980s provides ample evidence for the dynamics of the delocalization of firms and its consequences. At the time a great many organizations, mostly American but some also Canadian, shut shop on a Friday in their places of origin, only to open up somewhere south of the border the following Monday.

Low labour costs also mean that workers in these economies are not competent to the point where their skills would naturally command higher wages in competitive labour markets. This is a circular argument, one where companies search for low wage labour markets, but low wage labour markets are that because they are made up of unskilled undifferentiated labour that do not contribute much to the augmentation of value to production processes and products. That is why wages are lower and it is cheaper out there.

An unskilled and cheap workforce adds minimal value to goods and services, and the corresponding output coming out of manufacturing processes where it is used will only be able to generate low margins in very competitive export markets. In labour-intensive economic activities this is always the case, except of course unless that output is then branded with a recognizable label that commands the imagination and the preference of consumers worldwide, very much in the manner of the example of Portuguese and Italian shoes that was given earlier.

Another example is that of multinational corporations like Nike and Gap Inc. and others, which operate factories out of Southeast Asia. However, in many cases these organizations, whenever controversy arises on such sensitive matters as child labour or the treatment of women and the rights of workers in the workplace, just claim that they do not own these factories. In fact, some of these factories, which many refer to as sweatshops, manufacture exclusively for Nike and Gap Inc.

If entrepreneurs are not doing their jobs, that of constantly scrutinizing and monitoring the global environment for business opportunities, the only way that profitability is going to be achieved in competitive market environments and in labour-intensive sectors is by squeezing labour costs down even further. This corresponds to more of a downward spiralling effect than a circular motion, as a model anchored on low labour costs and labour-intensive economic activities is unsustainable in the short run, as witnessed by the thousands of bankruptcies of small businesses particularly in southern Europe currently. Other European economies are following suit with significant slowdowns in economic activity in Germany and the UK, the difference here being that not much remains in the way of a labour-intensive economic structure in these countries.

This downward spiralling effect that comes from the narrow mindedness of a search for productivity gains through the lowering of labour costs of unskilled workers is not sustainable in a European context, in the light of global competitive dynamics. Low-cost production leads to little aggregated value and negligible bases for differentiation of market offers, making impossible the acquisition of sustainable angles of competitive advantage.

This model is not viable for European economies and these will remain out of control until something is done to structurally alter this state of affairs. This means that there is an imperative for thinking about productivity and competitiveness issues in a different light, ensuring that production efficiency parameters are met upstream in manufacturing, but also guaranteeing that downstream at market level, organizations focus on the critical issues of value aggregation, image building and the creation and nurturing of the all-important asset of reputational capital and goodwill.

Coming back to the earlier example of the Italian shoes and the Portuguese shoes, both manufactured in the little town of São João da Madeira in the northwest of Portugal by the same person, using the same materials, working the same number of hours and with identical compensation of the labour employed in the manufacturing of both pairs of shoes, we conclude that the Italian shoes, whose only thing Italian is the logo, sell under a well-known brand for an incomparably higher price than that of the Portuguese shoe. Having approached this matter in the context of the productivity of workers, it is now time to analyse the impact of this story on the GDP of both countries.

When importing shoes from Portugal and selling them in the UK, the British retailer is contributing to national British GDP. The retailer aggregates value to a product whose manufacturing he was not involved with in any way, shape or form, but he did give it a name, a recognizable high-street retailer's brand, thus introducing a meaningful change in the supplied good that would prove to make all the difference. More to the point, British GDP increases by the difference between retail sales of imported products and the cost of importing the same goods. That is, by importing the pair of shoes and paying X for them to the Portuguese exporter, only to retail them for 5X in the UK, the impact on GDP of retailing imported products and aggregating value to them just by branding those shoes is anything but negligible, particularly as the British retailer had nothing to do with the actual making of the shoe.

This aggregation of value without any visible productive connotation upstream cannot be underestimated when GDP values are contrasted between countries as measures of national wealth. This is more so when, as a function of the disparities between the GDP of nations, this is precisely the argument that is used to stigmatize workers for being slow and unproductive, when they have little to do with the commercialization of products, in particular in international settings.

As GDP is a universally accepted measure of the wealth of a nation, and GDP per capita is the equivalent for the welfare of individuals, it stands to reason that countries whose basis for accumulating wealth is not founded on economic activities that aggregate value do not rank highly in the GDP pecking order of nations, whilst countries whose economic activities are closer to consumers, countries with brands and also branded countries, tend to rank much higher on GDP tables.

The crux of the matter is that without ever having intervened in the process of manufacturing shoes, the contribution of the British retailer to his country's GDP is incomparably higher than the equivalent of the Portuguese worker to the GDP of Portugal. This means that if productivity is a ratio of the value of output over inputs (productive factors), it is of little importance to consider output quantities generated for a given combination of inputs, but it is critically important to focus on the market value of that output. The market value of the Italian shoe is much higher than that of the Portuguese shoe, but the shoe is the same.

It is of course mandatory for organizations to strive for efficient combinations of production inputs in manufacturing if they want to remain a going concern, but what is really important is to think of creative ways in which to aggregate value to our products, even if they are not the best in the world or do not derive from the most efficient and state-of-the-art manufacturing processes in terms of the knowledge and technology that is built into them. Desirably, both market value and production efficiencies should come together but that does not always happen. One thing is for sure, a company can go on for some time not being the most efficient at what it does, but if it doesn't have any clients it won't last long.

In conclusion, what is relevant in a market economy, where consumers have money to spend, is that the value of a good or service is in the end a function of the willingness of consumers in destination markets, first to prefer our products to those of others and secondly to be willing to pay a premium price for the same product as a function of higher perceived value, irrespective of technological content or any other tangible dimension built into the product. What went into the product, how it was manufactured, and often, even the technical intricacies that characterize it, hold little interest for the savvy contemporary consumer who could not care less about those more complex dimensions of the product equation.

Northern European countries, those who rank highly in the labour productivity tables and the national competitiveness leagues, tend to see their top corporate brands occupying the most valuable places in global supply chains. In a spectrum that goes from production to consumption in any value chain, organizations in these economies prefer to be close to the consumer where they are able to derive higher value as margins are higher, particularly for branded goods of high notoriety and value.

This being the case, and again going back to the national productivity formula of output value over inputs used to generate that value of output in an economy, it is understandable why the low-cost manufacturing nations have lower productivities. Perhaps it is because workers in these economies are less skilled and competent, but in all certainty it is also because these unskilled workers do not have dynamic and pro-active entrepreneurs relaying to them the exigencies of foreign sophisticated consumers and training them to respond adequately to these. A workforce of this calibre and a non-existent entrepreneurial class combine in failing to augment value to manufactured goods, forcing the economy to occupy links upstream in value chains where competition is intense and operating margins are lower. This being the case it is still easier to have a presence upstream in the value chain than downstream next to consumers, as the latter requires a totally different set of organizational skills and competencies.

Branded countries with strong reputations, whose economies benefit from positive country of origin halos, are also the nations that have seen their economies build notorious, globally acclaimed and valuable brands. Organizations in these economies tend to dominate the positions downstream in key value chains. They do this by developing and nurturing strong and valuable corporate and product brands. Here, nearer to the consumer, the potential for differentiation and in particular for finding emotional differentiation expressed in branded goods is higher. The possibilities for value aggregation to products are also higher when operating downstream in value chains and next to consumers for marketing reasons, and finally, operating margins for whoever owns and controls the brand are also incomparably higher downstream.

The relative position occupied by key firms or even entire economic sectors in most global value chains counts. As we progress downstream in a value chain, the links where most value is concentrated are precisely the ones that are closer to the consumer. If a significant component of the economic activity of a nation is located upstream in a global value chain, or alternatively, if the principal sectors of activity in an economy are located downstream in the same value chain, this makes all the difference for the competitiveness of a nation and for its productivity levels. Not only that, it says a lot about the sustainability of the particular economic model of competitiveness of a nation.

Countries which have worked hard to progress downstream in key value chains of their principal sectors of economic activity, and have done so by working to establish credible and valuable corporate and product brands, anchored on positive country reputations, will naturally find it easier to build their GDP, whilst other economies who are incapable of identifying meaningful aggregators of value to their otherwise undifferentiated goods and services will have to build their exports component of GDP by selling enough goods and services abroad, rather than by aggregating value to their current export base.

The populations of the wealthier nations naturally enjoy better standards of living, as GDP is strongly correlated with widely accepted measures of human and social and economic development, including the provision of quality health and education systems. These economies have for some time now subcontracted low value-added, trivial, unattractive and most times environmentally-sensitive activities that belong upstream in value chains to low labour cost hubs, typically in emerging economies but not only.

When it is the case that the subcontracting of these activities with low value-added potential has been farmed out to other poorer economies within the European territory, and these have received them with open arms, this constitutes a clear sign that the governments and organizations in these European nations have totally missed the point, and have failed to understand what is really at stake here – the complexity of the country competitiveness game and the role of value chain management and control over it.

Being very efficient in labour-intensive economic sectors upstream in the value chain implies being adept at the manufacturing equation and having a keen eye for every possible aspect of cost rationalization and specifically identifying ways in which to reduce labour costs. This is not a sustainable strategic outlook for any European economy today no matter how low wages are in any part of Europe. Even if one is to achieve the pinnacle of manufacturing efficiency upstream, by being marginally or even much better than others at optimizing production efficiencies and input combinations in production processes, in the end it is a matter of time before one's competitive advantage is copied and hence eroded. This is particularly true in sectors of economic activity where technology is of easy diffusion and rudimentary knowledge is required and not difficult to obtain.

What any economic sector in Europe should aim for instead, and in the light of current global competitive dynamics, is to progress downstream in their respective value chains and focus sharply on the links that constitute effective value generators. The emphasis also needs to be on shifting the balance radically towards capital-intensive sectors of economic activity with the acquisition of sustainable competitive advantages founded on exquisite technological requirements that are very difficult to replicate, and that go hand in hand with top notch labour skills and competencies grounded on cutting-edge technical and commercial knowledge.

The characterization of economies as being capital-intensive, and ultimately anchored on reputable brands means that goods and services that are brought to market under these conditions are necessarily of high value, perceived by savvy consumers in sophisticated markets all over the world as superior to competing goods and services that perform the very same function, but somehow fail to capture the imagination of the consumer.

This value aggregation equation is achieved through marketing, branding and the enhancement of national, corporate and product reputations. In the case of national reputation the best way to achieve this is by nurturing positive country images next to external stakeholder constituencies, and this can best be done through recourse to numerous examples of constant consumption experiences of excellence with exceptional products that can be traced back to a particular brand and country.

This can only be achieved if the workforce is educated – meaning the exposure of a society to formal high-calibre schooling but also a society that is formatted to pursue lifelong knowledge and the acquisition of skills for the betterment of the individual. Only by doing this can a workforce be equipped with the kinds of both generalist competencies and specialist skills that translate into a more demanding citizenship in every respect and also in the context of consumption decision-making.

These collective skills, when mixed with technology and innovation in efficient goods, services and labour markets, under conditions of transparency and good governance, with a bureaucracy that aims to simplify and a judiciary that arbitrates conflicts and does not add to the entropy, create a hotbed for the true aggregators of value in the economic offer to kick in and thus make business environments more sophisticated. This of course requires a long-term strategic perspective and not ad hoc and short-term solutions driven by the whim of political cycles and their management to party political interests but not the interests of national competitiveness.

Take Britain and Sweden for example. They are both nations with strong industrial traditions but are currently strong mainly in the services sector. Both of these countries, albeit in different economic sectors, subcontract activities that are economically unattractive to them to countries such as Portugal, Turkey, India and others. These are productive activities in economic sectors that generate little value to the host country. They are undifferentiated activities, in that anybody can do them, as they entail few specific skills and competencies, and even these do not constitute significant obstacles for anyone wishing to enter the market to do so with a degree of probability of success.

On the other hand, emergent economies that possess an endless supply of cheap labour, apt for these types of economic activities, are unbeatable when it comes to their unlimited capacity for lowering their costs of labour even further. In addition to this, and probably linked to it, these nations present lousy records on human rights, the treatment of workers, women and child labour, as well as more sinister and dubious labour practices that are virtually impossible to monitor. Labour-intensive, low value-added sectors in the developed economies are particularly susceptible to competition from these emerging economies as they require undifferentiated manual labour as their main productive input.

Organizations operating upstream in value chains are forced to work on volume as margins are extremely tight in manufacturing. There is always someone with a better business model elsewhere, which in this case only means someone operating on a substantially lower labour cost structure somewhere across the globe. It is virtually impossible for European economies to compete in labour-intensive sectors, and when they do, and if these sectors show above average profitability, it is only a matter of time before a pack of competitors jumps onto the bandwagon to drive profitability down, through low-price strategies sustained by low labour cost structures.

These are also sectors of economic activity with tremendous environmental problems. The more developed nations and their educated populations tend to see these as huge problems, aware as they are of the significance of the environmental agenda for a new archetype of conscientious and sustainable economic development. The more sophisticated economies are not interested in having controversial and environmentally-sensitive economic activities in their backyard and for that reason these are farmed out to other nations that have no alternative but to accept them. These less developed economies do indeed welcome these less palatable activities with open arms, strapped as they are of any form of industrial activity and faced with legions of unemployed and the political pressure that comes with that.

There are examples of organizations that manage to go against the grain in their own turf and turn out to become global examples of true excellence. This is difficult as the tendency is one of perpetuation of the status quo, and it is really the intensity of the competitive environment that brings out the best in organizational excellence. The retail brand Zara is part of the Spanish Inditex group and is a good illustration of the point above. This organization is an example of shrewd strategic planning and efficient extrapolation of basic principles of supply chain and logistics management, as well as other methods imported from the automobile industry, namely Just in Time (JIT) techniques pioneered by Toyota in Japan, bringing them into the fashion industry.

Unfortunately there aren't too many Zaras and its equivalent in other sectors of economic activity around in southern Europe, with perhaps the exception of northern Italy where fashion brands proliferate and the odd company in Spain. Zara is an example of good practice and illustrates how the paradigm of north to south subcontracting of less value-added activities needs not be an inevitable fatalism. The Inditex Group effectively realized from very early on what the determinants of competitiveness and the drivers of profitability in the fashion business were. In doing that, they concluded that it was imperative to exercise full control over the elements of the supply chain that effectively generate value.

Zara accomplished this by introducing a hybrid system consisting of own production, coupled with local subcontracting in Galicia or northern Portugal to cater for unplanned demand in accordance with the fast-fashion paradigm that it had brought to the world along with Swedish newcomers H&M. In conjunction with this they also sourced from the low labour cost paradises in the Far East for planned demand where it could afford longer lead times. In effect Zara and the Inditex group, with its vast stable of valuable brands including Massimo Dutti, Bershka, Stradivarius and many others, were to revolutionize the fashion world and revoke the incumbent paradigm in the clothing retail sector at that time by introducing short supply cycles and lead times, copying well-known designer names with what were no more than cheap imitations of elitist branded products, in line with the values and aspirations of their core target markets.

If one walks into a Zara store today, there is a strong possibility that upon coming back to the same store only a couple of weeks later that the merchandise that was there before will no longer be available. Running the risk of not finding what one is looking for corresponds – in today's world of appearances, concern with image and rampant consumption – to a strong incentive to buy, an important element of induced consumer excitement and conversely a sense of loss if one just misses out on a unique opportunity. These are all traits of a great business model, patented by Zara, who have been doing this extremely well for over 20 years now.

Excitement and adventure are traits inherent to the buying experience, the importance of which cannot be underestimated for sophisticated consumers in today's world of fashion immediacy. Calculated risk-taking has always been part and parcel of the Zara blueprint. Excitement here translates into a positive state of anxiety induced in the consumer, which compels him or her to buy there and then and not run the risk of missing out on a great purchasing opportunity. Another element that corroborates the described paradigm shift in the fashion business relates to the idea of seasonality. Whoever within the sector still thinks in terms of well-defined seasons and seasonality in fashion, spring–summer or autumn–winter collections, is missing out on the all-important fast-fashion concept, a kind of consumerist immediacy that imposes flexibility and quick response as its structural pillars. The same thinking is valid for other sectors of economic activity.

In conclusion, it is important not to stigmatize the worker or to attribute the true reasons for low labour productivity levels solely to worker inefficiency. Entrepreneurs and governments have not revealed the necessary strategic acumen and vision to pursue growth models focussed on the real economy of production of goods and services. In lieu of that many European governments have opted for an obsessive focus on macro-economic issues and thinking as well as speculative financial economics that do not create wealth.

Few have failed to emphasize the importance of the control of critical links of key value chains in important export sectors – as described earlier that is the elements that effectively generate value in an economy. Rather than being landed with dangerous manufacturing facilities that most developed economies would refuse to have in their own backyard, the strategy for less developed European economies has long needed to be one of overriding emphasis on innovation, education and knowledge-creation, leading to more sophisticated business environments. This in turn would mean that stakeholders in an economy would impose stringent parameters of exigency from organizations, translating into a demand for goods and services of high aggregated value, implying that key sectors of economic activity would have to relocate downstream in the value chains of promising market sectors.

Instead, complacency, lack of political vision and entrepreneurial short-sightedness all meant that corporate and personal interests took precedent over national or sector strategic issues, or for that matter anything that remotely coincided with the collective interests of the community. Governments were complacent in at least not doing much to stop this from happening. This is true of the southern European economies, but rather than being exclusive to these nations, it has affected other European countries albeit to different degrees.

Entrepreneurs in these economies did not need to be competitive, at least according to the real determinants of competitiveness that in the final analysis are reflected in the ability at every moment and for every transaction of convincing export markets of the relative merits of goods and services in relation to those of competitors aiming for the same markets. Prices of exported products had to be competitive in markets where countries had an historical presence, and when they were not the usual exchange rate fix would kick in to save the day. Currency devaluation policy measures introduced under fixed exchange rate regimes after Bretton Woods would ensure that a nation's exports would be cheaper in foreign denomination and thus apparently and only apparently more competitive in the world stage. Exchange rate currency devaluation or depreciation worked like a drug under fixed and flexible exchange rate systems respectively, sorting the problem for a short period of time, but immediately making matters worse.

Unfortunately, although convenient and even effective in the short-term stimulation of exports, exchange rate policy instruments have in many cases little to do with the reasons that make a sector of activity truly appealing to foreign constituencies and competitive in global markets. On the contrary, currency devaluation, applied whenever things are tough going for a nation's exports due to ever more demanding and sophisticated foreign consumers, ends up seriously contributing to a collective feeling of complacency, dangerous relaxation and a lowering of the competitive guard. This is particularly true for the psychological effects produced on entrepreneurs in sectors that are dependent upon export markets, who end up losing touch with the changing needs and wants of foreign constituencies. This is of course in the fortunate cases where they were ever in touch with those needs.

Paradoxically, another fundamental problem afflicting nations today, which justifies the lack of competitiveness of many contemporary economies, is the deep-rooted entrepreneurial bias towards the tyranny of prices as the only determinant of competitiveness in key export markets. This has to do with decades of the ad hoc use of the currency devaluation lever of exchange rate policy in many European economies. These economies, many of them with significant labour-intensive sectors, were left stranded, stuck in the middle and halfway between the irrevocably lower labour cost structures of the emerging economies on the one hand and an innate inability to adequately differentiate their offer and aggregate value to their best products. They can as a result manufacture cheap goods better than anyone else in Europe, but they cannot make them cheaper than the new entrants coming out of the emerging economies in the Far East.

These southern European players do not have a problem of technological obsolescence, on the contrary, but they do not possess the branding prowess of the more competitive northern European economies. They have gotten away with manufacturing cheap goods and placing them in the more affluent markets at competitive prices, but this is only viable until such a time that a lower-cost entrant comes into the market and outcompetes incumbents on price. Again this inherent vulnerability has become a significant issue because incumbents have let price remain an overriding competitive criterion in retail buying decision-making and have failed to work hard on the intangible dimensions of supply.

Although labour costs have on average been lower in absolute terms in southern Europe than in northern Europe, they are still substantially higher than those practised in emerging economies that compete with them in labour-intensive sectors for the same export markets. However, the low costs of labour hid something a lot more sinister and profoundly marking of the problems with the economic development of southern European countries. This was that there are significant pockets of undifferentiated masses of unqualified and indistinct labour with no specific competencies to stimulate and to sustain the development of sectors of higher technological content and inbuilt complex knowledge. This was labour that for the most part could easily be found anywhere in the world.

Compulsory exposure to formal education up until a certain age has a significant impact on the intellectual abilities of individuals to continue learning throughout their lives. A workforce that does not engage in the pursuit of constant and systematic learning throughout the working lives of individuals is unable to develop abstract thinking competencies that would enable them to subsequently grasp complex skills and capabilities in later life. A workforce with such characterization will forever be condemned to a superficial grasp of complex contemporary issues, not only of a technical and specialist nature but also of more general, global and wide-ranging problems.

New methods and technology, innovative processes and procedures, technical and market challenges and the permanent defiance of the incumbent status quo is what brings out the very best in people as they are forced out of their psychological comfort zones. Societies who under-invest in education are confronted with realities where their citizens find it extremely hard to develop capabilities of logical reasoning and out-of-the-box thinking. An increasingly complex world will require more and more of a toolkit of skills that allow people in organizations to be comfortable in fairly heterogeneous situations both from the viewpoint of technology but also that of changing market demand.

Worker skills in the context alluded to herein do not refer solely to the world of labour and the corresponding competencies that a suitable workforce needs to possess in facing increasing technical complexity, but also to the set of mundane social competencies that are required in dealing and managing common everyday situations. This includes the ability to deal with ambiguity and making decisions in the light of extreme uncertainty in the workplace and in markets, outside-the-box thinking, working in unstructured work environments, making sound judgments and decisions with the information available, and developing a conscience of rights but crucially also of duties and obligations.

A failure to develop fundamental analytical skills traduces a lower ability to think logically about complex problems that require sequencing of thought processes in their resolution. At a stage of their lives when individuals are being shaped in their intellectual abilities, shortcomings of this nature constitute a disadvantage for life. High-calibre academic preparation has profound sociological and economic repercussions on the future of individuals and collectively on the future of societies, nations and economies.

A volatile world is made up of constant change. In the world of organizations, change is breath-taking. The emphasis here is not so much on the rate of technological change and how well organizations manage technology in the updating of production processes and techniques – this in itself is of huge significance for organizational survival in cut-throat competitive business environments – but market change and the imperative of keeping up with market trends and aesthetic preferences, and what from the perspective of the consumer constitutes value at each point in time is a more substantive challenge to organizations today.

The consumer needs to be understood as a dynamic entity, the most volatile of economic agents, whose behavioural profiling varies in accordance with predictable socio-demographic and economic criteria, but also following aesthetic and cultural nuances and societal values that are much less susceptible to modelling and forecasting. The study of socio-economic and demographic trends undoubtedly aids strategic planning in firms, but often the decision-maker is required to resort to a kind of informed intuition that emanates from a mixture of empirical evidence and experiential knowledge and schooling, a deep understanding of the reality on the ground but also of the theoretical advancements in a particular field.

All of this is of course important, only because markets are different in their characteristics both intrinsic and extrinsic. A selective approach to the markets, with a corresponding allocation of resources and a targeted offer that matches the particular requirements of homogeneous groups of consumers is critical for the survival of organizations in competitive environments. Where science ends and art begins in strategically approaching heterogeneous markets is difficult to know. Strategic market planning therefore relies on a finely tuned blend of science and art.

By scrutinizing the environment better than competitors, organizations are able to derive above average economic profitability. However, and given the rising complexity of the business macro-environment on every aspect that hinges on organizational performance, it has become increasingly difficult for organizational success to be solely dependent on the ability, knowledge and innate qualities of good management.

Reality Check...

Levi Strauss & Co

Levi's suffered from an acute lack of distinctiveness and confused positioning in the jeans business in the 1970s. A brand whose historical heritage lay on the values of the American west, founded on free-spirit, Levi's personifies the embodiment of good old American ideals of freedom and individuality. Back in the 1970s however, the organization faced a serious problem of lack of identity in its corporate brand and of confused and diffused values, embroiled as it was in a desperate attempt to be everything to everyone.

The hippie movement had lost its momentum and with the end of the war in Vietnam there were no obvious social, political and ideological struggles around, at least of the same magnitude and intensity of societal involvement of the collectivist ideals of the 1960s embodied in the peace and love mantra. There was a kind of emptying of significant and worthwhile causes in American society. The yuppie movement of the 1980s was also still a long time coming.

Levi's chose a confusing product line and nobody understood what was going on. Certainly their core customers had no idea what these new product lines were all about and they started to walk away. The company went through a bad patch in the 1970s, and it took them a while to recover. It was not really until the launch of the legendary 50s jeans that they were able to begin to recover from this slump. The 50s launch was a landmark for Levi Strauss and Co. and the campaigns at the time were to become a watershed in advertising history. Of particular notoriety was the Launderette campaign.

Through an extremely well succeeded communications strategy, Levi's would be able to overcome strategic brand positioning mistakes that it had been accumulating for over a decade. In a relatively short time span Levi's turned around a business liability, that of a complete lack of distinctiveness in the brand and unclear positioning to consumers, into a case study of marketing success. The innovative advertising anchored on exciting soundtracks were always critical to the Levi's image. With Launderette, Levi's' sales went up by 70 per cent in thesUSA alone in just one year. The Lee brand saw an increase in sales of four per cent in the same period, without them spending a dime in advertising. This was exclusively to do with people who never wore jeans before joining the jeans craze. They were not fans of the Levi's brand. In the end, even Levi's competitors stood to benefit from this wave of success.

In the process, the consumption of boxer shorts went up, when Nick Kamen showed up on TV wearing shorts in the Launderette ad. This was to leave its mark in advertising history. Nothing of this magnitude had ever been achieved in retail history. This was without precedent, and it proved a lifesaver for Bob Haas, the CEO of Levi Strauss & Co., who had only a few years earlier, risked the family fortune on a management buyout.

Levi's problem was not having noticed and anticipated the change in values that were beginning to take shape in American society at the end of the 1960s, and the beginning of the 1970s. This relaxed posture and lack of pro-activity characterizes many contemporary organizations. When business is going well, the tendency is to think that there is no reason for it not to do well forever. Bill Gates once said that it is precisely at those times, when companies are performing well, that one should question the status quo. The simple logic here is that nothing, good or bad, lasts forever. The idea is to capitalize on the good times, as you never know what the future holds.

As for Bob Haas, great grand-nephew of the founder of the compan, Levi Strauss himself, he became a multimillionaire, in part due to the appreciation of his holdings of Levi's shares. In little over ten years, Levi's shares would be quoted at prices that were 53 times higher than those at which Haas had purchased them. A BBC documentary, made over ten years ago on the success of the Levi's brand, would qualify this business turnaround as one of turning denim into gold, a modern day alchemy and one whose formula was patented by Levi Strauss & Co.

3

Workers, Entrepreneurs and Productivity

This chapter explores further labour productivity in the wider context of the national productivity debate, and the ideological exploitation of the antagonistic dichotomy of capital and labour in the Marxian dialectic, with the inclusion of a third stakeholder, that which Galbraith called technostructure (senior management) in multinational corporations. The argument that is sustained here is that productivity needs to be about more than the optimal combination of human and technological resources as inputs to the production of goods and services.

The productivity of an economy is the ratio of output over inputs used to generate that level of output in an economy over a defined period of time. The role of the technostructure in aggregating value to goods and services directly and favourably impacts on the numerator of this productivity ratio. In less market-orientated economies the role of management in aggregating value to goods and services and in constantly searching for an adequacy between different characterizations of supply and demand has been well and truly underestimated.

The intricacies of productivity is approached here as well as a generalized tendency for the stigmatization of workers or entrepreneurs depending on which side of the ideological fence one sits on in what is a more complex discussion than is often thought. Labour productivity levels in southern European economies are typically taken to be below that of the European average. However southern European labour abroad is generally well-regarded and highly productive. What then is the problem?

There may be alternative explanations as to why this is the case but perhaps as good as any is that when exposed to better management and a more efficient organization of the work effort, under the auspices of clearly defined rules and transparent mechanisms, southern European workers inevitably become more productive, as indeed any other worker would, under identical conditions. In essence, labour productivity has to do with the efficiency of management in the organization of the work process, formal education levels of the workforce, the wide diffusion of a culture of constant learning and the pursuit of specialist knowledge skills and competencies.

This is one side of the productivity equation, one where low productivity levels typically go hand in hand with the stigmatization of workers. The other side of productivity, which is less exploited perhaps for ideological reasons, is that of the lack of pro-activity and entrepreneurial spirit and what this does to entire sectors of economic activity which are not able to expand beyond their domestic markets.

Differences in productivity levels between national economies or sectors of activity in different economies may, *ceteris paribus* and assuming equivalent conditions of government bureaucracy and good functioning of the judicial and justice systems, be attributable to differing general levels of entrepreneurial initiative and pro-activity between the economies of nations. Differences in productivity levels between national economies may relate more to entrepreneurial spirit and less to peripheral considerations on culture and ethnic idiosyncrasies that stigmatize workers depending on such variables as country of origin and cultural traits. In saying that, it is nevertheless true that entrepreneurial spirit and initiative are also linked to culture, education and industrial tradition.

Productivity levels and salaries in an economy should desirably correlate at all times. It is conceivable that lower labour productivity levels have as much to do with the worker's failure to contribute to production processes in a distinctive and valuable manner as it is attributable to a technostructure that fails to aggregate value to goods and services, that does not know how to build and nurture valuable brands, or to entrepreneurs that fail to pro-actively reach out to new markets and create notoriety for unbranded products that otherwise have exceptional intrinsic value. Low productivity levels may be attributable to the absence of a set of unique skills and competencies of the workforce but other skills and competencies should equip the technostructure, without which great products will forever remain unknown cult secrets for limited domestic consumption.

Productivity may have little to do with the workforce, particularly in competitive markets, where there are ample opportunities for the aggregation of value to goods and services next to discerning consumers with high disposable income. This is less so in business contexts where exporting organizations are price-takers. If the labour process is well-organized and workers are equipped with the necessary competencies, their nationality is irrelevant to productivity. There are of course cultural specificities and work ethic-related issues that may characterize and stereotype workers from particular origins and that intervene to justify differences in labour productivities across different geographies.

However, what is intended here is the provision of a clear argument for the non-stigmatization of workers, offering an alternative perspective instead, one which puts the onus of responsibility on sound management and the role of entrepreneurship, underpinning a value-aggregation philosophy. This being said it is important that workers are equipped with state-of-the-art general and specific knowledge as there is a correlation between worker skills and competencies and labour productivity.

The concept of productivity has been defined in various ways. Samuelson and Nordhaus define productivity as:

> *A term that refers to the ratio of outputs and inputs in an economy. Total output divided by the inputs utilized in the production process is productivity. Total output divided by labour inputs used to derive that output is labour productivity. Productivity increases when by using the same quantity of input in the production process, higher output levels are generated. Changes in labour productivity occur when technology and worker competence improve. (Samuelson and Nordhaus, 1999)*

Productive is also defined as: 'The production of goods that have economic value' (Webster's Dictionary, Canadian Edition).

The ability to combine a long-term strategic vision with the tactical resolution of everyday problems is one of the rarest traits to find in organizational leadership, reflected at one in the same individual. To have the faculty to think the organization into the long term is particularly difficult in the current context of extreme uncertainty. The volatility of the macro-environment independent of whether its characterization is political, economic, technological or sociological, the unpredictability of crucial business variables including the changing nature of demand, the cut-throat intensity of almost every competitive environment and the ephemeral nature of competitive advantages, make it very difficult for organizations to think strategically. In many cases survival concerns obliterate any notion of strategic long-term thinking as a reasonable timeframe to operate within.

In this context, of particular relevance to contemporary organizations is the development of instruments that allow for the best possible characterization of demand, the complete understanding of the customer and its idiosyncrasies, and preferably that this is done in real time. The anticipation and satisfaction of customer requisites as the ultimate and overriding objective of the efficient and effective organization is the key idea behind marketing philosophy and practice. It constitutes the central theme in many a conference and keynote speeches of gurus and pseudo-gurus the world over. Everyone with varying degrees of authority talks and writes about customer satisfaction and the importance of managing and retaining customers as a proxy to organizational success.

There exists a vast literature that corroborates the importance of customer loyalty for an organization in many sectors of economic activity. A satisfied customer will recommend a company to between three to five potential new clients. A dissatisfied customer on the other hand is unlikely to return and to make matters worse he or she will tell an average of 14 people about the negative experience, particularly if it relates to bad service or to people in the organization being indifferent (Doyle, 1999).

Human nature is much better at propagating bad news and reinforcing negativity than in eulogizing good practice. This chain of negativity has perverse side-effects that are extremely difficult to quantify for an organization, as the only visible clue is that customers simply refuse to come back. Often before anyone inside the organization is able to do anything it is too late. This has become even more of an acute problem with the advent of the social media networks and blogging. Often the damage is simply manifested in customer alienation and preference given to competitors, who apparently provide the exact same product or service, but are perceived to do both better.

Customer retention and satisfaction is taken all too seriously indeed these days, and its study has progressed from just that of stating the importance of customer loyalty to organizations to the development of algorithms that allow for the estimation of the lifetime value of a customer for a particular organization. The calculation of the lifetime value of a single customer for an organization is done frequently today, with more or less rigorous methodologies, using complex algorithms and mathematical techniques. In effect, the ideas coming out of these studies are surprising, not so much for the novelty or sophistication of the concepts applied in the measurement of customer loyalty that are proposed in them, most of which corroborate common sense and intuition, but more because of what is now known to be the extreme importance of customer loyalty for the long-term sustained commercial success of an organization.

Armed with this evidence, companies have felt the need to give serious consideration to customer loyalty and to think about these issues as much more than sophisticated marketing gimmicks. Not alienating clients is the first and overriding purpose in the construction of long-lasting relationships between the organization and its customer base. Clients abandon a company due to negative perceptions of organizational arrogance or simply because the levels of service that are provided to them are judged to be pedestrian. Bad service is not exclusively down to the relationship between front-line employees and the client, but is instead a reflection of the totality of the experience enjoyed by key stakeholders that have a vested interest in the organization. Recent work on the management of corporate reputation clearly suggests that emotional involvement between the client and the organization expressed in customer satisfaction and retention is a key predictor of financial success.

People look at organizations in complex ways, but invariably the corporate brand asset is worth a lot more than the sum of the individual products that the organization brings to the marketplace. For many, the corporate brand is a sign of status, of belonging and social affirmation. For others, the organizational brand serves as a reservoir of value, a comfort zone in consumption, a mechanism that allows for the reduction of ambiguity in the buying decision-making process.

For some people, organizations are like old friends, buddies who they grow up with, and about whom they believe to know everything there is to know. That is why in the case of firms, in the same way as with friends, we are often taken aback by unexpected behaviour, actions that are totally out of character, whilst with others we tend to forget and forgive the odd mishap and wrongdoing as in our heart of hearts we know what the organization is really about.

For firms, like people, can be argued to also possess character and identity. Substantive deviations from expected normative behavioural patterns on the part of firms in relation to what consumers expect from them cause a cognitive dissonance. This corresponds to the gap between individual and societal expectations of the organization on the one hand and underlying corporate behaviours on the other. When the former are not met by the latter, consumers simply walk away and give their custom somewhere else. They leave often never to come back, and they do so while letting the whole world know what they think of the organization, its products and its levels of service provision.

In modern economies, firms are immeasurably more than sheer providers of goods and services. Excellent organizations with a strategic vision for the future operate as going concerns for the long term. These solid companies constantly search for a sense of adequacy between their ethos and identity and predominant societal values in order to remain relevant into the future and not ephemeral and short-lived as other organizations that end up disappearing off into oblivion. Great companies have something in common and that is that they tend to be better than average at reflecting the values and aspirations of a sufficient number of people who desperately care. Those consumers who do care tend to manifest their concern by continuing to buy product from these companies and tell others about it. In addition, those who are touched by these organizations at some meaningful level end up carrying the corporate flag, sometimes consciously, but often not. Their daily lives are inundated with corporate symbols and ideologies, traduced into forms of individual expression and identity, and this goes for individuals but also for societal groups.

People develop relationships with organizations and often refer to these in surprising ways, using unexpected adjectives and affective terminology when alluding to companies that they feel emotionally attached to. Sometimes firms are treated as family, and often the terms used in their characterization are intimate and caring, to the point where they seem dislocated as traits for non-human entities. For many, firms are a friend that they know well, in whom they entrust their custom and expectations and for whom they are more or less willing to forgive the odd mishap depending on past behaviour and track record. Organizations are for many much more than lifeless forms. On the contrary, they embody values, stand for something and have come to symbolize ways of life that find an embodiment in products that are put at the disposal of avid consumers who are only too keen to pay price premiums for what in the end are no more than aspirational metaphors of lifestyle and idealism for many who aim to tap into the value systems that these products personify.

Many corporate brands command the utmost loyalty from their stakeholders and in particular from their customers. The Harley Davidson brand, for example, embodies a set of values that configure a lifestyle that is very much its own, clearly distinguishable from everything else in the market, or for that matter in the world. The lifestyle suggested by the Harley Davidson brand is founded on well-defined values. These are the values that typify all of those that belong to the great legion of followers of the Harley spirit, the die-hards of the Harley Davidson brand. They share codes of conduct and mutually expected behaviours that are inherent to their condition and subscribe to values that dictate their membership of the group.

The organization itself has a vested interest in feeding this loyalty frenzy and does so through recourse to diverse initiatives, all of them sharing a common purpose, that of the development of a common culture and identity. The Posse Ride on Highway 66, where bikers ride across the US on their Harleys is its flagship cultural ritual. Such initiatives serve the purpose of uniting people around the Harley Davidson ideal, of which the product being sold is but a mere embodiment of common values and perspectives on life expressed in mutually accepted codes of conduct. The product is nothing more than a conduit of a slice of life and in some rare cases of a way of life that sufficient people with money adhere to.

In the case of the Harley Davidson organization, the whole thing extends well beyond the Harley motorbike. In reality, product quality, albeit not irrelevant as a purchasing criterion, is certainly not the most important aspect when it comes to buying a Harley. Naturally, product quality is always important. The product talks to the consumer. Harley Davidson has its own unique design, recognized by everyone the world over. This is founded on classic curvy lines and has been maintained for decades of successive generations of Harley models. The technological sophistication built into the product and the consequent performance of Harley machines can perhaps, and in comparison to some of its strongest competitors, be construed as a weak link in the Harley Davidson proposal, and a dimension of its market offer where the brand may show some weaknesses when contrasted with some of its immediate competitors, including the likes of Honda, Yamaha, Suzuki or BMW.

That being said however, nobody buys a Harley machine for its performance on the road, for its speed or indeed for its safety record. People who buy Harleys do it because they perceive there to be a unique and very advantageous cost–benefit relationship inherent to its purchase. The composite of whatever makes up for benefit here clearly comprehends much more than the set of tangible and unique technical elements that are intrinsic to Harley bikes, and can only be found in a Harley Davidson product. They relate instead to the unique set of values that are embodied in the Harley Davidson brand. In the case of Harley Davidson, and within reasonable parameters, product features are not a critical criterion to the average decision to buy a Harley motorbike.

There are of course minimum acceptable quality thresholds below which the experience begins to be compromised, thus dissuading prospective customers from future purchases. For the Harley Davidson organization however, an important part of its value proposition, and the way in which it is perceived by its constituencies, namely its customers, is measured by the intensity of a sentiment of belonging from those who uphold the Harley Davidson value system and identity and will buy the Harley Davidson brand no matter what. A feeling of belonging to something unique, a kind of counterculture, a legitimized and legal rebelliousness has to, of course, be part of a system of values that the organization and its brands need in turn to embody and personify. A feeling of belonging configures a situation where important dimensions of the identity of prospective customers blends in with the Harley Davidson corporate brand, to the point where the latter becomes the closest as is possible to the embodiment of the identity and values of the former.

This close identification between an abstract or non-human entity, the organization and its prospective customers, who see the firm as the ultimate embodiment of fundamental values and beliefs, is the Holy Grail of corporate branding. The Harley Davidson organization is no more than the sum of the complex relationships between people who work for the company and those who express their identity through consumption decisions to buy the Harley Davidson brand and not any other functional equivalent.

Consequently, buying decisions more often than not turn out to favour Harley Davidson motorbikes to the detriment of other functionally similar or identical machines that crucially do not cater to the same aesthetic requirements or, more to the point, fit in with the same value system that Harley Davidson stands for. In that way, product will keep being churned out successfully year after year, or at least as long as Harley Davidson keeps the illusion going.

By associating the corporate brand to a lifestyle, Harley Davidson stands a good chance of perpetuating the brand and its values over time, transcending generations and societal idiosyncrasies, although there are also perils inherent to this strategy, namely those of a kind of obsolescence of the particular lifestyle in question, and therefore of the role of the brand as a metaphor for that particular value system. The Harley Davidson corporate brand does not wish to be everything to everyone all of the time, but in attracting successive generations of potential consumers there is a danger of a lifestyle stickiness, to the point where there may come a time when people do not recognize themselves in the Harley brand. The risk clearly increases in the case of corporate brands that are also product brands, that is, product brands whose designations are homonymous with the organization, as is the case of Harley Davidson and many others out there. The risk is that the brand wears off on a new generation and the corporation then struggles to remain relevant beyond its incumbent constituencies.

When a brand is strongly associated with a way of life or psychologically attached to a generation and its fundamental values, defining it and its aspirations, and metaphorically symbolizing its identity, it may just happen that the next generation will assert itself precisely by recourse to opposing value systems and beliefs, subscribing to everything that portrays the antithesis of the values upheld by their parents. This of course means the rejection of the symbols that were the expression of the set of values which their parents embraced. This is very difficult for the organization which needs to continue to push product out of the door and finds itself no longer relevant as the incumbent generation gives way to the next one.

This generational gap is also a gap in values and beliefs, and its manifestations in consumption decision-making translate into the acquisition of brands that are meaningful to contemporary generations but not to preceding ones. This is because these brands codify the language of the time. Companies like Nike have mastered intergenerational relevance to a fine art and refined its market positioning strategy in order to avoid the trappings of being everything to a generation and nothing to the coming one. Nike positions itself in the market as a sports brand, not a fashion brand. The reason is a marketing one. Sport is eternal, fashion is not. Fashion is ephemeral and at best recurrent.

As a going concern, Nike simply cannot afford to be out of fashion for prolonged periods of time. It runs that risk if it positions itself as a fashion brand though. By positioning itself as a sports brand it offers an entirely different value proposition to its demanding and volatile customer base. As a sports brand it also stands to signify something entirely different for them. By having the best athletes endorsing its products, Nike knows that there will always be winners out there and there will always be people who love winners. People will not only always love winners they will always want to be associated with star athletes. The alternative would be for Nike to become a fashion brand. The risk is that what is fashionable today may not be fashionable tomorrow. It is simply too risky a strategy and Nike know it.

It is precisely when organizations are enjoying their greatest successes that there exists a reluctance in changing a winning formula. This is to be expected. Once found, a winning formula is like a magic bullet, adhered to no matter what, and there is a natural uneasiness in abandoning it. People do not mess around with a winning formula. But that shouldn't always be the case. The way to go about this would be to challenge the status quo precisely when things are going well. That is when there is time to think strategically about the organization, when there aren't any pressing and prevalent immediate survival concerns to take precedent over long-term strategic thinking.

However, the rationality and soundness underlining this thinking is one thing – another very different matter is that of a reality that is intrinsic to human nature, one that imposes the lowering of the guard when comfort sets in. Firms know that they need to think strategically for the long term but there is a human tendency to act on impulse when urgency dictates action and not to feel the need for change when things go well. Complacent organizations that fail to question the status quo, firms that do not scrutinize the fundamental reasons for their success, run the serious risk of not being successful for long periods of time.

Doyle (1992) points towards certain criteria whose verification in the life of an organization are crucial for its strategic success. In a context of permanent change, organizations have to find ways in which to adapt to volatile market environments that are characterized by a variety of macro-environmental factors, ranging from demographic issues to economic, political and cultural dimensions. Excellent companies, faced with the imperative of the macro-environment, develop an identity that becomes the organization and that in the end is a mirror image for its stakeholder constituencies, who see their values and identities reflected in the corporation and what it stands for. Every stakeholder, both internal and external, has a vested interest in the organization. Also important to the strategic success of the organization is timing and the idea that the outcome of strategic decision-making will necessarily be conditioned by the context and the timing in which it occurs.

All of the above links with the stigmatization and stereotyping of southern European workers as lazy, incompetent and less productive than their northern European counterparts, as a portrayal that is not only unjust but also fallacious. Not only is this assertion inaccurate but it worryingly forces these workers into a subordinate and less dignified position. There are in effect structural inadequacies in organizations and in entire economies that justify a less than desirable position of southern European workers in the labour productivity tables.

Low and inadequate formal education, insufficient technical training in specific and important areas of economic activity, inflexibility in the reconversion of labour competencies when market requirements change are some of the justifications for the lower productivity levels attained in southern European economies. Higher-order strategic-level issues that include the political inability of legislators and decision-makers to read the signs of the times and interpret the real determinants of productivity in the new global economy also account for the lower labour productivity levels and the stigmatization of workers in these economies.

Despite being perceived as having productivity levels that are below the European average, southern European workers are highly regarded when working abroad. Perhaps the most obvious reason for this is that under more efficient organizations of the labour process, workers inevitably become more productive. Crucially this has nothing to do with the worker at all. In most cases, if the labour process is well-organized the worker flourishes. There are many cases of success. Perhaps one example in a European context that best illustrates the point is that of Portuguese labour in Luxembourg. This is a country with one of the highest GDP per capita in the world. It is estimated that around 20 per cent of the population of Luxembourg is Portuguese or of Portuguese origin. The Portuguese worker is extraordinarily productive in Luxembourg. This is the very same worker that had to emigrate because he was unable to fully express his competencies and abilities in the workplace in Portugal, where training was non-existent and working conditions minimal. This is also the same worker that is highly regarded in South Africa, Canada and the US. There is therefore, and to the exclusion of other reasons, a set of specificities in the relationship between the Portuguese worker and the labour process in Portugal that determine his lower productivity in the workplace.

Obviously this is a complex theme, the approach to which demands a multiple and systemic perspective, in that there are many factors that contribute to this state of affairs. This is only an example amongst many that point to the macro-environment and in particular to the organization of labour and of the labour process in defining worker productivity levels. The reason why workers are more productive when working abroad in more efficient labour and organizational contexts, under comparable conditions of academic background and access to knowledge and technical training, is that the lower productivity of labour in their home countries has a lot less to do with the workers themselves than many people, for ideological or other more sinister reasons, would care to believe.

Lower levels of productivity should be attributable to workers as they are to an absence of strategic vision, incompetent entrepreneurship and sheer bad management. The fragile academic background and training of entrepreneurs often contributes to low productivity levels. This is true in various ways but the failure of entrepreneurs in exercising leadership and in showing initiative may be one of the most important contributors to low productivity levels in an economy. These traits, when they exist, correlate favourably with the capacity to think strategically in the long term, rather than just tactically and operationally.

Domestic rivalry in the economy, sometimes in unrelated industries, also contributes to the development of a state of heightened competition, thus leading to a search for an optimization of production processes but also ways in which to aggregate value to goods and services, both conduits to higher productivity levels. The examples of Rockefeller in oil and Carnegie in steel in the nineteenth century are a classic illustration of a competitive context that, with all its frailties and faults, particularly from the viewpoint of labour relations and the harsh treatment of workers, exemplifies the role of intense competition in economic development. Of course these frailties and faults in labour relations and worker conditions need to be looked at through the lenses of history and are not comparable to contemporary reality.

Often lower productivity levels are associated with short-sighted or absent entrepreneurial cultures, anchored on deep-rooted structural problems, namely what the entrepreneurial class expects from government and its role and scope of intervention in the economy. This is complex because there are fundamental questions of inefficiency of the bureaucratic machinery that constitute significant obstacles to the good functioning of organizations, but in the end it should not be the role of government to procure markets for products. That is the role of the firm and that of dynamic and pro-active entrepreneurship.

Government can and should ensure an environment of balanced regulation, a level of bureaucracy that regulates economic relationships but does not constitute a barrier to the functioning of economic activity or is not heavy to the point of constituting an unsustainable economic burden on the rest of society. All of this is also linked to the attainment of higher or lower national productivity levels. The argument against excessive government anchors on the natural tendency for it to expand uncontrollably, with consequences on the amassment of huge and unsustainable public debt, a burden that has been afflicting many contemporary economies in the developed world. The widely diffused notion of an ever-present, universal paternal provider, whose finished expression is the European welfare state, also leads to the withdrawal of any responsibility from individuals in society, who see government as a guarantor of their livelihoods from cradle to coffin. On the other hand, the sanctioning of outrageous and socially intolerable situations, of what is in essence no more than the reward of bad management and incompetence, in the public utilities or in other public sector organizations, is very detrimental to collective morale and to the perceptions held by society as to the pristine ethics and reserve that should characterize the conduct of the public sector.

There is ample evidence in Europe of politically appointed and incompetent senior executives who receive extremely generous compensation packages and whose only credentials are lifelong party political membership, people that have systematically seen their individual economic situations resolved through generous rewards for what is euphemistically called mismanagement. To cap it all, these pseudo gurus of empty rhetoric get landed with top job after top job in public administration. This happens in many European countries, and in particular in economies that do not generate enough wealth to sustain situations that configure such tremendous inequity, lack of transparency and outright corruption, that translate into unusual numbers of fat cats holding highly paid top-level public sector management and administrative positions.

There is a general tendency to have a collective attitude of exaggerated expectation as to the ability of government to solve everyone's problems. This paternalistic notion of an ever-present state is still very deep-rooted in certain parts of Europe, much more so than in the US. The state has, in many European nations, been a trusted entity, expected to provide the more traditional functions of justice and law enforcement but also to ensure widespread, and at times universal, coverage of education and health. In addition to this, people have come to entrust government with the responsibility for generating permanent employment for all in society, irrespective of whether the economy can objectively sustain full employment or not. In this context, only a few take performance evaluations seriously and care to think critically about whether the recruitment of people or the maintenance of current labour is adequate, or if indeed it is not, over and above diagnosed functional needs. All of this has had dire consequences on the competitiveness of national economies through oversized public sectors and the accumulation of unsustainable public debt, which has sparked the debate on the reformation of government and what it can do for people, a redefinition of its role and scope of action in the light of what are economically unsustainable social welfare systems.

Many Europeans look at governments first and foremost as a guarantor of their rights and privileges, the provider of universal education and health, defence and also of employment. This state dependency is exaggerated and differs from the North American view, where individual and corporate initiative in generating employment and wealth are the norm. The sociological antecedents to all of this are evidently much more complex than a superficial scrutiny of these matters suggests. One should also abstain from making very profound and objective value judgements on the relative merits of the different social systems and how they reflect contrasting societal views on the role of government. It may even be inappropriate to contrast systems that share very few similarities between them to begin with.

The American reality does not lend itself to much in the way of shedding light or indeed providing a deeper knowledge and understanding of European problems. It is also limited as a diagnosis of what can be done to improve the reality of a dwindling European economy. Furthermore it is improbable that the very notion of a European reality does indeed exist, one that is homogeneous and coherent, and that is perhaps the crux of the problem, that there is no such thing as a politically unified Europe and that, therefore and under these conditions, the full integration of national economies into a unified economic system is utopian. That such an ambitious edifice has been built on incredibly shaky grounds simply defies belief, but that is the situation in which Europe finds itself today.

In Nordic and Anglo-Saxon countries, although many complain of excessive and intricate bureaucracy, there is undoubtedly less ambiguity when it comes to procedure, and generally a more simplified administrative bureaucracy, perhaps reflective of more pragmatism in the characterization of the individual cultures in these geographies. By sheer observation, in southern

European nations the legislative and regulatory structures and frameworks, albeit comprehensive and exhaustive both in terms of coverage and level of detail sought, tend to be less effective in terms of the application and enforcement of legislation.

In effect, there tend to be generalized images of lower efficacy in the enforcement of legislation in southern Europe, thereby incentivizing regular members of society not to comply with the law,or to learn to evade its letter by finding loopholes and sophisticated escapist schemes. Perhaps the size of the subterranean economies in southern European nations, in some cases calculated in the region of 25 to 30 per cent of GDP, corroborate this view of a citizen that plays cat and mouse with its government institutions.

There is of course the added detrimental effect of a collective perception of an inefficient legal–justice system and in particular of a judicial system that fails to enforce the law. Perhaps even worse is the diffusion of a collective perception of a legal–judicial system that has different measures and weights in the treatment of white collar crime to that of regular crime. In light of this, people tend to find ways in which to deviate from the law, or evade its letter whenever possible, as they find the legitimacy to do so in a collective perception of unfairness which is so critical to the administration of the law and to the functioning of democratic systems. A collective perception of impunity is in all certainty a key driver of corruption, whose gravity is more attributable to perceptions of institutional inefficiency in failing to guarantee the enforcement of the law of the land than to the intrinsic traits of character of a society and its peoples.

Reality Check...

Productivity is Something We Can Work on: The Case of 3M

3M is an American company that invests substantially in research and development leading to a constant supply of innovative products. The company invests about 7 per cent of their annual sales in research and development (R&D) and new products are launched into the market at breath-taking speed. The investment in R&D is double that of the industry average. New products don't spontaneously and effortlessly happen. 3M commercializes an amazing 60,000 products at any one time.

The firm has an ambitious compulsory internal quota of 25 per cent of annual sales that are required to be derived from goods introduced into the market within the past five years. This in effect implies a serious financial effort in applied research, with the aim of achieving a constant flow of new products introduced regularly into the market. Such a stringent and ambitious internal quota makes 3M often discontinue profitable lines in favour of others that although not nearly as lucrative, ensuring that the organization keeps churning out new and innovative products all the time.

3M is in effect different from other companies in its approach to the development of new products. In its insistence for an internal culture of innovation, one that ensures a systematic and continuous flow of new products and ideas, 3M created many years ago what was known as the 15 per cent rule. This rule came to be known internally simply as bootlegging. 3M employees are required under this scheme to devote 15 per cent of their time to working on projects that are totally of their own initiative, and may be totally unrelated to their specific area of technical expertise. A 3M worker has time to think about alternative ways in which to execute his or her daily tasks and to flush out ideas that may lead to the improvement of processes, the development of novel concepts for products or to simply stimulate his or her creative fluids. The company benefits directly and indirectly from that.

4

Country Reputation, Productivity and National Competitiveness

There exists a general tendency to mentally associate supplier reliability and compliance with requirements and the expected quality of products with the general perceptions held about a country, including its level of industrial development (Schooler et al., 1987). Country stereotyping derives mostly from the preconceived notions held about aspects of the history, tradition, and political or social factors that in the absence of more accurate information contribute to the shaping of peoples' general perceptions about that country (Han and Terpstra, 1988).

Country stereotypes are inevitably transferred over to the products that emanate from that particular origin. These preconceived notions travel from product to product, crossing sectors of economic activity. Country stereotyping also encompasses collective expectations about the reliability and integrity of suppliers, which condition buyer–supplier relationships and crucially dictate such things as price ceilings for products that come out of countries with negative or neutral country of origin images, and for which consumers are unwilling first to buy them and second to pay price premiums for. In simple terms, if you are a top fashion retail brand from Italy or France, then money is not an issue for affluent and discerning consumers in sophisticated markets. If however your organization does not originate in Germany or the UK, your business is exporting automobiles or technology, and you have not been able to capture the imagination of aspirational foreign consumers with money, what do you then do?

There is ample evidence to suggest that country of origin is a strong cue in the formation of consumer perceptions and does indeed shape buying decision-making in both business and consumer markets. Take Japanese products as an example. In the 1960s they were considered to be of low quality, an image that in less than two decades was to change completely, to the point where today we look at Japanese goods as being of high quality in terms of their functionality, technological content and aesthetics, as well as the hedonistic benefits that their best brands are able to provide consumers worldwide.

It wasn't always like that and in effect Japanese products were not considered to be of a high calibre at all up until the 1980s, which in the context of the economic history of any nation is negligible as a timeframe. Positive country of origin stereotyping about the Japanese industrial economy has largely been a direct result of an obsessive and concerted national effort, aiming at the provision of quality and excellence in a wide array of goods and services that people all over the world recognize and are more than willing to buy.

This was largely achieved under the auspices of the Total Quality Management (TQM) philosophy, a school of thought which has included such remarkable people as Juran and, perhaps even more renowned, American statistician W. Edwards Deming, who influenced more than anyone the thinking and the actions of government institutions, and those of large multinational corporations in Japan, and whose collaboration with the Japanese political establishment and industry dates back to the 1950s. Deming was for decades an unknown quantity in his own turf back home in America. In Japan, the story was very different and his teachings were considered gospel for the large Japanese multinational corporations and economic groups, to the point where even today the most prestigious accolade to be bestowed on any Japanese company is the Deming Award for innovation.

Many examples coming out of the same area of the globe abound. For example, the countries that used to be designated only a few years ago as the Asian tigers, for example South Korea, have slowly but surely, over the last couple of decades, begun to alter the stereotypes that for years have stigmatized their best products, branded in the world markets as being low-cost and low-quality imitations. Closer to us, there are also good examples of significant turnarounds in country image and reputation, which in a relatively short timeframe have meant a shift in the way corporations, whole sectors of economic activity and even national economies are perceived by the outside world. Take the Czech Republic as an example, and what the collective stereotype held of its flagship automobile brand, Skoda, was like not too long ago. The litmus test with regards to Skoda is whether anyone remembers the image of a Skoda automobile as being anything other than shoddy, and in doing this one does not need to go back more than 15 years.

The argument that Skoda began to change its external image in the eyes of its most important stakeholders, its prospective customers, following its merger with Volkswagen is of course factual, and the reason why the Skoda brand image changed so much in such a short time needs to be examined. However, it is worth remembering that the automobile has, since the merger with VW and before that, always been marketed under the Skoda brand name, and is widely acclaimed for its stand-alone quality and reliability. Skoda was not a great brand at all. This has changed dramatically over the last couple of decades.

Skoda's image was that of a shoddy car, not far from its Russian equivalent, the Lada. The reason often attributed to the turnaround in consumer perceptions about Skoda relates to the association established with German manufacturer Volkswagen, and how it was that only from then on that Skoda's image and reputation began to change. It is true that the association with Volkswagen was pivotal in changing the fortunes of the Skoda brand, but it was also organizational perseverance and a constant pursuit for higher-quality processes and products that was to eventually lead to more reliable automobiles that were on a par and eventually better than some of its competitors in the market. With better cars came more positive consumption experiences, and these in turn led to higher consumer expectations about the quality of Skoda automobiles in a self-reinforcing spiral of more sophisticated and better products responding to higher market demands, commercial success and the progressive enhancement of the reputation of the Skoda brand, along with collateral positive spin-offs for other Czech products.

Italian fashion is generally taken to be highly creative and to possess exceptional design. Just across the border, everyone seems to have well-defined preconceived notions about the exceptional quality and exquisite taste of French fashion or cuisine for example. These generally tend to be very positive stereotypes. There is therefore a tacit belief that country of origin effects exist – generalized images held about certain countries which can be positive or negative. From the viewpoint of the exporting nations, these stereotypes inevitably need to be taken into account when formulating export strategies, as they differ from one country of destination to the next.

There are indeed many examples that illustrate the true importance of country of origin effects and stereotypes, how they stand to decisively shape consumer behaviour and in particular the propensity to buy products claiming a certain origin to the detriment of other products emanating from other nations.

What is relevant here is not so much where the product was manufactured but instead the origin of the corporate brand that the product in question carries.

In addition to all of this, the collective perception held by retail buyers and consumers in export markets of the level of industrial development of the country of origin of incoming products, and the way these thoughts and preconceived ideas are extrapolated and passed on to other often unrelated products claiming the same origin, is an important determinant of country competitiveness. They dictate why many economic sectors and national economies, no matter how hard they try, simply cannot win, unless they change their image and reputation abroad.

Before 1918, no one knew where products came from. In that year, Germany lost the war. As a form of retaliation and punishment to Germany, and with a view to warning European consumers at the time, German industry was forced to place on every product they exported 'Made in Germany' labels. Very soon the label became a sign of quality in the minds of European consumers (Morello, 1984).

A few years ago, Chrysler made a decision to manufacture some of their models in a new factory they had just opened in Mexico. Chrysler had set up a fine operation, put together the necessary infrastructure and trained its workforce in Mexico, providing them with the required competencies ready to begin production activities south of the border. However, when the first automobiles manufactured in Mexico began to appear in the market, the results were not what Chrysler had expected.

The US Government forced Chrysler to clearly identify the cars that had been made in Mexico and make that physically visible to prospective American consumers so that they would be able to easily tell which cars were made in America and which were not. In the knowledge that some Chrysler models were manufactured south of the border, many American consumers outright refused to buy those cars in particular.

On the other hand, the other very same make and model of the same automobile, but this time made in the US, did not see its sales hit a slump in the same way as their Mexican counterpart. The negative country of origin stereotype held about Mexico simply prevailed and got transferred over to automobiles made in this country. In effect, from the viewpoint of American consumers, a Chrysler car made in Mexico and the same car made in the US are not the same product and crucially are not perceived as offering the same consumption utilities.

It could be argued that there was a nationalistic effect here, to do with a heightened propensity of American consumers to buy all things American, but the truth of the matter was that many other foreign brands had always enjoyed significant success in the American market, in every sector of economic activity, and not the least in the automobile industry, ever since Japanese fuel-efficient models and makes made a dramatic break into the Detroit stranglehold on the industry back in the 1980s. Mexico was a different proposition though as far as cars and the American consumer were concerned.

This case is only one of the many that populate the literature on the consequences of country of origin stereotyping on buying decision-making, not only in B2C contexts but also in B2B. Chrysler made in Mexico is a good example of country of origin effects at work. Chrysler manufactured the same car models in the US and Mexico. It was the very same model and make that were manufactured in both countries, using the very same equipment and identical manufacturing facilities and infrastructure. The car made in the USA outsold the car made in Mexico for reasons that cannot be product related, that is if we are to define product as something limited to the core functional benefits and tangible features of the good in question.

Many attribute this preference for the car made in America by American consumers to a nationalistic trait in the collective character of American society, which makes them choose American products first and foremost. However this was certainly not the case in the 1980s when it came to Japanese cars and their astonishing success in the American car market. At the time American consumers preferred Japanese cars because they were fuel-efficient and perceived to be better than their American equivalent. The difference here is that consumers perceived there to be a tangible superiority of the Japanese offer on a key criterion, fuel efficiency, which they judged to be a sufficiently important dimension to warrant a switch in custom from American to Japanese brands.

With a hierarchy of decision-making criteria clearly established in the minds of the average consumer, the rational decision would have been to buy the best car irrespective of origin, and since cars made in Mexico and in the USA are identical, consumers should in theory have been indifferent to the origin of the automobile which they were considering purchasing.

However, they were anything but indifferent, and this is because consumers perceived the automobile that was made in Mexico as being of inferior quality, not because they knew anything about the car and its characteristics, but precisely because they knew of its origin. This was to become decisive in the lowering of the perceived utility of the car made in Mexico in the minds of American consumers. Nothing to do with the car, everything to do with its origins.

In reality, there is ample evidence to suggest that country of origin is an important cue in buyer decision-making, and the ways in which different stakeholder constituencies, and in particular consumers, perceive organizations and their brands as a function of the countries where they emanate from. Country of origin effects are thus decisive contributors to the shaping of buyer decision-making in most markets and sectors of economic activity.

The relevance of all of this to a country's economy, to its balance of trade and in particular to its export base, has not been given sufficient attention by policy-makers, entrepreneurs and management. In being present in international markets, it is a necessary condition for firms in export sectors to consistently demonstrate the excellent quality and superiority of their goods and services in these markets. The scrutiny as to what constitutes superior benefits is of course the privilege of sophisticated consumers who decide with their wallets. However product quality is not in itself a sufficient condition for success in highly demanding export markets where stringent buying decision-making criteria characterizes sophisticated consumers.

The aforementioned example of Japanese products is a case in point of products coming out of Japan being perceived as being of high quality in terms of their functionality, technological content and aesthetic value. However these exceptional products still needed to be anchored on valuable brands of global notoriety. This was done with recourse to an embedded philosophy pervading both government institutions and large multinational corporations, founded on pillars that can best be characterized as that of an obsessive and consistent emphasis on quality and excellence in the provision of manufactured goods to highly demanding consumers in foreign markets.

Under the ideological mantra of the total quality gurus, including people like Juran and American statistician, W. Edwards Deming, Japan was able to radically alter the way in which the nation was perceived by outside stakeholder constituencies and namely foreign consumers. Examples coming out of the same geography abound, economies that used to be designated as the Asian tigers only a decade ago, due to their astounding economic performances, including the likes of South Korea, have begun to slowly but surely alter the stereotypes that for years have tarnished their products as low cost and average quality imitations of the branded products coming out of the more developed western economies.

If, as an organization, one is on the receiving end of this, is there a way in which to avoid these negative perceptions? If foreign consumers have negative preconceived notions about a country, and if we accept as plausible the notion that these stereotypes extend beyond into the products that emanate from that country, that they do not remain restricted to a particular product and indeed jump from product to product and between sectors, then it stands to reason that any industrial sector may be tarnished with negative country of origin effects. This happens even in product areas that are totally unrelated, and every time adverse country of origin cues taint each and every product that comes out of that country. Negative country of origin effects are then difficult to escape once a whole nation is brushed with them, and they will extend to other sectors in the economy and products emanating from them.

If country of origin effects exist and they play an important part in shaping consumer perceptions in foreign markets, then inevitably they need to be acknowledged and taken very seriously indeed when formulating export strategies. If there is a perceptual gap between exporters and retail buyers in the country of destination of exported goods and services on the critical success factors that exporters need to possess in order to succeed and excel in a particular market, then exporters need to confront this head on and improve on the relevant dimensions of the choice process as seen from the viewpoint of industrial buyers and consumers in destination markets. Suffice to say, that in the final analysis, in a buying decision-making context, the only opinion that matters is that of the retail buyer, who in turn should to the best of his or her ability reflect the particular requirements of consumers who express their will with their wallet. The retail buyer's raison d'être and overriding purpose is to ensure that consumer preferences are met by providing the brands that cater to the benefits that consumers want.

If exporters are then able to clearly understand the decision-making processes of retail buyers, they will be in the unique position of knowing exactly what the latter look for in them as suppliers. This includes not only the tangible criteria related to product innovation, quality and design, but also the less palpable dimensions of the product equation, its less tangible features, including supplier responsiveness to specific requirements, compliance with delivery schedules, and the quality of after-sales service, amidst a myriad of other product enhancement possibilities that equate with value aggregation.

The collective perceptions held by retail buyers and consumers of export markets, of the level of industrial development of the country of origin of incoming products, and the way these thoughts and preconceived notions are passed onto other often unrelated products claiming the same origin, are important determinants of consumption decision-making in foreign markets. These perceptions dictate why in the end many economic sectors and national economies, no matter how hard they try, will always be on the losing end of the competitiveness game, unless they are able to change their country images and reputations abroad.

Collectively as a society, we tend to extrapolate from very little and often distorted information, quickly making up our minds over phenomena about which in reality we know nothing. We also stereotype people as a function of where they come from and make assertions about them and their cultures, inferring their behaviour on the back of superficial knowledge at best, and sometimes not even that. Popular sayings in their infinite wisdom illustrate human tendency to pre-judge, to draw the totality of an event or a person, often from not more than shaky clues and subjective interpretation of available information. Never judge a book by its cover is a good piece of popular advice in this context. Making quick calls on someone's character on the basis of superficial knowledge and hasty judgment is part and parcel of human nature. When this is extrapolated collectively to a country and taken to be its character and identity, then inevitably its exported goods and services will be judged in the light of such subjective country of origin cues.

This common tendency for the development of stereotypes may reside in what is perhaps a supreme difficulty in human nature in living with ambiguity and having to make decisions with imperfect information. In the light of ever increasing complexity in the quotidian lives of people in society, and with the proliferation of superficial information on everything under the sun, individuals feel the confidence to pass judgment on just about everything, forgetting that true in-depth knowledge requires time and dedication, specialization and further sub-specialization.

Instead, the individual intuitively develops sketches about what he reads or sees, and stores it in his memory for occasional reproduction when and where appropriate. The abundance of information available, paradoxically, only deepens the problem. Although one can easily arrive at the surface of most issues by resorting to the internet for example, the knowledge acquired via this method, albeit of immense importance, when contrasted with the collective ignorance of yesteryear, suffers from the danger of a deeply entrenched collective belief that this knowledge is equivalent in value to scientific scrutiny, when in fact this is not true. In effect this typology of relationship with widely available information is only susceptible of reinforcing stereotypes about things that are passed as proper scientific knowledge when it is no more than pseudo-science.

These determinants of country competitiveness, country of origin effects, are often overlooked, and their contribution to the attainment of sustainable competitive advantages underestimated. Much of what exists in terms of the goodwill associated with country reputation is not tangible, difficult to explain and reason through, and so people discard it as unimportant or inferior in the pecking order of the determinants of country competitiveness. One of the reasons why this happens is that perhaps they believe that not much can be done about country stereotyping, whether positive or negative, but this is not true.

Country reputation is critical and manifests itself in buying decision-making processes. Faced with uncountable solutions for the same problem, and with little time to choose amongst a myriad of alternatives, the consumer looks for immediate clues. Country reputation may be just the ultimate differentiating element, the one that will make a difference between buying in the first instance and then buying German or Italian for example, to the detriment of products claiming other origins. It may also traduce the willingness to pay price premium for products that otherwise would not be able to guarantee such high margins. It is therefore vital that national export strategies pinpoint the real reasons belying country stereotyping, as these will determine decision-making and choice criteria by foreign retail buyers and consumers. Country stereotyping inevitably shapes buying decisions as well as price-demand sensitivities for products claiming different origins, in other words how much buyers are willing to pay for the brand depending on where it comes from. Negative stereotyping will also determine the exclusion of products from a spectrum of consumer choice, simply because retail buyers believe that, irrespective of the intrinsic quality of those products, there are country cues that will simply put consumers off them.

Following on from this, the origin of goods can in itself constitute a reservoir of goodwill that is totally external to the tangible qualities and physical characterization of the product in question. In this context, and coming back to specific examples, the German or Italian origins to a brand can often be the sole reason for someone choosing that product to the detriment of a functional equivalent emanating from somewhere else. In addition to that, the fact that a product can claim a German origin may allow it to dictate a market price premium well over and above its functional value.

The origin of goods can therefore represent a reservoir of goodwill, an invaluable intangible with tangible benefits, an asset of the utmost significance and importance to an organization's balance sheet. In today's very competitive global markets, a reputable origin can constitute a crucial differentiating mark for the supplier. If there were balance sheets for countries, national reputation would be their most formidable asset, the equivalent of goodwill in balance sheets for organizations, an intangible asset which for many years did not show up on company accounts and now and for many organizations constitute their most important asset and one that they should carefully manage, nurture and cherish. There are no balance sheets for countries but national accounts and certainly GDP can benefit from positive country reputation in the context of value aggregated to the exports of goods and services, and the higher propensity to attract FDI that comes with tangible improvements in national reputation. The spin-offs for companies and their balance sheets of positive country reputations are also far from negligible.

Country of origin effects, or the stereotypical notions held in relation to foreign nations, their peoples and institutions, result largely from information that is assimilated about the history, culture, tradition, perceived level of industrial development and other significant country identity cues. This is not something innocuous or unimportant. It is also not cast in stone and immutable, as perceptions and indeed countries change.

These stereotypes, when negative, have devastating consequences to a country's economy, but there are cases of tremendous success in building reputational capital for a country, such as the aforementioned cases of Germany, Italy, France or Japan. Reputational capital may constitute an important dimension of value aggregation to country exports. It should not be a mere coincidence that these and other countries, that benefit from an aura of elitism in one or many valued dimensions of country character, carriers therefore of reputational capital, are precisely the countries that rank highly on GDP tables, competitiveness, FDI inflows and export rankings, and crucially also on barometers of human and social development.

Stereotype, albeit entrenched and deep-rooted in history, surrounded by the myths and beliefs held about a nation and its peoples, formed on the basis of subjective interpretation held by those who cross its path in some way, through commerce or tourism or just by reading about it, is by no means immutable. The image and reputation of a country from the perspective of its external stakeholders changes over time and often faster than what is historically deemed reasonable. There are cases of countries whose external reputation has been altered dramatically over a relatively short time-span. The Czech Republic and China are examples of economies about which there have been over the years serious doubts as to the quality of the products manufactured in these countries. These negative external perceptions, namely the low quality and unreliability of the products that come out of these countries, are being changed with much perseverance and absolute resolution, a determination to ensure stringent quality parameters for products coming out of these economies, and to do this systematically and over decades of discipline and rigour.

In the case of the Japanese economy, an unremitting commitment to total quality in sophisticated manufacturing processes and products is entirely accurate as a description of the focus on the development of external markets that has characterized the post-war Japanese economy. This was the only way in which Japan was going to survive if it was to be successful in key export markets, as they needed to counter the always vivid anti-Japanese sentiment in the west and in America in particular. The aforementioned countries were able to alter the preconceived notions held about them, and in the case of Japan they had to do away with a reputational liability that was the pending animosity that prevailed against them in the US following Pearl Harbour.

With regards to China, time will tell what will emerge from the new economic order and the viability of the coexistence of a dual system of political autocracy with state-sponsored capitalism. For all the transformations in its economic system, the provision of excellence and high-quality innovative products on the one hand and the word China on the other are difficult to reconcile in one sentence for now. This is the situation today, but it does not mean that it will remain the case for long.

Countries which have been able to counter negative stereotypes or shape and build positive long-term reputations, including Japan, have invariably done so with recourse to a clear and unreserved focus on quality, a recourse to state-of-the-art technology and innovation and appealing design, all combined in exceptional corporate and product brands of high reputational goodwill. This formidable mix however still needs to be anchored on a plethora of prestigious brands which progressively act to build notoriety in highly demanding and discriminatory international markets.

In the case of Japan, multinational corporations, including such notable names as Sony, Mitsubishi, Toyota and others, soon became established household brands, carrying the Japanese flag everywhere around the planet. In the case of the Czech Republic and Skoda, the brand quickly became known to consumers in the more developed western economies largely due to its association with Volkswagen, which meant that the original and deeply entrenched imprint of a low-quality eastern European automobile brand was soon to change.

Looking at the Japanese case in more detail, this is perhaps the best example of a country that has managed to completely alter its image and external reputation in a relatively short period of time, at least in the context of the histories of nations. The traditional image of Japan was for centuries that of a feudal nation with an insular mentality and isolated from the outside world. However, the Portuguese had arrived in Japan in the 1500s and the descriptions made of the Japanese at the time were in fact very different from the modern-day stereotype of an austere and insular culture of detachment and of a collective shying away from anything foreign. On the contrary, the Japanese were receptive of cultural exchanges, and a good example of that is that many Portuguese words managed to enter the Japanese lexicon and they have remained there until today. On a curious language footnote the Japanese word for thank you is *arigato*, a derivation of the Portuguese *obrigado* and this is true for countless other expressions in the Japanese vocabulary.

The Second World War ended with Japan facing complete destruction and wounded in its immense national pride. Nagasaki and Hiroshima are eternal testimonies to the tragedy and suffering of the Japanese people. In the post-war Japanese economy, and perhaps more importantly, when the nation's spirit was attempting to rise from the ashes and reassert itself, an American, W. Edwards Deming, played a very important role in what later was to become known as the

Japanese economic miracle, the rebuilding of the Japanese economy from the ashes without the aid of any natural resources.

As a consultant to what became mega corporate conglomerates, Deming worked hard with the Japanese companies and their senior executives, travelling back and forth from the US throughout the 1950s. Deming is today widely acknowledged as one of the major contributors to Japanese post-war economic reconstruction. He is still today, 20 years after his passing, venerated like no other foreigner in a country that is definitely not prodigal in eulogy and in particular to foreigners. The Deming Award is the most prestigious accolade that can be bestowed on any Japanese organization. This is an award that annually distinguishes companies for their innovation capabilities in manufacturing and for the excellence of the products that they are capable of bringing to the market.

Country of origin stereotypes are then a collection of preconceived notions that consumers create about products and services that emanate from particular countries. Often the stereotype is positive and favours the countries that benefit from this aura, allowing them to command the preference of consumers in export markets. They can also charge more for their products as a function of that. In other cases the stereotype is negative, and countries with a bad rap need to fight back against the negative stereotyping. In some cases, there exist countries that have a favourable image for a particular product or group of products, that have an established reputation in a particular sector of economic activity, or simply countries that excel in some area or form of cultural expression, and sometimes sport. Spain is an example of a recently acquired reputation for unmatched excellence in sport. It is in fact incredible what Spain has been able to achieve ever since the Barcelona Olympics of 1992.

In fact, over the last 20 years the level of success of Spanish sport is unmatched by any other country at any other time in history, if we are to take the breadth of sports where the Spaniards excel, in effect a plethora of totally unrelated sports. From club football to the national football team winning everything there is to win under the sun, amazingly, breezing through with ease and in succession every time there is a World Cup or a European tournament, to cycling with Indurain and Contador, to rally car driving and Carlos Sainz, to Alonso in Formula 1, the late Ballesteros and Garcia in golf, Nadal and others before him in tennis, or the basketball and handball teams in the Olympics. The amazing thing is that we are not measuring success in relative terms, factoring in direct investment in sports, country size or population, but even in absolute terms, the success of Spanish sport over the last 20 years is unmatchable. It would be interesting to assess the impact of excellence in sport on national reputation and as a spin-off of that, its impact on value aggregation to Spanish exports and to a higher propensity to attract FDI into the country.

Some countries may just have a feel good factor about them for reasons that perhaps relate to a privileged geographic location or an incredible climate. In other cases, a positive image in a specific sector may induce an unexpected positive impact in another sector of activity, without any real or apparent intersection or logical connection between the two sectors. The opposite of this also happens with countries holding a negative image in a specific area or sector, negatively affecting everything emanating from that country.

Countries like Germany or Italy have positive global images, but of course not for every aspect of the character of those nations. They also have good and bad dimensions to their reputations and the positive cues in both countries derive from different aspects of their national identities. Germany benefits from a solid reputation for the high level of technological content, sophistication and exceptionally high quality of its products. These are perceived to be of high technical quality and consumers tend to find them reliable. German brands are perceived to be innovative and of incomparable technical excellence performing at very high levels. This is particularly evident in hi-tech consumer goods where technological content constitutes a significant basis for product differentiation in the more sophisticated markets.

The automobile industry and the plethora of brands that German industry has in the high end of the global car market is perhaps the most poignant example of a solid reputation that has always benefitted Germany in just about every export market. Everyone the world over is familiar with Porsche, Mercedes, Audi or Volkswagen. The common denominator to all of these brands are the high-quality products that they embody, high performance levels associated with them, and the way in which they keep, time and time again, generation after generation, exceeding consumer expectations.

Exceptional product quality and positive cues about a country's image and reputation are important assets to have when organizations attempt to break into new markets. They constitute the basis for creating a sustainable and long-term competitive advantage for a product, a corporate brand and even for an entire economy. The development of a corporate culture that cuts across different sectors of economic activity, anchored on quality production and excellence in service provision, are critical requirements in reputation building. This is not enough however, and numerous examples of top brand names at last enable an association to be established between a product and its origin, hence creating a long-lasting reputation which is nurtured via constant and consistently positive consumer experiences. Crucially, in building a reputation for the exceptional quality of the brands that emanate from a particular nation, if consumers in foreign markets perceive this indeed to be the case, organizations in the exporting economies will then be in a position to demand much higher prices for products that essentially have identical functional value to those that originate from countries with lower reputational capital.

The positive image that we may have of a country as a result of the sum of our positive or negative experiences with products coming out it does not stay with that product or group of products. Image, positive or negative, transfers over to other products that are completely unrelated to the original product and which created the country's reputation to begin with. These collateral reputational effects may benefit or harm the exports of a country, depending on the underlying image being positive or negative. It is therefore possible to be in a position where one is considering the purchase of a product where technological content is irrelevant to the decision-making process, but the fact that the product in question can claim a German origin for example means that the image of reliability and exceptional performance that German products carry in general will positively influence the decision to buy and naturally bias it towards buying German. In effect, being of a German origin or not should be irrelevant to consumer buying decision-making processes, but in fact it is not. This is because national stereotypes again transfer over from product to product, often across totally unrelated areas. This leads to buying situations where certain product characteristics may even be objectively immaterial to that particular buying context but, albeit subjectively, the stereotypes held about the country will shape the outcome of buying decision-making of foreign consumers in export markets.

In reality, as consumers, and in the knowledge of the origin of a product, we easily extrapolate our subjective opinions from one brand to the next of the same origin and, if these notions happen to be positive, this aura of positivity crucially translates into a predisposition to buy from that country. This happens with German hi-tech goods as it does with those products of Italian origin in fashion, as well as anything to do with design, and in the case of French products, anything related to cosmetics, gastronomy, wines or the world of haute couture. The same goes for Great Britain and tradition, its democratic institutions, cultural heritage, education, industry and creativity. The same can also be said about Brazil and football, the Czech Republic and Bohemian crystal, Japan and technology and miniaturization and the extensive proliferation of consumer branded goods irrespective of sector of economic activity.

The tragedy is when a nation is not known for anything valuable, that is when consumers worldwide are virtually indifferent to its products because in effect this is an unbranded nation. Every product coming out of an unbranded nation is undifferentiated from the many others that compete with it for consumer attention in global markets. From a marketing and branding perspective, a nation is not dissimilar from a product in seeking global consumer attention. Nations are also faced with an identical dilemma to that of brands, in that in foreign constituencies, consumers have many alternatives from which to choose from. What needs to happen is for products coming out of a particular nation to systematically end up in the small consideration set of discerning consumers who have disposable income. This is the biggest competitive challenge facing contemporary nations striving for competitiveness in world markets. The problem is that of not being able to attain a sufficiently distinctive position in some significant market sector that will allow for it to attract a group of individuals with economic clout, that acknowledge and prefer a nation's goods and services and buy them to the detriment of other products, whilst crucially convincing others in their immediate circles to do the same.

Nations which are able to create clear imprints in the minds of prospective foreign consumers as to what they can do and the excellent quality of the products that they make will be able to positively detach themselves from others who shall remain largely unknown amidst the plethora of alternatives available to every worthwhile foreign consumer constituency. In a capitalist society, in a market economy where individuals can afford to discriminate between products of identical perceived functional value, very few are those that buy product strictly on the basis of its functionality, whether they are conscious of it or not. Buying situations where product function acts as a sole criterion or even as the dominating criterion in consumption decision-making are not the most common in market economies. In reality, many buy product because of its intangible cues. Even those who think that they are absolute functionalists, in that they buy product strictly for what it does – its core function, upon closer scrutiny are found to be influenced and manipulated by marketing messages and peer pressure.

In modern competitive environments, products and services are chosen by consumers to the detriment of others serving identical purposes as a function of the intangible elements that are anchored in them, thus augmenting the overall value proposition. Buying decision criteria clearly extend beyond the strict functionality of a core product notion, and there are instead cues or characteristics of the product that have no physical expression, but nevertheless inevitably shape the choice process in highly discriminatory markets where consumers have disposable income.

Crucially this immaterial dimension of the product offer can easily be mismanaged when it comes to foreign constituencies as it requires, from the viewpoint of suppliers, a profound knowledge of the idiosyncrasies and particular traits and characteristics of external stakeholders and namely prospective consumers in those markets. This being the case, organizations that truly understand the functioning of markets and the psychology of consumers in them conceive and manufacture products whose raison d'étre resides well beyond their function and comply instead with, or in addition to, hedonistic requirements of status and social aspirational cues amongst others.

The consistent provision of a wide array of benefits that coincide with the values sought by groups of consumers in target markets, benefits that are clearly perceived as distinct and valuable by consumers in foreign constituencies, has become the Holy Grail of organizations that have come to understand the complexity of the competitive game and have learnt to play it better than most. In many cases the real benefit that is being sought and the functional purpose of the product, the reason why the product was originally conceived, are two distinct things that rarely intersect.

When someone buys a Rolex, naturally the intention is not that of buying an exclusive brand and the values that are associated with it, if and when the benefit that is sought is that of a time-telling piece. If someone wants a device for telling the time, he can buy a Timex, or any other cheap watch, or indeed any other instrument that may indirectly tell the time as part of its toolkit of applications, including a mobile phone. A Timex fulfils the same function but it provides an entirely different benefit from that of a Rolex. The value inherent to a Rolex however may be the result of many things. A Rolex for a collector of rare and valuable watches is a timepiece that can never be substituted by a Timex, which is incapable of satisfying the very same benefit. A Rolex on the other hand simply encapsulates the value that is entailed in possessing the brand. In other words, for someone who acquires a Rolex, the value of the brand may be a strict function of the importance that the consumer attributes to the fact that he or she is seen wearing a Rolex, the price of vanity in other words.

There are of course no value judgments implied here. If people are willing to pay for vanity, then vanity is what will be supplied to them. What matters here is the embodiment of whatever is valued by prospective customers dressed in meaningful products and services that these acknowledge and prefer. Rolex stands for certain aspirational values that are incorporated into its prestigious brands, and to which sufficient numbers of people with discretionary income adhere to. What Rolex certainly does not do is limit itself to scoping its product offer to a positioning of strict functionality. In the case of Rolex, product function is not the most important criterion that consumers have present when purchasing the brand. Clearly, the same thinking applies to non-luxury brands, but perhaps with different weightings attributed to function versus the intangible characteristics of these particular types of brands. In other words function counts for more than hedonism in non-luxury goods.

Nike knows that 70 to 80 per cent of those who buy their sports shoes don't buy them for the purpose that they were originally designed and conceived for. The majority of young people who buy Nike basketball shoes will most probably never enter a basketball court, and the same goes for tennis shoes and other sports gear. Nike's argument is a marketing one. They make shoes and other materials for athletes, and if other people want to buy them what can Nike do but oblige. In reality, Nike's positioning strategy is one of the best marketing coups of modern times.

Through a systematic association with winners, all of them in competitive sports, including the likes of tennis great John McEnroe in the 1970s, basketball all-time greatest Michael Jordan in the 1980s, and 200m and 400m runner Michael Johnson in the 1990s, amongst many, many other true champions, Nike has been able to reduce the role and importance of product function as a choice criterion for its sports shoes, not exactly to a minor detail, but definitely a criterion whose importance has been shadowed in the average buying decision-making process by other vitally more important feelings of belonging to a family.

The brand embodies values that are widely recognized and adopted as symbolic expressions of a culture, in that a group of individuals purchase the brand because it means something to them within a codified and intricate system of values where group members know exactly what it means to go around wearing the brand. All of this of course is a far cry from product functionality. In the case of Nike, when consumers buy the brand they are also buying into a kind of collective sentiment of belonging to a group, not necessarily an elite but a collective of individuals who subscribe to similar values, which Nike personifies and symbolizes, and with whom consumers intend to have a close relationship with.

Successful organizations carefully scrutinize societal values and search for attribution of meaning by individuals in societies and only then proceed to deliver brands that embody and symbolize the values that are sought by sufficient groups of people with discretionary income. The values that rule the way in which individuals conduct their lives, when subscribed by economically empowered groups of influential people with social clout occupying leadership positions within social hierarchies and structures of influence, then have to be met by corresponding aspirational brands that people adhere to.

The Hush Puppies shoe brand is an excellent example of the power of opinion-makers that occupy pedestals within social and professional structures of influence, and what this can do to change the fortunes of a corporate or product brand. The very succinct story about Hush Puppies is that it was a dying brand back in the 1970s and mainly recognized in the American Midwest; a brand whose image was totally the antithesis of cosmopolitan New York. It was perhaps closer to the image of a hillbilly, redneck culture than the hip and urban ethos that it later came to embody. The turnaround came when some influential socialite New Yorker, upon travelling to the American Midwest came across the shoes, bought them and started to wear them in view of the (in)famous Studio 54 crowd, who began to wonder where these shoes came from. They proceeded to buy them as if there were no tomorrow and made sure that many others would follow. This meant the revival of a dying brand, the Hush Puppies brand.

Brands look for groups of people that share similar characteristics and that are homogeneous in some meaningful and valued way. It is then up to the brand to bring to life these aspirations through the embodiment of the values that it congregates into products that are sought by consumers all over the world. This is then communicated to key target markets and eventually endorsed by individuals who are seen as ideal personifications of the identity values of these well-defined target markets. Brands are finally bought by hordes of individuals who seek some form of expression of their identity. Paradoxically, brands cater to the individual aspirations of consumers, making them feel special and unique whilst at the same time selling as much of the same product as they can to as many people as possible, meaning that this notion of uniqueness is much more perceptual and one of market positioning than it is effective and real.

Companies like Nike or Italian Diesel, for example, scan their environment to seek out ways in which they can possibly be perceived as cool, because cool sells in their respective markets. Their products are then the materialized expression for everyone to see of the collective concerns and anxieties of society, as well as responses to the common aspirations of target market segments. These organizations design and conceive their products, and crucially, communicate them in a way that is consistently aligned with the values that are sought by their target markets.

This is not coincidental and corresponds in effect to a very carefully manicured strategy that requires a comprehensive market scrutiny and monitoring of societal trends and changes as well as an intuitive/informed feel for the particular aesthetics of individual markets. At the end of this long process, and only at the very end, does Nike devise a product idea that unites all that is sought from them, packaging it perfectly into a marketing mix of product, communications, distribution and price, which fits into the value system of the societal group of consumers whom they aim to target.

In the absence of great social causes, at least akin to hippie collectivism and yuppie individualism of the 1960s and 1980s respectively, faced with the relative ideological emptiness of contemporary times and in the light of a looming and deeply entrenched economic crisis, all that is left to the current generation, that has like all others idiosyncrasies, character affirmation anxieties and an indomitable will to change the world, is to find a landscape in which to express this ambiguity. Brands can serve that very exact purpose.

The secret behind a great brand is to make people feel that they are unique. In reality they are. They are unique until a new generation comes along, and that generation – like all others before it – again becomes unique, albeit in very different ways from preceding ones. A brand needs to tap into what constitutes this idea of collective uniqueness and the values that it embodies and that it purports to typify and cast in stone as the aesthetic paradigm of the times.

Branding today as the doctrine of an ideology for the times is the contemporary representation of the hippy philosophy of the 1960s or the yuppie era of the 1980s. Arguably, the ideological substance, as well as the underlying social causes and struggles, are today much less politically exciting. The economic payoffs are clearly not those of the flying 1980s but the challenges facing the world today should be more than intellectually appealing.

There are contemporary issues that attract the interest and attention of most and are hot topics in today's world. Environmental issues, sustainability, poverty, corporate social responsibility, transparency and corporate governance may not be as exciting as peace and love, or greedy Wall Street trading and investment banking, but saving the planet may be arguably construed as being ultimately more important than which side of the ideological fence one stood on in the choice of dichotomous political systems that ruled the world up until the mid-1980s. The quest for affirmation and individuality echoes in a system of societal values where being anti-status quo and anti-establishment is the embodiment of cool. The economic crisis will stand to legitimate these collective anti-establishment postures as the establishment has not been able to solve peoples' problems, nor have incumbent institutions been capable of matching their aspirations.

Companies communicate brands in ways that project the desired values sought by homogeneous groups of people with discretionary income and that express their identities in the consumption of products whose raison d'étre is to symbolize those values. These can take all shapes and forms, but in the case of Nike its corporate strategic positioning is about uniqueness and being counter-current, projecting a rebel essence and a constant will to fight the system.

Of course if you are a major player in the sports apparel market like Nike, then you are the system, which makes Nike's positioning all the more interesting. Nike follows this up by introducing into the equation that which can aptly be called brand ambassadors, opinion-leaders in relevant segments in society, people who personify the brand and touch those who desperately care to listen to what they are saying. These are the athletes, the people who win truly important and challenging things, those who tell us mere mortals that it is possible to fight and win our quotidian daily battles. These living symbols stand for the many who subscribe to the values of Nike. They embody those values and share a bit of their greatness with the common person and all for a miserly US$200 pair of Nike shoes. They may be expensive, but it beats the hell out of having to spend four years at university reading for a degree, or spending years in the gym working out to obtain a great physique.

This in reality is the alchemy of modern times. It consists of the complex skills and competencies that lead to the aggregation of significant value to goods and services, through the power of association and symbolism. It is less about the quality of products and their technological content, and more about complex, intangible cues that gravitate outside the physical realm of a core problem-solving capability.

The notion of value aggregation to the output of an economic sector or a whole economy constitutes an important contribution to economics in that it revokes Marxian thinking on value formation, which stipulates that value is a function of the remuneration of factors of production, namely labour and capital. Marketing and branding add a new variable to the value equation, that of the image alchemists, the opinion-makers and the market knowledge bearers.

Those who have developed tremendously valuable skills in understanding in depth what makes a homogeneous group of people with economic power dispose of their money to acquire brands because these are the embodiment and personification of the values that they subscribe to and live by stand to gain immensely in the light of contemporary competitive dynamics.

It is these brands, to the exclusion of others, that are metaphors and conduits for value systems that unite groups of people with enough disposable income, and that share similar characteristics that can be targeted with goods and services that personify those character traits and idiosyncrasies. The ownership on the part of brands of societal values through their embodiment in products that people want – which groups of individuals with economic clout recognize and see themselves in them, adopting brands as symbolic expressions of who they are – is something relatively recent, at least in its modern consumerist manifestations.

Economic theory has failed to account for this in the context of the importance of shedding light on the understanding and application of contemporary notions of value creation and brands' crucial role in the enhancement of output value in an economy, their impact on GDP via the balance of trade, but also on the rethinking of the truly crucial concepts in modern economics, including worker productivity and national competitiveness as we saw before.

The accounting profession has also only recently begun to acknowledge the value of corporate and product brands as intangible assets with tangible value, and reflect these on balance sheets as an asset aptly named goodwill. When one researches this and concludes that, for many well-known organizations, in every sector of economic activity their most important and valuable asset is the brand, and when some countries are more capable than others of developing industrial and consumer brands, and are thus able to augment value to their exports better than others, one begins to wonder why product, corporate and national branding as intellectual lines of enquiry into modern economic competitiveness do not indeed suffer a much more acute scrutiny than they do, given their importance to contemporary national economies.

Going back to the Nike example, the paradox as we saw earlier is that Nike positions itself as being anti-establishment and anti-status quo when, in terms of market dominance, Nike is the establishment and the status quo. Nike is of course the IBM or the McDonalds of the sports apparel and shoes world. Nike's positioning strategy is undoubtedly shrewd. Again, how can the brand purport to be anti-regime when it is in fact the regime? How can they be rebels, when they are in effect the establishment? The secret lies in simulating a form of separatism or exclusivity that is rebellious and anti-system when there is nothing rebellious and anti-system about Nike. They are not only an integral part of the system, in many ways they are the system, and whilst walking this tight rope they stand to make huge amounts of money in the process.

The paradox is then that a positioning that includes words such as cool, rebel and unique, leads to a kind of, not necessarily elitism, but clearly an idea of exclusivity or perhaps more aptly a feeling of belonging. The problem with the notion of exclusivity however, and unless one is operating in the super-luxury end of the market spectrum, relates to sheer numbers. As cool as it sounds, if it is too exclusive then there aren't going to be enough people out there to buy the product. That is of course unless exclusivity translates into exorbitant prices that only a few people with serious money anxiously wait to pay for, in order to perpetuate in lifestyle the uniqueness of their condition. In sports shoes this is difficult to envisage and it is certainly not the case with the Nike brand. In any modern market economy, the role of corporate and product brands is critical to value aggregation and, by extension, country of origin effects and their impact on organizational and national competitiveness needs to be emphasized strongly. However, in reality, corporate reputation and branding issues are not the exclusive of market economies as many may believe to be the case.

There is a story that is told of the former Soviet Union, the land of no logo and no brand. During those days, products in general were pretty much undifferentiated, at least by conventional methods and brand recognition cues. There were no logos in other words. This, however, did not dissuade people from wanting to know where good quality products came from for future reference and, of course, there not being brands and logos, people had to find alternative cues to what brands and logos normally do, and that is to allow for instant recognition and inference on product quality and credibility. Branding was novel to those executives who had ascended directly from the *apparatchik* onto the upper echelons of companies like Gasprom or Lukoil, at the time of *perestroika* and *glasnost*.

A story is told of how branding, albeit unconsciously, was important for the way in which people bought car tyres in the former Soviet Union. There were no brands of tyres, but some tyres were of a higher quality than others. Better tyres came from certain manufacturers who did not carry any tyre brands that would allow for immediate recognition of which were indeed the best tyres. This however did not present a problem for the average consumer. Different tyre manufacturers made different tyres with different tyre marks. The only way of telling tyre manufacturers apart was through the marks that particular tyres left on the road. This was good enough for the consumer in that it allowed for the establishment of a hierarchy of tyre manufacturers and corresponding preferences were made based on perceived quality.

That in essence is what a brand is and what it does. A brand is anything that allows consumers to tell products apart. By looking at specific tyre marks, potential consumers were able to tell the origin of tyres and locate a particular manufacturer. Whilst there were no brands, there were ways in which to tell different manufacturers apart, and that which brands allow for, namely the identification of a manufacturer, and the possibility of the establishment of a hierarchy of choice as a result of an acquired reputation for excellence in critical dimensions of the product equation.

A particular tyre mark could be traced back to a single manufacturer, his were the best tyres around, and crucially more people would buy them as a result. In the particular case of the former Soviet Union one cannot perhaps talk about consumers paying top rouble for reputed tyres as these, as well as any other product, had prices regulated and fixed administratively, but consumers certainly chose more of the tyres that they liked to the detriment of others that they did not think were of acceptable standards of quality and reliability.

Brands act as guarantors of product quality in the eyes of consumers and are crucial cues in establishing consumer confidence. This is reflected in buyer decision-making when consumers are required to choose between competing alternatives.

In the same way that people develop comfort zones in relation to everything, they also look for the reduction of ambiguity when deciding amongst competitive alternatives for the satisfaction of the same need. Consumers progressively gain confidence in a certain brand through continued positive and systematic experiences in quotidian consumption. The same happens in relation to the decision to buy brands originating from certain countries to the detriment of equivalent products emanating from other countries.

The image held about a country, its reputation, as that of an organization or product, acts as a warranty against deception, which consumers adopt in their quest not to take risks. If they have continued positive experiences with branded products emanating from a particular organization or country, they establish a bond with that organization or country, and they continue to buy from the same origin. The brand acts here as an identifier, a reducer of ambiguity and a guarantor of the consumer experience. If all goes well, this translates into a higher propensity of prospective consumers, to buy more of this brand, and crucially of other brands of often unrelated products claiming the same origin, organization or country, and not of others from other firms and national origins.

Countries that, through their flagship organizations, are able to consistently deliver high-quality experiences associated with corporate and product brands, that are capable unlike others of capturing the imagination of consumers worldwide, brands that have acquired global notoriety and that not only meet, but consistently exceed, customer expectations thus gaining the collective trust of widely differing consumer target groups, have economies that are better equipped than anyone else to face the challenges of national competitiveness in the twenty-first century.

Being competitive in export markets translates into significant improvements in the balance of trade of a nation. This is also a good indicator of the importance for national economies of the development and nurturing of their country, corporate and product brands. If these are solid and reputable brands, their positioning will necessarily be distinct and valuable in the minds of target foreign constituencies, consisting of affluent consumers who have at their disposal a plethora of alternative options to choose from.

In this context, if consumers have preconceived notions in relation to certain countries they will pass these on to the products that emanate from those countries. As we saw before, when those perceptions are positive, people are willing to pay a premium for the privilege of buying goods whose origin is a guarantee of quality, excellent design and state-of-the-art technology. This is of course independent of the intrinsic merits of the product in question, and whether it fulfils any or all of these expectations. It is of course crucial that the consumer is not disappointed by the brand experience, as it does not take much for people to change their opinion as a function of negative consumption experiences. As retail guru and owner Philip Green used to say in the context of the fashion industry: 'You're only as good as last week, forget last season. It is not relevant.'

Brands that claim elitist origins that are widely recognized as such by consumers, who see them as excelling on critical buying decision dimensions, benefit from the very beginning from a capital of goodwill that resides within the prospective buyer. This is either because these brands have unambiguously demonstrated a clear differential advantage and superiority on perceived product quality to other functionally equivalent goods, or that they have been able to establish clear and distinctive positive images and a solid reputation next to their most important customers in export markets. In extremely competitive markets and in a globalized world, this is by no means negligible.

Competitive advantages that are based on reputational capital are not easy to achieve and sustain. They are even more difficult to replicate. These advantages derive from strong favourable prospective consumer perceptions that in turn are founded on both factual knowledge and stereotype about the country of origin of underlying branded products. It therefore makes sense from the viewpoint of the supplier to develop a profound understanding as to what shapes country stereotyping, including the way in which country of origin perceptions are formed next to external stakeholder constituencies.

Country of origin effects are the result of stereotypes that everyone develops about countries, people and institutions for which often very little is known. In the light of ambiguity, people create their own idealized stereotypical notions and expectations of these countries and what they are supposed to be about. How country of origin effects are formed, how they are shaped in the eyes of consumers in export markets by cultural variables and societal values, should be crucial aspects in the definition of an industrial strategy targeted at export markets, whose success depends on the sustained ability of a country in competing with other nations in cut-throat competitive and dynamic market settings.

Positive country images are probably the most important value aggregators to products and services in today's consumer society, and crucially act as differentiators that are impossible to replicate. These stereotypes impact the balance of trade of open economies and they should command a compatible attention on the part of academics and practitioners alike. For some obscure reason micro-economic issues and in particular organizational and national competitiveness still play second fiddle to macro-economic policy concerns, even in cases where countries have little if any latitude in effecting change, as they do not manipulate any of the levers of macro-economic or exchange rate policies. This is the case in the small economies in the eurozone which are destitute of any exchange rate policy levers, cannot issue money, nor can they set and control reference interest rates. Yet policy-makers continue to ignore the micro-economy of the firm and organizational competitiveness in these economies. At a time of deep economic crisis, itself largely a consequence of an excessive emphasis on virtual and speculative financial economics, the real economy of the production of goods and services should play a much more dignified and prominent role in government economic policy agendas.

There are however only a handful of cases of success in the formation of positive country images and reputation. Not many countries are able to benefit from positive stereotyping. Most nations are not known for anything, good or bad. Neutral collective perceptions are held about them by external stakeholder constituencies. Other nations are faced with negative country of origin images, resulting from lack of political maturity, dictatorships or systematic human rights abuses. These are negative country images that act detrimentally against a country's exports, its ability to compete abroad and to attract FDI into its shores.

However it is not only about negativity in prospective consumer perceptions, it is also about the former case of neutrality in positioning or the absence of any positioning in the minds of consumers in developed economies. It is safe to say that only too frequently there is nothing that distinguishes countries and the products that emanate from them. These are nations that are not known for anything of value, anything that consumers in export markets think is worth paying for. This is tragic for these nations as they are unable to create a distinctive imprint in peoples' minds.

Not being able to create distinction is a capital mistake in contemporary globalized economic relationships, as in the absence of a well-defined positioning and a positive imprint, any event can potentially trigger a latent and much dreaded negative stereotype. The positioning of most countries abroad is neutral, and foreign consumer perceptions are often erroneous and demonstrative of a complete lack of knowledge of the most basic of facts regarding these nations. That could be construed as little more than a problem of low self-esteem for the exporting nations that others elsewhere would not know about them and their existence. It is however much more than low self-esteem. It means in the first instance the difference between being able to export to these markets or not, and when successful to charge premium prices for branded goods. Exporting economies are thus highly dependent upon positive country reputations when placing their products next to foreign constituencies, but it is precisely the consistent and systematic provision of exceptional experiences that will contribute to the shaping of positive country reputations and the improvement of national competitiveness.

There is an inherent difficulty in living in ambiguity in relation to many things in life and, in the absence of detailed information about the reality of a country, stereotype kicks in and replaces factual knowledge as to what that country is about. Things have been changing in the last decade or so and particularly the advent of low-cost flying has allowed the middle classes and even the working class to have mobility without precedent in the history of humanity, and thus be exposed to different cultures and societal realities.

In truth, the economic consequences to an open economy of a number of negative stereotypes can be potentially devastating. The notion of structural backwardness is mostly founded on the idea of cultural periphery and parochialism and has profound negative effects on the reputation of a country as a way of example. Beyond the subjective questions of collective self-esteem, the economic consequences of these negative reputational effects are anything but negligible.

Simply put, the cosmopolitan consumer in London, Paris or New York cannot associate a preconceived notion of periphery and parochialism related to an unknown and unbranded country to the values sought in his particular brand of mainstream cosmopolitism, and that necessarily need to be imprinted into a branded good, originating from a country whose association with these values would be expected, logical and natural. As we saw before, the product itself does not need to be made in that country. In effect it doesn't really matter where the product is manufactured. What matters is where the brand comes from and whether it is recognizable and does indeed embody the subscribed values that wealthy consumers aspire to and emulate.

Ideas, concepts and products emanating from an unbranded country are not expected to be at the vanguard of cosmopolitism, when in truth very often they are both aesthetically and in terms of quality of the highest calibre. Consumers simply don't care, as these ideas, concepts and products do not even cross their spectrum of choice of product, as well as their consideration sets. Foreign consumers may stereotype certain nations that are incompatible with their own aspirations on cosmopolitism and what is seen as 'chic' as well as expectations regarding technology and so on. This stereotyping is reflected in consumer decision-making by a refusal to purchase products emanating from these countries.

The tragedy in country competitiveness is that often stereotypes not only do not conform with any known underlying reality, but also the values that these countries personify simply do not intersect with the value system that is sought by affluent consumers in export markets. Products emanating from these countries can never, from the viewpoint of these consumers, embody the societal values being sought. This being the case, products cannot act as symbolic expressions of these values and therefore lose their intangible value and goodwill next to discerning consumers.

There is enough room in this vast world however, for nations to adopt a strategic positioning based on strong niche brands, where a country is known for something, a kind of elitist secrecy that offers possibilities for distinction, akin to what the financial sector or the watch industry does for Switzerland. This kind of positioning on specific sectors does not have to be in areas that are fashionable for a while, but can indeed be about something more permanent and for which a nation acquires a reputation.

A fashionable, yet temporary national brand positioning would be a dangerous strategic way forward for the external positioning of a country in that what is fashionable today may not be fashionable tomorrow. Fashion is not eternal and a country's reputation built with a view to improving its balance of trade or attracting more and better FDI has to be founded on much more solid pillars. Countries need something a lot more constant and long-lasting as strategic positioning platforms.

Sometimes countries position themselves by making geographical analogies, using cues that only make sense in the context of their original applied versions. When applied in other countries and other geographic and sociological contexts, these analogies simply do not work. In other words, the literal extrapolation of positioning cues from one reality to the next is doomed for failure, as people simply do not understand what is implied in these comparisons.

An example of this happened a few years ago when the Government of Portugal launched a massive communications campaign with the aim of divulging and promoting the notion of Portugal as Europe's west coast. The intention was to inculcate this idea in foreign constituencies in the hope of attracting tourism money and FDI into the country. In principle it seemed a good idea to draw upon the metaphor of the American west coast, but it appears upon closer scrutiny that the west coast as political, economic, sociological and ideological realities and concepts in Europe and in America are not comparable constructs. In effect, the only related dimension is territorial and is based on the irrefutable fact that Portugal is in the west coast of Europe, but that is not enough for the collective psyche to make the necessary and desirable transition between the American west coast and Europe's west coast, carrying with it all the implied meanings traduced in the former.

The aura and underlying values that go with the notion of the American west coast also do not seem to travel well, in other words the idea of the west, or the specificity of its American assertion, cannot be easily extrapolated into a European context. There is a singularity and complexity that conditions the idea of immediate transferability of the west coast ideal from America to Europe. It is of course much more than geography.

What is meant here is that the positioning of Portugal as Europe's west coast only makes sense when glued to the set of values that make up for a whole ideology and way of life including, crucially, the collective posture towards entrepreneurship and risk-taking in California as a way of example. Outside this, the comparison simply does not hold true. The crux of the problem is that the extrapolation of this set of values to the west of Europe simply does not hold, as it is not a matter of geography. It is cultural, it is economic, and the key factors for success simply cannot be replicated as they are profoundly about human nature and its desires and aspirations. One would have to replicate the sociological dynamics underlying the phenomenon that led successive hordes of people arriving in Ellis Island, New York to push west in the quest for better living conditions. That being utopian, it does lead to the assertion that there is a west coast of Europe, but there isn't a European west coast.

The American west has been for centuries a repository of hope for millions who crossed the land looking for new opportunities in search of the all-American dream. Pushing the frontiers to the west happened to those who were often the last wave of immigration, who upon arrival in America would be confronted with already entrenched and at times deep-rooted social and economic structures, often based on family history and presence in the new territories however recent those were. In the light of this they simply had to push west.

Hierarchical cues such as property ownership served the purposes of social and economic stratification, and newcomers had to search elsewhere for opportunities. Although America was still very much in its infancy as a nation, many of these recent arrivals into the new land of hope and glory found no alternative other than to go west, where there was land, gold and opportunity. The West was the land of milk and honey. This is clearly not the case with contemporary Portugal or Spain.

What made the American west coast different are the pure and hard facts of life. If California were to be an independent country, and not one of the 50 states of the Union, it would rank way up there on comparative world GDP with the wealthiest economies. What is missing in the west coast analogy with reference to Portugal is of course that Portugal has no equivalent of the Silicon Valley, the technological hotbed around the San Francisco Bay area, the business buzz of Los Angeles, and up north, still in the west coast, Boeing and Microsoft in Seattle, Washington and Nike in Portland, Oregon and countless multinational corporations of worldwide notoriety that are based in the American west coast.

There is therefore a deliberate intent to replicate, in a European context, a profoundly American business ethos and underlying sociological and economic realities based on a strong spirit of entrepreneurship and risk-taking, and this is utopian, not credible and therefore people do not intuitively buy into it. This is, however, the litmus test of success of any national strategic positioning, whether enough people are willing to buy into the intended country idea. All of this of course cannot be replicated in a kind of social laboratory, and its credibility and worth is very much a function of the deeply held beliefs about freedom, adventure and territory that are associated with the idea of going west.

A communications campaign, however masterful the means deployed in it and creativity entailed, simply cannot do the trick.

In the end it is not about resorting to tasteless kitsch when positioning a nation brand. It is about carefully delving into the idiosyncrasies and the worthwhile aspects of the national collective character and identity, and using them to assert distinctiveness next to foreign constituencies who are constantly bombarded with similar messages coming from all over the world. It is not about using the collective traits of a nation and its character and identity as foundations for a commercial business model for the country's economy, which some would perceive as tasteless and even less dignified, but it is rather about using its uniqueness as a platform for differentiation, valuable singularity and inimitable distinctiveness.

In so doing countries are able to establish a platform upon which a nation builds an economic imprint on the world, and on the back of which it trades goods with other nations, augments value to its exports and attracts FDI to its shores. In order for any of this to have significant economic expression, country positioning needs to be valuable and distinctive, and acknowledged by key constituencies the world over, translating into a consistent preference for products that emanate from that particular nation and a consumer willingness to pay comparatively more for these goods than those of others.

In intensely fought and highly competitive global markets, and in the light of comparative parity in perceived tangible benefits with products emanating from other nations, consumer choice is decisively shaped by country reputation cues. The aggregation of value to goods and services attributable to a common knowledge of foreign constituencies that these are of a well-defined origin is the Holy Grail of successful nation brand-building and should be the cornerstone of any successful export strategy.

Reality Check...

From Japan to La Coruna and How to Do Things Differently at Inditex

The Inditex Group is an excellent example of the importation of the best organizational practices from around the world, put to good use in very different economic and cultural contexts. Founded in La Coruna, in Galicia, and therefore far away from the decision centres of Madrid and Barcelona, by señor Amancio Ortega, the Inditex Group very soon came to the understanding that the road to success was paved with hardship and obstacles, as the extremely competitive world of fashion was undergoing tremendous change in what constituted its competitive pillars. The ability to overcome these obstacles by daring to revoke the incumbent paradigm in fashion retailing was to underpin the future viability and commercial success of corporate brands like Zara, Bershka, Stradivarius and others.

Ortega realized early on in his business life that if he was ever going to succeed he had to ensure that to the best of his and his company's abilities he needed to guarantee control over the links of the supply chain that effectively generate value in the fashion business and those, he knew only too well, were the ones that stand closer to the consumer. In other words, he knew that at some point he had to go downstream in the supply chain and create his own retail and product brands. This of course meant that the Inditex group would have to start their own retail businesses at some point. The closer they were to the consumer, the bigger their slice of the retail fashion business pie would be.

Ortega of course extended his business empire to the retail sector, demonstrating from a very early stage a profound understanding of the power of branding and that of staying close to the consumer with what were to become household names, including Zara, Bershka, Stradivarius and other very successful fashion retail brands, not only in Spain but also abroad. The rest of course is history.

Just south of La Coruña, the Portuguese textile and clothing industry, with few honourable exceptions, did not follow the same strategic path. It was of course not easy to do what the Inditex Group had done. On the contrary, it was difficult and expensive. The risk associated with building a portfolio of clearly differentiated brands with distinctive market positioning platforms, that have different meanings and that signify effective value to heterogeneous groups of consumers is high.

The fashion sector is very competitive and the investments needed to make any significant impact in it substantial. The Inditex group, however, clearly understood that there was no strategic alternative other than to go downstream in the value chain and control those extremely valuable links with the consumer if it was to take off or at least if it wanted to remain a going concern in the light of a very competitive environment, and faced with low-cost supplies from the Far East.

Many Portuguese companies in the textiles and clothing sectors simply failed to see the future of the business in the same way, for reasons that can be traced back to a hopeless and innate inability to think strategically on matters of competitiveness by incumbent market players in the sector. The tragedy of course was that the same was to happen in most other sectors of economic activity.

Zara and other Inditex corporate brands managed to successfully enter the cut-throat, yet very lucrative, British fashion market because, amongst other things, it was able to overthrow two essential pillars of the business paradigm that had long been gospel in the sector and that clearly conditioned the strategic options under consideration both for market incumbents and new players alike.

The two competitive pillars that had sustained incumbent business models in fashion retailing for decades had been, on the one hand, the deterministic nature of seasonality in fashion, and on the other, the inevitability of low-cost supply from the Far East. These were for many insurmountable obstacles, and any strategic outlook on the retail fashion business had to be subjugated to these two imperatives if one wanted to successfully compete in the global market.

These two quasi-inevitabilities and, particularly, low-cost production from the Far East were extensively used as arguments for justifying the competitive problems of the sector in southern Europe and in particular in Portugal. Many entrepreneurs would make constant appeals for government intervention and protection against what they perceived to be the unfair competition from the Far East, translated into cheap products coming from China and India, and from other countries with very low labour cost structures and often an unspoken tradition of child labour, and other ethically and morally condemnable labour practices that nevertheless went on unhindered in these economies.

The Inditex Group threw all of that away. It contributed to bringing down the pillars of a paradigm that many thought was there to stay for many a year. Zara and other Inditex brands very soon instituted their own version of what fashion retailing was to look like for decades to come. Through a planned international expansion strategy, Zara, along with Swedish retail giants H&M, enacted a radical change in fashion retail by introducing a new business model, founded on the principles of flexibility, quick lead times and fast-fashion. Seasonality in fashion and low-cost supply from the Far East, as the Inditex Group was only too keen to show the world, were not unbreakable rules. In the process, Amancio Ortega was to amass a formidable fortune and eventually became one of the wealthiest men in the world.

As Phillip Green, owner of British Home Stores, was quoted as saying, for many years fashion was sold in department stores much in the same way as toasters. There were two seasons, a Spring/Summer collection and an Autumn/Winter collection. In the early 1990s, retail giants Marks and Spencer chose grey as the colour of the season. At Zara and H&M today little can be found to remind the consumer of the idea of seasonality in fashion retail. In reality, the consumer walks into a store and sees something she likes. If she doesn't buy it there and then, there is a serious risk that the item will not be available the next time she visits the store. This induces a strong implicit appeal to consumption, one that is difficult to resist. It is also a departure from basic traditional retailing rules and techniques that consist of making the product widely available to the public as well as communicating its existence through sophisticated and expensive means.

On the contrary, Zara spends little on advertising and what is at stake here is an idea of stimulation of consumer demand as an intense psychologically-induced process, where people manifest an appetite for the brand and want to make sure that they buy it before the retailer runs out of stock for the particular item that is sought. A perception of scarcity in the supply of the brand makes people buy it just in case the item never again shows up on Zara racks.

Large and long-established household names with strong retail track records and market presence, such as Littlewoods or Dutch C&A, were soon to lose prominence in the British retail scene, and more recently Woolworths would declare bankruptcy after 100 years of retail activity in the UK. Woolworths was the company that, together with Tiffany's, were the pioneers of the one price only policy, as we know it today, the quintessential fashion retail operation if there ever was one.

The second pillar of the incumbent business paradigm to have been taken down was that of the inevitability of low-cost supply from the Far East. Of particular relevance here was the challenging by Inditex of the supposed superiority of the low labour-cost argument over the importance of quickness of response for their particular brand of fast-fashion retailing.

Fast-fashion required quick response and this was novel, whilst low-cost labour models in the supply of these goods had been an anchor of competitiveness in fashion retailing that had remained unquestioned for decades. Challenging the status quo and the incumbent business model was the difficult thing to do, as the tendency is always to perpetuate the traditional ways of doing things, even if they have led nowhere for ages.

As a corollary to this, and in perpetuating the pillar of competitiveness of low-cost structures, European industry in general cried foul and warned governments and policy-makers of unfair competition and dubious labour practices in the emerging competitor economies, calling for government protection and the imposition of quotas, tariffs and other restrictive measures to the inflow of foreign cheap goods into European markets. The Chinese threat, as it was commonly referred to in the trade, and unfair, unregulated and unchecked competition were to blame for the virtual disappearance of the textile and clothing sectors, particularly in the southern European economies, as in northern Europe any idea of a manufacturing textile and clothing industry was a thing of the past.

Zara and H&M however had different thoughts on the matter. Zara was able to innovate by keeping its supply sources very close to home, monitoring quality parameters both in Galicia, where it had been based since its inception, or in northern Portugal, a stone's throw away. In so doing, they of course had to incur incomparably higher labour costs, but having production closer to home was instrumental to the quick response business model which was to become the cornerstone of their commercial success. JIT techniques, imported directly from the Japanese automobile industry, which car manufacturer Toyota had pioneered, were crucial in phasing out the old ways of doing business and introducing a new business model based on short-lead times, quick response, low inventory and flexible supply logistics.

Zara felt that in order to survive in a cut-throat competitive environment, as has always been the case with the fashion retail business, ever-crowded with shrewd global players who know the market inside out, it would have to have, as part of its strategic mould and intent, quick response supply mechanisms, a business model that could put out product into the market very quickly without putting itself in the position of being too uncompetitive on cost in the process. In addition to that, it needed to innovate when it came to scrutinizing consumer needs, thus fine-tuning its understanding of buying decision-making processes in key target markets.

In the case of Zara, understanding the customer was something that meant the combination of ingenuity and a little use of technology. Celebrities who wore Zara clothes were also instrumental in stimulating consumer demand. People like Kate Moss or Victoria (Spice) Beckham were, for many young people at the time, the closest they could come to the aspirational lifestyles that those characters embodied. By having celebrities wearing the brand, it meant that these would inevitably condition and influence others into wearing the very same brand. Some celebrities who could easily afford Versace or Prada would still be seen wearing Zara, and that did a world of good for the Spanish brand.

From very early on the company clearly understood the volatility of the fashion world and how ephemeral and short-lived the whole thing really was. The key then was to always be on top of the game, riding the fashion wave with different collections and ideas but always with a common purpose, that of remaining relevant to successive generations of consumers. This wasn't done through advertising, as Zara does not spend money on advertising, but in being contemporary and relevant – the whole of the backroom process had to be streamlined and fine-tuned and nothing could really be left to chance. Here technology and its role in production and supply logistics, but also in marketing and in the constant and real-time monitoring of consumer needs and wants, was to prove critical. Technology at Zara meant that customer-facing employees were equipped with hand-held computers and information on everything that was sold in any store, anywhere in the world, got fed to La Coruña immediately. There they would proceed to ensure that more of the items that sold got manufactured and not of the ones that did not sell. This meant that very low stock levels were indeed kept at any one time, and certainly less than the industry average.

The overriding idea was also one of emphasizing customer retention and loyalty by ensuring that the customer remained interested and curious about the brand and its products. Zara was able to create a tangible proposition, based on a strategy aligned with the psychology of the times and anchored on logistics that fitted the bill. The company also based its logistical systems on an intelligence that allowed for a systematic scrutiny of market trends, including the less obvious ways in which consumers made decisions to adopt new products, thus refining the role and use of celebrities and their endorsement of corporate brands.

Zara had to think of different ways in which to generate and sustain interest in its brand in what is an overcrowded world, having to go up against competing messages from everywhere, for pretty much the same product offer. The company, as stated earlier, does little advertising, and yet in the UK, an average consumer will walk into a Zara store 17 times a year, contrasted with the average for the fashion retail sector which is calculated at four times. These figures report to fashion retailing a decade ago, but it is probably a fair assumption to state that things have not changed much since then, as Zara continues its success story in foreign markets. This is how Zara creates an insatiable appetite for its products. The message is that you either buy it now, or if you come back next week, there is a fairly good chance that you will not find what you came looking for. In a world of immediacy and consumerism, this sends a very powerful message to punters out there.

In the case of Zara, by importing best practices from Japan, where they have been used in very peculiar organizational contexts and specific sociological and cultural worlds, they could potentially have faced hidden dangers in applying these conceptual frameworks and practices in the realm of the Galician sociological reality. However, this not only did not constitute a problem for them, it turned out to be the cornerstone for their logistics, an important component of their strategic competitiveness and long-term organizational success. The use of JIT methods and techniques and their application in the Zara supply chain worked well for them in La Coruna, and there is no reason to believe that, if proper caution is exercised on adjusting to local realities, imported managerial practices should not work in alternative organizational, cultural and sociological contexts.

In the eyes of a kind of centralist pseudo-cosmopolitan view of the world, very little happens outside the capital city in most countries. In reality, a lot goes on in rural towns and villages, outside the major decision centres. Even this idea of a certain kind of parochial or peripheral rural feel to a place can be cleverly exploited abroad, if well treated and communicated. It can in effect be a unique, distinctive and valuable positioning platform for an organization or a nation. It wasn't necessary for Zara to have come from Barcelona or Madrid, and had the company originated in one of these cities, it would perhaps not have had the same success that it eventually was to have for several reasons. In all probability, the complex network of relationships, created from nothing and nurtured continuously by the company, with suppliers in Galicia and in the north of Portugal, would never have materialized elsewhere.

The trick is to challenge the status quo precisely when things are comfortable. People like Bill Gates of Microsoft and Phil Knight of Nike firmly believed in this. Bill Gates once said that it is precisely when things are going well that he begins to worry, wanting to know exactly why the company is doing well. Phil Knight, at one time worth $5 billion, said once that there were nights when he was just not able to sleep, worried sick that his competitors would overtake him for consumer preference. He once summed it up by saying that when people wake up in the morning they don't get up, walk out and buy a pair of shoes from each company. They buy one pair of shoes, and for Knight this meant that he had to make damn sure, that the pair of shoes was going to be Nike. This implied having the best products, with the best cushioning and design but also having the best athletes endorsing those shoes, and the best ads when communicating them to the public. They both personify an indomitable will to compete.

5

On Leadership, Entrepreneurial Spirit and the Search for Sustainable Competitive Advantages

One of the greatest challenges that senior management confronts today is that of a commitment with a long-term vision for organizations and to think strategically in times when immediate survival and tactical acumen are also paramount and have to be of foremost concern to all. Akio Morita, who was Chairman and CEO of Sony for decades, identified early on a latent need in the market for what he was to designate as personal portable sound. Morita had to overcome suspicion and scepticism inside Sony, where his colleagues began to doubt the elderly gentleman's once exceptional faculties.

In effect Morita's idea for personal portable sound was to be the genesis of the concept that gave rise to one of the most successful Sony products ever, the Walkman. Organizational leadership and the traits of great leaders and the link between these and the pursuit for sustainable competitive advantages in organizations are approached next. Are there character traits that are common to these prominent people? What is the role of individual drive and commitment in overall organizational performance?

As an undergraduate student Richard Branson was not your run-of-the-mill studious type. From an early age Branson had a strong inkling for business and running the school magazine was one of his first projects. He showed from very early on a strong entrepreneurial spirit. The school magazine was followed by other projects and in the 1970s, and riding on the punk wave that had swept across the UK at that time, he decided to create the Virgin record label. One of the first bands that he was to sign for the Virgin label was punk band, the Sex Pistols. If, even to the liberal eyes of today's world, Sid Vicious' antics and those of the Sex Pistols are still capable of raising controversy, one can only begin to guess what the fuss was like back in the 1970s when young Branson did not hesitate to link the Virgin brand to the punk music band. It was far from consensual at the time that this was the right thing to do, or that associating with the Sex Pistols was ever going to be good for business and for Virgin.

In the beginning it was complicated, as the registering office did not want to patent the Virgin name, considering it to be a bit on the rude side. Eventually Richard Branson managed to register the name. Virgin it stayed. This was an appealing and controversial name, and something that was perceived to be on the edge and risqué, with anti-status quo and anti-establishment undertones. It was nevertheless guaranteed to more than raise a few eyebrows. More to the point, it was bound to shake the conservative British establishment of that time. The Virgin name was to become associated with many products and areas of business that were completely unrelated to each other. Many from the very beginning claimed that it would be difficult for the Virgin name to travel across different products and business areas and still manage to keep a distinct and recognizable identity.

History was to demonstrate that none of that was to ever become a problem for Branson and for Virgin, and the company was to establish itself as a credible corporate brand across a variety of business areas, ranging from civil aviation to railway transportation, spirits, bridal wear and financial services. In the latter case, criticisms were apportioned at Virgin for entering a business that in the eyes of many critics was impossible for it to go into, as it lacked the specific competencies and knowledge, as well as the technical acumen that was required. Those critics made their views known, that financial services were a specialist business that required particular technical skills and an in-depth knowledge of the ins and outs of the world of finance. Prudence was strongly recommended and many waited for Branson to fall flat on his face.

As it turned out Richard Branson ended up entering the financial services business. When confronted with the opinion of critics, he simply stated that there was no reason for the idea of Virgin financial services not to work. Although the modus operandi of the business was different and demanded specific technical knowledge, the organizational values underpinning all Virgin ventures were the same, a sense of adventure and fun, as well as courage to confront the sceptics and enter business sectors that upon first glance were very different in terms of market requirements and implied organizational competencies, but in the final analyses, all shared the common imperative of the satisfaction of customer needs at a profit.

The issue of value incongruence within the various Virgin organizations could have in retrospect been a problem for Branson, as financial services are not normally the kind of goods that one associates with fun and adventure, which were perhaps more intuitively in tune with Virgin vodka. On the contrary, for most people, financial products are dull, detailed and conservative stuff, characterized by the kind of consumer involvement that forces one to deal with these matters when instead he would rather have someone else handle it for him. Financial services certainly do not appeal to most people, but rather to a restricted few.

Virgin's challenge to the incumbent paradigm was in defying the status quo on who in accordance with established thought should be allowed to trade in financial services, in short, banks. For Branson, what was critical was for the organization to keep its core values and ethos intact when dealing with different businesses in varying areas and sectors of economic activity.

Entrepreneurship values with roots in Victorian ideals that had historical precedents in the Rowntree, Lever Brothers or Cadbury families were the basis of much of this thinking. An entrepreneurial philosophy founded on strong religious values, sought in work ethic a conduit for happiness, and the ideology was shipped to the new world where it found fertile ground for its propagation in yet unstructured societal values. The universe of Quaker belief systems preferred chocolate to alcohol and salvation on earth through the pursuit of a solid work ethic, discipline and rigour to a more relaxed attitude to work and life in general.

That and the Weberian ideal of a protestant ethic, that not only legitimizes, indeed strongly encourages the pursuit of happiness and the meaning of life meaning on earth, calling everyone to the duty of making and shaping their own individual destinies through work, discipline and rigorous lifestyle principles, are the historical foundations for this particular brand of entrepreneurship. Exemplary social conduct and deep-rooted societal values and concerns were to find their materialization in modern entrepreneurship ideals and manifestations of this philosophy in the new world.

These values can be traced back to such people as Rockefeller in oil or Carnegie in the steel businesses respectively at the end of the nineteenth century. In the case of Carnegie there are strong points of contention as to the purity of his social ideals and principles, namely when contrasted against the harsh treatment of workers in steel mills in Pennsylvania. As a side story, history documents Carnegie and his right hand man, the legendary Mr Frick, as attempting to cut labour costs by reducing wages and increasing working hours to inhumane levels in an attempt to drive up the profitability of the steel business, obsessed as Carnegie was with his arch-rival, oil tycoon Rockefeller. In the process they were to bring in the Pinkerton brigade to impede workers from striking, resulting in the death of nine workers and the injury of countless others who were picketing outside the steel mill. There is always of course a romanticized version of history on the one hand, and the cruel and harsh reality of events on the other.

In the case of Branson, in the end he was only to apply his core beliefs, values and philosophy to the running of a successful business. In doing that he derived lessons from what the Japanese had been doing for decades, and that which was part of the architecture and raison d'étre for their post-war economic success. Branson has spoken highly of the *kieretsu* organizational philosophy, groups of companies in different areas of economic activity, many of them unrelated, yet with significant coordinated strategic collaboration between them in international markets.

Within the Victorian entrepreneurial spirit, a company that people have learnt to trust for decades, that builds a reputation based on lasting relationships between clients and the organization, is much more than a company, it is almost a friend, from whom we expect the utmost loyalty, someone who will never disappoint us. Branson responded to those who accused him of brand stretching by stating that his idea was really simple and that people in Japan, for example, had no problem in driving a Mitsubishi to work whilst at the same time withdrawing cash from a Mitsubishi bank.

There is however a risk of a corporate brand having a strong reputation for excellence in a particular business area but not in another. In this case it is often very difficult for the public in general to recognize the brand outside the business context in which the corporate brand's reputation was initially built. This has not been sufficient to deter Virgin, Mitsubishi, Yamaha or other brands that are simultaneously corporate and product brands.

To be able to draw on the strong notoriety of established and valuable brand names makes economic sense. There are risks however associated with brand stretching. Perhaps the most important of these risks is the negative image held about an organization with respect to its performance in a certain area or sector of business, and the way this may negatively impact other areas and businesses sharing the same name. There is a risk of contamination of the brand due to negative comment or bad product experiences in one area of the business that extrapolates onto other often unrelated areas, whose only relationship or connection with the former is the sharing of the corporate brand name.

Virgin had a problem with its Virgin Rail brand in the rail transportation business. Virgin entered this market at a time when the British railroad infrastructure was decrepit and significantly more backward than that of France or Germany. The railroad infrastructure was particularly antiquated, provoking delays to every operator, and Virgin Rail was not an exception. People who used the Virgin rail services began to experience frustrating delays. With time and persistence, however, Virgin was able to overcome these problems which Branson claimed to be related to the decrepit railroad infrastructure in the UK and began to compete effectively also in this market.

Although not always successful in every business that the Virgin brand entered into, Branson never allowed the incumbents to dictate what he could or could not do. Whenever someone told him not to get involved, or that he would not be able to make it in a particular business because it was difficult, the technology was complex or because the big boys of the establishment would not allow it, Branson would take this as precisely the kind of inducement that would drive him and his business forward.

One of the greatest challenges facing senior managers today is the imperative of leadership and strategic vision. Akio Morita, former Chairman of Sony, had it in his mind that there was a latent need in the market for what he designated as personal portable sound. Morita had to overcome suspicion and scepticism at Sony, where senior executives believed that the elderly gentleman had passed his sell by date and had by then lost some of his at one time exceptional faculties. Morita persisted and the personal portable sound idea became the Walkman.

Exceptional leaders like Jack Welch of General Electric, Phil Knight of Nike, Herb Kelleher of Southwest Airlines, and a few others have as personality traits, amongst other qualities, a resolute obstinacy in the pursuit of objectives and an obsession with winning. Many stories are told about these characters and it is often difficult to tell truth from tale, to dissociate the person from the mythology. These people share a common denominator though. Exceptional leaders, such as the ones mentioned above, are invariably individuals that tend to combine a long-term strategic vision with a fine tactical acumen. These leaders are charismatic and inspirational and that is why people will follow them.

Phil Knight, a sports buff with a particular interest in track and field, was never himself a top athlete and was never able to win anything as a runner at the University of Oregon. He never quit though and an obsessive will to win became deeply engrained into Knight's character. At college, Knight wrote a paper which he called Blue Ribbon Inc. about a sports apparel and shoe company. This was to become the Nike strategic blueprint. The paper did not receive a satisfactory grade but that did not dissuade Knight from ploughing away towards his destiny. On the contrary.

Selling sports shoes from the boot of his car, Phil Knight was probably the only one who believed he could make it. Deliverance came in the form of what was to become the largest sports apparel company in history. Of course it wasn't as easy as that, and many obstacles were to be faced by Knight and the early Nike people on the way. In reality, to keep believing when others have quit long ago appears to be common to all of these legendary characters that permeate the history of great ideas that became great organizations. Companies need charismatic leaders who have a strategic vision and the ability to share it with everyone else.

It is obvious that European economies, no matter how cheap labour is in some of them, cannot sustain a set of competitive advantages based on low costs of labour. It simply cannot happen, which means that in order for European economies to be successful they need to focus their energies and resources on capital-intensive and knowledge-based models of economic development. European firms cannot sustain labour cost advantages and that which has allowed some European economies to be price competitive in their export markets no longer holds in the light of a globalized economy.

Countries that now compete with European industry for export markets have always had lower cost structures than those of any of the European economies, even when compared to the lower wage economies in southern Europe. Wages in these economies are of course lower than those of their northern European counterparts, but they are still going to be much higher than those of emerging economies that compete with them for the most appealing and profitable export markets.

In addition to this, there are also obligations as to the compliance with labour practices to which European organizations are legally bound, as well as the moral and ethical principles that they are required to adhere to, which contrast with the much less rigid requirements and flexible labour practices of the emerging economies. Ethical behaviour and stringent codes of conduct differ substantially in European and Far Eastern labour contexts. This includes the unequivocal rejection of child labour practices as well as the treatment of workers in the workplace in European economies, which is much more susceptible to monitoring and control by labour organizations than in the emerging economies of the Far East. Whilst acknowledging this, in effect all is not pristine and transparent in Europe as labour conditions have progressively deteriorated with a deepening of the economic crisis.

Understandably, entrepreneurs complain about the unlevelled playing field and the unfairness of having to compete against industries of nations where human rights abuses are treated lightly. These emerging economies compete against European export sectors in what used to be traditional strongholds for European economies. It is also true that Europe has progressively lost competitive ground to countries where there is insufficient monitoring of labour practices, but in a free-trade environment it is simply impossible to ensure that players in the Far East comply with European standards on labour relations and practices in the workplace.

Labour in many sectors of economic activity, and this is particularly true in southern European economies, is often unskilled, with low levels of formal education and little specialist training, and consequently undistinguishable from mass unqualified labour anywhere in the world. The problem with this typology of labour is that it can easily be found anywhere in the world and even cheaper. The low wages that are paid to workers only reflect their indistinct nature and low level of specialization, probably in line with the characterization of low-tech sectors of economic activity in these nations.

However, sectors of economic activity that are characterized by higher technological content and that comply with state-of-the-art knowledge requirements, seen as having much potential in the future, including the areas of renewable energies, information technology or the environment, require a qualified and specialist workforce. Any European economy, whose principal basis for competitive advantage is anchored on low labour costs, should be hearing alarm bells and serious warnings against the inappropriateness of such a strategic paradigm in the light of the easy availability of cheap labour resources in the global economy.

In thinking strategically, a vision for the European economy is required. A strategic perspective needs to be anchored on strong political leadership and has to stand well above party politics and surpass ideological difference. This is not utopian as a view on reality. The less competitive European economies are characterized by having low levels of formal education of their populations. These economies are particularly vulnerable to the low-cost emerging nations.

This type of workforce is not very likely to respond well to change in terms of its reconversion potential when having to deal with new conditions and higher technological complexity in novel and innovative sectors of economic activity. An uneducated workforce simply finds it too hard to cope with change of the kind that it has not been trained for. This does not refer to the acquisition of any new specialisms in particular, but more to the inability of an uneducated workforce in thinking outside the box and in acquiring complex knowledge and information.

A largely uneducated workforce does not know how to learn and hence does not possess the intellectual capabilities that simplify the acquisition of new knowledge, not only of a technical nature but also commercial knowledge of customers and markets. A workforce of this calibre finds it difficult to deal with the requirements and sophistication of higher-order economic activities that are the only ones that can aggregate value to goods and services in contemporary economies.

These activities require the development and application of knowledge, and crucially from the viewpoint of the workforce, a thorough understanding of the philosophy of value aggregation to processes and products. Achieving this means attaining success in a critical dimension of global competitiveness in contemporary economies. Reality in the low-cost European economies demonstrates that only a few tried to go against the grain, in that traditional sectors of economic activity with some export potential have invariably been in low-tech sectors. These are not susceptible to much in the way of value aggregation.

A workforce with a low level of formal education is unable to develop skills that are inherent to activities that require analysis and critical thinking. For society as a whole this means the proliferation of a population that does not question the status quo, that follows but never leads and whose behaviour is the antithesis of truly democratic systems. This has consequences that extend beyond those directly associated with the economic crisis, unemployment and negative GDP growth. These are manifested in a profound crisis of societal values characterized by the absence of inspiring and valid ways forward, leading to social unrest and despair.

In addition to this, the characterization of whole nations as unable to exercise critical thinking has devastating effects on the way in which they are perceived by foreign constituencies. The creation of stereotypes in relation to countries have, as a consequence, that their most representative products benefit from, or are alternatively harmed by, respectively positive or negative notions held about the countries in question.

As has been amply demonstrated in countless studies over the years, the impact of country of origin on consumption decisions is not negligible. Consumers seek to mitigate risk and avoid less than positive experiences with products whose origin does not represent a warranty of quality or does not guarantee a positive performance on the dimensions that are considered to be relevant in the buying decision-making process.

There often exist criteria that unify the consumption profiles of different groups of people and that cut across geographic boundaries. The profiles of target groups may indeed intersect different geographies and cultures. Economic globalization means that effective communications strategies need to recognize cultural difference. However, and in acknowledging cultural and aesthetic diversity expressed in different structures of preference, it is also true that individuals in different cultural settings and geographies share a lot more with each other than they care to imagine, and this is reflected on consumption decision-making.

The need to be relevant at a global level has meant that the knowledge of target markets has taken on a whole new meaning, requiring an understanding of the nuances that characterize individual markets. This implies the acknowledgement of the frailties and shortcomings of traditional profiling mechanisms that aggregate consumers according to socio-economic and demographic criteria when other variables need to be sought.

Although still very valid as segmentation variables, socio-economic and demographic criteria need to be refined by the scrutiny of cultural filters when targeting key export markets. That being said, cultural and country differences are not in themselves indicators of significant differences in consumer behaviour. Heterogeneous lifestyles and subcultures within countries or even regions are perhaps more important cues for exporters.

There is a proliferation of urban cultures each with its own specificity and aesthetic expression. There are cultural niches that are defined in terms of commonalities in music, the arts or anything that may potentially aggregate people around a unified set of values. In effect, geographical boundaries are often irrelevant in the definition of consumer groups that share similar characteristics.

Organizations placing their products in key export markets need to recognize this to acknowledge the idiosyncrasies of particular markets but also, crucially, that in which they intersect, and in the end reflect all of this into a market offer that caters to the interests of those consumers and not of others. This needs to be done as consumption decisions made by savvy and worldly consumers are much more about the acquisition of universal symbols that satisfy specific groups of buyers that recognize and adhere to the values personified by meaningful brands than with anything related to core product functionality.

Universal brands constitute excellent metaphors for the satisfaction of the needs of groups of consumers that are homogeneous in their preferences but may be dispersed across different regions of the world. In the end it is all about the power of universal brands that are able to unify consumers that share meanings and symbolism as reflections of societal values, despite originating from varying cultures and geographies.

What underlines the categorization or stratification of both domestic and foreign consumers are often the same criteria. What can feed and give substance to the set of values that translate into elitism, being anti-status quo, anti-establishment, counterculture, or any set of values embodied in valuable brands, to which a group of consumers with economic expression adheres to, may be the same for both the domestic and foreign markets.

Societal values may be the same but the processes in which the brand is communicated may differ, and for organizations this is significant in that they need to translate the intended values that the corporate brand carries next to key target markets into codified languages that accommodate the cultural singularities and societal values of their countries of destination. For truly global organizations, acknowledging and effectively dealing with this is critical. Adaptation to societal values is also a dynamic process as these quickly change across key target markets.

The idea is to identify enough individuals with disposable income for the consumption of goods and services which they choose to the detriment of other equally valid consumption alternatives. These individuals should be willing and economically able to buy brands that are expressions of their identities and aspirations, and do so in the knowledge that those brands will cater to their needs and provide benefits that extend well beyond their core functional purpose. An important group of consumers is also one whose influence upon others in society is both unusual and disproportionate. In this context, being individuals with disposable income and social kudos, they have the potential for dragging others and influencing them, setting trends for others to follow.

Foreign markets are critical for small open economies with a significant dependence on export sectors. The inability to create a clear distinctiveness in the brand proposition is often the consequence of the inability of the country image to aggregate significant value around its best products and services. For many countries, being successful in their export markets is not a question of the intrinsic quality of the goods and services that emanate from their sectors of economic activity. Many countries are able to manufacture exceptional quality products but nobody has ever heard of them. They are thoroughly incapable of projecting an adequate image for these products abroad or to surround them with an aura of value that is compatible with their intrinsic quality. In other words, firms in these economies are more than capable of manufacturing exceptional products but consumers in foreign markets don't even know that they exist.

Companies in these economies make products of the highest quality but they do not know how to create and nurture excellent corporate and product brands and how to consistently build up accounting goodwill by making these brands the most significant assets on corporate balance sheets. Critically these economies do not benefit from positive country of origin effects that could aid their best products. This takes time to build as it is largely perceptual, although anchored in the experiential realities of consumers that are consistently exposed to excellence in branded goods and services emanating from a particular country.

It also takes time to achieve a positive country reputation as all of this of course needs to be achieved next to foreign constituencies.

In general, and with the odd exception, firms and institutions in the less developed European economies, and in particular in the southern European countries, have failed miserably in that most crucial of areas, the marketing of their best products. The absence of a strategic vision on the part of institutional and organizational decision-makers, government and top management in organizations, and the collective failure in dealing with the challenges of globalization and its manifestations on consumer preferences, aesthetics and dynamics, are the reasons why these economies can't keep a decent balance of trade. This has afflicted some more than others but it is clearly evident with the southern European countries. In many cases these economies have exceptional products but no one knows about them. In a cut-throat globally competitive environment this has to be a cause for worry.

There is widespread concern about the indiscipline of the public finances of European economies and the dangers inherent to successive and historical budget deficits that have culminated in extraordinary levels of accumulated public debt. This has also obscured the critical need for a focus on the real economy of production of goods and services and for the constant search for ways in which to improve national competitiveness. In maintaining unsustainable lifestyles, countries have run successive public deficits and accumulated debt, but over and above the surreal level of indiscipline in the running of the public finances, and the levels of wealth creation that these economies are capable of generating, much of this are but symptoms of the structural lack of competitiveness of some European economies and their consequent inability to augment their frail GDPs.

Much of it is also reflective of a very unhealthy dislike of what are considered to be the soft elements of the economic equation, in other words, the real economy of goods and services, in contrast with the speculative economy of financial transactions that adds no value nor does it create any real and tangible wealth to the economies of nations or in any way benefits the livelihoods of individuals in societies. Again the role of education in building productive citizens that are effective contributors to society and that can tell the difference between the real economy and institutional financial speculation cannot be underestimated. In the final analysis, the economic purpose of education has to be that of the constant search for adequacy between the skills and competencies of individuals, and their applied expressions in the lives of organizations on the one hand, and the satisfaction of the current and latent needs of a consumer society on the other, allowing for the optimal detection of what consumers need now and what they will possibly need in the future.

In a competitive context where there is ample choice, organizations need to search for angles of differentiation in the supply of goods and services to selective key target markets. These angles of uniqueness in the product offer need to be part of the toolkit of intangible cues that need to be built around the core product offering. At this level and sophistication of consumption, marginal differences in product quality become diluted and are immaterial for consumers. In reality, quality differentials between alternative offers are often not even perceived by consumers in that quality is taken for granted and effectively a pre-condition for entering the marketplace to begin with. Without excellent quality products and services, companies should not even bother to show up as the market will simply not allow it.

In competitive consumer markets the most important decision-making criteria are often the intangible cues in the product offer that are difficult to imitate. What successful organizations do is to think in the way that the average consumer in that target thinks, understanding clearly the drivers of consumption for each market and for each situation. If consumers tend to value certain criteria, those are the criteria that need to be part of the offered package, as those are the criteria that constitute worthwhile and valued difference from the viewpoint of the consumer. It means needing to identify the criteria that dictate consumption, that are the make or break of purchasing decisions. These intangible cues shape the decision-making process and are either tangible and form part of the product's characteristics, or more likely they are reputational and derive from an established history and track record in markets, or are a result of planned corporate or product brand communications.

In the same manner that the intrinsic quality of products that are placed in external markets is sometimes not adequately augmented by image and reputation and branded to form a formidable offer, countries are often unable to create any reputation, good or bad, as they are not known for their political maturity or level of industrial development, or even for any cultural idiosyncrasy, positive or negative. In the final analysis, the products that emanate from a nation's economy can be possible forms of expression of the collective identity of its people, and in that way they are also unique and not susceptible to imitation by others.

In order for this to happen, however, a product needs to be much more than its function or what it does. It needs to be the embodiment of societal values that others in some way aspire to emulate or buy into. This singularity is what people look for when they buy something other than function and are willing to pay premium prices for a distinctiveness that stands out amongst a clutter of confusing messages. In essence, others can copy a nation's offer but they cannot imitate a nation's soul and collective identity embodied in desirable and valued branded goods. The difficulty is in transferring these intangible cues to products and services in ways that are credible next to foreign constituencies.

In reality this is not about nations trading on their character idiosyncrasies but more than anything it is a tacit concession that, given the state of the world today, the idea of neutrality in what concerns the external perceptions held about a country and its products is no longer valid or desirable. Positive country of origin effects are compulsory if the aim is for a nation's economy, or key sectors of economic activity in it, to be competitive on the world stage, where others with perhaps more obvious advantages, due to the size of their economies and wealth generation potential, compete for the same export markets.

Positioning a nation or an economic sector within a nation distinctively for the purposes of making it commercially appealing is not a concession to any idea of disrespect for, or playing around with, the collective dignity of a nation, nor is it an adulteration of national identity as if the collective character of a nation could ever be subjugated to a business purpose or an economic imperative. What is desirable is the quest for commercial affirmation of a nation in the world in a way that its cultural and economic interests are not dichotomous and mutually exclusive. There is unfortunately a pervasive notion that these worlds stand poles apart and are also mutually exclusive as expressions of the identity of a nation abroad. One is institutional and dignified whilst the other is commercial, vulgar and ordinary. This of course makes difficult the notion of a concerted strategy for the projection of a country brand in the world and neglects the economic benefits to a country that would accrue from that.

A clear and distinctive positioning should be the ultimate objective of any well thought through strategy for national economic development. This notion of institutional entrepreneurial spirit still has what can be euphemistically termed as a singular interpretation next to policy-makers in certain countries, who think it is beneath them to project national image and reputation for what they see as commercial purposes, when in effect these are key dimensions of the balance of trade of an economy. These are often precisely the nations that fail to aggregate value to their exports.

A positive starting point for the competitiveness of nations is to focus on the things that they know how to do well, sectors where there is an established and well-grounded history and tradition or clear geographical or territorial advantages. If a country makes fine wine and has a tradition for its gastronomy, or if most of its territory is bathed by the ocean, then tourism and modern fisheries are obvious cues for the anchoring of national competitive advantages that are difficult to imitate, as nobody can replicate geographical position or the weather.

Traditional sectors may then benefit from the introduction of higher-order activities that challenge incumbent ways in which these sectors have been strategically thought of in the past in terms of their perceived economic potential. This means the incorporation of economic value to activities that make these sectors competitive globally. Fisheries and sea-related activities, including different forms of tourism, are obvious choices in this case, but what often needs to happen is that these sectors need to be approached in a different light. They need to be reinvented in a way that allows for the aggregation of value to products and services that emanate from these sectors. These are situations where the resources exist, they just need to be looked at from a different perspective, one that recognizes alternative ways in which to aggregate value to tasks and activities along the respective economic value chains.

Often these are areas of immense potential for the economy of a nation, they have always been there, but they need to be thought of in a different light. What needs to happen is for these sectors of economic activity to be scrutinized thoroughly for the full exploitation of their corresponding value chains, their effective but also latent potential, traduced in the development of new products and services, leading to the satisfaction of current and future needs.

In simple and objective terms, it is about the constant pursuit of value possibilities given a fixed endowment of natural resources, for example the sea, and their translation into economic value in the worlds of modern fisheries, gastronomy and tourism in imaginative and creative ways, in the knowledge that countries need to make do with what they have and not fantasize about idealistic lifestyles that are not sustainable under current conditions and limited potential for wealth creation.

The brief description above is perfectly suitable to many European economies and their governing institutions and should be the kind of strategic thinking about the real economy of goods and services that is most needed in lieu of what seems to be a pervasive obsession with macro-economics and monetary policy, over which governments in small nations in the eurozone have absolutely no control.

The creation and nurturing of corporate and product brands often offer the platform, or the necessary impulse, that leads to dynamic and globally competitive export sectors in key areas of economic activity. The ultimate aim needs to be that of creating brands from the ground through many examples of excellence and consistent supply of supreme quality products and services, anchored in effective and clever communications, in distinct areas of intermediate or final consumption. Consumer brands are ideal for the purposes of acquiring global notoriety in that the brand name is closer to those who matter, the consumers. This is clearly the case with the German and the Japanese models, which consist mainly of a conscious investment in building a systematic supply of excellent branded products and services in a widespread array of sectors of economic activity, typically operating next to the consumer, which in turn translate into the creation of a positive national aura and reputation.

Without a consensus on the definition of a strategic path for key sectors of economic activity, any debate on national competitiveness is no more than a mega exercise on creative national accounting embroiled as policy-makers are on the workings of macro-economic variables and objectives. The absence of a blueprint and lack of definition of a clear strategic path for the development of a competitive national economy inhibits a focus on three or four key strategic sectors that could, with the necessary adjustments and fine-tuning, act as drivers of national competitiveness for the coming decades. This applies to many European economies.

The efficient allocation of productive resources and the development of specific competencies and skills needed for this purpose mean that, in successful cases, the real determinants of competitive advantage are thus developed and deployed, leading to true long-term competitiveness in key sectors of economic activity operating in global markets. The choice of economic sectors for strategic focus has to abide by criteria of value aggregation and international market potential. Technical know-how and market knowledge are critical for successful export strategies in that their presence impacts positively both on levels of intrinsic product quality but also on the likelihood of successfully positioning products in a distinctive manner in the minds of foreign consumers in global markets.

The imperative for countries that do not possess a distinct positioning platform in globalized markets would be the development in the medium to long-term of sectors of economic activity with aspirations to worldwide notoriety, with a view to establishing a reputation of excellence abroad in key economic sectors. This is the way forward in building a country brand. These positive country of origin effects need to be built upon many examples of excellence in the provision of quality goods and services linked to product or corporate brands. With persistence, time and a constant willingness to learn from mistakes, by producing high-quality consistently, communicating effectively and ensuring that brands become synonymous with excellence, key economic sectors in a country can slowly but surely build a capital of reputational goodwill next to demanding foreign constituencies.

Consumers abroad in the more sophisticated and discerning markets begin to recognize the origin of goods and services that are associated with their brands of preference, and acknowledge their comparative quality by paying premium prices for superior consumption experiences, tracing these back to the country of origin of the brands in question. The positive associations between these experiences and the country of origin of the brand is what follows. In subsequent purchases, when consumers are again confronted with a choice to buy brands originating from a country with which a personal history of positive associations has been established, even if this track record refers to entirely unrelated product areas, the positive cues have already been transferred over to the new purchase and the buyer is naturally positively conditioned by this. These are what are called country of origin effects and they shape buyers' views and perceptions of products that they have never come into contact with or experienced in any way.

The nature and sophistication of consumers in destination markets is very important to the likelihood of success of export strategies. The more elitist markets include in their make-up opinion-makers who exercise a marked influence upon the rest of the world. These consumers shape public opinion in other markets that are often unrelated culturally or in any other way to them, but they are somehow able to influence the consumption patterns of the less developed economies due to sheer aspirational cues that are implied and a kind of subservient attitude on the part of the less developed economies towards the more developed nations, as well as a collective tendency for subsequent imitation effects to emerge. Breaking into the more elitist, sophisticated and affluent markets is indeed vital for the export sectors of the less developed economies, but it is also extremely difficult. Wealthy and sophisticated markets are characterized by patterns of consumption that are in accordance with the educational levels and the high disposable incomes of the individuals that make up these markets.

In achieving notoriety in these more sophisticated markets, the next stage in the formulation of a successful strategic blueprint for an open economy is to approach the higher ends of other less developed markets, with the capital of goodwill accumulated next to sophisticated and wealthy consumers in the more developed economies. This is only achievable if we are somehow able to gain the confidence of the opinion leaders in these more sophisticated markets, who buy our brands and grant them the legitimacy and credibility that subsequently acts as an umbrella of goodwill, next to wealthy segments of consumers in the less developed economies.

Sometimes all there is to this phenomenon is a kind of whispering campaign, where the word is spread around and consumers in the less sophisticated markets, avidly aspiring to what they perceive to be better standards of living in the more developed economies, naturally become enchanted by the prospect of accessing those symbols, expressed in products which they perceive, perhaps naively, as conduits for the aspirational lifestyles to which they would like to subscribe.

When McDonalds opened its first restaurant in Moscow, miles-long queues would form outside and Russian consumers would be more than willing to dispose of half a month's worth of wages to buy a Big Mac and a Coke. In this way the adoption of branded goods in the less sophisticated markets simply derives from establishing distinction in the more sophisticated markets, which legitimizes consumers with disposable income to purchase these products in the less developed economies.

The absence of a strategic blueprint for the social and economic development of a nation also has the pernicious effect of creating the latitude for a political clientele of a kind that is not too interested in thinking the country strategically, but instead subjects a national long-term orientation to the short-term interests of economic groups and those of individuals, with all the negative consequences that are inherent to that. Having an export strategy means to develop an understanding of the different consumption profiles in export markets, a deep knowledge of the aesthetics and preferences of the different markets, including tastes, culture, demographic variables, disposable income and an inkling for determining price-demand sensitivities at all times and for different market contexts.

Barriers to export markets may be of a technological nature or they may be related to commercial knowledge shortcomings and both will impact on the competitiveness of an economic sector of activity in these markets. In labour-intensive manufacturing sectors anyone can have access to the latest technologies or manufacturing processes that are widely available. These are there to be acquired in industrial fairs the world over, and anyone who wants to enter any market may potentially do so with a modicum of technical skills and competencies. The problem emerges when someone attempts to enter the higher ends of markets where the significant differentiators are not strictly technically-based but rather depend on a fine balance of possession of knowledge skills and commercial acumen, whose ultimate expression is the building and nurturing of valuable brands.

On the other hand, accepting product quality unambiguously as a critical success factor in any manufacturing sector, the quality differentials between alternative market offers, although not negligible, are beyond a certain threshold not decisive for consumers in the context of purchasing processes. Beyond price and threshold quality levels, retail buyers and crucially consumers begin to pay attention to other choice criteria in the buying decision-making process.

To have good quality products is a necessary condition for entering the competitive game, but it may not be a sufficient condition given the intensity of competition in almost every manufacturing sector of any expression, and even more so for sectors of global interest and exposure. On the other hand, if everyone is able to supply high levels of product quality in a given market, differentiation will need to occur on other dimensions of the product offer and other criteria will emerge as relevant in the buying decision-making process.

The other way of achieving sustainable competitive advantages in any national competitive strategy consists of having preferential access to raw materials that are critical to the production processes of economic sectors. These advantages are often circumstantial and the strategic acumen and skills required here are fundamentally those of making economic sense of the natural endowment of national resources by constantly pursuing ways in which to aggregate value to them.

If, for example, we happen to be born near an oil well and if oil is a critical input in production processes that lead to products that people the world over need and use, then it stands to reason that a natural competitive advantage is attained by exploring oil in all its economic possibilities. However this advantage will be more or less sustainable depending on how long the implied resource lasts or remains valuable to the world, both in itself as a raw material or as an intermediary input feeding into production processes of higher-order activities and economic value.

This happens as by virtue of geographical accident we effectively control the provision of fundamental inputs for the manufacturing processes of economic sectors the world over, and it makes sense to base national wealth creation strategies around the fixed endowment of valuable resources available, thus exploring the limitless value creation possibilities that it offers in subsidiary industries and sectors.

In having preferential access to raw materials, costs of production are lower and supply can be adjusted and monitored to control prices and escape the determinism of intense global competition, thus rendering the position of daring competitors as unsustainable until, that is, someone discovers oil in their own backyard or until, and continuing in our example, different energy sources are found that signify clear improvements to the incumbent resource, or that even revoke its use, which is somehow analogous to technical obsolescence in the context of knowledge-based technological advantages.

In the same way that Porter referred to the three generic strategies that are at the disposal of organizations, namely cost-leadership, niche or focus, and differentiation, countries can think strategically following a similar rationale. In the case of differentiation and its role in national competitiveness, beyond certain quality thresholds, marginal quality improvements are insufficient to differentiate a nation's goods and services from those of other competitors in key target markets as they are not often even noticed by the consumer or not perceived as significant improvements to the market offer.

The cost–benefit analyses implied in improving the quality of manufactured goods may prove to be disadvantageous to further investments on the intrinsic and objective qualities of manufactured goods. In other words, the marginal costs that are incurred in incrementing the quality of manufactured goods may not be recouped in business or consumer markets. This is particularly true when those marginal increments in product quality are not matched by corresponding consumer perceptions of value. This means that the value aggregation that is implied by those increments in quality is simply not perceived and understood by consumers in markets, who refuse to pay more for them, leaving only what become in effect and from the viewpoint of manufacturers more onerous cost structures and more narrow margins in which to operate.

This being the case then, rather than investing in the tangible cues in the product equation, it would be best if the export strategies of firms, economic sectors or even entire economies, could be anchored on the investment of time and economic effort, to what are for that product, sector of activity and key market the true aggregators of value. These tend to be in high-income, sophisticated markets elements of the supply package that are conducive to a better image and reputation of the nation and which then transfer over to the goods and services that emanate from that country.

With all of this in mind, what is important here is to concentrate effort and energy on improving the performance of other variables that constitute, from the viewpoint of retail buyers and consumers in foreign markets, the true deciders as to what gets purchased and what does not. These include reliability of delivery in the case of the relationship between retail buyers and suppliers in foreign markets, a focus on innovation, good design ideas, or the ability to respond quickly and efficiently to specific requirements from the organizational buyer.

Much more important than to search for objective or tangible differentiation cues, based on hard, visible criteria, but that which consumers often fail to see, value, or both, and that others can easily replicate without incurring the steep upfront costs in research and development that are necessary, would be to understand, in each case, what the key drivers for buying product are at retail or consumer level. In high-income markets, discerning consumers will inevitably go for brand rather than function and for emotional difference rather than the hard core rational and quantifiable criteria entailed in a product or service.

Consumption criteria in high disposable income markets extend well beyond product-related dimensions and, although this is common knowledge, manufacturers still do not work these marketing and reputational cues effectively or hard enough. Intangible criteria based on a set of values which export markets recognize as distinct and superior to those of competitive offers in the same market are what export strategies should strive to excel in. These relevant dimensions or consumption criteria that need to be built into the product offer also have to be seen strictly from the viewpoint of the consumer. It is this insularity of the supplier that needs to be broken in order to overcome the gap between suppliers on the one hand and organizational buyers and consumers in foreign constituencies on the other.

Understanding that both societal values and the market characterization of consumers and their needs and wants are volatile and susceptible to change, and that they do indeed change over time and often quicker than organizations are able to recognize and adapt to, means that the skills and competencies that firms and economic sectors are required to develop, more than product or process-related, refer to an obsessive, organized and systematic attention that needs to be paid to market determinants of consumption, and what they are every time and at all times.

The relevant dimensions of supply consist of the set of intangible cues aggregated to a product or service, that which goes beyond what the product does or its functionality. Critically this notion of what the product does also needs to be looked from the consumer's perspective. The product only makes sense from the viewpoint of the consumer. The product is what the consumer makes of it. In external markets this implies that success goes to those who are able to understand better than others the idiosyncrasies that characterize groups of consumers with disposable income, and the nature and specificities of consumption of these groups of affluent consumers in foreign markets.

Those singularities of consumers in foreign markets, that which makes them different, are not cast in stone, including the cultural dimensions of the marketplace, the implicit and explicit codes, that shape consumption and that are not written anywhere but which evolve over time and with changes in the demographic make-up of a nation. This is where it gets complicated and where the peripheral and parochial nature of manufacturing sectors in emerging economies attempting to break into the more sophisticated consumer markets begins to stick out like a sore thumb. They can make the products but they cannot break into the value systems and idiosyncrasies that are peculiar to particular brands of cosmopolitism, urban lifestyles and other cues that have underlying explicit and implicit codes and that determine consumer choice in the wealthy segments of the more developed market economies.

These low-cost economies can indeed manufacture good-quality products, but they are still unable to capture the imagination of sophisticated consumers who discern amongst alternative offers as a function of a lot more than core product benefit. These consumers instead focus on the intangible benefits that are entailed in the product offer and the way to get to them is to emphasize the cues of emotional differentiation and brand values that are sought.

This is also where entrepreneurs from the less developed and emerging economies that are beginning to work with foreign markets show tremendous shortcomings. Not understanding exactly what export markets want, and not being philosophically formatted to think about intangibility in supply, they are naturally unable to cater to stringent demands adequately. By not knowing what the intangible cues in market demand are, they cannot really devise a product offer that caters to the requirements of those markets.

These exporters are of course familiar with socio-demographic and economic criteria, but they are less knowledgeable of lifestyle issues and how these shape buying decision-making, as well as being ignorant of the complexity of modern consumption dynamics. Often the hard criteria used in market profiling are insufficient as evidence for determining the right mix in approaching these markets in differentiated and effective ways.

Probably the strongest motive for this lack of understanding of the subliminal aspects and nuances in consumption patterns in foreign markets is the traditional insularity of entrepreneurs in emerging economies. The subliminal aspects of consumer profiling in the more developed economies, where there is discretionary income, are in effect the critical dimensions of consumer choice, those that make or break a viable commercial relationship. Crucially these are often the most obscure and unknown criteria for the entrepreneur.

In the world of fashion, for example, understanding the particular aesthetics of a culture, what people go for at each point in time, the relevant demographic variables that may impinge on consumer choice, what the implicit and explicit criteria for social stratification are in particular markets, the role of money and how people relate to it, education, cultural orientation, pragmatism or bureaucratic bias, functionalism or hedonism, all of these will be part characterizations of retail buyers' attitudes and that of the consumers that buy our products.

The relative importance of each criterion varies within the same market and from market to market. These may seem unimportant to the outside observer but they are precisely the market nuances that, whilst appearing to be negligible and unimportant to the untrained eye, turn out to ultimately matter. These are the deciding factors when foreign discerning consumers choose our products to the detriment of others, as well as when they are willing to pay premium prices for our goods and not for others as a function of higher perceived value.

Insular entrepreneurship is a contradiction in terms and if entrepreneurs are not out there looking for markets and trying to understand how they function they will not be successful. It is extremely difficult to incorporate all the variables without being present and developing an informed intuition as to the idiosyncrasies and specificities of export markets in the dimensions that really matter.

The failure to do this is attributable not only to a geographic but also a psychological insularity that makes it hard to understand consumers in foreign markets. Perhaps a graver form of cultural insularity is one promoted by educational systems that perpetuate the status quo and do not induce pro-activity and a go get it mentality in individuals, creating a society that waits for others and in particular the state to sort out the individual problems of its members.

The other reason for the lack of understanding of foreign markets by entrepreneurs in emerging markets is one of economic need. Often entrepreneurs in these emerging economies have not been trained to be intrinsically and naturally competitive. What this means is that for many years, economies that are dependent on export markets for building their fragile GDPs, and in this way ensuring minimum indicators of social and economic development for their populations, did not develop a sense of emergency in the light of dwindling export scenarios, independent of sector of economic activity.

The critical reason for choosing products emanating from these economies to the detriment of alternative offers from other countries was, as a rule of thumb, lower prices. When the prices of manufactured goods ceased to be competitive in foreign markets, export volumes would immediately feel the sting as foreign buyers would prefer other competitors' products. What would then happen effectively typifies the inappropriate use of the macro-economic levers of exchange rate policy in these economies.

Policy-makers would proceed to devalue the national currency, thus making exports cheaper in foreign denomination in what turns out to be one of the most detracting policy measures with respect to what should be a critical aim of economic policy anywhere, and that is the psychological entrenchment of a feeling of complacency that is the antithesis of a competitive philosophy that should always be present in entrepreneurs and their firms. A competitive philosophy means a focus of key stakeholders in the economy, and in particular exporting organizations on the real determinants of competitiveness in foreign markets, in short, the reasons why foreign consumers really decide to buy our products and are ultimately willing to pay more for them.

With currency devaluation a nation's products become comparatively cheaper than those of its competitors fighting it out for the same export markets. The economic sectors where the exports of a given economy are concentrated are in this simple and straightforward way made competitive through a legislative act. The problem with applying ad-hoc legislation in economics is that markets may not see it that way and currency devaluations become in the end artificial distortions to underlying market conditions.

The other, perhaps even more important issue, and one that few seem to allude to, relates to what successive currency devaluations seem to suggest, the message that policy-makers appear to be giving the entrepreneurial class, and that is that they should not worry. Should all of a sudden they become uncompetitive in foreign markets, the legislator is sure to step in and intervene, devaluing the national currency. In addition to this, the other wrong message that currency devaluation gives entrepreneurs and their firms is that price is the only relevant criterion out there, or always the most important criterion shaping the purchasing decision of the average consumer. The reality for most consumer markets is that it is not, that for most markets there are always going to be a wide array of segments, whose consumption profiles range from strictly price-based to elitist niches where price is immaterial for prospective consumers.

Legislative action may therefore exert a profound impact on the dynamics of trade, but measures to incentivize exports that are restricted to the manipulation of the exchange rate mechanism do not truly reflect the dynamics and complexity of contemporary consumer markets, and to a certain extent that of industrial markets, where such criteria as relationship building and networking have become critical dimensions in the choice of supply sources.

Policy-makers seem not to be able to understand that currency devaluation makes products cheaper abroad, but not necessarily more appealing. Countries that adhered to the euro currency and consequently lost control over monetary and exchange rate policy mechanisms were rendered toothless when it came to their ability to command the destinies of their already vulnerable economies. To make matters worse, these nations were not prepared to switch gears towards the development of a sharper focus on firm competitiveness and micro-economics, as policy-makers and entrepreneurs alike were not formatted to think and act in ways that would make organizations competitive in a global context.

Without the exchange rate lever to make economies artificially more competitive in the global markets, the expectation would be that a truly entrepreneurial attitude would kick in to incentivize real competitive behaviour. This in essence would translate into a heightened awareness of entrepreneurs as to what are the real determinants of competitiveness in foreign markets, leading to an improved ability of national firms in outperforming global competitors on the supply dimensions that are considered to be the make or break of consumption decisions in foreign markets.

Given the financial crisis and its ramifications on the real economy, these are probably not the times to exhort the virtues of the free-market and its non-interventionist underlying philosophies. It has become heresy to do so but in the less developed European economies excessive protectionism from central governments and state intervention in the functioning of the markets has meant the distortion of the criteria that lead to the true competitiveness of economic sectors. Exchange rate policy with a view to arbitrarily increasing economic sector competitiveness is, alongside excessive and inefficient bureaucracy, the most significant obstacle to the true competitiveness of firms in the global economy.

It seems however that amidst an ideological spectrum that stretches from free-market purism on the one hand, and a tight fist on the regulation of economic activity on the other, there may just be an equilibrium point somewhere in the middle. This equilibrium should coincide with a state whose philosophy, whilst non-interventionist, is still capable of regulating the functioning of economic activity so as to enhance the conditions that lead to increased competitiveness, but no more.

The point here is that state intervention is required when the pursuance of individual interest is mutually exclusive with the resultant common good.

In this case the latter needs to prevail at all times. In times of profound economic and social crises afflicting some more than others, it has become commonplace to call for forms of government intervention, thus repeating historical mistakes of yesteryear, erring on excessive state intervention that leads to overwhelming bureaucracy and inefficiency. As Obama stated at the beginning of his first mandate, it is not about more or less government, it is about good or bad government. There is a fundamental distinction between the two.

Ad-hoc currency devaluation, at the whim and convenience of the legislator, will normally produce an immediate positive effect that translates into an improvement in the export picture of an economy. The magnitude of this effect is dependent upon the structure and composition of a nation's exports and the particular price-demand sensitivities of consumers in its key export markets. Whenever there are difficulties in the placement of goods in export markets, because there are cheaper alternatives out there, governments devalue national currencies in order to make goods produced in the economy cheaper in foreign currency. By using exchange rate policy to arbitrarily devalue their currencies, nations are able to artificially lower the prices of their exported goods.

Cheaper exports expressed in foreign currency denominations means that a demand–supply equilibrium that was temporarily lost through the entrance of low-priced competitor goods into the market is restored with a nation's goods again becoming competitive on price against those of foreign competitors in export markets. This solution however is not ideal and there are costs to the economy in the medium and long terms. In sophisticated markets, where there is disposable income and people buy as a function of the intangible elements in products, an economy whose productive structure is organized to compete solely on price, in labour-intensive sectors, is doomed for failure. This is particularly true if that economy happens to be in the European geographic space.

The gravest consequences of ad-hoc currency devaluations with the purpose of enhancing the competitiveness of a sector of economic activity or the whole economy of a nation, however, are the pervasive detrimental psychological effects on the behaviour of a whole entrepreneurial class, who simply begin to believe that it is not up to them to be resourceful in acquiring the skills and competencies that lead to a heightened state of awareness when it comes to identifying and pursuing market opportunities, as well as always being on the lookout for improvements in production efficiencies and the optimization of processes. They simply do not need to do that.

In the final analysis there will always be a safety net from government that will kick in, if and when necessary. In reality, when this happens entrepreneurs inevitably feel the protecting hand of the state, and in the knowledge that government will intervene to sway the game to their benefit when necessary, they refuse to confront the real determinants of competitiveness head on. Using a football analogy, if the pitch needs to be sloped towards the opposition's end, or if the opponents goal needs to be made bigger then so be it. In the end, entrepreneurs in these economies are not formatted to understand a basic tenant of the philosophy of competitiveness which states that success goes to those who are better at satisfying the needs and wants of demanding consumers in sophisticated and discriminating markets.

In the absence of this and in the comfort of the exchange rate cushion, entrepreneurs know that, within reasonable parameters in relation to the harder criteria, including the quality of their products, they do not need to do much to be competitive in external markets that are critical to the balance of trade of a nation and its potential for wealth creation. Whenever undone in export markets on such crucial criteria as the quality or price of their goods, these organizations would begin to lobby their respective governments, persuading them to throw their weight around and bail them out when necessary. This idea of a government, whose economic mandate it is to bail out firms and economic sectors artificially, leads to the creation of an intolerable culture of relaxation with negative consequences for the future competitiveness of sectors of an economy and for entire economies.

In reality, entrepreneurs do not effectively need to compete according to the real determinants of market competitiveness. They do not need to be constantly on the alert to export market trends and its immense volatility, nor do they need to make an effort to understand the idiosyncrasies and specificities of those markets. They know that if they ever run into trouble the government will bail them out in the name of safeguarding employment, and this has clearly become a problem not only in the less developed economies, but also in others.

Reality Check...

Nike – Why Do It?

In the 1980s, *Fortune* magazine wrote something to the effect of there never having been a clearer sign that the Nike organization had lost its bearings than to have paid US$ 500,000 for a basketball player fresh out of the University of North Carolina. That player went by the name of Michael Jordan, and he turned out to become the best basketball player of all time, and single-handedly responsible for one of the biggest corporate turnaround stories in history.

Nike was at the time competing head to head with one of its strongest rivals, Reebok. Many years later, Nike would sign an endorsement contract with basketball player, LeBron James worth US$ 90 million. LeBron has since joined the exclusive list of all-time greats in the history of the NBA, but when Nike signed a millionaire contract with the young LeBron he had just come out of high school. Also around that time, Nike took some risks by signing Freddy Adu, a young, up-and-coming soccer prospect. This was a risk, in that soccer is not a love affair with Americans as a spectator sport, although it is regularly practiced by millions every weekend particularly by women. Nike's investment on Freddy Adu was substantially lower than that made in LeBron, somewhere in the region of US$ 1 million, and the returns were disproportionately even lower, as the promising early years of the young Adu never materialized into soccer superstardom.

In the case of LeBron, Nike again overtook Reebok. Reebok offered more money to LeBron James but when they met up with the player, Reebok executives allegedly showed up with sketches of the sports shoes they intended LeBron to wear and associate his image with, and what these would eventually look like. Nike, in turn, showed up with the finished product, a new model of basketball shoes made especially for LeBron James, and took these over for him to have a look at. LeBron naturally chose Nike.

Nike has historically used controversial athletes to endorse its products. McEnroe and Cantona both had what can euphemistically be termed as a strong personality. They also had an edge to them, erring on marginal and at times uncontrollable behaviour. Sometimes things would just get out of hand with these characters. The common denominator, uniting any Nike athlete, anyone that has ever endorsed and personified the brand throughout its history and has contributed to the projection of Nike brand values the world over, has been that every one of these athletes has at one point been a winner, and in some cases has come to dominate his or her respective disciplines. All of them without exception have also come to embody the ideal of winning, anchored in the supreme philosophy of a heightened competitiveness and an indomitable will to win.

Individuality, rebelliousness, defiance of the status quo – they all align with societal values which the brand wishes to emulate, symbolize and embody. Its target audience subscribes to a set of values which the brand personifies and caters to in the form of products and the intrinsic and extrinsic benefits that they promise and indeed fulfil. It doesn't really matter that consumers who buy the products never really go onto a tennis or a basketball court, a football pitch, or that they never really engage in any sporting activity. This is irrelevant as far as Nike is concerned. As long as people continue to buy the product, it is good enough for the corporation. They make sports shoes, and if other people want to wear them great. Lucky Nike.

It is of course very difficult for a company that is as mainstream as IBM or McDonalds in the sports fashion apparel world to maintain an aura of being anti-status quo and anti-establishment when they represent the status quo and they are the establishment, but that is what Nike does. Nike argues that the sports shoes retailing business is not about fashion. It is about sports. Fashion is ephemeral but sports are eternal. There will always be winners, and there will always be people out there that will want to be associated with champions and wear the symbols that these exceptional star athletes have come to personify.

Many agree to disagree with Nike on the fashion and sports positioning dichotomy, arguing that Nike is indeed a fashion company. Nike believes it is far too risky to position itself as a fashion company, as what is fashionable today will not be fashionable tomorrow. Sport is a far less risky positioning proposition for a company like Nike, who has always made it a point of associating itself with the very top athletes, not only in track and field and basketball, but also in soccer and other world renowned sports.

Never has this been as true as in the Atlanta Olympic Games of 1996. Reebok was the official sponsor of the games. Nike decided to sponsor the athletes, including Michael Johnson, who eventually won the 200 and 400m men's track. Sports Illustrated, probably the most prestigious sports magazine in the world, and certainly the one with the widest readership in the US, had a picture of Michael Johnson, fresh out of winning the 200m final, holding a pair of golden Nike shoes right on the front page in his hands and next to the golden pair of running shoes and showing prominently, the famous Nike logo with the word whoosh written across it. As a BBC documentary later put it, it was game, set and match for the swoosh. Phil Knight, CEO and founder of Nike, would at the time state that 'we don't have enough money to buy adverts on the last page of Sports Illustrated, but we do have the athletes that show up on the front page.'

For Nike, first was the product. Nike executives always aimed at developing the best sports shoes, with better traction, lighter, more comfortable, with special cushioning and soles, with the ultimate aim of improving the performance of the great athletes who they paid handsomely to wear them in competition, but also at public social events. There had always been a strong investment in R&D aiming at better new products as well as improvements in the performance of existing product lines. Many allege that Nike shoes are not in reality the best athletics shoes in the world. But does that matter? On the one hand, we are talking about a type of product whose technological content, although increasingly sophisticated, still has clear thresholds and limitations as to what it can possibly allow that can translate into tangible performance improvements. The technological ceilings in sports shoes manufacturing are much more defined and restricted at least by comparison to high-tech products, for which technological content acts as a much more obvious discriminator of consumption decision-making.

There is a threshold as to the impact and role of technology and what it can do to a sports shoe, but many beg to disagree on this one. Although technology constantly revokes incumbent production processes and products, that are in turn linked to the betterment of the performance of top athletes, much of this role of technology is rendered a little more than redundant in the context of buyer decision-making, as the consuming masses fail to acknowledge technological virtuosity as a critical differentiator in such mundane purchasing decision-making as that of sports shoes.

People will buy sports shoes for personal everyday use and not to practice the sport for which it was originally designed and conceived although Nike also beg to disagree on this one. They believe that they make exceptional sports shoes for athletes,and if regular people want to wear them then Nike will not stop consumers from buying Nike sports shoes that were made for athletes to wear. This is a great marketing ploy but the truth of the matter is that most Nike brand faithful will never enter a basketball court or an athletics track. When confronted with this evidence, a Senior VP responsible for Marketing at Nike at the time of the Atlanta Olympics simply responded by saying something along the lines of: 'We don't care. We design for a purpose. We conceive products for athletes. If other people like them and they want to buy them, great. Lucky us.' Apart from the apparent cynicism that is latent in this statement, its content makes a lot of sense.

Nike designs shoes for athletes. It is obvious that the shoes that athletes wear when engaging in professional sporting activity at the highest level will not be the same shoes that are placed in the market for consumption by regular customers. However that is irrelevant for the Nike organization. The argument that Nike permanently reiterates on this issue is again that they make sports shoes for athletes. If other people want to wear their shoes, are they supposed to do anything to avoid that?

The alchemy for Nike consists in building brand value through the positioning of the corporate brand as a sports brand and not as a fashion brand. Again sport is eternal but fashion is not. There will always be winners. On the other hand, what is fashionable today may not be fashionable tomorrow.

The history of corporate or product brand endorsement by famous people, who stand to embody and personify the values of all kinds of brands, has not however always been one of success. Pepsi spent millions on an advertising campaign with pop star Madonna only to have it cancelled when controversy broke out because of her use of crosses and other religious symbols in music videos. People believed that it all had been in very bad taste and offensive of certain religious sensitivities.

On another stage there was an outcry over actor Bruce Willis and his alleged abuse of alcohol at the time when he was the spokesperson for Seagram's wine coolers. Other cases that spring to mind include late performer Michael Jackson and his association with the Pepsi Co, culminating in the eccentric behaviour of the singer and the public exhibition of his child, dangling dangerously outside a balcony of a hotel in Berlin, in what some believe to have been one of the worst publicity stunts ever, or at least something in very bad taste indeed.

The infamous case of O.J. Simpson, one of the greatest American football players of all time, who whilst acting as spokesperson for car rental company Hertz, was accused of having murdered in cold blood his ex-wife Nicole Brown and her then boyfriend, is yet another example of an unfortunate post-hoc corporate blunder. Post-hoc in the sense that organizations cannot control human nature and spokespeople are mere humans with their frailties and shortcoming like everyone else.

What organizations are looking for are the positive aspects of their public personas, but sometimes they get landed with the full monty. In the case of O.J. Simpson, the plot included a Hollywoodesque escape number from the crime scene and a car chase which was broadcast live by virtually every television network in America. This was not good news for Hertz at all.

6

From Popper to Soros and the Downfall of Economics

In *Free to Choose*, Milton Friedman embodies the thinking of neoclassical monetarists from the Chicago school, who were met as adequate metaphors in the political arena by Reagan, Thatcher and Mulroney, in the US, UK and Canada respectively. A good part of the Anglo-Saxon world shared a common ideology that advocated individualism, the rejection of excessive government and of a protectionist state, the exacerbation of materialism expressed in the yuppie ethic, well personified by the City and Wall Street, of quick fortunes made in the financial markets, and traders who retired at 30, never needing to work for a living for a single day more in their lives.

Galbraith, the renowned Canadian economist, had warned in his acclaimed works *The New Industrial State* and *The Affluent Society* of the emergence of a new class that was to play a prominent role in the structures of multinational corporations, that of senior management, which he was to aptly designate as technostructure. These senior managers in multinational corporations had tremendous decision-making power, yet they were non-proprietors of these organizations and according to Galbraith they would be pivotal in the functioning of modern organizations and the economies of nations. They would play, according to Galbraith, a crucial role in modern economies and constituted an additional protagonist (the senior manager) to that of the dichotomist Marxist system, which only considered two factors of production, capital and labour, and two actors, the owner of capital and the worker who owned his labour force. Drucker was another anchor of management thought and he spoke of the end of capitalism, pointing towards the emergence of a new knowledge society that would dominate the 1990s, where those who succeeded were those who had ownership and control over knowledge, whom he designated as knowledge gatekeepers.

With this in mind the approach here is to highlight the frailties and shortcomings of current thinking in economics, and its abject failure to shed light on contemporary issues and challenges. In an attempt to give the science of economics the scientific dignity and perhaps the legitimacy of the exact sciences, there has been a bias on the part of the scientific research community in economics towards the widespread use of deductive reasoning and the adoption of quantitative methodologies grounded on a positivistic epistemological stance. This has proved at best insufficient and probably wrong as a methodological posture for enquiry into the social sciences and in particular for economics. What is argued here is that the inadequacy of methods of enquiry used is perhaps one of the crucial reasons for the historical difficulties of the economics sciences in predicting anything with a modicum of credibility, including its endemic inability to forecast macro-economic variables with any reasonable degree of accuracy.

Model building attempts in economics grounded on methodological approaches that are characteristic of research programmes and traditions mainly to be found in the exact sciences are in all probability not adequate for the social sciences, and this partly justifies the low predictive capabilities of economics as a science. Along with the revoking of methodological approaches, a new epistemological stance for the social sciences perhaps needs to be instigated at this critical juncture, one that finds a closer adherence between the postulates of economic models and a recognizable underlying reality, in the hope that their findings and outcomes also resemble and explain reality in much more truthful and meaningful ways.

A perspective on economic sciences founded on a system of pseudo-truths claiming universality, and one that is based on the wrong premise, that the idea of methodological rigour of the kind that is essential for the life sciences should be adequate and fit for research into economics issues, is dangerous and indeed tautological with the fallacy of the postulates and assumptions upon which economics models are founded.

This implies an urgent call for an epistemological rethinking of the economics sciences, and more critically for a questioning of the policy consequences deriving from the application of pseudo-sophisticated analytical tools and procedures that lead inevitably to little more than post-hoc rationalizations of economic phenomena and poor forecasting of macro-economic events, both flaws that the discipline has become known for.

One of the problems with theoretical construction in economics, and perhaps one of the fundamental obstacles to a more legitimated and credible economics science next to crucial constituencies, policy-makers and practitioners alike, resides on the underlying assumptions that are inherent to model building, the set of conditions and axioms whose adherence to any known reality is virtually inexistent, and the parochial manner in which the use of surreal axioms for the building of complicated mathematical models is treated as secondary or outright unimportant.

If axioms and starting assumptions in model building in economics are farfetched and detached from reality, then the models themselves as mere idealizations or simplifications of underlying realities are rendered useless in their essential capacity as predictors of future outcomes. More critically their analytical consequences as proxies to explaining and predicting reality and informing decision-making have to be dangerously flawed.

Soros illustrates clearly the fallibility of the incumbent deductive method in economics enquiry, blaming this methodological stance for the failure of the economics science in getting it right more often than not, as a true science should. In his critique of economic theory in *The New Paradigm for Financial Markets*, Soros alludes to the insurmountable problems with economics as both a theoretical apparatus that aims to explain an underlying reality and a credible instrument for predicting future outcomes, thus acting as an invaluable instrument of policy, aiding decision-makers in governments and organizations. Of particular concern to Soros was the poor use of economics as an instrument and barometer for forecasting macro-economic indicators with any acceptable accuracy.

Soros of course has the personal legitimacy that comes from a degree of abnormal success at playing the financial markets, showing a brand of pragmatism that has in the end been traduced into a handsomely rewarded understanding of economics. Soros has been able to amass a formidable fortune that can be measured not only in accumulated wealth but in the unparalleled consistency shown over decades of playing the stock market game. Of course in having built a fortune, Soros can indeed afford to take the moral high ground to the theoreticians and academics that did not really put their money where their mouths were.

It would be immensely preferable to rethink economics as a science that is capable of diagnosing with far greater rigour, social and economic phenomena, and a discipline that allows for better mechanisms to emerge, that act as warning signals to policy-makers and market strategists alike, instruments that permit more accurate forecasting and far better predictive powers in the scrutiny of socio-economic phenomena.

The scientific edifice of economics needs to be advanced and, in order for this to happen, the current paradigm needs to be revoked. The science of economics has to deal head on with the clear failure of the incumbent positivistic epistemology that has prevailed for decades and provide solutions of sufficient quality to address the challenges of contemporary societies and their economic problems or it will run the risk of not being taken seriously by policy-makers or, crucially, the public at large.

Contextual truths are momentary and hold until they cease to remain satisfactory portrayals of underlying realities. As Popper postulated, truths are apt for the times and are only waiting to be falsified by other better truths that emerge now and again as better solutions to problems, solutions that fit better with constantly changing contexts and problems. Rather than absolute truths there are momentary truths that are always waiting to be revoked by new and better truths that constitute significant improvements as explanatory schemata to the underlying phenomena under scrutiny. There are therefore no absolute truths. Instead there are truths that are more apt and adequate explanations of contemporary issues than others, who were better truths before in the sense that they sufficed in their explanatory power of underlying socio-economic realities.

This holds for economics, as it does for any other social science, and it can be argued even for the exact sciences. From Copernicus, to Galileo, Newton and Einstein, physics of the universe has gone through successive paradigm shifts from geocentrism to heliocentrism, to Newton's gravity and Einstein's relativity theories, yet as the incumbent paradigm has evolved, the universe has remained (relatively) stable. Often, as in the social sciences, the revoking of a prevailing paradigm is conditioned by the particular characterization of the underlying socio-political context and situation.

In the case of physics and the role of Copernicus and Galileo in its advancement, the Roman Catholic Church certainly played a part in prioritizing whatever truth suited its interests better to the exclusion of others. This may explain why Ptolemaic geocentricism as a theory of the universe took so long before it was revoked by the heliocentric paradigm. The dissuading mechanisms that resist paradigm shifting may differ in time and space but they will always be there as witnesses to the tensions between the incumbent views of the world who naturally want to remain perpetuated as the prevailing truths and the newcomers who want to revoke the existing paradigm.

The problem with economics as a science is that it doesn't seem to be able to get it right. In effect the ability of the discipline in generally being able to forecast macro-economic variables, however strong the methodology and powerful the forecasting methods used, is pitiful. If any national government, the International Monetary Fund (IMF), the World Bank or any other credible institution is off by 3 or 4 per cent on projections on unemployment or negative GDP growth, or indeed on any other macro-economic indicator, this is not a failure in getting it right by about 3 or 4 per cent. It is instead a complete and utter flop in the forecasting of crucial macro-economic variables. This happens all the time with the most credible of institutions the world over.

The Queen of England was to witness the frailties of the economics science firsthand when she visited the London School of Economics at the height of the financial crisis. Her Majesty addressed an eminent professor at this prestigious institution and asked him why was it that nobody had foreseen the crisis, alluding to the by then full-blown crisis of the financial system. No satisfactory response was forthcoming, which probably led the Queen to believe that they knew as much about it as she did. There is every reason to believe that this embarrassing silence is more than a metaphor for the forecasting problems of the science of economics, whose credibility problem is unfortunately not limited to the realm of the English monarchy.

The wider community crucially begins to detect the vulnerability of the science in explaining phenomena that concern us all, and the inability of economic sciences to diagnose reality and predict it, at least in the light of state-of-the-art methodologies and instrumentation. A discipline with enhanced forecasting capabilities that is more effective in aiding institutional and organizational decision-making is no small achievement, but in the end it is conceivable that forecasting accuracy may be utopian as a scientific quest in that the unit of analysis in the social sciences is the individual human being.

Whilst accepting this as irrefutable, the science of economics still needs to search for better methodologies that are more capable of incorporating individual and collective behavioural idiosyncrasies, and consequently more realistic scrutinies of the way in which these variables interact, thus providing a much more useful instrument for diagnosis and forecasting of underlying socio-economic phenomena with a modicum of accuracy and realism.

There are various examples of the surrealism in the use of axioms with no adherence to any recognizable reality in economic analyses and model building with a view to simplifying economic realities, but a good one may be that of the work in market structures where the axioms of perfect information and the rationality of economic agents are at best debatable and in all probability cannot be found in any known socio-economic reality.

The concept of rationality is in itself a complex philosophical construction and outside the realm of this text but for the purposes of illustrating a point, the inference that economic agents behave rationally when pursuing strategies of maximization of their respective utilities and that these may be aggregated in linear and straightforward ways is at best simplistic and most probably outright wrong. Economics undergraduate students learn how managers in organizations operating in oligopolistic or monopolistic environments arrive at optimal prices and quantities of production by equalizing the derivatives of both their revenue and cost functions. Who, in the real world, independent of the particular characterization of market structures, consciously or not, analytically or even intuitively, determines the point at which it should cease production or determines optimal prices by equalling marginal revenue with marginal cost functions to determine optimum prices and quantities manufactured?

Yes it is about model building and the simplification of reality, but how does it simplify reality? Would it not be preferable to focus on the dynamics and idiosyncrasies of demand and its multitude of heterogeneous expressions, and how to meet those experientially and by approximation, instead of identifying surreal axioms for the sake of pseudo-analytical beauty and the pursuit of universal laws that simply do not hold in the social sciences?

This may appear to be simplistic or naive but the manner in which these things are relayed to first-year economics students the world over suggests to them that this is effectively what goes on in the day-to-day practical life in organizations. Many come out of university thinking that this may just be what goes on in your average pricing department or in production units in organizations, envisaging the moment when they themselves will sit around a table optimizing prices and quantities and deriving revenue and cost functions.

It is all done for the sake of simplification of reality, an essential requirement in model building, true, but until a degree of realism and closer adherence between the postulates used in model building and the known realities that they intend to explain and forecast is achieved, and fundamentally until such a time when the science accepts that human beings and their individual and collective manifestations, interactions, dynamics and mutual interdependencies in societies are not susceptible to modelling with a view to predicting behaviour, then the science of economics will continue to get it dramatically wrong on such notorious events as predicting financial and economic crises, or in getting macro-economic forecasts drastically wrong and off the wall.

It is not the purpose of these writings to make a critique of the choice of axioms or propositions used in model building in economics, but beyond simplistic and often wrong, these axioms indeed suffer from the niggling detail of failing to have any adherence to the reality that they purport to explain and critically fail to forecast. The arguments sustaining the defence of mathematical modelling and the extensive adoption of the deductive method in economics are somewhere along the lines of models only being oversimplifications of reality, and the scientific quest for the constant pursuit of universal laws as a form of legitimation of economics as a science.

However, if the founding propositions or axioms are distant from reality to the point where they are completely unrelated to the phenomenon they purport to explain upstream, how can models claim any explanatory or forecasting power down the line? The plausibility of the axiomatic conditions may possibly correlate strongly with the more or less predictive power of a model, and that absurdly appears to be irrelevant for some.

The obsession inherent to the thinking that in order to legitimize economic science there is an underlying imperative on the adoption of the deductive method of the exact sciences, forces a subordinate role to behavioural variables and a difficulty in incorporating the human dimension in the scrutiny of economic decisions. In the end this is what it is all about, economic relationships between people, and if it is very difficult to model individualized human behaviour, it is even more complicated when this behaviour is expressed collectively in social groups and societal systems.

This of course has as its main consequence the inability of economic sciences in forecasting future realities with a sufficient degree of accuracy, and this has to be a strong epistemological limitation even in the light of the increasingly sophisticated methodological instrumentation that is available. What also appears to be happening is that the pseudo-sophistication of method has become an objective in itself, replacing what should be the sole purpose of a good methodology, that of allowing for the best possible scrutiny of the problem at hand, one that is an improvement on incumbent analytical and explanatory schemata, ultimately a better whilst equally scientifically rigorous portrayal of an underlying reality. What has happened is that method has become an end in itself.

The economics science is riddled with what end up being completely erroneous predictions of reality and forecasts that are totally off the wall. More often than not, credible institutions including the IMF and the World Bank, as well as national governments and unsuspected bodies like the Federal Reserve Bank get it completely wrong. The discipline of economics also has a nasty tendency to engage in post-hoc justifications of phenomena rather than accurately forecasting events in ways that would benefit policy-making at government or organizational levels.

The human element as the object of study and its collective expression in groups, societies and nations introduces entropy to the point that it makes it virtually impossible to model socio-economic phenomena with any hope of attaining reasonable forecasting, at least in the light of state-of-the-art methodological instrumentation and thinking in the contemporary social sciences.

Much progress has been achieved in economics though with the importation of conceptual frameworks and analytical methods from physics and biology, which have been added to the scientific edifice of the economics sciences, both to aid methodologically but also in terms of the underlying systemic thinking that they allow. Neural networks and life sciences principles are common in financial and organizational studies for example, but somehow the predictive powers of the science remain flimsy at best.

Perhaps one of the central problems with the discipline of economics in general is that in pursuing scientific legitimacy, it does so by searching for the Holy Grail of deterministic causal relationships between variables, linearity, generalizability and the extrapolation of results to contexts that are often both inappropriate and inapplicable. Judging by the recent performance of the economics profession, there is every reason to believe that this is indeed not the way forward for research in the economics sciences.

Alternatively, economics as a science would truly enhance its social and political kudos and credibility if it were able to improve on its forecasting capabilities to the detriment of a position that has traditionally been one of explaining economic phenomena post hoc. In the end it would be important to have a discipline of economics that, whilst keeping its analytical rigour, could do so by incorporating, in a more effective manner, behavioural dimensions into the scrutiny of social and economic issues.

This would be an economics discipline that, whilst remaining analytical and quantitative rather than descriptive and qualitative in its method and fundamental approach, would still be capable of relating to its object of study, people in societies engaging in economic relationships. This would be a science more capable of incorporating the behavioural unpredictability and idiosyncrasies of economic agents acting individually and collectively.

There are grounds for believing that the obsessive search for methodological pseudo-sophistication that appears to dominate the editorial criteria of prestigious scientific journals, not only in the research areas of economics and finance but also in such areas as marketing and others, favours a quantitative approach and an obsession with statistical methods and mathematical models to the detriment of the quality of the ideas and the formulation of interesting problems in conducting research in the social sciences. Even when qualitative methods are employed, there exist a plethora of statistical software that in the final analysis beat the purpose of the very nuances of qualitative research, and often only barely reflect the knowledge and experience of those who are being scrutinized.

Statistical analysis has ceased to serve the purpose of improving the interpretative quality of research findings to become itself the sole purpose of the exercise, in that the pseudo-sophistication of the research technique, rather than improve the understanding of the problem, becomes in itself the objective of the research. All too often the pseudo-sophistication of statistical techniques and their use in overbearing statistical analyses replaces elegance and analytical simplicity, and fundamentally withdraws the focus from the quality of ideas. And that can't be good.

It is urgent that behavioural nuances and the idiosyncrasy of the research object are devolved to the forefront of economics and finance research, as well as research into other disciplines in the social sciences as, in the end, the object of study is people and people in societies. This runs counter to a kind of fundamentalism that has pervaded research in the social sciences, biasing it towards the prevalence of the quantitative paradigm.

Following from this, it is urgent that novel research methodologies and new ways and insights into problems are developed that substantially improve on the effective understanding of pressing issues and allow for the withdrawal of lessons that are truly useful for economies and societies now and in the future. All of this is of course much more complex than it appears on the surface as research agendas are often conditioned by corporate interests whose role in a financially deprived academia is far from negligible.

One needs only to look into the structure of university funding in North America and to a lesser extent in Europe to infer the intricate interdependency between the worlds of corporations and universities, and how often research agendas are shaped by corporate funding directly or indirectly via the contributions of alumni of prestigious institutions of higher learning, now occupying prestigious positions in renowned corporations with deep pockets. This is paradoxical in that academia should be the exact forum and the proper place in which to challenge incumbent paradigms and established ways of thinking.

Unfortunately this is often not the case, and the academic publishing circuit is at times closed, self-fulfilling and circular, with well-defined traditions, codes of conduct, networks and political structures of influence. This perhaps helps to explain the perceptual gap between the way in which academic researchers in the management and economics disciplines see themselves, and the way in which they are perceived by practitioners. Of particular concern is the little use that the latter make of the former and their research. Until a new paradigm looms on the horizon to replace the dominating and prevailing truths this will remain the case.

In addition to this, most reputable scientific publications are of American origin and, strictly from observation, it may well be that there is a content bias towards research issues that are mostly of interest to Americans, although there is no hard evidence of that. This is important in that Europe has its own specificities and idiosyncrasy. The publications game, however, is nothing more than that, a game intrinsically linked to individual academic career management, and of course to university funding by governments. Instead it should be about illuminating the world of practitioners with new theories that would become better practices, thus making organizational life and the lives of societies better.

A complementary approach to that should incorporate in the evaluation of the quality of research output, the use that practitioners make of academic research, and how and where it is applied in organizational reality. In economics and business research, a good proxy to research quality and its impact on wider society should be the interest manifested in its findings by specialist publications, or the buzz generated next to key practitioners.

Academic research should also be measured by its potential for acting as a driver of change, revoking old ways of doing things and inducing new practices in industries, renewing and shifting them with better theories that in turn would induce better practices. The wider impact of academic research needs to be measured against the potential for incorporating and transferring knowledge to the economy and to the wider society. This means a stronger emphasis on applied research leading to the effective improvement of quotidian business practices, processes and everyday organizational applications, as well as in strategic policy formulation by organizations and governments. This would be a much more relevant barometer of economics as a science, and a contributor to a fundamental objective in science building, that of deriving from its findings and conclusions ultimate improvements to the lives of organizations, people and of the societies in which they live. This would also be the validation of the assertion that there is no better practice than a good theory.

The indiscriminate use of methodologies of the exact sciences in social sciences without any regard or concern for adequacy or relevance is a mistake. Epistemological positivism and the deductive method are characteristic of the exact sciences, where the requisite for proof is done through the scrutiny of systematic causal links between variables in closed systems.

Universal laws are derived from observation and deductive analyses in the light of immutable systemic conditions. The aim is to verify the nature of relationships and the interdependency of variables in systems. In the social sciences this is not exactly the case as the object of study does not remain immutable, and this constitutes a serious problem when modelling the behaviour of these variables.

In defence of the economic sciences, these are in effect harsh times in which we live in, with an intensity and degree of variation that often makes redundant the application of theoretical knowledge and frameworks to the study of underlying economic realities. The known mechanisms for leveraging macro-economic policy measures, the stimuli that are believed to kick-start recession-laden economies, do not function as they are expected to in these troubled times because underlying their effectiveness are conditional requirements of collective confidence that are difficult to induce artificially.

The current socio-economic context is typified by certain traits or characteristics that are unique, at least in recent history. Although the collective sentiment is one of insecurity, this is not unchartered territory for the western world. The current crisis is however something that has not been experienced by most, who have not come across anything remotely similar to it in their lifetimes. From the viewpoint of the legislator, this shift in the macro-environment offers additional problems.

Measures that are effective in normal times may not necessarily work when low collective confidence and mistrust in institutions prevail. Central banks lower reference interest rates to incentivize private investment and inject liquidity into the economy with the aim of incentivizing private domestic consumption. All of these are of course measures that are conceptually sound when isolated from complex sociological dynamics of widespread lack of confidence, but when the context changes they simply fail to work.

The effectiveness of economic policy measures however is directly related to the predictability of the behaviour of economic agents and this is a thought that should illuminate economic research that aims to revoke the incumbent quantitative paradigm. The collective feeling also has its own dynamics that are difficult if not impossible to manage. In this way, the effectiveness of macro-economic policy is conditioned by context, defined in terms of the collective societal and cultural cues that lead to higher or lower levels of collective confidence and how this impacts on the very effectiveness of macro-economic policy in the economic systems where it is applied. The change in context thus makes all the difference to macro-economic policy measures and their effectiveness.

Monetary policy measures attempt to incentivize private investment and consumption with a view to heating up an ailing economy. Central banks have lowered interest rates to historical minima, unthinkable only a few years ago, as has happened in Japan and the UK not too long ago. Yet these and other developed economies fail to pick up, submerged as they are in crises of collective confidence. These are also times of opportunity for rethinking old formulae that no longer apply in a changing world. This constitutes a unique set of sociological and economic conditions of exceptional instability and unpredictability that have no known recent historic precedent.

A careful scrutiny of the financial crisis of 2008 and its ramifications into the real economy as well as future developments to the world economy will offer the bases or structuring principles for what will come next. It would have been important, especially in the current context, to have developed research programmes that are centred on the search for innovative ways of kick-starting stagnant economies, mechanisms that are not just old hat regurgitations of worn-out formulae with low potential for contemporary applicability in modern economic systems.

Salience should be given to research into the changing needs and problems of contemporary societies and how economics may respond to those. There should be an emphasis on such crucial topics as business ethics and corporate social responsibility, a sharper focus on technology, innovation, globalization and international trade, insights into new ways of doing business, and a rising prominence of micro-economics to the detriment of macro-economics in government policy agendas. An emphasis on anything leading to the understanding of the sophistication of business environments is critical as these, alongside innovation, are the drivers of competitiveness of national economies today. In the end it is all about firms and the competitiveness of firms.

Research into the crucial role of government in restoring the levels of collective confidence in times of crises would be most relevant. There isn't however a laboratory where these things can be replicated. Crises of consumer or investor confidence cannot be artificially induced for social research scientists to stand aside and observe the behaviour of economic agents and take notes. Here is then and once again a crucial difference between economics and the exact sciences. Much the same applies to research into management studies. The search for exact answers and intercontextual formulae may be vain and utopian as the context, irrespective of how it is defined, is deterministic of the outcome of social phenomena.

Popper elaborated on the concept of verisimilitude, a kind of approximation to the truth, a constant search for a better truth, not an absolute truth but a truth with better adherence to the reality that it purports to explain. The search for the best truths available, the ones that best explain phenomena at a given point in time rather than the permanent quest for absolute truths is most likely the proper way forward in the advancement of knowledge in the exact sciences, and in all likelihood the same applies to the social sciences.

A constant search for alternative and improved truths that better fit the times seems to be the right thing to do, rather than look for intercontextual magic bullets, one size fits all pseudo-solutions. In challenging the incumbent paradigm, the new set of truths has to unambiguously and at all times demonstrate its epistemological superiority. This is a balanced stance, one that refutes absolutism, authoritarian views and manicheistic perspectives of the world in the building of scientific edifices. Falsification of the incumbent paradigm is thus a convenient and progressive way forward in the construction of knowledge, and ideal in business and economics research.

An epistemological positivism built on causal deterministic relationships between variables, anchored on the premise that everything is susceptible of proof, finds insurmountable obstacles in the systemic nature of management, and paradoxically in another superior form of determinism, that of randomness that comes from the contextual essence of social and economic phenomena. Contrary to the exact sciences, the social sciences in general, and the management sciences in particular, should acknowledge that the application of identical techniques, methodologies and knowledge in different contexts will most likely produce different results depending on where and how they are applied. The learning outcomes in management are therefore a set of techniques that are effective in the contexts for which they were developed, but only susceptible to extrapolation after a scrutiny that comes from an iterative process of adaptation to new realities. This is mostly done by trial and error, and the knowledge derived although susceptible to systematization is also largely intuitive and experiential.

The vectors that define context are cultural, political, demographic and economic, and particularly shape the societal values that characterize the time and place in which they occur. It follows from this that for someone who researches management issues, what remains is a body of scientific-intuitive knowledge of organizational reality in its interface with societal stakeholders, other economic agents, governments and wider society.

Multidisciplinarity is ever more important for a complete and profound understanding of organizational problems and issues. The nature and content of organizational problems has roots in various disciplines and systemic consequences that stretch beyond a particular domain or field of knowledge. However, and perhaps by way of convenience, tradition or because these have been the requirements of the industrial establishment, the dominant paradigm appears to be that of compartmentalized specialization, translated into functional areas of expertise. In organizations, as in life however, problems are systemic and intertwined, and they are only made sense of through multidisciplinarity and integration.

A matter that appears on the surface as belonging strictly to the financial or marketing domains is in reality seldom strictly a financial or marketing issue. It is always a problematic with multiple dimensions and consequences. It has roots and manifestations on the totality of the firm and its surrounding stakeholder constituencies. Organizations, consciously or not, put together structures according to functional criteria and silos of knowledge expertise as ideal representations of the best ways in which to handle the complexity of the economic riddle that is posed to them.

Throughout the nineteenth and twentieth centuries, functionality and departmentalization became deep-rooted in early industrial organizations and towards the latter half of the twentieth century most organizations had clear-cut functions overseeing their marketing, finance and human resource activities, with these being autonomous areas within the business. MBA programmes the world over typically include in their academic curricula marketing and finance disciplines and it is very rare that these and other disciplines intersect in a systemic body of knowledge that could perhaps constitute a better reflection of organizational problems and challenges, and principally of the most effective ways in which to tackle them. Organizations and universities are in dire need of urgent change in order to accommodate societal transformations and an impending reality that is pervaded by political, sociological, economic and technological volatility of a kind whose comprehension requires knowledge integration and multidisciplinarity.

Organizational structures have already begun to introduce and reflect the kind of change that is referred to above. It is common to find job titles at credible institutions which were not there before, including that of Senior Vice President for Premium Value/Customer Experience at American Express or a Director of Corporate Reputation at Telefonica, the Spanish telecommunications multinational. There are an abundance of examples of unusual job titles in contemporary organizations, and they are only strange because the challenges that their holders address were not there before. These new job titles are reflective of a deliberate search for adequacy on the part of firms, between their domestic resources, skills and competencies and what they understand to be the true essence of the problems and issues that need to be confronted.

Contemporary challenges are of course dynamic and they keep changing all the time at a breath-taking pace.

The nature and characterization of organizational demands and requirements by key stakeholder constituencies is changing all the time. Organizations need to constantly search for new and improved ways in which to respond to stakeholder demands. Universities in general and business schools in particular, along with faculties of economics the world over, have traditionally been split along well-defined functional areas, and this has perhaps not been the best fit between academia and the world of practitioners.

The case study method of teaching business management pioneered by the Harvard Business School reflects the need to understand business problems in ways that encompass their totality and complexity, yet when they are taught in MBA programmes the world over the tendency is to explore what in essence are systemic organizational issues strictly from the perspective of the functional discipline under scrutiny, missing out on the totality of the organizational situation or problem.

The case study approach makes salient a breadth of management competencies, knowledge that when used adequately can be important contributors to the solving of business problems in multidisciplinary contexts. In the constant search for better solutions, it is important to bring to the forefront an epistemological stance that is much more than a doomed quest for absolute and intercontextual truths, giving body to a management and economics discipline that incorporates behavioural variables in the scrutiny of the economic dimensions of sociological phenomena.

Economic systems are first and foremost constituted by individuals with unpredictable behaviours that are impossible to model through mathematical formulae for the sake of simplicity and convenience. This is particularly true when these individuals are aggregated and interact collectively in societies. Theoretical construction in the economics science would do well to incorporate behavioural variables and disciplines more, whilst allowing for an empiricist and inductive approach that would search for less deterministic causistic methods of enquiry.

The neoclassical monetarist paradigm had a deeply entrenched belief that the markets would in due time accommodate any and every artificial distortion via the price mechanism. Unfolding events clearly demonstrated that the world needs to understand better the power of sociological dynamics and how these stand to shape the economies of nations. From the intellectual compromise of bounded rationality, a kind of conditioned rationality as proposed by Herbert Simon, to Adam Smith's invisible hand, to the antagonistic Marxian dichotomy of capital and labour, perhaps something fundamental has escaped or been underestimated by all these great thinkers and theoreticians. People, their idiosyncrasies and the collective manifestations of these in changing societal systems may have been the missing link that explains the failure of economics in shedding light on very important contemporary phenomena.

As happens periodically in scientific query, both in the exact and the social sciences, a more rigorous epistemological stance would suggest that prevailing paradigms are only waiting to be falsified by an improved scrutiny of phenomena and the emergence of more powerful explanatory schemata anchoring better truths. The strength of the new paradigm is in its explanatory capacity of the same underlying phenomena. This leads to the notion that there is currently in economics a need for revoking the incumbent paradigm as the prevailing truths are unequivocally insufficient in shedding light on current socio-economic phenomena. The litmus test is in the adequacy or failure of the current apparatus in providing answers to contemporary problems. The latter appears to be the case today.

The mistake of many a policy-maker is that not often enough do they adopt a critical stance, one that comes from a profound knowledge and deep sense of history. The mistake of many academics is one of abdication from a posture of constant scrutiny, a methodical doubt that should always characterize knowledge creation and societal development. This idealized epistemological stance should always aim to stand above the pseudo-objectivity of universal laws in the social sciences, acknowledging that the object of study is mobile and indeed very difficult to model, particularly when expressed collectively in relationships between individuals in society, in labour relations and in consumption.

The sociological dimension of economic relations should impose that in the search for valid outcomes and conclusions the subjectivity of context is recognized to the detriment of an obsession with generalizability. The explanatory superiority of contextually bound findings should be preferred to the quest for universal truths and laws. The context is in truth, a deterministic or at least a conditioning factor, dictating or shaping the unfolding of socio-economic phenomena.

In this way, best practices and methods work well in certain contexts but not in others, and it is up to the practitioner to have the discretion to extrapolate from general principle and find the necessary adequacy between these and his own particular reality, applying the necessary filters when and where appropriate. Theoretical frameworks, best practices and methodologies in economics and management need therefore to be contextualized in all their relevant dimensions, sociological cultural and others. In reality, the globalization of economic relationships, beyond signifying a greater interlinkage between economic agents, configures something much more important, an interdependency of economic systems represented globally.

Competitive advantages are ephemeral and ethereal disappearing with much more ease than the effort incurred in attaining them. The market is a dynamic concept, where change is the only constant. Where people are entailed, change is not straightforward and always difficult to manage. Change may be of a demographic or sociological nature, or it may be in the particular characterization of economic relations. In the final analyses, it is always a chore to model and predict human behaviour, individually and as economic agents in societies. Unfortunately for social scientists, but not for the rest of us, rarely can human nature be trusted to behave in expected ways.

The internal context, as well as the macro-environment that surrounds the organization, do not remain immutable for long. The rate of change in most markets today is breathtaking. Sound management should have the ability of navigating the organization according to the seas. There is therefore an imperative of adaptation to changing contexts and a necessary emphasis on core organizational qualities and competencies that accommodates change as best as possible. First and foremost amongst these leadership traits is the management of change in turbulent times and dealing with ambiguous and unpredictable macro-environments. The cultural, linguistic or interpretative contexts surrounding contemporary issues and phenomena present such a widespread complexity that the very analyses of economic phenomena interferes with the outcomes of these phenomena and their consequences. In resorting to the football analogy, not only do the rules of the game change but also the goal posts are moved now and again, and often just as our deadly striker is about to score.

Organizations, as people, have their own history and aspirations, and like people, struggle to deal with complex surrounding environments. Just like people, organizations need to constantly adapt to changing environments and likewise, success very much goes to those who are best at monitoring and managing the volatile macro-environment in which they operate. Indicators of success may be different for organizations than they are for people, including in the latter case the inclusion of such objectives as the pursuit of happiness or professional and personal success, but the metaphor of the organization as person continues to remain perfectly viable and adequate in understanding the shortcomings and contingencies of organizations, as well as their aspirations and collective anxieties.

Doyle (1992) concluded that successful firms operate in what he referred to as a tolerance zone of objectives, where no objective in particular is maximized. Top management behave in a way so as to satisfy the often irreconcilable requisites of various stakeholder constituencies both within the organization as well as those that gravitate around in its external environment, including customers, suppliers, governments, shareholders and others. In the case of a key stakeholder group, customers, the very notion of what constitutes value at each moment in time is a dynamic concept that has to constantly undergo a detailed and profound scrutiny on the part of firms and managers as to the cues that make up for value in the minds of consumers at each point in time and for each context. What consumers value today they may be indifferent to tomorrow. Amidst this chaos, survives the values of an organization, what it represents, expressed in its mission and strategic vision, and crucially, in the way it is understood by its key stakeholder constituencies.

Paradigm shifts occur in the social sciences as they do in the exact sciences. Taking the earlier example of physics, from the geocentric paradigm grounded on the Ptolemaic system to the heliocentric apparatus of Copernicus and Galileo and on to Newton's theories of gravity and Einstein's relativity, the theoretical building in physics was constantly revoked to accommodate better truths. It is however undoubtedly the case that whilst theoretical construction and paradigm revoking occurred not in continuity but in occasional shifts, the relationships between forces in the universe have remained constant, at least for the time-span of the duration of the incumbent paradigms, and these sufficed as explanatory schemata for the times.

In the case of the geocentric paradigm, its rejection as a prevailing paradigm had to confront the strong opposition of the predominant political and societal powerhouses of the time, namely the close scrutiny of the Roman Catholic Church who tended to adopt what can euphemistically be described as dissuading methods on whoever sought to refute incumbent institutional truths, and attempted their replacement with contributions to the scientific edifice that ran counter to the political, economic and sociological dimensions of the establishment. In reality, anything that was perceived to somehow shake the prevailing status quo and orthodoxy would be dealt with accordingly, meaning such aberrations as burning people to the stake, or condemning anyone who dared to challenge the established orthodoxy, such as the one that postulated that the earth was indeed at the centre of the universe, to fates worse than can be described.

Safeguarding for the necessary distances, there are points of contact between this reality and that of how incumbents protect their own turf today. If we care to adjust for the times, and if a medieval bonfire is replaced with budgetary restrictions in our metaphor of restrictions, then the conditionings of political and corporate agendas along with economic boundaries mean the explicit or implicit discrimination of those who dare to think outside the box and challenge the incumbent paradigm. This restrictive philosophy on research programmes and prevailing agendas is not too dissimilar from the political and sociological conditionings of the middle ages, albeit the contemporary version it has to be conceded is cleaner and more aseptic.

If this is the case for physics, it is certainly also the case for the other sciences, and principally for the social sciences, where the object of study, the individual, is susceptible to change and virtually impossible to model when it comes to behavioural unpredictability. Thus the variability in the object of study contributes to the explanatory frailties inherent to the social sciences and the futility of serious attempts in the pursuit of forecasting accuracy in economics.

If the forecast for annual GDP growth is 2 per cent, and if by the end of the year GDP has decreased by 1.5 per cent, then the forecasting error may statistically be one of 3.5 per cent, the net difference between actual and projected figures but in reality it is much more than that. A deviation of such magnitude in the forecasting of a crucial macro-economic indicator implies the difference between economic growth and a technical recession and crucially millions of people out of a job. When these kinds of estimates are totally off the park, as they often are, this can only be reflective instead of a complete inability of the apparatus of the economics science in forecasting GDP growth with its current gamut of pseudo state-of-the-art methodological instrumentation and tools. A science that does not predict is only useful as a post-hoc diagnosis of past phenomena and offers no lessons for the future.

The problem is that the social sciences do not handle future events well, and even less their estimation, at least in useful ways, so as to aid corporate decision-making and government policy formulation. Many of these mathematical models and their assumptions are not mere simplifications of reality as they purport to be. They are deturpations of any known reality. Economic models claim to forecast macro-economic aggregates, including unemployment, inflation or GDP, but if one is to look at institutional forecasting of these aggregates by credible bodies over the years, upon sheer observation and memory the record is simply abysmal. In addition to a poor track record when it comes to forecasting underlying realities, the absolute lack of understanding and insensitivity of those who, not being from related scientific areas, end up taking these models and crucially their findings to the letter, treating them in a decontextualized way, is not only inadequate, it is also dangerous.

In forecasting macro-economic indicators that are supposed to aid government policy formulation and organizational decision-making, cultural filters need to be factored in. By failing to acknowledge the idiosyncrasies of the collective psychology and character of a nation and its sociological underpinnings, any estimates about future macro-economic variables are probably going to be completely off the wall. Macro-economic forecasting needs to therefore somehow incorporate the subjective conditions and behavioural characteristics of the people and the societies in which the exercise is embedded.

Policy-makers who fail to acknowledge the critical importance of cultural filters and the subjective and behavioural dimensions of the problem will always make the wrong decisions in organizations and governments, with dire consequences to the economy and to wider society. There is ample evidence of this over the last decade, and it is no wonder that outcomes on otherwise well-intentioned macro-economic policy measures are often disastrous. If this is indeed the case, what is then the alternative to macro-economic analyses and forecasting as it currently stands, given that the quantitative predictions emanating from otherwise credible institutions do not seem to hold and be doing the trick? In answering this question, a possible way forward is to go for a blend of art and science, of accepting the outcomes of mathematical models as valid, but taking into account the contextual subjectivity that characterizes the underlying realities that they purport to explain and predict.

Of the 43 companies chosen by Peters and Waterman as America's best, in their best-seller In Search of Excellence, *only 14 showed a good performance 5 years later, and only 10, 10 years later. Many of them had disappeared. (Doyle, 1992).*

Of the 12 companies identified as the best in the United Kingdom between 1979 and 1990, only 5 survived in 1996, and only 1 was still a high performer. (Management Today)

Management literature and practice in the 1980s and 1990s offered here and there a vigorous attempt at a kind of organizational alchemy, a search for the philosopher's stone, magic recipes and corporate formulae that stood to guarantee organizational success in any market sector at any time. In this context, there began to appear in MBA programmes, in scientific journals and in management and practitioner publications, degree courses and articles deriving principles from the engineering and biological sciences and applying them to the functioning of organizations.

Obscure concepts out of cybernetics, including the idea of black boxes of input resources, were to be found in the organizational literature. There was an accepted view that it would be possible to establish universal laws in the management sciences, that the usage of the deductive method to be found in the exact sciences was possible and indeed desirable in research programmes in the social sciences, and that its application gave the latter a legitimacy and corresponding credibility akin to that of the exact sciences.

This was largely due to an insatiable appetite for deterministic rules of cause and effect, linear relationships and the quest for predictability in the diagnosis of organizational realities and the forecasting of economic events. This kind of scrutiny would produce outcomes that would have in the jargon of scientific research, external validity, meaning that they would be susceptible to extrapolation onto other unrelated economic and sociological contextual realities. The future however would prove bleak for forecasting and, if anything, it was demonstrated that in the social sciences, more than searching for solutions that are inter-contextual and applicable everywhere, the aim should be for a less ambitious agenda, a more humble quest for a truth for the times, attained by iterative experimentation, in other words a pursuit for the accumulation of knowledge through trial and error.

When Peters and Waterman published their seminal work, *In Search of Excellence* in 1982, their intention was to identify a set of criteria or organizational traits that were transversal to every company whose performance excelled in comparison to that of others. The verification of these characteristics or traits in firms would inevitably lead any organization to achieve economic success in any market at any time.

To that effect, the authors alluded to an archetype of organization whose traits, behaviour, underlying characteristics and attitudes constituted secure indicators of success, irrespective of the sector of economic activity in which they operated. Other companies could, in the light of the identified set of criteria for excellence, follow these magic formulae in the quest for the Holy Grail of exceptional organizational performance in any market at any time. Those were the times of organizational alchemy, the constant search for the philosopher's stone and magic recipes for success, whose formulae would guarantee excellent performances independent of sector of economic activity, time and space.

Parallel to this thinking there was a branch of the management literature that applied research on cybernetics and concepts from the engineering sciences to the study and functioning of organizations. There was talk of such concepts as viable systems models and people alluding to organizations as if they were living organisms. Methodologies and concepts taken out of the leaves of the biological and the exact sciences would be imported into the complex and chaotic world of organizations, in a permanent quest for linear relationships between variables. A conviction reigned in certain academic circles that it would be possible to establish universal laws in management, very much akin to the phenomenological approaches found in the exact sciences. This was largely substantiated by notions of deterministic causality in relationships between variables, linearity and a search for a yet untapped predictive potential of the management sciences.

It was widely accepted amongst members of the academic fraternity that organizational and economics research could and indeed should resort to the deductive method, and that it would be possible to infer general conclusions about the behaviour of economic agents and other stakeholders, both internal and external to organizations. The output derived from scrutiny of this kind would have external validity, meaning that it would be susceptible to extrapolation onto other economic and sociological realities irrespective of the context of where they were applied.

The application of cybernetics to management and its use in organizations had some staunch proponents. The Viable Systems Model (1989) created the metaphor for the organization as a living organism. The 1980s and

1990s were, in the light of this, fertile ground for attempts at modelling organizational reality in such a way as to be able to predict it. Complex models would be devised for the forecasting of social and economic phenomena with a view to deriving formulae and recipes for organizational success, susceptible of extrapolation to any sector of economic activity, company or geography.

These mathematical models were to signal a constant search for order where there was disorder, and logic where there was chaos, a general set of valid principles that would transverse different types of organizations, independent of economic, cultural and geographic contexts. The future if anything demonstrated that in the realm of the social sciences more than a search for solutions that are inter-contextual and applicable everywhere, scientific enquiry should perhaps strive for truths that are apt for the times, and not universal laws that cut across time and space.

The application of infallible formulae, techniques, magic bullets or methodologies needs in this context to be pondered well. The specific context in which these are used is deterministic as to the quality and nature of their intended outcome. This is also something that clearly needs to be part of the educational agenda and training of future managers in business schools and management programmes. In many ways the Harvard Business School case study method is founded on the exposure of the prospective manager to as many different potential business situations as possible, involving and requiring different toolkits of skills and solutions. This is also a deliberate attempt at replicating the complexity entailed in the real life of organizations in the light of an internal endowment of corporate resources as well as external constraints vis-à-vis the dynamic interface of organizations and a constantly changing surrounding macro-environment. All of this needs to be done in ways so as to accomplish the overriding objective of business education, that of enhancing the practical competencies of future managers in heterogeneous organizational realities and contexts.

An in-depth scrutiny into the criteria that will determine an organization's ability to survive and indeed excel in a new context is what is at stake here, as new contexts and environments are unpredictable at various levels. The application of a set of general principles of management in alternative organizational and macro-environmental contexts should be treated with caution as it is precisely context, however it is defined, that will determine the viability of the proposed solutions.

When extrapolating from a theoretically grounded set of principles, even when they are founded on solid empirical observation, there are no guarantees that they will remain valid in other realities and that indeed their applied outcome will remain satisfactory in these novel contexts. The same goes for the importation of management methods, techniques and principles that have proven successful in particular economic, geographic or cultural contexts, but that are all formulae whose success still needs to be scrutinized in alternative contexts. This being the case, the onus of responsibility for making the whole thing work is increasingly on the manager, who needs to incorporate in the right measure, acquired knowledge skills and the intuitive and experiential competencies that are needed in the interpretation of the relevant contextual cues. In the end, practical experience should tell the manager what is worth retaining as well as what should be discarded.

As a way of example, if we were to take the concepts of JIT from supply chain management, as they are used by Toyota and the Japanese automobile industry, and extrapolate them into a different organizational setting and national reality without regard for cultural context and geographic specificity, the outcome would not necessarily be a satisfactory one. JIT aims for the rationalization of stock levels and the reduction of costs by ensuring that inputs are supplied just as manufacturing processes make use of them. The optimization of resource allocation and rationalization of costs is thus attained through the lowering of stock levels to the strictly necessary. This is achieved through a sequencing of production and supply chain management activities, whereby the logistics that link suppliers and manufacturers are fine-tuned, aligned and coordinated to the point where supplied inputs into the production process are used when and only when they are needed in the production process, thus rationalizing inventory levels and keeping inventory costs to a minimum.

There are cultural specificities that make it difficult to extrapolate organizational philosophy, methods, systems and modus operandi from one country to the next. A distinct reality will require a particular concern for the specificity of context to which these new methods and ways are to be applied. Beyond the differences that are easily visible on physical infrastructure, roads and communications, the direct extrapolation of novel or even well tested conceptual frameworks and methodologies from one country to the next is made difficult by what are in essence different ways of approaching not only the world of organizations and labour but even, and fundamentally more important, different outlooks on life and divergent philosophies governing the quotidian of people in society.

There are therefore cultural imperatives that act as obstacles to simply adopting formulae supposedly leading to organizational success in a particular geography and culture, and applying them in other completely unrelated contexts. Sometimes exceptionally successful organizational practices, including different ways of doing things, best practices, methodologies or alternative techniques in one context, do not work in other contexts simply because the timing is not right for them in the newly found reality. They make sense in a particular cultural and time context but not in another, at least not yet. This of course does not invalidate the critical importance of learning with external best practices, both within and outside the particular sector of economic activity. It is however critical that the necessary cultural filters are applied in order for these imported methodologies and processes to make sense in one's own backyard with all that this means in terms of a much needed adjustment to the local macro-environment, as defined by culture, economic settings and implied societal dimensions. Sometimes it is not about substantive cultural differences, it is about a kind of heterogeneity that is not easily registered, such as idiosyncrasies of the collective character or specificities in markets that combine to ultimately determine the success of these imported practices, independent of their intrinsic qualities and merits.

It is often the case that people in other industries or indeed in other countries have been able to figure out better processes and ways of doing things on otherwise equivalent activities, best practices that can be imported as benchmarks for doing things in one's own backyard. But the whole thing does not end there. Better business practices that are derived from a permanent search for the optimization of the modus operandi of organizations can never be dissociated from the cultural cues and societal values in which they are embedded, and the way in which individuals in societies conduct their lives and their relationship with work. One has to take into account that there may be very valid reasons, albeit not often easily perceptible to the naked eye, for organizational practices to be effective and successful in a particular context only simply not to work in other business and cultural contexts. Timing is also of the utmost importance here, and what may work at a particular point in time may be an abject failure when applied earlier or later.

The quest for universal laws in the social sciences is complex, and attaining inter-contextual truths from what are no more than occasional regularities are difficult in economics and management. The derivation of universal laws from the observation of economic phenomena is probably a lost cause. The acknowledgement of this is important for organizational thinkers and practitioners alike in that experiential knowledge, gathered in the implementation of foreign (to the industry and to the country) methods and processes, needs to be given its rightful importance in this debate and in the hierarchy of skills that are needed to make best practices work in new cultural contexts. The substitution of these pre-conditions of permanent adaptation to the prevailing context for an idea of generalizability and less regard for the idiosyncrasies of culture and geography is often accompanied by a lethal mixture of arrogance and ignorance, with grave consequences to organizations and economies, and to the daily lives of people.

The economic sciences have clear limitations in forecasting, and the prediction of future outcomes is still very much informed guesswork and crystal ball stuff. Events in the last decade have shown just how limited the forecasting capabilities of the science of economics really are and, in truth, the limited effectiveness of the existing theoretical apparatus in predicting what the future holds for economies and societies. This was amply demonstrated with the debacle of the financial markets in 2008 and its subsequent impact on the real economy of the production of goods and services.

Of particular relevance was the inability of the economic sciences and its most significant constituencies and actors in warning the incumbent political structures of the time of what was to come our way, as well as the subsequent repercussions to the economy and to the lives of us all of an unprecedented crisis. There will always be those who say that they had warned us all, but apart from one or two isolated cases of academics, who wrote and spoke about certain warning signals that had been looming in the horizon for some time, including a pending real estate bubble that had been threatening to burst for some time, we end up never knowing who these people are and where they were.

Concluding on the importation of techniques and best practices from one sector to the next, often across unrelated areas of economic activity, it would be ideal if these techniques and methods could be applied indistinctly to different countries as well as economic and organizational realities. However this is simply not possible. The archetypes of solutions that are susceptible of extrapolation from country to country, or sector to sector, have to undergo the subjective judgment as to their reasonable adequacy and fit into local realities. Only by subjecting these solutions to the filter of localized scrutiny can one unquestionably judge whether something works or doesn't in alternative contexts.

It is never a call on the absolute merits of a theory, methodology or practice. It is about an idea of effectiveness in the importation of best practices being conditioned by the particular set of circumstances in which they are subsequently to be applied. The science here is more of an art in that it is up to the manager to make the call on where and how imported best practices should be implemented. In so doing, the manager resorts to a mix of theory and experiential sensitivity, acquired through permanent exposure to reality, thus gathering practical knowledge in the process. This is an informed intuition that allows for the best decision possible to be made at each moment in time in accordance with the specific context in which it occurs. Openness to new challenges and a permanently inquisitive posture is thus critical.

Reality Check...

Nothing is Sacred: A Dispassionate Perspective on Government Deficits

Not too long ago the world-renowned Harvard economist Robert Barro, of the monetarist tradition, published a book, which he decided to aptly name *Nothing is Sacred*. In it he dealt with an area of intellectual query that has always attracted the interests and opinion of many an economist and commentator from all sides of the ideological spectrum. In effect there has been for some time a hot point of contention and controversy surrounding government compliance with target public debt and budget deficits. In recent times, given the truly alarming debt problems afflicting not only eurozone economies such as Greece, Ireland and Portugal, but also, and most critically, the US and Japan, there are more and more calls for strict spending and debt reduction policies.

In the cases of the smaller EU economies, including Greece, Ireland and Portugal, the debate, albeit important, is somewhat redundant as these and other economies no longer enjoy any room for manoeuvre. Incapacitated in their ability to formulate or even influence macro-economic policy and unable to manipulate exchange rates, these economies cannot not issue money. In sharing a common currency they are not allowed the lever of currency devaluation that would make their products cheaper and more competitive in export markets outside the eurozone. Often in the smaller economies in the eurozone ad-hoc currency devaluation had arguably contributed to the perpetuation of a culture of competitive relaxation. This in essence aided companies with limited strategic vision who would lobby successive governments for the devaluation of the national currency. This would artificially make local products cheaper in foreign currency and more competitive in export markets. Of course what this also did, and perhaps their most detrimental collateral effect, was that these successive devaluation measures only served the purpose of creating a false sense of security, deviating attention from the true determinants of global competitiveness. These remain as always a country's ability to export products that consumers want because of their quality and not only because they are cheap. This is particularly true in market economies where individuals have disposable income and are able to discern between competing offers. In a way, successive devaluations only help to take the eye off the ball of the true determinants of organizational and national competitiveness.

For the countries within the eurozone, the European Central Bank conducting monetary policy means that it is no longer feasible for the particular interests of an economic sector, or those of a group of companies, to condition the monetary policy of individual state governments. This is particularly true for the small economies. These are left with running fiscal policy. On the revenue side of the equation we have taxes and on the other public spending. With regards to fiscal efficiency, governments attempt to create effective mechanisms of tax collection, namely by improving the crossing of sources of information. This ensures a more rigorous monitoring of tax collection leading to a reduction in tax evasion and a more effective and equitable fiscal process.

Faced with no latitude in the formulation of macro-economic policy, national governments are left by default with micro-economic policy. This translates into the imperative for creating the best possible conditions for companies to operate in an open economy. These conditions include such critical areas as the efficient running of justice and better education, the absence of both of which can constitute obstacles to FDI, but whose adequate functioning on the other hand can signify a critical contribution to organizational and national competitiveness. The other crucial problem is the cost and difficulty of financing of small and medium-sized firms in the small and debt-ridden economies and the interest differentials between companies based in these markets and others who have to compete with them in the same currency zone for the same markets.

The strategic role of government in formulating micro-economic policy is important but it is still peripheral to what are the higher-order responsibilities of entrepreneurs in actively seeking to excel on the determinants of competitiveness that matter in individual markets. The idiosyncrasies of consumption across different markets can only be met by sharp and cosmopolitan entrepreneurs who are willing to take risks, go out of their comfort zone and make an effort to understand others. Price is critical in non-discriminating markets whilst in the more affluent markets, where consumers have higher disposable income, price is often not the most important consumption criterion.

Branding and brands are critical in the buying decision-making process in affluent societies. Understanding the specific essence of local cultures and its particular manifestations in consumption, the reasons why discerning consumers decide to buy something to the detriment of an alternative offering that complies with an identical functional benefit is perhaps the most remarkable competency that an exporter needs to possess in order to be successful in a sophisticated foreign market. Understanding the collective psyche of an affluent target group, the social cues and hierarchies that typify and characterize a group of people, the urban subcultures and their implicit and explicit codes, the cosmopolitism and clues of a place and fundamentally how all of these are aggregated and expressed in consumption decisions are critical competencies in contemporary markets. This understanding remains infinitely more important as a success determinant in export strategies than the quality of products, their packaging or even their functional benefit, what they do. The tragedy is that only a few see success in export strategies expressed in this way.

Ireland, Portugal, Spain, Greece and others were the recipients of substantial European aid, with a view to recovering from a severe structural backwardness at the time of entry. The jury is still out on how all of this money was spent and the story is narrated differently in the three countries depending on which side of the ideological spectrum one sits on, but it is a fact that large amounts of European funds were terribly mismanaged and frequently deviated for purposes other than what they were originally intended for, a euphemism for stolen. In a nutshell, these countries, albeit to different degrees, threw away a unique opportunity of developing new skills and competencies by not having a clear and well thought through strategic outlook. Had this been the case, the structural aid invested rationally would have allowed the poorer countries to become truly competitive once the rug was removed from underneath their feet. The magnitude of the failure in taking advantage of this window of development opportunity differs from country to country but the thinking is valid for the poorer European countries.

The end recipients of these funds were also corporations, many of them that have since gone bankrupt. These organizations were not incentivized to search for competencies and solutions that would have enhanced their competitiveness in a global and more sophisticated marketplace. Still to this day, and with national governments ridden with debt, many corporations continue to demand for protectionist measures from their governments and further funding from what they think are the deep pockets of the EU. In so doing they demonstrate that old habits die hard whilst tacitly acknowledging their incompetence in understanding the determinants of competitiveness in a changing world.

Few looked at structural aid as an opportunity to invest in enhancing the understanding of a changing marketplace and world. To be more specific, sustained corporate success has always been about the consistent provision of goods and services which consumers, domestic or foreign, are willing to acquire to the detriment of other goods and services that apparently do pretty much the same thing in terms of functional benefit, but to which consumers do not ascribe as much value. In export markets, where disposable income is higher, consumers are willing to pay a premium for something they perceive to be of higher utility. It is in the understanding of this that the success of export strategies lies today.

Consumers in these more affluent societies often buy product not because of its functionality but for its intangibles, or that what goes beyond the functional benefit that the product or service offers. In the light of this, the perceived value of an economy's goods and services has to clearly outweigh the effective value that comes from its strict functionality or benefit of usage. In truly competitive markets, the ultimate determinant of choice is widely seen to be the branded image of a product or that of an organization. Its reputation next to its most important constituencies is of increasing importance too.

If enough organizations in a particular sector or across economic sectors of activity are competitive in the global market, if their brands are widely acclaimed for their quality, then the country's reputation is enhanced. As a country becomes more positively positioned in a distinct and valuable manner in the minds of foreign consumers, organizations find that they have the leeway to charge premium prices for their products and services in export markets. That is the wheel in which the poorer European economies need to jump into. However, and in most cases, this notion of competitiveness is so alien to entrepreneurs in these countries that the genesis to this problem has to be educational and its solution morose and strategic. Until this philosophical distance is reduced and its educational causes effectively tackled, the idea of a homogeneous Europe is anathema and the wealthier nations are left to deal with the symptoms of a disease rather than with its antecedents.

Europe faces a need for absolute discipline on public spending and compliance with budget deficit goals. Rigorous management of the public finances and the strict adherence to budget deficit objectives are common objectives for every EU country. However there is a recurrent debate amongst economists and commentators on the hindrance to economic growth of rigorous austerity and public finance discipline. In particular there appears to be a lack of consensus on the idea of severe austerity detracting from economic recovery when budget discipline and the overriding objective of keeping a low deficit are attained at the cost of lower public investment.

In the absence of the possibility of being in the presence of two alternative monetary policy paradigms, it is acceptable to economists, whether they are monetarists or Keynesian, that governments should conduct high budget deficits in times of recession or war. Recessions are bad times for tax revenue collection, and in times of war public spending is, for obvious reasons, substantially steeper. As thankfully the war scenario is not imminent let us focus on the first scenario.

On fiscal reform, Barro (2003) points to the famous IMF study conducted by two economists, Alesina and Perotti that empirically observed the experiences undertaken on budget deficit reduction in 20 economically developed OECD countries during the period between 1960 and 1994. Barro points towards some interesting results, not only with regards to the success or lack of success inherent to fiscal reform that was effected in these countries, but essentially as to the structure or composition of these measures, and their impact both on the revenue but also on the expenditure side.

The authors refer to Type 1 reforms, which are in fact more permanent adjustments, in that they tend to focus on budget items, such as the salaries of public servants and expenditure on social programmes, as these tend to increase uncontrollably. In contrast, there are Type 2 reforms, typified by the authors as those who after empirical scrutiny have been found not to be successful. These reforms focus on cuts in public investment. These reforms show on the part of government a tactical, non-reformist posture, a short-term perspective and principally a view of the economy that suggests a priority for the management of political cycles and a less than desirable will to observe fiscal discipline.

In conclusion and still following on from Alesina and Perotti's study, the undertaking of economic growth under Type 1 reforms is quicker for the cases that have been scrutinized, as it is accompanied by higher investment and an increase in exports. The authors attribute a significant part of the improvements witnessed on country economic performance to the credibility of governments, and the signals that these send to economic agents. These signals appear to be key drivers when pursuing the objectives inherent to sustained fiscal reforms.

The authors of the study refer to governments that are willing and disposed to confront the more delicate and open variables of the budget debate, such as public sector salary increases, restrictions on social security programmes and other popular forms of government spending on social welfare. All of these may signal a more serious attitude towards the overriding purpose of fiscal reform.'

Alesina and Perotti point towards the Italian case as that of a typical Type 2 (unsuccessful) case where deficit reductions have been attained by focussing on the tax revenue component of the budget and less on public spending cuts, with the added disadvantage that these cuts had been effected on public investment. Still, in a deep recession, rigorous fiscal policy is needed for sustainable future economic recovery. That much of the discipline in public finance and deficit containment is obtained through public investment restrictions and less through the capping of public servants' salaries and a rigorous rationalization of social programmes is a clear indicator of a worrying compromise of future economic recovery.

On the one hand, public investment signals a more serious and permanent intention on the part of governments to promote economic growth. On the other, public finance is not a bottomless pit. On the contrary it constitutes an unacceptable burden of debt unjustly imposed on future generations. Government decisions on public investment should be seen in a more ample and systemic framework, one whose focus should err on the imperative of national strategic interest.

7

Rationality vs. Emotion: Funny Tasting Coke in the Land of Georges Remi (Hergé)

When Peters and Waterman published *In Search of Excellence* in 1982 they identified a list of companies that had as common characteristics a set of unifying criteria which made them exceptional performers. Little did the authors know that it wouldn't be too long before most of the 43 organizations that were originally identified in their research as being remarkable and picked for their excellent market performance had simply withered away and disappeared.

Reality would subsequently show that the idea of magic bullets of organizational success, the identification of criteria that are meant to be inter-contextual in the portrayal of the archetype of a successful organization, would end up being refuted and made obsolete by evidence, a fate shared by the companies that they supposedly were to characterize. Reality also imposes an imperative that is much more poignant than that of the temptation of searching for regularities, and from them extracting and proclaiming conclusive universal truths about the behaviour and performance of organizations in an economy.

There is a variability and at times randomness about the whole thing that makes it impossible to model economic systems, at least in predictive ways that allow for accurate forecasting of the underlying phenomena that they purport to explain. It is thus impossible to derive universal truths from contextualized query as the specificity of the context limits the potential for extrapolation of those truths in alternative realities.

A few years ago in Belgium and northern France, people began to complaint about nausea and dizziness. Hundreds felt sick and began to pack local hospitals. Many complained of having drunk Coca Cola just before beginning to feel nauseous and awkward. More than 100 people were hospitalized including children. Faced with a very probable public relations disaster as its name kept popping up in the media, and with developments unfolding, Coca Cola's kneejerk reaction was to first deny that its products could have possibly been the cause for what was beginning to look like an epidemic.

The answer came quick, and governments in five European countries decided on an immediate ban of all Coca Cola products, forcing the company to withdraw every one of them from the commercial circuit until further notice was given. Seven days after the first case was reported, and before governments began to intervene, Coca Cola had finally decided to withdraw all its Belgium-bottled products from the market.

They conceded then, that although from their perspective there was no issue of public health for which they could be apportioned blame and responsibility, there was something wrong with the CO_2 used by one of its bottlers, and that a fungicide used in the treatment of pallets may have had come into contact with products and somehow tainted them. On the eighth day of the crisis, the problem began to escalate into a major debacle in France where 80 people near the Belgian border had fallen ill. The French Government ordered the immediate withdrawal of all Coca Cola products from the market, irrespective of whether they had been bottled in Belgium or not.

It became abundantly clear that the justification given by Coca Cola for the funny tasting Coke was not credible. On the tenth day, the problem had escalated and hit Switzerland, Germany and Spain, countries where the brand began to be banned from trading. As events unfolded, scientific data was being actively collected and scientists were working overtime in an attempt to explain exactly what had happened.

The whole thing became even denser when scientific evidence proved inconclusive on the nature and origin of the problem, and crucially on the potential repercussions to public health that could derive from it. Coca Cola simply and unequivocally could not be blamed for endangering public health, as nothing was found in their products that would lead anyone to that conclusion. Coca Cola then took an unprecedented and historical step forward in the face of what appeared to be a mounting crisis that could soon get out of control, and made what was to be an important decision.

Although there was indeed no evidence linking Coca Cola products to issues of public health, nor any evidence of misconduct or wrongdoing on the part of the company, Coca Cola in Belgium offered to pay for every medical bill of everyone that had been affected. This proved to be a landmark decision, as on the fourteenth day of the crisis, full page ads began to appear in the Belgian press, with Coca Cola apologizing for what had happened. On the fifteenth day, the Belgian Government lifted the ban on Coca Cola products, and similar action was to follow in other countries.

What had been the problem then? There was to begin with a collective environment that can best be described as one of hysteria in the food sector at the time, a climate of impending suspicion over food products and their origin, with consumers particularly sensitive to issues of the public health forum. BSE, more commonly known as mad-cow disease, was a major concern at the time and there was a general reluctance on the part of the public to accept the arguments and reasons of government officials on matters perceived to potentially lead to the endangerment of public health. Nobody really knows what summarily happened in the Coca Cola in Belgium case, and if there had indeed been a problem with the product or if this was merely a phenomenon of mass hysteria that had sadly gotten out of control.

Coca Cola's defence, that there had been no real problem, was construed by the public as reflective of the firm's uncaring attitude as well as a sign of lack of respect for its customers, something that was totally uncalled for, in bad taste and potentially damaging to the company's reputation as it meant the alienation of its most important stakeholder, the customer. It translated into a subliminal and subtle message, that in the final analysis the organization did not really care for its customers or their health, and that profit was the overriding concern for the firm.

In the end the episode cost Coca Cola US$60 million in immediate lost sales and withdrawal costs of the product from the market, but the evidence showed that long-term sales did not suffer. Once again, it became abundantly clear that an organization is indeed much more than the sum of the products that it puts out in the market. An organization upholds values and has responsibilities towards its surrounding stakeholder constituencies, its customers, employees, creditors and governments.

These stakeholders have expectations about the organization and its behaviour towards wider society. This implies that the organization has to correspond to the promise that derives from its social mandate and is reflected in the way it interacts, involves and manages the relationship with its stakeholders. This means that at times, in making what appears to be the rational decision for the company, this may not coincide with the interests of the wider community and surrounding stakeholders as they are perceived by these, and so perhaps an alternative course of action needs to be taken. It may not be a question of who is right and who isn't, or of fact versus fiction. It is an issue of managing expectations and perceptions, always bearing in mind that the overriding objective is for the organization to be a going concern into the future.

Peters and Waterman in *In Search of Excellence* (1982) identified 43 organizations based in the US that, according to their analyses, complied with the most stringent criteria for what they believed to be the archetype of an excellent organization. In effect, five years later, only 14 of those 43 companies were still commercially successful in the US and only five had survived and were still in business ten years on.

It is impossible not to stumble upon the harsh evidence of how ephemeral the life of organizations can be. Companies are cells in complex systems, dependent upon the characterization of the macro-environment and its dynamics, unpredictability and how all its variability inexorably shapes corporate outcomes, often not coincidental with the aims and aspirations of organizations that had up until then been very successful in the marketplace. Given that the surrounding context is something that changes all the time, organizational success depends very much on the ability of the organization in adapting to change in its macro-environment, monitoring it the best way it can, and wherever possible inducing environmental change in its favour.

Many of the companies identified in Peters and Waterman's text had disappeared not long after it was published. The reality is that the aim of the exercise, which was to pinpoint the archetype of the ideal organization and its characteristics, was merely academic and condemned to failure. The quest for the identification of a set of criteria that unite every successful organization is rendered futile as higher-order contextual variables take precedent, which makes excelling on those criteria redundant in the light of changing market conditions. What this means is that just as the formula of organizational success has been identified, the times have already moved on and so have the determinants of success changed.

Peters and Waterman attempted to search for convenient and deterministic regularities, drawing conclusive and generalizable universal truths from the observation of organizational characteristics, which they saw as being associated with companies that excelled in their respective sectors and showed above average market performance in them. From this, they inferred that those traits and behaviours had to be the universal determinants of organizational success and were not therefore context specific. The truth of the matter is that it has been impossible to derive universal truths when it comes to organizational excellence, in that context is deterministic as to the behaviour and performance of firms and thus limits the potential for the extrapolation of findings that correspond to character traits of excellent organizations. These traits of excellence may be irrelevant in other organizational realities and contexts.

This thinking and the importance of context applies to organizational reality and firm performance, as it does to macro-economic forecasting, and this probably explains why governments and specialist bodies and institutions get it so wrong in predicting macro-economic indicators most of the time. Policy measures may be effective in a particular social and economic reality but not in another. The determinism of context, whatever form and shape it takes, and the impossibility in modelling human behaviour, particularly when expressed collectively in societal relationships, makes it extremely difficult to come up with formulae for corporate success that are inter-contextual and go beyond the particular reality of the firm, or at best the sector under scrutiny.

Sadly, what has been going on in the social sciences for decades is the persistent pursuit of the holy grail of success, the search for corporate traits that typify every successful organization, irrespective of sector of economic activity and time, in the belief that if other organizations, in other geographies or at any other time replicate those behaviours, they too will be successful. The supreme importance of the social actor at the centre of a system, where he is not a passive object but instead a conscious intervener, at once manipulator and manipulated, an agent that is conditioned by reality but also subverts reality according to what he perceives to be his own interest and benefit at each moment, needs to be considered.

In the end the social sciences suffer from a basic ailment, a fundamental flaw that makes them absolutely different from the exact sciences. The object of study, the human being, expressed individually or collectively in society, is mobile, not static, and does not easily lend itself to mathematical modelling of a kind that we can easily infer future behaviour, at least in ways that aid decision-making for governments and organizations alike.

The reason for this lies precisely in the unpredictability of human behaviour, independently of the methodological sophistication and analytical rigour in its study. The attempts have been many, including the importation of principles of physics and biology, chaos theories, neural networks and overpowering intellectual constructions, anchored in complex mathematical models to study human economic behaviour. The overwhelming majority of this acquired knowledge finds a natural outlet in scientific publications that have little impact on the underlying reality that they purport to explain and modify.

In the management sciences for example, and unlike other disciplines including medicine, the object of study, organizations and people in organizations, go about their business in a parallel track to that of the academic world, and these worlds seldom intersect. Foremost amongst the reasons for this apathy and limited impact of these scientific publications on everyday organizational life is that many of these models appear not to have any adherence to the objective reality of the social systems that they claim to simplify, explain and whose outcome they purport to predict. Often these models are also poor when it comes to their forecasting abilities, and frequently when those who work with these models attempt to predict future outcomes, they tend to fail miserably as the object of study invariably slips away from underneath their feet.

These limitations have been brought to evidence recurrently in the world of financial markets, or indeed every time the IMF, the World Bank or national governments attempt to forecast economic growth, or any other major macro-economic variable, thus pre-empting the need for an urgent revoking of the incumbent quantitative paradigm in economics thinking. A recent prominence of behavioural economics is only the beginning, as there is still what can best be described as not more than lip service paid to behavioural variables in the study of economics.

This probably explains the absolute inability of the social sciences in general, and economics in particular, in predicting social and economic phenomena with any degree of accuracy. One does not need to go far to corroborate this view. From central banks to faculties of business administration and economics, to research departments in large corporations, they all find it difficult to pinpoint what will happen next, as well as forecasting major macro-economic indicators with a modicum of accuracy.

There has been a prevalence of the quantitative paradigm in research into the economics sciences and little attention has been paid to the behaviour of economic agents, the business context or the determinism of the surrounding macro-environment. This has contributed to an economics science that, whilst aiming to be more effective in explaining underlying sociological and economic realities, is thoroughly incapable of forecasting economic phenomena with acceptable accuracy. Furthermore, the science of economics is increasingly perceived by policy-makers and economic agents alike, not to be able to get it right most of the times, with dire consequences to its credibility and legitimacy next to key stakeholders.

If the economics profession does not find ways in which to enhance its capabilities for forecasting macro-economic variables then it loses legitimacy as a credible and worthy science. This is crucial, as a perceived inability in forecasting economic phenomena and their sociological ramifications, with a reasonable degree of accuracy, will detach economic agents from any idea of reliance upon the economics profession and academia for knowledge that contributes to better and more informed policy formulation and organizational decision-making. Better forecasting capabilities would also mean that governments as well as organizations could plan more effectively, and that individuals in society would be able to improve on their consumption decision-making processes.

A few years ago, Warren Buffett, Chairman of Berkshire Hathaway, a renowned guru in the world of financial markets and investments, and one of the wealthiest men in the US alerted the few who cared to listen to the then recent arrival into the stock market of a new type of investor, one with no sympathy for the long term, speculative in intention and serving no foreseeable social purpose in his deeds. Buffett emphasized also what he perceived to be an insufficient focus on the part of investors on the core fundamentals of business and the failure to use these as the overriding criterion for the choice of a portfolio of stock.

In the end, Buffett was referring to good old barometers of business performance including such crucial indicators and questions as: Has the company been well managed? Could someone else do better under similar conditions? Does it have a track record and a history for continuously developing new products and services? Is it perceived by its publics as an innovative organization? Are the company and its products positioned distinctively in different markets, and do they serve attractive market segments effectively? Is the company a going concern and will it continue to make products that people want in the foreseeable future?

All of these are questions that somehow, and amidst the rising prominence of an apparently complex world of speculative financial economics, have become unfashionable to ask, when they in fact have always remained the vital questions that needed to be asked. Buffett stated back then that he had never invested in companies whose businesses did not make commercial sense. When he invested in a company, he had to understand its underlying business idea, its products and what current or latent future consumption needs they stood to satisfy.

One cannot mistake the failure of the current apparatus of the economics science in diagnosing the present and inability to forecast the future as something unimportant and worthy of a mere footnote in history. It is not unfortunately something intermittent and without historical precedent. In 1973, at the time of the second oil shocks, the inverse relationship between inflation and unemployment that had held constant for decades, something that resulted like so many other theoretical constructions and concepts in economics from empirical observations and tracking of the historical behaviour of economies, ended up being refuted as new conditions emerged on the supply side of the economics equation with input resources into production processes and in particular raw materials becoming more expensive as a result of a sudden scarcity. In that year, rather than an inverse relationship between the two variables, what the world witnessed was a simultaneous occurrence of unemployment and inflation.

The Phillips curve had postulated an inverse relationship between inflation and unemployment, something that was supposed to hold constant. An economy heated beyond full employment, notwithstanding structural unemployment, would naturally suffer inflationary pressures caused by an increase in the demand for its goods and services. On the other hand, when an economy undergoes harsh recessionary times, demand slows down and there is a downward pressure on prices. As organizations reduce their activity, naturally and as a consequence, unemployment levels rise.

The idea of inevitability in this relationship subsisted for decades and was taken to be universal, independent and irrefutable, until the oil shocks came into the forefront. Suddenly, as oil prices began to increase, the cost of raw materials rocketed and firms found it hard to absorb these extra costs, passing them down instead to the consumer. The net result was a general increase in prices, or to put it simply inflation. There was therefore a phenomenon of co-occurrence of inflation and unemployment. The phenomenon originated unexpectedly from the supply side, whereas up until then the Keynesian apparatus only foresaw demand-side inflation. This occurred as raw materials, which in modern economies are all too closely tied to oil prices, became more expensive. Some of these raw materials became indirectly more expensive including oil derivatives, others directly in the form of energy inputs into manufacturing processes. Scarcity of raw materials led to exorbitant costs of factors of production and a rise in consumer prices of goods, whilst simultaneously the world bore witness to a slowing down of economic activity which naturally led to higher levels of unemployment in the economy.

The incumbent paradigm at the time was dominated by demand-side economics, founded on the post-war Keynesian tradition. Unfolding events brought to evidence that what contemporary economic thinking and state-of-the-art methodological query had not accounted for, or at least not reflected sufficiently upon, and that is the relationship between inflation and unemployment, and specifically what would happen to this relationship in case of an exogenous variable hitting the supply side of the equation which was what increased oil prices did to input factor costs.

In the absence of a theoretical apparatus that would allow for the forecasting of a simultaneous occurrence of unemployment and inflation, how would economists square the circle? In the end, the scientific community resorted to creative terminology and decided to call the phenomenon 'stagflation', a term never heard of before, and hastily defined as the simultaneous occurrence of unemployment and inflation. Subsequently, and faced with an unforeseen state of affairs, various conceptual and theoretical advancements came forth in the economics scientific literature, including ideas on rational expectations and non-accelerating inflation rate of unemployment (NAIRU) to explain the occurrence of stagflation.

Eventually Edmund Phelps would introduce the long-run Phillips curve, concluding that in this particular case the Phillips curve was in effect vertical, and that there was no trade-off between inflation and unemployment, ideas that earned Phelps the Nobel award in 2006. It would have undoubtedly been a much more grandiose and useful achievement from the viewpoint of economics, and its legitimacy as a science with predictive capabilities, if it was able to foresee what would happen to economies that were hit by sudden supply side shocks.

It would have been infinitely better to have an economics science much better equipped at forecasting economic phenomena rather than explaining them post-hoc. In the case above, an economics science with predictive powers could have warned policy-makers and senior management strategists in organizations alike of what would loom on the horizon should a sudden shortage in the supply of raw materials ensue as a result of cartelization phenomena or any other set of policy measures, leading to an immediate shortage of input resources in key sectors of economic activity. In particular, it would be interesting to have an economics science that was capable of predicting that under certain conditions of abnormal pressure on the supply side of the economy, in the case of a sudden increase in the costs of raw materials, production costs would necessarily go up and thus inflationary pressures would occur along with unemployment.

The study of economics is in this regard not dissimilar from that of other social sciences. The discipline mutates along paradigm shifts as social and economic phenomena are no longer explained adequately by current state-of-the-art knowledge and analytical capabilities in the field. A new paradigm emerges to replace the existing views of the world, a new and better fit to an underlying reality, apt for a particular point in time and context, an explanatory structure that serves better than the old schemata the purpose of shedding light on contemporary issues by improving on incumbent explanations of pending phenomena.

The Keynesian paradigm has been recurrently visited, particularly by the European left wing of the ideological spectrum, in the context of the current reflection on the spending role of the state, seen as the ideal mechanism for the kick-start of stagnated and recessionary economies. The Keynesian school of thought, and later the neoclassical monetarist supply-side tradition, dominated economics thinking for most of the twentieth century.

Neoclassical, supply-side economics, whose intellectual pillars were first and foremost to be found in the Chicago School of Economics, and whose most prominent figure and key ideologue was economist Milton Friedman, became synonymous with the values of liberalism, the ultimate expression of which was what became known as Reagonomics, a political and economic ideology which dominated policy and thinking throughout the 1980s in America and the UK.

Milton Friedman and John Kenneth Galbraith are two key protagonists in contemporary economics and they have shaped the economics science and economics thinking in the twentieth century. Friedman and Galbraith were to be found in the antipodes of the paradigms that sustained their philosophical stance. Although contemporaries, their vision of the world and of society, the role of firms, education and crucially the role of government was widely different.

In *Free to Choose* (1979), Friedman put forward the thinking of neoclassic monetarists from the Chicago School, concurrently endorsed in the political plane by Reagan in the US, Thatcher in the UK and Brian Mulroney in Canada. Those were times when it was believed that the individual's ability to shape his own destiny was unquestionable, where the markets feverishly acted as demi-gods, and where names like JP Morgan or Merrill Lynch were a dream come true for those who had just graduated with business degrees from the top and not so top institutions of higher learning, searching for the excitement and quick money in investment banking and the thrill of the financial markets. Keynesianism had long been thrown out of the window and, as Keynes himself had once put it, in the long run we are all dead. The incumbent paradigm was that of immediacy, quick accumulation of wealth and not much in the way of scruples in the process.

Galbraith, on the other hand in *The New Industrial State* (1967) and *The Affluent Society* (1958) warned of the emergence of a new dominating class in organizations, that of managers which he would designate as technostructure. These key senior decision-makers, non-proprietors of the companies that they worked for, would play a crucial role in modern economies and constituted another protagonist (the senior manager) that needed to be factored into the equation and added to the dichotomist system (capitalist and worker) of the Marxist dialectic.

Drucker spoke of the end of capitalism as we know it, and pointed towards the emergence of a knowledge society that would dominate the 1990s, where those who succeeded were going to necessarily be those who possessed and controlled knowledge, which he termed knowledge gatekeepers. A deeper knowledge of the philosophy of sciences, a more rigorous epistemology and a more humble yet inquisitive posture, would have allowed at least for the posing of pertinent questions, including whether the economic growth of the years leading up to the financial crisis of 2008 was indeed sustainable and could have been maintained *ad aeternum*. Not many dared to challenge then British Prime Minister Gordon Brown when he announced to the world, on the eve of the financial crisis, the end of economic cycles of boom and bust as we had always known the economy to perform. These would be replaced in this brave new world by permanent economic growth, founded on new technologies and new methods of doing business.

This new paradigm was anchored in the globalization of economic activity, the new world of the internet and the immense possibilities that it offered and what it meant for the approximation of market players, the availability of goods and services, and the opening of new economic spaces. An idea of permanent growth would undoubtedly have been a desirable vision for a changing world but completely unfounded when contrasted with the deterministic reality of economic history. This instead suggested an alternative view of the world, one where cyclical crises are historically the norm.

On the supply side of economics there have recurrently been phenomena of cartelization that lead to increases in the costs of key input factors of production, thus putting inflationary pressures on economies that depend on these inputs for their industrial activities. In this context, it is also plausible to expect a reduction in economic activity due to a shortage of demand attributable to political or social instability. In the end, general trends in the economy are possible to roughly estimate, but pinpointing the impacts of changes in the macro-environment on the performance of economies is certainly difficult to do.

Currently available methodological tools make it difficult to determine with any degree of accuracy and reliability the magnitude of these environmental effects on the economy, and consequently the ultimate purpose of applied knowledge in economics, or any other science, which is to aid policy-making by governments and decision-making by senior management in organizations, is defeated in the light of this complexity. Ascertaining the size of each of these effects, and crucially how they will impact on economic activity, simply means that any forecasting is rendered useless.

Often crises emerge due to causes not totally untraceable as to their roots but highly unpredictable as to the degree and severity of their consequences. This is perhaps the case with the 2008 crisis in the world financial system, whose only historical precedent would be the 1929 stock market crash, albeit with different antecedents to both phenomena. However, and given the complexity and the systemic nature and characteristics of modern economies, it is difficult to determine even well into a crisis what are its exact consequences to the real economy and to the lives of individuals. Futhermore, what would have been really helpful was the existence of a scientific apparatus capable of warning economic agents of a looming and impending g crisis, thus helping policy-makers and agents in the economy to prevent it. A post-hoc science is useless.

There is undoubted merit in attempts at modelling human behaviour in economics. Modern economics is grounded on Marshall's architecture of mathematical rigour applied to the understanding of the economics problematic. This has resulted in an economics science that is based on rigorous mathematical analyses anchored on the deductive method of scientific enquiry, and this has how economics has been taught and learnt in the cathedrals of higher learning of capitalistic societies in market economies as well as other economic systems.

The construction of sophisticated models founded upon starting assumptions that have no adherence to reality as a proxy to the simplification of that reality can only lead to outcomes that are as farfetched as the starting assumptions of the models on which they are based. The justification that is often used, that economic models are mere idealizations of reality and that their underlying assumptions are indispensable axioms that are required for the development of these models, does not explain why these axioms should be so detached from reality. If the starting assumptions in economics models are absurd to the point that they have no adherence to any known reality, then the model itself can never be expected to be a useful instrument in predicting reality, and consequently its use to policy-makers is very limited indeed.

An epistemological stance that is grounded on a positivistic view of the world imposes the existence of formal and measurable relationships between variables that social and economic phenomena simply do not possess by virtue of their essence and that of their object of study, human beings and their relationships in open societal systems. In the end, model building with a view to explaining and predicting economic realities that are not moderated by the formal acknowledgement of the behavioural effect of human action, expressed individually or collectively in society, is bound to be rendered as a mere academic exercise of no practical use whatsoever. It is however always in this contextualized way that economic phenomena occur, and it is always in this way that they have to be interpreted when shedding light on contemporary social and economic matters.

In an attempt to give the economics science the legitimacy of the exact sciences there has certainly been a bias on the part of the scientific community towards the adoption of deductive methods of enquiry and methodological traditions that are inherent to research programmes and methods that are to be found more commonly in the exact sciences. As a way of example, the axiom of rationality of economic agents in the analyses of the behaviour of market structures in a situation typified as one of perfect competition is a starting assumption for the purposes of model building that does not conform to any known reality. It is not surprising then, that faced with the shortcomings of theoretical models in economics and their abject and utter failure in explaining underlying phenomena, that the science of economics often needs to resort to compromise solutions.

Herbert Simon's theory of bounded rationality is a good example of a kind of conditioned rationality, one that is limited by the availability of information and one that acknowledges a more humble quest which states that the objective of the exercise does not need to be one of optimization of the economic solution to a problem, as would be the case with a purist Marshallian approach. The difficulty in incorporating the unpredictability and erratic nature of individual and collective human behaviour expressed in groups and even whole societies gives research in economics an added complexity.

In reality the economics sciences are confronted in many cases with the non-verification of two fundamental conditions of scientific scrutiny, namely the absence of external validity in research findings and the inadequacy of the discipline as an instrument for the forecasting of macro-economic variables, at least to the extent that they can significantly aid policy-making and everyday decision-making in economies and in organizations.

Reality is simply too messy and complex to be modelled with the aim of forecasting macro-economic variables, at least with the degree of certainty and accuracy that would constitute a valid tool for organizational planning and policy-making for national economies. The variables in question are mostly idiosyncratic of human behaviour, meaning that the object of study easily drifts away from control and the search for regularities in the relationships between the variables turns out to be a futile exercise more often than not.

The scientific edifice in economics is built through successive paradigm shifts that occur as social scientists seek improved solutions on incumbent ways in which to solve contemporary problems. By way of example, circumstances that will force a shift in paradigm in the economic sciences may derive from the tacit acknowledgement of the eminent shortcomings of mainstream economics in forecasting the financial crisis of 2008 and the consequences to the real economy that soon ensued, at least in a manner that would constitute a clear warning to policy-makers and economic agents alike.

The current state of the art of methodological sophistication and scientific scrutiny into economics issues has not allowed for a better scoping and explanation of contemporary reality and has not aided significantly the forecasting of future outcomes in social and economic systems. The theoretical and conceptual frameworks that sustain the incumbent paradigm have simply failed to account for so much and such diversified variance, and the economics profession struggles to project whatever will come next and the measure in which it will impact on the lives of individuals in societies.

There is a need for a paradigm shift, the revoking of a set of truths that once fitted the bill and were deemed adequate for the purpose of shedding light on social and economic realities, but that are now in dire need of replacement by others, that offer better explanatory capacities to an underlying reality that has changed in the meantime. The falsification of a truth that was apt for a time but has now been revoked by another better truth, one that is a widely accepted improvement on the understanding of current phenomena, is what is required. Better truths that adhere more closely to a contemporary and volatile reality are what the epistemology of the social sciences requires to ensure that the respective disciplines remain relevant and influential.

Methodological pseudo-sophistication, in attempting to model social and economic relationships, including theoretical delving into such complex apparatus as chaos theory, neural networks, bounded rationality and the incorporation of these in economics thinking, and into the theoretical edifice of economics, do not appear to have shed light on the complexity of the behaviour of economic agents and certainly have not done much for the predictive powers of the economics science. However, and even with the adoption of the most sophisticated statistical tools around, including structural equations modelling and other intricate methodologies, it is still impossible to overcome the laborious and erratic unpredictability of individual or collective human behaviour, and that which John Kenneth Galbraith termed the tyranny of circumstance in the description of how sometimes social and economic phenomena simply envelop in the ways that they do.

The critical issue here is that the inherent complexity of social and economic systems makes it awkward and perhaps even impossible to model human and social relationships with a view to predicting individual or collective economic behaviour. It defies belief that this most crucial of shortcomings seems to escape policy-makers in governments and those involved in strategic planning and decision-making in organizations, and not receive much attention from the general or even the specialist media either. The advancement of theory should not be compromised but we cannot collectively afford to underestimate experiential knowledge and a kind of informed intuition in the construction of the scientific building, however unscientific and unpalatable to the traditional scientific scrutiny this may seem.

Clearly, as a way to inform organizational decision-making, complementarity between practice and theory is perhaps the best way to approach the balance of contextual determinism that is imposed by business context on the one hand and a quest for universality in business solutions that tends to be the norm in scientific enquiry into the management sciences on the other. In the end, what matters is that whatever mix of theory and practice is adopted, it should be the best possible way of shedding light on underlying phenomena whilst also contributing to improved forecasting of economic and business issues.

In the end, rather than standing horrified at what is believed to be an impossible concession, an abdication of the criteria of rigour and discipline of the scientific method in its application in the context of the social sciences, perhaps the scientific community needs to begin to question the purpose and validity of an epistemological stance that is grounded on methods of enquiry that belong to the exact sciences but do nothing for the social sciences. The litmus test of any science, exact or not, has to be the ability to diagnose phenomena and, equipped with that, forecast future events and outcomes with a view to improving decision-making.

If we were to randomly ask someone to look at a portfolio of stock with the ultimate aim of picking the optimal choice of company shares in that portfolio the one combination that would be most likely to outperform all other possible combinations for a specific period of time would possibly be unpredictable. It is highly conceivable that the most intellectually gifted and financially versed academics would probably not pick better stock than 50 people chosen randomly from off the street.

On the one hand, there are the infallible mathematical models of Merton and Scholes (Black–Scholes), and on the other, the kind of scientifically shaped but more intuitively informed guesses of people such as renowned investor George Soros who has learnt the art of making money often at the expense of disregarding scientific counsel. What this means from the strict perspective of the optimization of a chosen portfolio of stock and the propensity for predicting its behaviour over time, better, more accurately, and more often than others, is that scientific knowledge helps but may not be the overriding, or even perhaps the most important criterion, in getting it right.

In the end, people like Warren Buffett or George Soros, however idiosyncratic their personalities and particular brand of knowledge that they embody, founded or not on traditional scientific scrutiny, are equipped with something other than the deterministic laws of scientific enquiry, and are perhaps able to combine in one person the statistical average that is the outcome of common sense reasoning, that which comes from asking 50 people randomly on the street about the future performance of stock. To that they add their fundamental knowledge and experience in an amalgamation that perhaps accounts for them getting it right more often than others.

In reality Buffett or Soros have by virtue of their life experiences been able to combine in good measure good old common sense with scientific knowledge, and have refined this into a disciplined alchemy of informed intuition, and this may just perhaps explain why they get it right so much more often than others. This includes probably just about every finance professor in the world, researching and teaching in the best cathedrals of learning in business schools across the world, and it is not a question of unequal access to information.

In effect, there is a fairly good chance that Soros and Buffett would especially get it right better and more often than financial specialists and academics as the way in which they perceive and deal with financial risk may differ from that of scientific risk. The fact that people like Soros have done so much better than anyone else over the past 20 years shows that there is a gap between scientific knowledge and the toolkit that is necessary to optimize performance and investment behaviour in the financial markets.

The filling of this gap and its materialization into an instinct that is undefinable but much sought after and very rare indeed is something that is difficult to instil into individuals, by recourse to conventional learning methods only. It is an acquired skill and can be learnt but it is perhaps more experiential in nature, and the underlying skills that it requires do not derive from formal learning techniques.

The difficulty here is in packaging this toolkit of intuition or acquired skills and capabilities or whatever it may be, and sell it in as an integral part of an MBA curriculum in a top business school somewhere out there. In such things as predicting the market behaviour of a portfolio of stock, the problem is that nobody has thus far been able to model the impact of intuition on stock market investment strategies and investor behaviour.

Since the object of study is the human being there is a fairly good chance that this cannot be replicated in a laboratory and simply cannot be neatly modelled and organized into knowledge, at least with an acceptable degree of accuracy, that would allow for a set of rules and procedures to apply in each context, with a modicum of guaranteed success, when it comes to making investment decisions in the financial markets.

Many of the so-called purists, mostly academics in elitist cathedrals of knowledge the world over would in crude terms become very wealthy if they only knew how to systematically beat the stock market. Some of course do, but perhaps not more than the average individual in a given population. The debate should therefore not be as much about the superiority of the arguments of the theoretical versus the practical camps, but about paradigm complementarity. It is about perceptions of financial risk versus intuitive risk, scientific scrutiny of risk against feeling the market and intuiting its behaviour and evolution, and drawing inferences and patterns for future reference.

The randomness of the whole thing justifies an intuitive and experiential approach and confers legitimacy to this notion, which is as valid as any in shedding light on the erratic complexity and pure madness of financial market behaviour. The intricacy of these phenomena can certainly be given scientific scope and structure, but it is probably impossible to attempt to derive deterministic conclusions or even search for causal relationships between the variables and model them in neat ways that lead to predictable outcomes.

Most probably it is impossible to model most aspects of human behaviour with a degree of accuracy that allows for pinpointing future events, or for the kind of forecasting that would serve policy-makers and strategists alike. Attempting to draw deterministic causal relationships and modelling human behaviour, individually and collectively, expressed in societal dynamics, that are shaped by variables whose behaviour is uncontrollable, that relate to cultural diversity and differing aesthetics, very likely amounts to an exercise that is condemned to failure.

It is probably a good approximation to the truth to say that it is impossible to model human behaviour when it is human behaviour really that is the object of the social sciences. Any credible attempt at predicting the behaviour of stock markets for example needs to incorporate the dynamics of human behaviour, expressed collectively in the interactions of individuals in society and their resultant economic transactions. Group dynamics are difficult to understand and to predict, who follows who and why, calculated behaviour, spontaneity, risk-taking, who belongs in which camp, and how many there are of each, at any particular point in time and how influential they are.

All of this is impossible to model, as is power asymmetry and structures of influence in groups, peer pressure, the erratic and unpredictable behaviour of individuals and societies, and the dynamics underlying investor behaviour. In essence, the random, casino-like atmosphere that characterizes this complex system of interconnectivity and relationships cannot be made sense of, at least in ways and with the kind of accuracy that suffices the certainty requirements of investors.

Some argue that they can indeed make sense of this all and with carefully manicured arrogance make the rest of us mere mortals believe that the level of intellectual sophistication entailed in seeing the light has not been democratically distributed. But what is at stake here is again the irrefutable fact they simply cannot get it right. They are unable to forecast the future behaviour of macro-economic indicators better than anyone's wild guesses, and they are simply unable to outperform the average punter on stock market investments, at least in ways that would justify the cost of the marginal time and effort put into the acquisition of their particular brand of knowledge.

There are obviously those who very legitimately live in constant pursuit of the holy grail of neat models, who strive for a kind of simplicity that is inherent to direct causal links and relationships between variables and who avidly seek and wholeheartedly believe in structure and linearity when attempting to shed light on complex social and economic phenomena. This is most probably a utopian quest for universal pseudo-truths for all times, when instead what scientific query should aim for is verisimilitude, approximations to the truth. This is a permanent search for better truths, truths that are more apt for certain times but are only waiting to be refuted and falsified and replaced by new and better truths, better explanatory schemata that approximate as much as is possible the changing nature and requirements of contemporary societal issues and problems. In formulating economic policy, not understanding this simply means that measures that are conceptually adequate in particular contexts, and are introduced in the pursuit of certain objectives, end up having perverse effects and often ones that are contrary to what was initially intended.

Not too long ago there was a fair degree of controversy when a southern European government decided to liberalize fuel prices. The legislator wanted to ultimately benefit the consumer with measures, whose aim it was to open up the market and introduce real price competition at the retail level of the business. The superiority of the argument of free-market competition as the supreme mechanism for obtaining optimal retail consumer prices, an instrument for guaranteeing that the demand and supply of fuel products were adequately and justly reflected by market prices made theoretical sense. In this particular case however the outcome was not what the policy-maker intended or expected.

The theory went that in an open market environment, incumbents would compete unhindered and freely. Market players would supply a homogeneous product, with little latitude for relevant differentiation and thus had to be competitive by deriving efficiencies that would in turn translate into lower retail prices to consumers, who in turn buy strictly on price. Conceptually, these measures make absolute sense in that this is indeed a market with great price sensitivity – punters switch easily as petrol is close to being an undifferentiated product – in a business where there is little room for brand loyalty, and thus a strong propensity for substitution of the retail provider exists. But this was only conceptually.

Policy-makers expected to generate what economists designate as consumer surpluses. The consumer would benefit in the form of lower retail prices. Did that happen? It clearly did not. What came into fruition instead was that the petrol companies collectively (a parliamentary commission was not able to establish whether there was indeed a concerted effort at cartelization) began to increase consumer fuel prices when oil prices went up but were much more reticent in dropping retail prices when crude prices decreased again.

The problem was then literally one of viscosity. The price mechanism was much more oiled when it came to increasing retail consumer prices than when lowering them. There was clearly a greater reluctance on the part of retailers in lowering prices than in increasing them. Various explanations came from the sector as to why this was happening, some more complex than others, but essentially pointing to the fallacy of looking only at recent oil price variations as a proxy to the determination of current fuel retail prices.

The explanation pointed towards the price of fuel at any point in time being a function of complex algorithms, and that in order to understand pricing in this industry one would have to incorporate other variables, including crude prices that date back to three or four months before, when the fuel that is now being sold in petrol stations was in effect purchased. Once again this argument does not explain the greater reluctance in reducing fuel prices when contrasted with the easiness with which fuel prices tended to go up in the light of increases in crude prices.

In this case, even in the absence of variations in the prices of oil, retail fuel prices still increased, which was unexpected as the intended policy outcome had precisely been the opposite. By liberalizing retail markets, fuel prices were expected to go down but they never did. The perverse effect of a well-intentioned measure was that prices not only did not go down, in effect they went up.

There may have been several reasons for this phenomenon, and there certainly was no shortage in the way of explanations for it to have occurred, but perhaps the most poignant reason for the unexpected outcome for a well-intentioned policy measure is that when policy is formulated, the underlying context in all its dimensions, social, legal and cultural, needs to be understood clearly as to its possible ramifications and how it stands to impact on the intended policy outcome. This means thinking through every possible way in which contextual macro-environmental dimensions are likely to subvert and undermine the ultimate aims and objectives that are inherent to the formulation of policy in the first place.

These are not times for magic potions and universal solutions that are inter-contextual and susceptible to extrapolation from organization to organization, from sector to sector and from country to country. More and more the study of economics and the management sciences should be grounded in the analysis of best practices and the context in which they occur, and how and why they stand a good chance of being successful or indeed not.

These best practices need to be subsequently adjusted to the specific requirements and characteristics of the economic sector in question, as well as the specificities of the organization and the culture in which it is embedded. Best practices also need to be scrutinized as to their adequacy in terms of the socio-economic and demographic contexts in which they are embedded, and with respect to every aspect of the macro-environment that may contribute to organizational success, or be blamed for the lack of it.

There exist a number of organizational stakeholders whose interests are complementary but often also antagonistic. Top management in organizations need to constantly balance the conflicting interests of stakeholders. These are in effect the various publics that surround the organization and have a vested interest in it, including its shareholders, customers, employees, suppliers, managers and any other entity with manifested explicit or implicit interests in the functioning of the organization.

Organizational objectives need to therefore be managed with a view to walking a tight rope, a fine equilibrium that requires a multiple perspective, one that harmoniously balances the often conflicting interests of stakeholders. The organization has to be seen as a going concern and this ultimately depends on its ability to constantly align the interests of stakeholders to the point where they coexist and are mutually re-enforcing.

The balanced management of the interests of organizational stakeholders forces a shift away from traditional thinking about the role and purpose of organizations embedded in the incumbent paradigm of economics that dates back to Marshall and which stipulates that the overriding objective of firms should be that of profit maximization, subject to production function restrictions. In reality, the interests of organizational stakeholders are often not sufficiently aligned, requiring instead balanced solutions, leadership, negotiation and strategic vision, rather than the maximization of any particular objective.

A successful organization needs to be able to adapt to change, even to welcome change and incorporate it as perhaps the only constant variable in corporate life. Change management is particularly important with regards to monitoring the macro-environment surrounding the business. The organization needs to constantly challenge the status quo, be intolerant to complacency, be able to harmonize the internal and external perspectives of key stakeholders, and fulfil its expected role in the functioning of the economy and the betterment of the lives of individuals in the wider society.

Reality Check...

Häagen Dazs

An example of exceptional value aggregation through branding has been that of another American company, Häagen Dazs, and how it came to defy every rule in the food marketing book when it came to Europe. This stipulates that merchandise needs to be made available to as many prospective customers as is possible. Häagen Dazs entered the European market through a whispering campaign, whereby using what could be loosely termed as brand ambassadors, influential individuals and unsuspected opinion-makers, they managed to effectively spread the message around.

As they brought their brand to the European market, they began to achieve notoriety in closed circles, an awareness created casually by these brand ambassadors who were seen consuming the product or in some way associated with the brand. At the same time, the brand would be sold in exclusive shops in Covent Garden, or the Champs-Élysées, and in other elitist neighbourhoods of the principal European capitals. Häagen Dazs took some pages from the book on how to successfully market luxury goods and applied it to food marketing.

In particular it drew some lessons from the luxury end of the perfume sector, offering samples to people who wanted to try the product, getting people to spread the word, thus starting a whispering campaign. Soon everyone was listening. The brand would gain an unprecedented notoriety, progressing from cult status to becoming a well-known and established brand in the European market where it had no previous history.

As an interesting point, the words Häagen Dazs have no etymological meaning or are in any way grounded on any family of languages. They are gibberish, but they phonetically resemble and suggest a German or Scandinavian background, Nordic qualities, an aura of mysticism, enigmatic secrecy and purposeful ambiguity. Häagen Dazs is in effect an American brand.

8

Bernanke and an Urgent Need for a Paradigm Shift

Ben Shalom Bernanke, Chairman of the Federal Reserve Bank, stated at the height of the financial crisis that not to have intervened in the solvency of the institutions of the financial system and to have allowed important constituents of the system to disintegrate would have been a fatal mistake, with unimaginable consequences to the real economy. It would have been a popular decision in the short term and a welcomed one next to certain sectors of opinion, but nonetheless a decision of irreparable consequences.

To have allowed the financial system to break down would have been a decision that would have harnessed some votes for populist politicians, but it would equally have been a demagogical decision, demonstrative of a lack of understanding of the complexity, interconnectivity and central role of the financial system in the functioning of modern economies. By way of an intricate set of complex links, much of them marginal to the real economy, a severe disruption of the modern financial system may indeed cause indescribable mayhem to economic activity.

In times of diminished collective confidence in economic systems, individuals and businesses are confronted with obstacles in establishing creditworthiness and obtaining loans, starting businesses or pursuing quotidian economic activities. On the other hand, the interface between organizations and the financial system also manifests itself in dubious and often sinister speculative operations that fatally fall outside their modus operandi and core business activities.

When someone asked Bernanke to explain what had happened to the world's financial system in the course of the current crisis, and particularly to justify the unequal treatment given to its institutions, namely the bailing out by the American federal government of banks and other financial institutions when organizations in other sectors of economic activity did not benefit from the same privilege, he had a good answer.

For Ben Bernanke, the son of Jewish immigrants from eastern Europe, simple God and law abiding folk, running a small business in the middle of nowhere, this would be a pertinent question, as people like him, with a family background of hard work and difficulties ascending the social ladder, would be precisely those who would benefit from measures supporting small family businesses and not the huge bail outs of corporate giants and banks. Bernanke, however, used an interesting analogy which helps to explain the priority of financial institutions when it comes to injecting liquidity into the system, with a view to retrieving any type of normality to the economy.

For Bernanke, any institution of the financial system in trouble is akin to a house engulfed in flames in a neighbourhood of wooden houses. The house is on fire because the neighbour, drunk, fell asleep having lit a cigarette. The fire anecdote is a metaphor and for the purposes herein the house is a bank. In fact, the neighbour's house catching fire is in a strict sense not our problem. Yet we still need to call the fire department. Not for moral or ethical reasons, but because if we do not there is a serious risk that the next house to be set alight is ours. In a neighbourhood of wooden houses, a small house fire becomes all too quickly a community catastrophe.

Despite not having any direct or indirect responsibility, as we are not drinking companions of our unruly neighbour, and having given up smoking many years ago, or not having smoked ever, we are still in trouble. We may condemn his behaviour or find his moral and ethical conduct reprehensible but we are nevertheless an integral part to the consequences of his act.

Paradoxically, should we fail to cooperate in extinguishing the fire consuming his house, the consequences of our inaction imply that we are co-responsible by not acting in accordance with the circumstances, thus making us part of the problem. Our house burns down along with those of others who are also peripheral to the initial cause of the problem, people that had never met the neighbour before, many of them non-smokers, and most with a track record of being on their best behaviour all of their lives. That is the crux of the matter and makes Bernanke advocate a different approach when it comes to the constituent institutions of the financial system. Because if they were to fall we would all fall with them.

With organizations it is different. There are complex links, interactions and economic relationships within corporations and between corporations and other economic actors. The domino effect created by firm bankruptcy and the interdependency of organizations in competitive and intertwined markets requires a different approach to the consequences of a systemic failure of organizations in the real economy to that of a blanket failure of the institutions in the financial system.

The institutions of the financial system are interdependent but not in the same way. Whilst companies in the real economy are competitive but often complementary in their activities in that they may operate at different levels of the value chain, financial institutions have a more intricate interdependency, one that results from the peculiar nature of their business activities and the products they trade in.

Banks are financed by other banks and buy financial products from other financial institutions. They mitigate risk by engaging in financial operations traded by global financial institutions operating in several countries. Banks invest the savings of depositors in financial products in markets worldwide, following a complex and intricate logic whose common denominator is the fluidity of capital, a mobility that is unparalleled in the history of human economic relationships. The ease with which this is done is fuelled by revolutionary technology in the domain of electronic commerce that has forever changed the landscape of financial transactions. Its main consequence is a drastic reduction in distance between actors in this complex landscape, both psychological but also geographical and time distance.

People buy and sell from other people and organizations the world over, instantly, as psychological barriers, as a result of cultural estrangement, are easily broken down by a common understanding of new codes of conduct in commerce. A complete absence of barriers to the trade of financial products, whose principal characteristic is intangibility, an absence of physical expression and often intractability characterizes capital flows in the sophisticated financial marketplaces of today. Intangibility is critical here as it often equates to intractability. If it can't be seen, it is much more difficult to trace.

Organizational financial risk exposure is dependant, along with other variables, upon corporate objectives and of course management and leadership style, but it is also most critically dependent upon shareholder pressure for healthy financial results. Shareholders tend to be very receptive to annual dividends and enjoy an appreciation of their own stockholdings, but are much more critical of losses in firm market capitalization.

Beyond intangibility and fluidity, financial products are also characterized by being less homogeneous than other products. Financial products have no physical embodiment and are heterogeneous in their composition, making the tracing of their origin a much more difficult endeavour. Financial products are often composites of other products of varied origins.

Returning to Bernanke's burning house analogy, we may not smoke in bed or drink uncontrollably, however the direct consequences of our unruly neighbour's behaviour affect not only himself or his family but all those who live nearby, and eventually everyone in the community. This is true irrespective of the fact that we have never met this person before nor would we willingly engage with him in any form of social interaction. The extrapolation of this part of the analogy to the financial markets leads to the notion that, independently of whether or not we have money invested in high-risk and toxic financial products, the viability of the financial system is always of concern to us all.

Of course, had we invested in toxic financial products, then the fire would have reached us first. However, even if we have not invested in high-risk financial products and all we have are sound investments in long-term deposits of guaranteed capital, the insolvency of the financial system would be sure to hit us as soon as we were to need credit to finance business projects or for real estate purchases. Quite simply the financial system is the lifeblood of the real economy. In this anatomical analogy, the sectors of economic activity are organs of the economic body and corporations are cells in this system. If critical organs fail, given the systemic interdependence of most aspects of the human anatomy, there is every likelihood that the very survival of the individual is jeopardized. However there is always the possibility that the failure of individual systems may be limited to those systems. With the circulatory system it is more complicated as it irrigates all the other systems and organs in the human body.

The analogy is also adequate in the sense that sector crises are rarely autonomous and their consequences are often systemic. Crises in the automotive, textiles, clothing, footwear or semi-conductor industries will have a detrimental impact on other sectors of economic activity. A decrease in demand for products and services in a particular sector will cause rising unemployment in other sectors of the economy, with overall consumption diminishing as a result of lower disposable income and less spending in the economy. This is made worse in small geographic areas as an interdependence of relatively few economic activities implies that the crisis spreads quickly.

Rising unemployment and the loss of disposable income reduces demand for products that originate in other sectors, and the crisis of one sector will negatively impact others and often the entire region. But the analogy of the circulatory system serves mainly to emphasize the notion that the institutions of the financial system are not in this respect just like any other corporation operating in other sectors of economic activity, whose sole purpose of existence is the provision of ordinary goods and services. The financial system is the lifeblood of the economy and in normal conditions constitutes a good barometer of the health and prosperity of an economic system.

Exploring the analogy a bit further, had everyone in the region built wooden houses and had wind conditions been ideal for the propagation of the fire, it would have been highly unlikely for it to have been contained and restricted to only a few houses. A disaster would have inevitably ensued. The consequences of an otherwise innocuous fire would turn out to be catastrophic. This means that even in the most optimistic of times, prudence and a conservative posture to risk management are good qualities to keep in mind. It also means that these systems are interlinked and mutually influence one another.

So, in conclusion, ideally one's neighbour should not smoke in bed, nor should we need a government to closely monitor his behaviour. In an ideal world we can do without irresponsible neighbours whose behaviour jeopardizes our lives, but it is a fact of life that now and again, in the course of our lives, we do come across people like that. When that happens in a democratic society, where the rule of law applies, we allow the judicial system to work its ways. The metaphorical arson that was the relatively recent crisis of the financial system should fall into this category. Moreover, the analogy seems adequate in that it serves perfectly to explain what has happened to the world's financial system since 2008 and its disastrous impact on the real economy.

It should be noted that in this story the houses were all made of wood, a crucial point, in that it refers to the mutual interdependency and intricate links between the constituent institutions of a financial system that is characterized by complex relationships between parties that operate globally. The rapid spread of the fire relates to the globalization of economic activity and the fluidity of financial transactions.

Business opportunities arise from perceived and real differences in economic development and disposable income in different regions of the world. The relative ease with which capital flows across global markets from Tokyo to London or New York mirrors an environment of such economic interdependency that it has now become impossible to define geographic boundaries for money and rights of property, and difficult to pinpoint its origins and where it is invested. Technology and electronic funds transfers have made this easy. This raises issues of jurisprudence and has made salient a gap between judicial architectures the world over and the challenges of economic and financial globalization.

In completion of the analogy, the wind refers to the unique meteorological conditions that have prevailed at a particular point in time and thus have uniquely contributed to the crisis spreading to most developed economies in the world. These conditions were particularly favourable to the occurrence of a global crisis in the financial markets at this particular time, in an environment of weak regulation and after years of permanent growth when cautionary guards tend to come down and complacency creeps up.

In this atmosphere of euphoria and perceived unlimited economic growth, the then British Prime Minister Gordon Brown at one point promised an end to the cycles of boom and bust, and a brighter future of permanent economic growth. With this kind of endorsement, financial institutions felt the political backing to legitimize what turned out to be unreasonably risky behaviour. Not that they needed it but it helped. This would prove fatal and serious consequences to the world economy soon ensued. On the other hand, corporations began to misrepresent their true essence, nature or purpose as productive entities, taking their eye off the ball and of their raison d'être, beginning instead to engage in what turned out to be no more than financial speculation.

The systemic nature of global economic activity, the impact of Wall Street on the global economy, the size of the US economy, its real and psychological importance to the rest of the world, have meant that there is an intricate interdependency between economies and economic systems worldwide. The fact that recent economic powerhouses, and most notably China, whose principles and beliefs on the economy have so rapidly travelled from feudal bureaucratic autocracy to the embracement of a form of state capitalism deep-rooted in millenary merchant traditions, has meant that this interdependency is now truly global.

A crisis such as that caused by the sub-prime fiasco in the US could not but take on a whole new meaning in the light of the intricate networks that characterize global economic and financial relationships. The proliferation of high-risk toxic financial products, stemming from the most sophisticated financial system in the world, was more than likely to have devastating effects on the rest of the world.

These effects were compounded by an underestimation of the unpredictability and erratic nature of human collective behaviour, the difficulties in conveniently modelling it and its role in contemporary economics, all issues that have begun to be scrutinized now but are still not regarded in high esteem by the prevailing quantitative paradigm in economics and finance research.

The culture of the US financial system and its constituent institutions, from the Fed to the investment banks and the rating agencies, has had a knock-on effect on the rest of the world that goes beyond the global pull of the US economy, even by its mammoth standards. The psychological underpinnings to the influence of the US financial system and the behaviour of its constituent institutions have meant that traditionally strong institutions with conservative ideologies expressed in responsible postures to risk have allowed themselves to get carried away by promises of an Eldorado of unlimited payoffs, having in many cases ultimately decided against their better judgement to engage in risky behaviour that ran counter to any sound analysis of the economic fundamentals.

Bernanke's analogy was made in an interview given at the peak of the financial crisis. It constitutes perhaps the best contemporary justification for government intervention in the financial system. Governments can these days ill-afford to enable institutions that have committed serious errors through the greed and incompetence of those who serve them to carry on as if nothing has happened.

These institutions and their top executives are beginning to emerge yet again as paladins of a pseudo-elitist unregulated and unchecked brand of corporate culture, when the current architecture of modern economies demands responsible and competent constituents in a new and more efficient global financial system. To have allowed the core institutions at the heart of the financial system to fall would have had profound consequences to the real economy globally, but to subsequently endorse the very types of behaviours that brought us to where we are is beyond comprehension.

In 1929 the New York stock market crash was very soon followed by the Great Depression. The consequences for the American economy were devastating. A meltdown of the core of the financial system in 2008 would have seen disproportionately more severe consequences than in 1929, given the global interdependency of markets and economic flows today. The intricate interconnectivity of the different elements and components of the financial system, the mobility of capital and the globalization of economic activity would have meant that a severe disruption of the nucleus of the financial system would see disturbing consequences to economic activity worldwide.

Interestingly, when queried on the matter, Bernanke conceded that we had indeed been close to a meltdown of the financial system when Lehman Brothers was allowed to collapse by the government institutions that could have but did not step in to intervene. Bernanke, perhaps not coincidentally, has the advantage of carrying a personal wealth of expertise which perhaps makes him the right person for the job. Bernanke was appointed Chairman of the Federal Reserve Bank at a time when the historical precedent that most closely matches the situation that was experienced in 2008 was the 1929 crash and the Great Depression that ensued soon after. Bernanke's doctorate at Harvard and the scientific area of scrutiny that he was to devote his scholarly time to subsequently was precisely that of the great financial crisis of 1929.

A failure to have intervened in the institutions of the financial system thus ensuring their solvency would have certainly dragged down others with unfathomable consequences to the real economy of production of goods and services. Interestingly, Bernanke is well-known for being a fierce opponent of highly paid but incompetent top executives and his anger legendary when confronted with the obscene bonuses paid to executives of companies with little more than poor business performance records to show for their achievements. This was clearly the case with AIG, for example, but not only. Bailing out the likes of Lehman Brothers must not have been a palatable decision for the Chairman of the Fed.

Bernanke proposes a third way to the dichotomy of market purism on the one hand and ad-hoc government bailouts of individual acts of sheer managerial incompetence and often criminal behaviour on the other. It does not have to be a choice between the market working its ways on the one hand and the endorsement of bad management on the other as two opposing and mutually exclusive alternatives. The government has leeway to acknowledge and pursue a third option. He proposes a gradual disintegration of those corporations that make no business sense, organizations that fail to meet the criteria of economic feasibility now and in the future.

The advantage to this approach is that it allows for the gradual absorption and dilution of the consequences of the disintegration of corporate giants with tentacles in various sectors. The political and social advantages to a gradual and progressive dismemberment of these corporations are manifold, as a progressive loss of employment is more easily manageable and absorbed than the alternative of brutal cut-backs of tens of thousands of jobs, often in circumscribed geographical regions.

The constituent institutions of the financial system have become the ugly duckling of modern economies, and strategic decisions to bail them out have not been popular. However, despite public animosity, even if only in principle against government intervention in the banking system, it is nevertheless paradoxical, albeit not irrational, that investors that have incurred substantial losses with the financial crisis but at one time enjoyed handsome returns on their investments be the ones to claim that the government should come to their aid, a government whose intervention they once vehemently opposed and indeed considered anathema.

Many only too quickly began to understand the impact on the real economy of a possible collapse in the financial system. Those were the very same people that have begun to reconsider their position on the role of government and its duty to intervene in the economy if and when required. The ramifications of a possible meltdown of the financial system would have extended to all sectors of the economy, causing vast unemployment through a dramatic contraction of economic activity, job insecurity and instability about the future. The difficulty that governments have under these circumstances is in activating credible economic recovery mechanisms, given the breach of trust in the financial system and its constituents.

Taken aback by the ease with which we have reached this state of affairs and the permissiveness of government in allowing it to happen, ordinary people rationally revert to short-term economic survival strategies as important pillars of social equilibrium are damaged beyond recognition. This is particularly true of government institutions but also of the institutions of the financial system, banks with whom regular people had entrusted their lifesavings and pension funds, safety nests arduously built supposedly to take them into later life.

Once broken, the emotional bond of trust is irreparable, at least with the same systems, mechanisms and people around.

The economic and social costs of a breach of trust in the financial system and its impact on the lives of citizens should not be restricted to the measurement of the impact of a slowdown in economic activity. There are deeper and more sinister consequences. A lower efficacy of traditional monetary policy instruments in stimulating economic recovery in a context of low confidence in political and financial structures is one of the principal costs of an institutional reputational breakdown.

Trust is thus a crucial yet underestimated criterion for effective macro-economic policy formulation. Without trust, individuals revert to basic economic behaviour, tending to their personal survival and that of their families as primary individual and collective concerns. Survival in a climate of lack of confidence in the institutions of the political and economic systems means a rush to liquidity in an attempt to maintain similar standards of living to those that one has been accustomed to in the short or medium term. If this is not possible the citizen gradually abdicates of aspects of his lifestyle, prioritizing expenditure and, wherever possible, continuing to pay the mortgage and keeping children in good schools. Until that too is no longer possible.

Often, given the ease with which they have climbed the socio-economic ladder, the downward path naturally becomes extremely painful. The problem is that more often than not the former upward mobility of individuals had been built on very shaky foundations and this typifies the lives of citizens in many uncompetitive economies that are riddled by debt. Given the precariousness of employment and the untenable levels of private debt incurred over years of conspicuous consumption, mainly attributable to the explosive mix of an irresponsible concession of consumer credit by the retail banking system and a profound lack of common sense, the situation has quickly become unbearable for many.

Many of the very serious insolvency situations that we witness today would not have happened were there to have been regulatory mechanisms in place that would have imposed credible credit restrictions, thus ensuring responsible credit engagement on real estate purchases and consumption. The speculators would also not have lived the Eldorado of the 1980s and 1990s had this been the case. That said, nothing replaces common sense and the fundamental notion that it is bad counsel to engage in conspicuous consumption, especially if there is no economic basis to justify it.

This applies to countries as well as individuals. For the average citizen this simply means that it is never advisable to overspend consistently unless one is investing in one's education and training with a view to generating future marginal income. Of course blame for irresponsible consumption should be apportioned to the individual first, as the abdication of responsibility and its resting with government, and the easiness of credit concession by retail banks or any other external entity are obvious signs of a serious shortcoming in the collective relationship with basic notions of active citizenship and personal freedom.

Government is responsible for the provision of education to its citizens, and this includes a fundamental understanding of the dynamics as well as of the pitfalls of modern day consumption and its idiosyncrasies. In some of the smaller European economies, including Portugal and Greece, but not only, governments did little to curb the widespread enthusiasm that naturally came with economic growth and the blessings and promises of continuous prosperity that the 1990s offered.

Much of this, of course largely unfounded, as an underlying real economy of production of goods and services, simply failed to materialize, which tragically led to artificial and unsubstantiated affluence. On the contrary, many of these countries were encouraged upon accession to the European Economic Community (EEC) to dismantle the industrial infrastructure they had in place at the time in the name of a services Eldorado that was supposed to have ensued.

The financial crisis of 2008 and its consequences on the real economy will rest high in the agenda of governments for years to come. First governments need to search for more effective methods of market stabilization and perhaps find mechanisms that dilute the dependency of the real economy upon the vagaries of financial institutions. Secondly governments should be able to better monitor the behaviour and scope of intervention of these organizations on the economy and the lives of people.

Finding a balanced regulatory environment that allows for the functioning of the institutions of the financial system and other constituents in the real economy, whilst ensuring that they do not exceed their brief or at least operate within the boundaries of accepted ethics and practice, does not seem to be asking for the world. This is a major task for the legislator but there is yet another concern which should occupy the agenda of governments for years to come. It is a concern for the long-term, strategic rethinking of the interface between financial institutions and the real economy of production, and between these institutions and the lives of common people, all issues that deserve careful scrutiny as a model of financial speculative pseudo-development is all but exhausted.

Of particular concern is the arduous reconciliation between the diktat of global finance and its most representative institutions and the functioning of democratic systems. Recurring protestation, gatherings at world leader conferences, rallies against the IMF and other supranational organizations show at best a public unease with the institutions that have come to symbolize capitalism. In Europe citizens come out in hundreds of thousands protesting vehemently against severe austerity measures in debt-ridden economies. Many see these very restrictive limitations on their livelihoods as vindictive and unfair impositions from the institutions that are under the thumb and control of the bastions of capitalism on these societies.

A few years ago at a meeting of the G20 in London, and later in Pittsburgh, many came together to challenge the ideas of capitalism, the free-market, the growing inequality in income distribution and the ever widening gap between the rich and the poor of the world. Strong protests and social unrest soon ensued. The intensity of these protests and the blame apportioned on what people perceived to be a set of fundamental beliefs, entrenched in the ideas of pure capitalism, have received wide acceptance in these troubled times. The belief that the rich nations can no longer turn a blind eye to inequality has been such that the leaders of these nations cannot but give these protests their undivided attention.

Whilst these events are recurrent and anti-capitalist animosity appears to be as strong and intense as ever, the degree of violence in these conferences looks to be increasing. People are fed up and the tolerance threshold appears to have been reached. They have protested in the streets of London, Madrid, Lisbon or Athens, stoning windows of banking institutions, retail multinationals and everything they see as a symbol of a system that they perceive to be the root of all evil.

This particular brand of capitalism traces its modern-day political and economic foundations to Thatcher and Reagan, whose ideologues,

Milton Friedman and the School of Economics at the University of Chicago, successfully endorsed their own-brand of neoclassical monetarism, free-market fundamentalism and radical emptying of the role of government and its scope of intervention in the economy.

Philosophically grounded on the principles of government non-intervention that quickly translated into the deregulation and privatization of key sectors of economic activity, this model for many years unquestionably offered unparalleled economic development to the world and put money into the pockets of ordinary people. This should not be underplayed, as the idea of disposable income for the masses is historically a recent phenomenon.

However, and as things began to go sour, with collective memory being short, capitalism was soon to epitomize everything that was wrong in modern-day contemporary social systems, an intolerable ideology, synonymous with human exploitation, and the genesis of unparalleled inequality. It didn't really matter that all of this was historically inaccurate or that never before were so many enjoying standards of living that were unimaginable only a few decades earlier. A deep animosity towards capitalistic ideas had gained firm roots, fermented in an ideological soup ranging from environmentalist groups and the radical left wing to what became known during the Blair years as the so-called third way.

The abandonment of the Keynesian paradigm and its underlying conceptual architecture, where government intervention in the economy was pivotal, was followed by neoclassical monetarism and supply-side economics. The core ideologues and intellectual substance feeding this movement came from the Chicago School of Economics, who had since the early 1980s served as the ideological platform of economic science behind political Thatcherism in Britain and Reaganomics in the US.

The chronological simultaneity of the manifestation of this doctrine in these two very powerful nations and their theoretical grounding on the monetarist conceptual paradigm, created both in the USA and the UK a disturbing and dangerous belief that the market had an in-built capacity to self-adjust, regenerate and find long-term equilibriums following imbalance and distortion.

With unemployment reaching worrying levels in western Europe and unprecedented economic crises that have led to the intervention of the IMF and the EU in Ireland, Greece, Spain and Portugal, in some way or another, the future looks bleak for what was not too long ago a dreamlike world for the citizens of these countries. These and other economies are riddled with public debt and have no credible, sustainable strategies for getting out of the mess that they are in.

The problems afflicting these countries can be traced back to different roots, with Ireland for example clearly being a poignant case of a failure of the financial institutions in exercising a degree of conservative caution and the others in failing to take advantage of successive aid packages to invest in the determinants of real competitiveness in their respective economies. However, and to different degrees, all of these countries suffer from a structural lack of competitiveness in their economies that makes it difficult to attract FDI or to follow the path of value aggregation to the exports of goods and services emanating from these economies.

A past of EU subsidization, bailouts and a deep-rooted dependency culture is not alien to the problems that these countries are currently experiencing. The window of opportunity that constituted the EU structural aid packages was not properly and strategically made use of to make these economies much more competitive in world markets when the rug was to be removed from underneath them at a subsequent stage.

These countries along with others have a public-debt problem, but the real problem that these economies have is that they are not focussed enough on the real economy of production of goods and services. These countries have deep structural imbalances in their economies and a strategic misconception as to what are the determinants of economic recovery and how to go about improving on these. A historical lack of fiscal discipline, heavy public sectors, disproportionate public spending in relation to underlying economic realities and a distorted view of the road to economic recovery are deep-rooted problems afflicting all of these countries.

Portugal is a good example of all of the above. There tends to be an excessive emphasis on national accounting and the public finances by the intelligentsia and the technocrats and not enough on the micro-economy. A dangerous underestimation of the role of firms in the economy, a failure to understand the idiosyncrasies of market demand in sophisticated environments and an underplaying of the critical importance of value aggregation to goods and services typifies these economies. There is also a general reluctance in going out of a protective and bureaucratic comfort zone to compete globally and fight stagnation through exports.

One of the problems with the recent intervention of the triad of the European Commission, the European Central Bank and the IMF was the difficulty found in establishing exactly the nature and composition of overall public debt as data on the spending of the municipalities and public transportation corporations had not been fully accounted for. The case of Greece before that is indicative of the dangers and the fallacy of relying on country statistics that are often fudged to political convenience or to what is euphemistically labelled as the national interest.

The financial crisis of 2008 arose from inordinate risk-taking behaviour and the aggressive postures of important institutions in the financial system whose consequences gradually propagated to the real economy. Businesses and families were as a consequence faced with enormous difficulties in obtaining credit, despite successive reference interest rate cuts from central banks. The climate of insecurity about the future and the collective lack of trust in the institutions of the financial system meant that individuals began to resort to conservative behaviour, a preference for liquidity and an aversion to investment and risk.

Those living off their wages placed their savings into bank deposits of guaranteed capital return. However, a climate of pending economic instability and unprecedented vulnerability, at least by modern standards, with threats to the livelihoods of people and horror stories about the institutions and organizations that they had learnt to trust, has meant that many have rightfully assumed that nothing is safe anymore, including banks, despite government guarantees on deposits and the safety of the capital invested. Public confidence in the banking system significantly eroded and the reputational capital of banks was damaged with the financial crisis of 2008. Collective suspicion on the banking system has allayed since but it will take a long time before things return to normal, if ever.

Governments have not acted prudently in the regulation of the activities of the financial institutions, or that of organizations, which in the pursuit of profits that are untenable in their core lines of activity simply decided against their better judgement to deviate from their businesses and vocations and engage in risky speculative schemes. These complex ventures in which many sank into were indeed murky waters, areas of economic activity whose principles and criteria for success many simply did not dominate or understand.

The fact that corporations from every sector of economic activity would engage in speculative investment activities of varying degrees of risk, that demanded little in the way of competitive competencies in core economic functions, only meant that the eventual collapse of major institutions of the financial system, were it allowed to happen, would have hit the real economy even harder as it meant that the speculative financial economy was intertwined with the real economy of production of goods and services.

The Lehman Brothers debacle, or to a lesser extent that of Barings Bank, and their real as well as psychological impacts on the economy and the lives of ordinary citizens was disproportionate and unacceptable. The same thinking goes for the shenanigans and corporate wrongdoings that characterized much of the 1990s, including the WorldCom, Enron, Arthur Anderson or AIG cases. Most of these signified more than corporate mismanagement and were indeed found to have criminal ramifications that were to be dealt with by the judicial system. Much of this was endorsed by a culture of unregulated permissiveness that was purportedly tautological with the virtues of the free-market system. In fact it was all but that.

People just got fed up with all of this. The main reason for an animosity of the magnitude of that which occurred a few years ago at the G20 summit in London was the collective perception of intolerable interference in the lives of ordinary citizens, from institutions that were clearly not mandated to exert that kind of destructive influence on society. Add to that the idea that governments did nothing to prevent the instruments of unbridled capitalism to operate freely and without restriction against citizens and it all begins to look and feel a lot like conspiracy or incompetence depending on which side of the ideological fence one sits on. Perhaps both would be a fair diagnosis of the situation.

Such permissiveness in relation to the modus operandi of these institutions has only occurred due to ignorance or omission or perhaps more aptly due to the absence of an effective regulatory function overseeing the activities of financial institutions that were given carte blanche to reign as they wished for too long. Few dared to question the neoliberal paradigm which posited the free functioning of markets and regarded state intervention as a remnant of obsolete totalitarianism, buried since the fall of the Berlin Wall and *perestroika*, and therefore anathema, retrograde and not open to discussion.

The unwillingness to use its regulatory arm perhaps rests on the philosophical remnants of free-market fundamentalism and deregulatory obsession dating back to Reaganomics and Thatcherite economic ideology. Here the state abdicated from its responsibility of monitoring a set of speculative financial activities, processes and procedures that had a high potential for over-spilling into the real economy, thus putting in grave danger the livelihoods of millions. These activities included the creation and trading of high-risk financial products with no economic substance and backing to them, whose societal value and benefit were marginal at best and turned out to be outright disastrous in the end.

Embedded in a spirit of adventure, grounded on the idea of continued economic growth, and the promised demise of historical cyclicality in economic activity, or the end of the cycles of boom and bust, as Gordon Brown, then British Prime Minister put it, people began to undertake risky behaviour, buying financial products that they did not fully understand or engaging in risky stock market operations. This was to have dramatic consequences.

Given the recent track record of government inaction in disciplining the institutions of the financial system, an abdication on the part of the state in enforcing its regulatory responsibilities, economic agents are now very wary of a comeback of a free for all, everything goes mentality, giving free reign to the institutions of the financial system to go well beyond their remit and provoke inordinate damage as was the case in 2008 and 2009.

Furthermore, the credibility of government in promoting genuine economic recovery is jeopardized if a collective perception persists of its inability to deal with financial institutions, their risky behaviour and principally its consequences to the average member of society. Coupled with the need to discipline markets and to convince the average punter that things have in fact changed are the pressures on government to fully exercise its social role, that of ensuring that the basic rights of the citizens are safeguarded and protected from the vagaries of corporations who go well beyond their remit and what is deemed reasonable.

There is a feeling of collective anger when thousands of families are confronted weekly with the repossessions of their homes after failing to meet their mortgage commitments through loss of employment. They realize, perhaps naively, that in their case there is no one to bail them out. The anger reaches worrying proportions when they realize that banks have been treated very favourably indeed by the government. These are the very institutions that failed to meet their own commitments in the past. All of these are controversial points of contention but other philosophical issues on the contemporary role of government, what is expected from it and what is a reasonable degree of state intervention, are being debated now more than ever.

The notion of a welfare state as we have known it since after the war has shown more than just signs of lacking sustainability in the short term. A bastion of European social democracies, there is strong evidence for doubting its viability into the future, at least in its present form and for various reasons. These include adverse demographics, ageing populations and low birth rates. This is important in that the system has to pay for more people for longer and there will be fewer of us of a working age to support it. Of course this can be offset by recourse to migratory flows but it is not that simple.

It is also difficult to forecast socio-demographic patterns due to the positive impact of technology and scientific progress on demographic dynamics, life expectancy, decreasing infant mortality, migrations and other variables. All combine to the accrual of uncertainty in modelling and forecasting the demographic evolution of contemporary modern societies.

Any reliable forecasting of the sustainability of a welfare system, and specifically whether there will be an economic resource pool for distribution to the next generation of retirees, is also very much conditioned by the volatility of the financial markets where pension funds are placed in so-called safe investments but which are in effect funds of varying risk. The financial crisis of 2008 showed that in many cases the extent of the problem was not fully known across the different economies and systems. This notwithstanding, the future behaviour of the institutions that manage these funds needs to be monitored carefully by the legislator as these are matters with potentially deep social ramifications, too serious to be left to the whim of the free-market and in particular of financial institutions.

Having stated the case for regulation and enforcement thereof, it is fair to say that the free-market and its advocates are not to blame for everything that has happened to the world economy over the latter part of the last decade. Blame should also be apportioned to what in effect are the deliberate actions of individuals who lack moral and ethical stature, that were left unleashed to destroy the lives of millions of people, who through hard work had built what they thought was a decent nest for themselves and their families. These citizens rightfully expected that they would be protected against what in the end were proven to be no more than white-collar forms of crime.

Regular citizens were exposed to deception and outright criminal behaviour which saw millions dispossessed of their homes and their livelihoods and with very bleak immediate or indeed long-term prospects, thus providing the clearest indictment for a closer scrutiny of the activities of financial institutions by governments. In the end purely speculative action that lacks a productive dimension and any resemblance of a societal purpose, and which on the contrary may well jeopardize the basic existence of many, needs to be monitored effectively as to its potential detrimental effects. Pure and simply the idea of a hand of God, Smithian-like notion of natural equilibrium is anathema.

Striking a fine balance between the virtues of the free-market and government regulation with a view to ensuring that personal gain coincides with collective welfare is indeed tricky, but recent events demonstrate unequivocally that the pursuit of individual gain will not necessarily intersect with the collective welfare of society. Somewhere along the line the invisible hand does not work, and in order for societal and economic development to go hand in hand there needs to be adequate regulation and effective enforcement thereof. People are simply too greedy.

To limit the analyses of the fallout of the financial crisis of 2008 to a series of events whose consequences were at some point just passed onto the real economy is to miss the whole point of what happened. The financial crisis coincided with the economic crisis at the precise moment when businesses began to renegade on their core activities and what they knew how to do, to alternatively engage in speculative tasks and activities that had nothing to do with their core businesses and for which they had no vocation or particular acumen.

A paper economy has the fragility of the foundations used in its construction. In this case, the true economic value of this paper economy was infinitely smaller than the underlying market capitalization of the corporations that make up this economy. The excess fictional value of this market capitalization in relation to the true value of firms in the economy was entirely attributable to financial speculation. This is the tragedy in this parody of errors. A paper economy founded on simplistic, albeit effective pyramid architectures, always allows for the potential for someone out there to be willing to enter the system at the bottom of the pyramid. The scheme works whilst there are takers, but there comes a time when enough people understand the speculative nature of the game and decide to jump ship.

These reflections are highly topical today but in fairness would not have deserved more than a footnote of attention if made only a few years ago. Certainly the specialist media would be highly sceptical of these considerations. These remarks would be snarled at and rejected as the exact demonstration of the inability of the ordinary mortal in embracing the conceptual complexity of the world of finance and financial products, and debate its idiosyncrasies and virtues, next to an intellectual elite of the calibre of its proponents in investment banking, academia and government policy-makers.

Antagonistic views to the financial diktat of the 1990s would be construed by these pseudo-experts as precisely the corroboration for the need for exclusion of a kind of intellectual peasantry that simply failed to understand the role and virtues of the market, and its immense potential for value creation. In the end and for the common man, nothing but misery came out of pseudo-elitist vanity and greed.

Unfortunately for some of these artisans of the financial wizardry, life has a way with things. Instead of the infallible and mathematically-proven promise of a brave new world, where economic growth was independent of such mundane minutiae as an economy of goods and services, reality would clearly show that behind market fundamentalism and its joys, lay a financial paper economy whose incumbents happily engaged in high-risk transactions, fully knowledgeable that given their crucial importance to modern economies, governments would come to their rescue should things go sour. And indeed they did.

Furthermore, corporations merrily engaged in financial market operations unrelated to their core or even peripheral economic activities, under the auspices and gaze of contemplating governments, are often the very same characters in different costumes. These corporations of the real economy would pursue promises of unlimited gains, tragically taking their eye off the ball and the focus from their central purpose in life, their core business. That would prove to be tragic.

Similarly, arrogant city and academia types would bring society into a dead-end alley. Those who heralded infallible mathematical models, built on ridiculous assumptions, whose grip on reality was non-existent at best, would hail from the top of their marble modern-day equivalent of the pharaonic pyramids of yesteryear, the offices of investment banks in New York, Toronto or Frankfurt, the unquestionable virtues of their autocratic rule whilst crying heresy against those who dared to denounce the fallacy of their artificial constructions.

What seems to have been absent in the process of building complex financial products and their underlying mathematical models, and in a wider context in economic policy formulation, was the failure of acknowledgement of the niggling and intrusive nature of the human element, and its erratic and unpredictable character and behaviour.

People were always an imponderable variable for theoreticians in the construction of these models and a frustrating intrusive that only added to their fallibility. There had been more than enough attempts at incorporating the human element and its unpredictability or 'irrationality' in theoretical construction in the field of economics, but much of it unsuccessful as predictors of the behaviour of socio-economic variables and failing to have the accuracy necessary to pre-empt social and economic crises.

In the past when people, particularly expressed in groups in societies, have been the object of study, attempts at modelling their behaviour have proven not only untenable but also undesirable. Sinister yet powerful political regimes, often legitimized by formal democratic scrutiny, have failed to control people for long periods of time. Even the most hideous characters in ancient and contemporary history were not able to model and control societies forever.

The architects of this spectacular fall from the magnificent pedestal upon which they placed themselves are also often those who advocate a residual regulatory role for the state and its abdication from any idea of intervention in the economy. Not because they hold strong ideological beliefs either way but because a stronger government constitutes undesirable monitoring of the activities that go on in the name and on behalf of what has euphemistically become known as market forces at play.

A more interventionist role for government simply means a stronger scrutiny over the seedy tasks of those who, through greed and irresponsibility, have endangered the solvency of pension fund schemes or even the lifesavings of those whose sole purpose was to see off their days in peace and dignity. This is therefore no longer a debate about more or less state, or differing ideological stances as to the scope of state intervention, the powers of government, or even a tussle over the role of ethics in economics and business or the moral acceptability of such niceties as the obscene payments to fat cats in corporations in Britain, the US or indeed in every capitalist nation in the world.

It is instead the desire for an informed debate about a deeper societal concern, one that demands a notion of government as promoter of economic development and social stability, reconciled with its responsibilities for overseeing and regulating a financial sector whose raison d'être has been distorted beyond recognition, and whose speculative spin-offs have come to endanger these all important societal objectives.

The wider debate centres on the virtues of economic liberalism and its coexistence with ideological frameworks that safeguard the role of government in the economy. As Obama put it in the inaugural speech of his first mandate in 2008, it is not about more or less government, it is about good or bad government. It is about striking a fine balance between adequate and excessive regulation as a proxy to balanced social and economic development. As we cannot afford to trust the power of the invisible hand in acting to the benefit of society, we need to at least guide it in the right direction.

Ben Bernanke's analogy of the financial system as a burning house was given in a rare interview and justified by the extraordinary times America and the world were living in then. Bernanke stated at the time that until the world and particularly the US were able to stabilize the financial markets, there was no possible recovery to the real economy. What Bernanke did not state at the time for logical reasons was that, in addition to the financial crisis, there was also a crisis of economic confidence which inhibited the effectiveness of macro-economic policy. Debt-ridden economies and deep structural problems in the competitiveness of nations presented frail prospects of economic recovery in much of the western world.

Bernanke knew that trust is indeed the most elusive of ingredients, and whilst every proper and adequate measure may be taken to correct policy trajectory, economic recovery is not as simple as that. One cannot simply resume a normal agenda if there is a collective suspicion on the functioning of institutions and a common perception held by economic agents that nothing will ever be the same again in the kingdom of Denmark. This is especially true if there is a societal view that regulatory institutions were too relaxed and permissive in allowing a new kind of 'technostructure' to come to power in business and finance.

Nothing that Galbraith, the renowned Canadian economist, had not warned us all against many years earlier. He was a man ahead of his time.

A close scrutiny into the conduct of the institutions of the financial system whose activities, when not monitored, may have disastrous consequences on the real economy and the lives of common people, is not only recommended but mandatory. In this sense a profound reflection upon the role and scope of intervention of regulatory institutions is required. A structural reform of the system and the introduction of mechanisms that lead to the redefinition of the social contract between financial institutions and their stakeholders are necessary to avoid the future recurrence of the kinds of disruptions that have pervaded financial institutions over the last decade. This would mean for example the imposition of threshold levels of risk exposure for financial products, which by their nature and objectives should not have disproportionate risk profiles, when underpinning the likes of pension-related investment funds or savings plans for retirees.

The financial markets were inundated with such products at the break of the financial crisis and entire institutions were unduly exposed. A case in point was that of the British police pension fund scheme and its intricate link to Icelandic financial institutions who had sought to manage these funds in a less than conservative way by gambling them in high-risk toxic financial products.

As the Icelandic economy fell down like a deck of cards and its financial system dangerously approached bankruptcy, the Icelandic Government simply came out stating that it could not guarantee the solvency of the British police pension fund scheme. From the viewpoint of the British police this was unthinkable and exactly the kind of thing that simply could not happen. That was also to be the perspective of the British Government.

It is understandable that pension fund managers should want to maximize returns for their investments as any other rational investor would do. The average police officer though, unaware of the intricacies and pseudo-sophistication of investment strategies, whilst keeping the streets of Britain safe, would preferably do so with the knowledge that his or her retirement fund is safely and productively invested. This is not a high-risk profile client and neither should his pension fund be.

The average British police officer is certainly oblivious to the rules of engagement in pension fund management, and not much interested in such vocabulary as market volatility and risk exposure. This is a pension fund whose constituents are policemen and women who serve the British people. If the average police officer were to be queried on the importance of the security and safety of his pension fund, this would most certainly been given priority as an investment criterion to the detriment of aggressive market behaviour and unacceptable exposure to high risk.

In a country of the economic stature, democratic tradition and political maturity of Britain, the police were far from thinking that the security of their members and their future could even but remotely have been questioned. In effect, and given the outcome of this conflict, one is led to believe that the integrity of British police force retirement pensions could easily have been jeopardized.

When the Icelandic economy collapsed because of the careless exposure of the financial system to what were subsequently and euphemistically designated as toxic financial products, it was concluded that the pension funds of the British police were in danger. The Icelandic Government went public, stating that Iceland could not guarantee the solvency of these pension funds. The sequence of events that unfolded shows that the rules of engagement in normal times do not apply when serious interests are at stake, the protection of which requires drastic measures to be taken.

British Prime Minister Gordon Brown, to the dismay of Icelanders, threatened to enforce the Anti-Terrorism Crime and Security Act of 2001, an exceptional piece of legislation with the purpose of seizing the assets of Icelandic banks in Britain. This legislation had indeed normally been reserved for the IRA. Few would hazard a guess as to the practical consequences of this, but suffice it to say the British Government left no doubts in the minds of its Icelandic counterparts as to whose responsibility the default on the pension funds of British police officers was. The pension funds of the British police had to be guaranteed and so they were.

People like the British police officers are precisely the type of people that will benefit from a structural reform of a kind which pinpoints the nature, scope and extent of the activities of the institutions of the financial system, thus limiting their perverse externalities on the real economy and the spin-offs of speculative activity that is of peripheral interest to most and certainly fails to fulfil a recognizable social function. A structural reform of the institutions of the financial system should start by rejecting what appears to have become commonplace in the current mandate of these institutions, that of playing irresponsibly with money that is not theirs. The legislator will certainly need to be ever more vigilant in the future.

If the pension funds of an institution as traditional and conservative as the British police were subjected to such a high degree of exposure to market volatility and unacceptable risk profiles for what should have been a conservative investment, one can easily infer that the notion of a safe investment is no longer what it used to be. Knowing that money flows with incredible ease and speed, effectively at the push of a button, and that the regulatory environment has not dissuaded excessive risk-taking for far too long now, it is safe to conclude that much needs to be done in this domain.

Years of irresponsible behaviour, managing pension funds, not as a risk-averse and conservative portfolio of products, but in a manner akin to the casino-like atmosphere that typified the times, would inevitably have led to the mess we are in today. The dust having settled it would be a safe assumption to believe that the future would necessarily have to be different, but unfortunately there are worrying signs coming out of Wall Street as some old habits are simply too hard to kick.

The impact of the recent financial crisis on the management of pension funds should have kick-started a wholly different, more conservative and risk-averse approach, one that balances the real interests of those whose sole purpose is to ensure a decent standard of living upon retirement, with a genuine attempt at maximizing investor returns on what should effectively be low-risk investments.

There is also an inescapable determinism here, the acceptance that less risk-taking correlates with lower returns on investment and this means that unless other variables are introduced into the equation, the welfare system is not sustainable, at least not in the way that we have known it since the war. The storm that hit the global financial system will surely prevent risky behaviour in the immediate future of the kind that was witnessed in the 1980s and 1990s, and should radically change the definition of what constitutes acceptable risk in managing funds that are by nature and purpose conservative applications, or so we hope. Having said that, one should never underestimate the short collective memory on these and other matters of relevance.

The extent and severity of the financial crisis and particularly its impact on the real economy will certainly need to introduce much needed change on the definition of the boundaries, of what is permissible for institutions, whose impact on our lives goes beyond the social and economic mandate for which they were originally created. Banks clearly fall into this category.

Unemployment and the impoverishment of the middle and working classes for reasons that are beyond their knowledge and comprehension requires a fundamental philosophical change on what societies believe to be the regulatory role of government. This is not about an ideological abrogation of the role of the private enterprise substituting it with totalitarian government control, or even a statement on the degree of ideal government intervention in economic activity. It is a deeper concern than that and relates to the acknowledgement that the government has fundamental responsibilities towards its citizens, including its duty to protect not only the more vulnerable amongst us, but simply those who are decent law-abiding individuals.

If the use of the term vulnerable seems farfetched and excessive here, that is because historically it has only been used in describing a narrow remit of the social agenda of the state. That is the notion of protecting the human and social rights of those with physical or mental disabilities, which in many cases constitute recent societal and legal conquests. This is another kind of vulnerability and given the inaccessibility of the common man to the intricacies and complexity of modern financial riddles, and their disproportionate detrimental consequences to the everyday life of common individuals, the problem is paradoxically similar. A feeling of impotence is what is left in the minds of many.

The state has an obligation to rid society of the pseudo-knowledgeable that operating under the cover of unfettered capitalism, profoundly lacking in humanity and destitute of ethical or moral barriers, cynically proceeds to undermine the livelihoods of many ordinary citizens who simply did not ask to be part of the process. Many of that kind of technocratic intelligentsia were no more than puppets at the whim of higher-order interests. The examples abound.

From Bernie Ebbers to Maddoff, from WorldCom to Enron and Arthur Anderson, we were led to believe that the elusive elitism of the silk tie and suit brigade grounded on obscene bonuses was nothing more than a genuine portrayal of just what can be achieved through honest hard work and legitimate means. We were wrong. The trading floors of London or New York were simply the arena for a more mundane, yet still sinister, white-collared form of legitimized pillage and dishonesty as some of these corporations traded freely on crooked books. Rating agencies did not help as we know today.

At this point, it is only fair to mention those who erected these idols with feet of clay and elevated them to the status of contemporary alchemists. These were the scholars that had pontificated on the pseudo-science behind all this, attempting to dress the whole thing up in colourful attire and embed it in valid theoretical substance in business schools and economics departments the world over. Many of the corporate idols of the 1990s and early 2000s, who ended up in jail, including Ebbers and Maddoff, were portrayed as corporate heroes and true exemplars of what became known as the new economy.

Their corporations were also hailed as examples to look up to for all those who aspired to do well in business. Bernie Ebbers of WorldCom was a revered management guru and his company a reference case study, a true embodiment of a new generation business paradigm. We all had to follow the man. If you wanted to be at the cutting-edge of management in the twenty-firstcentury than certainly the Ebbers lesson on cost-cutting and expansion had to be a must learn. The bastions of knowledge in the Ivy League cathedrals of business and economics higher learning portrayed him and others as such.

Thus, and by constructing seemingly complex financial products for which there always had to be risk-takers, akin to the architects of pyramid marketing schemes, and with the gentle charm of infallibility, they built the great illusion of our time. That being said, all of this could only have worked properly,with the tacit seal of approval of a passive government, and that too was conceded. Government, in compliance with the new rules of engagement of a wider paradigm reigning in the new economy, had abdicated from exercising its regulatory role and mandate.

Rather than exhausting the reader with fastidious stories about epistemological paradigm-breaking, Michael Moore's film *Capitalism: A Love Story* makes a poignant metaphor of the 1980s and 1990s when showcasing the then Merrill Lynch Chairman, Don Regan, as he abruptly advises US President, Ronald Reagan to wrap it up as he was well into a public speech. More than the content of what was said, and the tone in which it was said, it was the audacity in the manner in which the President was addressed that is perhaps the best indictment on the relationship between government and the world of investment banking and finance.

In order for all of this to work there also had to be the illusion-takers, those who believed wholeheartedly in unlimited growth and effortless success. There was an abundance of those around in the 1980s and 1990s, and right through the first decade of the new millennium. Unsuspecting, and fleeing from an uncomfortable determinism, one which life always imposes, that of under normal circumstances nothing worth having comes our way easily, effortlessly, and unless work ethic and discipline are involved, these people began to amass outrageous personal wealth on pure market speculation. Of course, unusually high investment returns had to be corresponded by substantial underlying risks. In the end, many were clearly much better prepared for the benefits of the former, than for the plight of the latter.

Warren Buffett of Berkshire Hathaway, who knows the financial markets better than most, had been warning for some time of the dangers of embarking in boundless and unjustified enthusiasm founded on the simplistic idea of unlimited economic growth, and perhaps advised by an informed intuition derived from having witnessed many of these bubbles burst in the past, he warned of the dangers of what was to come.

Buffett warned of what he saw as speculative behaviour in the stock markets, a characterization of a state of affairs whose purpose and essence he thought deviated from a more fundamental notion of organic corporate growth, the true barometer of firm market capitalization. In particular, Buffett failed to understand how and why people would invest in businesses and ideas that did not make sense, in companies whose products nobody wanted, companies with no history of great products or brands, companies that people had not wanted in the past or envisaged wanting in the future, and sometimes companies that never manufactured a widget or put out a service of any kind.

Returning to the recurring idea of regulation and better governance, it is crucial that society must never again allow for the resurgence of the WorldComs, Enrons, Arthur Andersens, Barings, or of characters of the calibre of the Nick Leesens, Bernie Maddoffs, Bernie Ebbers and countless others. These are of course only a small fraction of the dozens of corporate scandals that occurred in the 1980s and 1990s and if they are mentioned here it is because they suffered the intense scrutiny of the media at the time. There were thousands of others. Simply put, the nature and consequences of a collective perception of impunity may jeopardize something much more poignant than the health of financial markets in the present and in the future.

The credibility of the institutions of the financial system or even that of large corporations, employing millions of workers across the world, depends on how the criminal justice system is perceived to deal with acts of deliberate wrongdoing. The rigour with which the judicial system is perceived to enforce the law will dictate how much leeway there is for similar behaviour were it to recur in the future.

Many of these pseudo-gurus of the financial system acquired social kudos through the amassment of unjustified inordinate economic wealth. Worse still, because of their economic prominence, many were vested with an intellectual legitimacy of a kind that derives from a less than rigorous scrutiny of their true abilities. The naivety of some in academia and many in the political establishment did the rest.

The development of effective mechanisms of transparency and good governance in markets is inevitable. Only then, gradually, and in a climate of trust, can the financial markets become effective barometers of economic activity, a mechanism for evaluating the true market value of companies, and not a mere reflection of the consequences of speculative corporate behaviour. Even worse, when one can't tell financial wizardry from true underlying economic fundamentals then something has gone radically wrong with the system.

Transparency thus acts as a guarantor of market capitalization of a publicly quoted corporation effectively being an adequate reflection of its true market value. What has happened over the last decade or so is that speculative strategies and an artificial and often illegal distortion of market rules (WorldCom and others) have caused the valuation of corporate stock in markets to tell very little about the current strength or future economic prospects and performance of organizations.

Effective regulatory frameworks and mechanisms and the transparency that these bring into the inner workings of financial systems will contribute to the restoration of a climate of greater trust in institutions. A perception of transparency and good governance in the functioning of the institutions of the financial system has an invaluable impact on the confidence of the other agents in the economy, thus aiding macro-economic policy objectives. Confidence in the system is a valuable asset in contemporary economic systems.

The constituent institutions of the financial system play a crucial role in the functioning of modern economies. The ramifications of a bankruptcy of a major financial institution, as we saw only too clearly with Lehman Brothers a few years back, are so pervasive and the ramifications of its consequences so deeply intertwined with other sectors of economic activity that the state must stand to intervene to ensure the solvency of these institutions, thus avoiding a risk of systemic failure.

The constituent institutions of the financial system cannot be regimented conveniently as if it were just another sector of economic activity, whose scope of intervention is bounded geographically or in territorial terms. The financial system, more than mediating or facilitating economic relationships in society, has become an end in itself, one, where at times one struggles to find the slightest resemblance between what goes on under its operational spectrum of activities and any recognizable form of a productive and tangible economic and social function.

Thus, a paper or virtual economy has replaced the economy of production and substance. Precisely, the extent to which this is real, by how much the paper economy exceeds the real economy of production, resides the true level of speculation in the system. The WorldCom case shows that at times of unbridled excitement it becomes very difficult to separate fact from fiction. These are also the times when they all want to shoot the messenger.

Many of these toxic financial products resemble in their raison d'être, functioning and the underlying collective psychology and involvement some of the rudimentary pyramid marketing schemes that have been around for years. The logic is simplistic, one dependent on an endless supply of illusion-takers, where as long as there is someone down the line buying into the scheme, it just keeps going, the latest entrants perpetuating it and providing the necessary fuel to keep the wheels in movement.

The analogy with toxic financial products relies on the premise that where we read fuel for a fire, we are to read an uninterrupted flow of risk-takers that guarantee the perpetuation of the scheme. As paper circulates, new risk-takers enter the system only too willing to invest in these toxic high-risk financial products in the hope of trading them at a profit later. It all looks apparently very healthy but the system is already ill as nothing of value gets traded. In the end it is just about risk being passed on with no underlying economic value to even mitigate it. Once the chain is broken it won't take much for the whole building to come tumbling down. It happens with financial institutions but it also happens with publicly traded corporations.

The WorldCom case, albeit different in its particular idiosyncrasy, was a mere fudging of the books with ill-intention that led to the distortion of the market capitalization of the firm, with Wall Street knowingly buying into the whole thing as it meant artificial added value in the form of WorldCom shareholdings and profits for those who traded on shares of this company.

The Barings Bank scandal had more to do with an absence of control mechanisms in place and a casino-like atmosphere that characterized the world of financial institutions at the time, and that was the antithesis of what should have been the conservative essence of the banking sector. In enforcing the law, the criminal justice system should dissuade corporate engagement into what is effectively illegal behaviour of a kind that has exceptional detrimental consequences to the well-being of society. The creation of mechanisms to monitor and prevent the recurrence of anti-economic behaviour of this kind into the future needs to urgently follow.

When AIG executives decided at the height of the financial crisis to hand back the annual bonuses that they had earned, something unthinkable only a few years back, they obviously sought to appease the unbearable collective pressure that had been mounted and the threat of the direct and indirect consequences to their careers should they have failed to do so.

In the end it was an economically rational decision for them to make, that of returning their bonuses or to outright refuse them, for they knew that the losses that they stood to sustain in the medium to long term would far outweigh the immediate bonuses that they were entitled to, no matter how exorbitant and illogical these were. In effect, it could be argued that an important psychological threshold of societal tolerance was about to be crossed if top management at AIG was to receive benefits for what was no more than mismanagement of the corporation. Shrewd top management instinctively realized that and wisely resorted to better judgement.

There have been over the years numerous characterizations of the incestuous relationships between American administrations of the past and the incumbent dominant institutions of the financial system in the US. A few years ago cinematographer and social pundit Michael Moore denounced the promiscuous nature of these relationships and exhibited the disproportionate and rather unusually large contingent of Goldman Sachs executives with prominent positions in previous American administrations as an illustration of a closer than desirable *entente cordiale* between the world of finance and investment banking and government.

In contemporary times, these dubious relationships between the mammoth institutions of the financial system and American administrations were best exemplified by the aforementioned Don Regan, former Chairman of Merrill Lynch, who went on to become Secretary of State under Reagan. No one really knows what the situation is like under the current Obama administration with regards to top job promiscuity between Wall Street and Capitol Hill.

However, as world-renowned economist Paul Krugman warned not too long ago, there were signs of Obama giving in to intolerable pressure from the financial institutions soon after being sworn into his first mandate as President of the USA. This was evident more than ever when a few years ago in Pittsburgh, the European Commission tried to suggest a closer scrutiny on the remuneration of top executives, only for Obama to give the idea the cold shoulder. The pressure and the intricate links between Wall Street and Washington are simply too strong to break.

To ensure the fairness of the system and thus monitor the pay cheques of fat cats is not demagoguery or populism. As a society we simply cannot continue to pay princely and unjustifiable sums of money to public or private senior executives without seeking for a closer monitoring of a sense of adequacy between the social and economic impact of what they do on the one hand and how much they earn on the other. In addition to giving the wrong signals to the economy, this also ratifies intolerable discrepancies in income distribution as many struggle to survive with a modicum of dignity whilst others live lavish lives, and this in the so-called developed world.

The cynicism inherent to all of this arises from the knowledge that many of those involved in unwise corporate decision-making, or just deliberate wrongdoing, have often been rewarded with healthy bonuses for their troubles. In addition to the perceived social injustice that this entails, rewarding failure simply makes no economic sense. It is also in extremely bad taste to reward executives, particularly in the public sector, for managing their organizations poorly. The same line of thinking applies to the hefty bonuses paid to senior executives in the public utilities sectors, operating virtual or real monopolies. It simply makes no sense at all.

The only economic argument for paying hefty bonuses to top executives is to reward their exceptional managerial abilities. The economic performance of the organizations that they lead and run should be a barometer for how well they do and corresponding remuneration should ensue. However there is ample evidence to suggest that this was not always the case, amidst the fat cat bonuses of the corporate euphoria of the last decade.

Thus, beyond a question of equity and social justice, there appears to be a higher-order issue here, and that is the business imperative that forces an unambiguous correlation between top executive performance and compensation, that is, if we want to send the right signals to the rest of the economy, and if we want to promote the overriding idea of an ethical and just society founded on meritocracy.

At the beginning of his first legislature Obama instructed his Treasury Secretary, Timothy Geithner, to use any means necessary and within the law to impede the payment of bonuses to AIG executives, the intention being to convey a direct message to corporate America that there was indeed a new sheriff in town. For Obama, whatever legal mechanism was deemed necessary, bonuses would not be paid to AIG executives. If that failed, bonuses would be taxed at 90 per cent. They got the message. Unfortunately, Obama wasn't able to keep up the pace and match rhetoric with action as time went by.

The idea of eradicating from corporate America the notion of reward for poor performance and incompetence has to be a good one and this applies in good measure to Europe. The bonuses to be paid to AIG executives were in the grand scheme of things, peanuts, but the consequences of the ratification of their payment by the American Government were not negligible. Were these obscene bonuses to have been allowed to stand they would have represented a rejection of a crucial message in the Obama agenda, that of the moralization of top executive remuneration in large business conglomerates.

One of the electoral platforms of the Obama ticket for his mandate was that a new and fairer America had to be one where performance and reward should be intrinsically linked, thus countering the numerous corruption scandals in top executive compensation and bonus rewards that typified corporate America over the last decade. Rewarding AIG executives with scandalous bonuses would have been the antithesis of a message of restraint that needed to be spread to America and the world.

However the subsequent behaviour of the Obama administration and its reluctance in ratifying the ceiling limits for the remuneration of top executives in large corporations does indeed mean that, in the end, everything was to be no more than mere rhetoric. As Krugman put it, the pressure is simply too much and entering a second mandate there is not much hope that this state of affairs will improve.

The ideas of transparency and corporate governance are concerns that were high on the 2008 electoral platform and the agenda of the new Obama administration. The award of the Nobel Prize for Economics to Ostrom and Williamson, distinguishing a body of research in the area of governance, attests to this. The economic situation, as it has enveloped since 2008 in most of the developed world, has only exacerbated an already robust collective feeling of animosity towards large multinational corporations and their top management, leaving little leeway and tolerance for a perception of opacity in the ethics of corporations with tentacles all over peoples' lives.

There also appears to be a very low political and indeed societal tolerance threshold to emerging corruption scandals, in line with the many that occurred over the last decade, not only in Wall Street but throughout corporate America and Europe. The harmful effects of successive corporate fraud cases and the incompetence of governments in scrutinizing and monitoring governance processes are disturbing, and the economic costs difficult to quantify. In addition to these, there are the added costs of a collective breach of confidence in fundamental institutions of the economic system.

The costs of a loss of collective confidence are impossible to quantify in all their dimensions and ramifications but certainly act detrimentally as serious obstacles to economic recovery. This is because, in a climate of widespread distrust in institutions, individuals in society do not react to macro-economic policy stimuli, both fiscal and monetary, the way that policy-makers would expect them to.

Here again a wrongful assumption of pseudo-rationality on behalf of economic agents means that policy measures do not obtain desired policy outcomes at least in the ways that are predicted by economics textbooks. Successive reductions in central bank reference interest rates that were intended to induce more investment, higher consumption and a lower propensity for individuals to hold long-term savings deposits in banks, appear not to have attained much desired outcomes. With interest rates hitting historical lows, people are more cautious than ever. They did not invest and they were careful with anything that they construed as consumption of non-essential goods.

In times of uncertainty and mistrust in the political and economic institutions, a collective lack of confidence mitigates and often annuls the intended policy outcomes that are inherent to monetary policy measures. As the prime concern is one of ensuring survival in the short term, what is truly important is to have enough liquidity to meet immediate financial obligations.

Finally, in the context of economic crisis, any perception of glaring social inequality is exacerbated. A small group of individuals receiving disproportionate compensatory rewards, undeserved and detached from any comprehensible barometer of organizational performance, are naturally opposed by a vocal majority of the masses who struggle to survive and simply fail to understand these discrepancies outside a framework of moral corruption and unethical and unjust systemic behaviour. And so they protest.

As metaphors for the malaises and inequities of contemporary corporate life, the case of Worldcom and its CEO Bernie Ebbers is a must read. The same goes for the demise of accounting giant Arthur Andersen. Vast and profound analyses and writings have been conducted on high-profile corporate scandals as the cases are plentiful and multifaceted over the last couple of decades.

Nick Leeson and Barings Bank, also known as the Queen's bank, the Enron debacle, and more recently Madoff and his at one time highly acclaimed number on financial alchemy are also compulsory illustrations of a merry go round of corporate criminality. In between, one may seek to delve into the cases of financial insolvency of the Icelandic state, the infamous savings and loans tragedy in the US and the sub-prime crisis, which many believe to have triggered the current economic crisis.

The list of cases of corporate corruption and scandal is endless and endemic to the last decade but not exclusively Many believe that what we are witnessing today is the fallout and the full development of the last consequences of a philosophical paradigm of economic deregulation, begun in the 1980s in America under Reagan, with correspondence in Thatcherite Britain in the same period. An intense calendar of deregulation of economic activity, and in particular that of the financial system, has culminated in the anarchy of the financial institutions that was witnessed in 2008, and its consequences manifested in the frailty of any prospect of economic recovery today in much of the developed world.

This black list of corporations and fraudsters has gradually but surely been thickened as the magnitude of the problem has received the attention of the world's attentive media. In an explosive mix combining lack of judgment and criminal intent we arrive at the mess we are in today. There is an unequivocal need for a new paradigm that puts a higher onus on the role of government regulatory action and the enforcement of corporate ethics, one that strikes a more harmonious balance between effective regulation and the benefits of free-market competitive dynamics. Thus, what is required is a regulatory role that does not stifle economic activity and ensures fair competition whilst acting as a guarantor of transparency and good corporate governance.

Corporate life has produced numerous cases of incompetence and outright corruption in the last decade, enough to demonstrate unequivocally that markets do not self-regulate. Recent events have also shown that neither transparency nor good governance are achieved through self-regulatory means. Left without the proverbial leash, and feeding on a frenzy of greed, these people would go to any extent, including the destruction of the lives of others, if they felt that there were profits to be made in the process. In all of the cases enumerated here, a common denominator emerges, and that is one of just the right mix of incompetence, illegality and ill intent, all combined in self-interest and disregard for others.

Nick Leeson and Barings Bank constitute an astonishing example of how a simple, run-of-the-mill trader was allowed to operate with unchecked autonomy and, in effect, had the institutional backing that allowed him to bring a reputed institution to its knees through an incredible web of casino-like operations, conducted in the Asian markets, through an intolerable, yet possible exposure of the bank to extreme risk.

Barings Bank had up until then built up a peerless reputation for its conservative old-school banking tradition. Leeson had obviously been offered free-reign autonomy over trading operations in the Asian markets, perhaps because of the technical incompetence of his superiors in exercising any visible control over his activities, but more likely due to their insurmountable greed throughout the whole time that he was consistently bringing handsome profits into the organization.

The absence of formal monitoring and control mechanisms, or if there were any, the reluctance in exercising them effectively, particularly when profits were sizeable, only makes sense in the context of a top management that has to be in on everything that had been going on at the time. Abnormal profits without historical precedent would have aroused suspicions, particularly one would expect from old-fashioned conservative bankers who were only too knowledgeable of the profitability levels inherent and expected from regular banking activities. Of course, all of this falls by the wayside when profits are astronomical and there is a natural reluctance to rock the boat, or when one does not really understand the ins and outs of the business. If the money keeps coming in, why bother? And the money was coming in like never before.

There is however a fundamental problem here arising from the improper treatment of stakeholder constituencies, including shareholders and clients, who had their lifesavings deposited in Barings Bank, those whose interests should have been paramount to the institution and present at the very top of the bank's agenda. They were not. No one at Barings Bank dared to question, with some degree of effectiveness or relevant authority, the actual or apparent risk to which the bank was being exposed. The lack of effective mechanisms and controls that would denounce and impede the outcome of what was to ensue is what is at question here, and is tautological with the times in which this process occurred.

The process itself was shameful from beginning to end, but it is the atmosphere that led to its occurrence that is most worrying. This was most apparent when Leeson, in a desperate attempt to recover the huge losses that he had spectacularly amassed, began to enter into an all or nothing gambling downward spiral, dealing in ever higher-risk products, unremittingly and irremediably exposing the bank.

When finally the top executives at Barings Bank agreed that action was necessary, it was way too late to save the institution. The bank had run up astonishing debts in the volatile Asian markets and was declared insolvent soon after. No wonder that a few years later, when Her Majesty the Queen visited the London School of Economics, the question that came to her mind, and that she indeed posed to a startled economics professor standing next to her, was: 'How could you have not foreseen this?' Many would have asked the same question.

Barings Bank was known as the banking institution of choice of the English monarchy. It was in the eyes of many the cornerstone of British institutional conservatism and of a traditional banking system. It was inconceivable that it could possibly disappear into thin air just like that. In effect, Barings Bank was the quintessence of conservative tradition in an ancient, solid and highly procedural banking system. The facts churned out something entirely different. The players in this full costume drama were anything but conservative in philosophy, and in the end this event brought out the particular archetype of the city trader, a character that could not be farther from the idealized figure of the conservative banker of yesteryear. That was common knowledge in the financial circles but to the great public, not versed in the vagaries of investment banking and its activities, the whole thing came as a huge surprise.

Amidst all of this, one thing that one could always count on was the immeasurable greed of the top executives at Barings Bank who, armed with mounting evidence of massive profit earnings, were only too keen to endorse the game fully, not having to worry much about the contours, details and underlying assumptions and fundamentals of the business. Good old-fashioned banking rules, such as continuous checks and balances on financial transactions and activities, including the monitoring of undue exposure to risk, soon went out of the window.

One cannot afford to ignore a certain reserve on the part of the top executives at Barings Bank in relation to what they considered to be complex financial instruments, products that they perhaps did not even vaguely understand. These products had strange names, such as futures, derivatives, swaps and others. Underlying them were complicated mathematical models whose technical complexity went far beyond the understanding of the conservative bankers of yesteryear.

Much of this constituted a substantial departure from the classical training of traditional bankers. They were simply a breed apart, a different generation of bankers imprisoned in a knowledge and technological time warp. On the other hand, and this is just a basic trait of human nature, as unimaginable gains mounted there was little willingness to exercise caution and institute monitoring mechanisms to oversee what could possibly go wrong.

However, it was precisely this kind of hard-nosed, old-time scrutiny that was demanded of them. As bankers from another era, they were privy to a rule as universal and timeless as any, and that is that high investment returns in normal circumstances correlate with high levels of risk-taking. Thus, in an explosive mix of technical ignorance, pure greed and misjudgement, the epitaph of one of the oldest and most reputable banks of Great Britain was written.

Examples of lack of transparency and bad corporate governance, particularly in the US, over the last decade are innumerable. Many of them have had disastrous consequences extending beyond their own backyard, inflicting incalculable damage to the world economy and impacting detrimentally on the lives of us all. In some cases, and given the size of the corporations concerned, these effects were direct and immediate. Lehman Brothers is a good case in point but many others have occurred outside the financial sector. In the end it is safe to say that the rules of engagement in many large corporations across a widespread spectrum of economic sectors, such as that of American telecommunications or the banking sectors in Britain and the US, have been deeply tampered with.

The size of these organizations, the breadth of their tentacular activities and the geographical scope of their operations has meant that a knock-on effect was inevitable, one with profound economic consequences felt across different sectors of activity and geographies. There were also impacts on corporate governance as smaller organizations were to interpret this as a concession, warranting them the moral latitude for assuming unethical and socially irresponsible behaviour, and coming to accept it as normal practice.

As other players in the telecommunications sector were unaware of the real source of WorldCom's competitive advantage in this market and what its astounding business acumen and success could be attributed to, they believed their inability to compete was their problem and began to respond blindly by cutting costs and laying-off employees. This was certainly the case with corporate giants AT&T and Sprint in the American telecommunications industry.

There is a recent history of irresponsibility and criminal intent characterizing corporate life. There are many cases of both and mostly concentrated over the last decade or so. Enron and WorldCom, Barings Bank and Arthur Andersen illustrate the point. Ebbers and Madoff are only metaphors for the many other cases of senior executives that were accused, tried and convicted in American courts of law for embezzlement and corporate fraud.

Ebbers and Madoff were the same individuals who, in their heyday, were presented as genuine pillars of outstanding competence and honesty in their communities, to whom people looked up to and whose success and lifestyle they aspired to emulate. It may sound farfetched now but both Ebbers and Madoff were seen by many, including their competitors, as examples of what exceptional management in the new economy was all about.

For all these reasons, and because it is imperative that a society needs to base its present on a profound sense of history, we need to collectively remember the magnitude of the economic and social impact of corporate mismanagement and wrongdoing, and the hugely detrimental impact of white collar crime on the lives of regular people, in order to avoid repetition of such behaviour in the future.

Much of what we are witnessing today is a direct consequence of the ineptitude, malice and sheer greed of the upper echelons in management in the large corporate conglomerates in various sectors of economic activity, all in the name of the free-market. It is particularly important not to allow for the prevalence of the idea that all of this is simply empty and unsubstantiated rhetoric, that what is happening in the world today is merely business as usual, another day in the erratic game of corporate life, that in a competitive world, in a modern, open and global economy, there are winners and there are losers. It is not business as usual when the competitive conditions that ultimately stand to determine the winners and the losers in this game have been adulterated by criminal action that has falsified the true and accurate picture of the organization and consequently the nature and rules of engagement vis-à-vis all the other players striving for success in the same market. This happened regularly throughout the 1990s and the first decade of the twenty-first century without much hindrance on the part of the regulators, perhaps because that was the paradigm of the day.

It is precisely here, in regulation and its enforcement thereof, that a paradigm shift is needed, one that rethinks the role of government in protecting the welfare of its citizens. A new order needs to be built upon an idea of dynamic harmony between government regulatory intervention where appropriate, and the many virtues of flexibility and agility of market mechanisms, thus allowing for free-market forces to compete but not without supervision and control.

The whole thing is of course a question of degree and of the agility of bureaucracy in accompanying the breath-taking dynamism of the free-market. When Obama alludes to better government rather than more or less government, he is perhaps addressing just that. Genuine competition has served economic growth well over the last half a century, and that should not be forgotten. In the end, a desirable outcome is one where the distinction between bureaucratic distortion of market competition on the one hand and a carte blanche given to corporations to do as they wish on the other is clear and unambiguous. There needs to be a fine balance between the two opposites of the spectrum.

Economic protectionism is undesirable but, if anything, recent times have shown that as dangerous to the common good as excessive government intervention is a brand of free reign, unchecked capitalism, and an absolute reliance on the pseudo-altruism of its proponents. For some, there is no legitimacy in advocating extensive government intervention in the economy. So-called market purists argue that by endorsing the inefficient hand of government, the effective gains from a free-market economy are irrevocably jeopardized. That said, good or bad government, not more or less government is again the question at hand. Striking a good balance between effective regulation and the gains of the free-market is also the true mark of great political leadership. It is also the greatest challenge in the formulation of economic policy in current times.

Reality Check...

Jack Welch's Mother on Transforming a Bad Hand into an Opportunity

Jack Welch was for many years Chairman and CEO of American corporate giant General Electric. As a child, Jack had a pronounced stutter and whilst at school he was bullied because of this and children can be particularly cruel in these circumstances. When he mentioned it to his mother, who meant everything to him, she had an answer that was to stay with him for the rest of his life. What she said was something so important that, throughout his life, he repeatedly told the story at numerous conferences and corporate interventions the world over.

His mother told him that he did not stutter. It so happened that his brain worked so much faster and processed information so much quicker than that of others, and indeed faster than his own speech, that when he spoke, his words simply could not keep up with his brain. According to his mother, Jack was so much more intelligent than others that when it came to verbalizing his thoughts, the words simply did not come out as they should. That is why Jack stuttered. The young Welch faced life with a renewed optimism after hearing that.

As he later reflected upon these things, and knowing that he really did have a bad stutter as a child, a condition that had nothing to do with thinking quickly or not, he realized the good that his mother had done to his self-esteem as a child. Jack Welch's mother had transformed a disadvantage into a strength, building into his character a capital of confidence of immense value, a trait which was to serve him well later on in life during the many years at the helm of General Electric.

9

Bernie Ebbers, WorldCom and Other Corporate Tragic Comedies

Corporate incompetence in financial institutions and in particular that of top executives in investment banking is typically not one of a lack of understanding of the technical complexity of financial products, or their exact nature and purpose. Technical ignorance in the upper echelons of management in financial institutions, and its contribution to a shameful and tragic outcome to the world's financial system, was not a decisive factor. It certainly did not help the cause that many top level decision-makers in financial institutions did not know much about the likes of swaps and derivatives or futures and options, along with all the other technical nomenclature that typifies contemporary financial lingo. But the key to what happened was an abandonment of old-fashioned rules of conservative banking behaviour and common sense.

Most were too ashamed to admit to a lack of technical knowledge on such matters of critical importance in today's business world. They were also hesitant to make much of an effort to understand these complex financial products in any depth, as what really mattered was being delivered, with traders keeping the money flowing in, earning these banking institutions unprecedented and astronomical profits. All of this continued right up until the casino economy began to obey the random laws of gambling. These stipulate an inevitable order where at times one wins and other times one loses. High returns meant that high risks were being undertaken and the downward spiral was as swift as the upward trajectory that preceded it. We were then privy to the unthinkable, that of reference institutions of investment banking disappearing overnight such as the aforementioned Barings Bank as well as the once prestigious Lehman Brothers. Some may argue that this is a gross oversimplification of reality that it is not its totality, or even a fair portrayal of what has effectively happened in the world's financial system. This analysis may indeed be construed as stereotypical and subjective.

On the other hand it can be argued of course that reality is a construct, susceptible of modification by virtue of the intervention of social and economic agents who are not mere observers of reality and as such behave as social actors with a vested interest in moulding reality to their advantage. As the economic agent engages in decision-making, he does so with a plethora of biases and preconceived ideas that in effect are his interpretation of the underlying phenomena. An intervening actor manipulates and modifies reality according to what he perceives to be his own interests. Critically, and accepting the principle that the actor is not a mere observer of reality, he will influence the outcomes of reality, adapting and adjusting those outcomes to what he perceives to be his own economic benefit.

When this thinking is extrapolated to the financial markets the manipulating role of the investor is not that of a mere observer of reality either, in the sense that the investor modifies his behaviour along the process as he acquires knowledge and experience, adjusting all the time to changing underlying conditions. The investor acts with a kind of informed intuition that results from years of accumulated knowledge and experience. The actor is an observer but is also part of the process, influencing it in a way that coincides with the pursuit of his own interests.

Soros (1998) makes this crucial distinction to explain the concept of reflexivity in describing what he considers a fundamental problem of contemporary economic theory. For Soros, this is the inability of established thought in the economics science in accepting that economic agents are not mere observers of reality, they are also actors and, fundamentally, they are manipulators of reality, shaping it and directing it towards what they perceive to be their individual self-interest.

It is critical not only to make this distinction but also to evidence the role of the manipulative actor to the detriment of the impartial observer. The actor accumulates knowledge in the process and is part of an elaborate script, sharing his biases and prejudices, stereotypes and views of the world. In the case of the financial markets the distinction between intervening investor and mere observer of reality is crucial to a better understanding of the financial system and why it sometimes behaves in ways that run counter to the principles of pseudo-rationality.

Soros uses this line of argument to explain the debacle in the financial markets in 2008. To think that the introduction into the market of an array of toxic financial products should be construed merely as a market response to a perceived demand for these products, and not to understand that the very proliferation of non-backed financial products could indeed have been the genesis of a profound crisis in the financial sector, with ramifications to the rest of the economy, was naive at least, and most probably riddled with criminal intent when all is said and done.

Young and ambitious researchers in investment banks were only too keen to develop complex mathematical algorithms that were the underlying conceptual foundations to toxic financial products. Their real purpose was to pass risk along a complex chain of risk-takers only too willing to buy into this pyramid scheme convinced as they were of permanent economic payoffs. The mathematical complexity of these products discouraged senior executives from scrutiny and monitoring, who, as a result of their incommensurate greed, collected the money and thought no more of it.

Left to their own devices, and on a long leash, these investment bank researchers and traders had the leeway to fully express their basic instincts of money-making and avarice at any cost. The idea was that the market would eventually sort things out. There would be winners and losers as is always the case, but nothing more than that. Hollywood would perpetuate the myth, and in the 1980s, the motion picture *Wall Street* featured a young Michael Douglas playing Gordon Gekko, the quintessential Wall Street maverick, who at the height of a climax of cynicism claims that 'greed is good', certainly a good epitaph for that particular brand of capitalism and an apt synthesis of the times.

Traditional bankers, who had learnt their trade in a different world, one of much more rigour and control over the scope and consequences of financial activities, found it difficult to adjust to the ways of contemporary times. On the one hand, there wasn't anybody around from the time of the 1929 crash and, on the other, those traditional bankers never felt perfectly at ease with a new lexicon and even less so with a culture that they simply failed to understand. The former included such dense terminology as futures and derivatives, strange and weird names, including plain vanilla swaps, call and put options and others, whose content did not disclose much to the uninformed and certainly not to the technically ignorant. These names were sexy but not understood by most, and hid an unknown world where money flowed in abundance.

Inasmuch as these traditional bankers were trained to concentrate on the fundamentals of the business, the promise of a new world of unlimited profits, easy money and the incredible notion that all of this was achievable with minimum risk was too attractive an opportunity to miss out on. It was in that way, that oscillating between shameless avarice and pure dishonesty, we all found out to our despair that the emperor wore no clothes. Very quickly the scandals involving the Arthur Andersens, Barings, WorldComs and Enrons of this world began to appear before a startled corporate America and beyond. More would follow.

The dishonesty of some bankers and the corruption of some politicians and top-level executives in large multinationals were fertile ground for those who, out of ideological conviction, had always understood the regulatory role of government as needing to be somewhat more than symbolic and toothless. The anathema of market self-regulation, the belief in internal market solutions tending to market equilibrium, the philosopher's stone of an invisible hand that would kick in to restore balance where there was imbalance, and normality when chaos ensued, all came tumbling down amidst surprise and collective fear.

All of this created the moral legitimacy for a dangerous u-turn in favour of turning back the tide towards a more meaningful role for government intervention in economic activity and specifically a tighter control over financial markets. This call for more government was not so much about the healthy monitoring and enforcement of the rules of engagement of stakeholders in the economic building but a more fundamental shift towards a more interventionist state. As always it is in finding a virtuous middle-ground that the answer resides.

The basic premise was that, in the end, the market would, through the alchemy of an invisible hand, expurgate bad behaviour whilst rewarding the good guys. Academia would provide the theoretical and intellectual legitimacy to this thinking and contribute to this rather naive view of the world, by casting in stone in the minds of young aspirers to the economics profession, the redeeming fatalism of a regenerating market, a market that has inbuilt into its essence the internal mechanisms to restore equilibrium and solve all of our problems. Curricular academic programmes in economic theory would end up with pacifying chapters aptly termed general equilibrium. The future would demonstrate that the invisible hand would indeed prove to be invisible and elusive.

To think that these ambitious investment banks in Wall Street or in the City of London, including such powerhouses as J.P. Morgan, Merrill Lynch or

Goldman Sachs, would limit themselves to withdrawing maximum gain from this reality and not influence it to their own benefit was naive to say the least. To think that they would not interfere in the markets to the point of distorting their logic and underlying fundamentals if they saw in it the opportunity for further gains was utopian and demonstrative of a collective inability to understand the real genesis of what was at stake here.

The problem is one of basic human greed, and the historical imperative for a tight monitoring of the activities of those who stand to gain most has to necessarily imply the introduction of mechanisms that make, insofar as that is possible, individual gain coincide with the collective welfare of society. This should be ever present in the minds of policy-makers.

The same applies to the belief that in the absence of effective regulatory mechanisms, banks would be guided by principles and practices of self-discipline and caution. The huge profits that these institutions were earning were simply too tempting and any perception of risk was diluted by the unfounded, yet popular idea of limitless growth, and worse, grounded on the premise that all of this could easily be achieved with a modicum of risk exposure. A new paradigm, of all gain and no risk, was given credence to, and everyone seemed to embark on this journey of effortless and unlimited success, with no questions asked, particularly by those who should have been asking all the questions.

To have believed that the downturn in this paper economy would not have clear and dire repercussions on the real economy of production, and that all of this was in the end no more than market forces at work, the resultant of the actions of economic agents coming together freely and individually pursuing self-interest, was to say the least naive. This was a much more complex process than it is thought and portrayed even today. It was, in essence, an interventionist process, one that acted and distorted market conditions and modified them beyond recognition. Not fully comprehending this was to be the downfall of many.

Warren Buffett of Berkshire Hathaway stated in a rare interview given to Ted Koppel of ABC Nightline that, when investing in company stock, the organizations that he carefully picked for investment had to make business sense. A fundamental condition for Buffett and indeed one that needed to be verified when investing in a company was that he needed to understand the business, its purpose and objectives.

Buffett had to believe that the business made sense otherwise he would not put his money or that of his investors into that business. It seems common sense and straightforward as a suggestion, but to pay attention to the fundamentals of a business became in the years leading up to the financial debacle of 2008 more the exception rather than the rule when picking stock, as a tendency for speculative behaviour had become deeply entrenched in the world of financial markets.

A company's strategy and its presence and position in the market or its great products should ultimately be the cues that potential investors need to look out for, but often all of this falls by the wayside as speculative behaviour, short-term tactics and a search for speedy financial results that attract further investment take over. Understanding the market and the organization, fully comprehending its products and customers, what needs, current or latent, the former cater to in this or other markets were the key investment criteria for Buffett. In a nutshell, investment decisions were, for the Chairman of Berkshire Hathaway, about an absolute imperative, that of the organization making commercial sense.

Buffett was adamant on this and he relayed his views unequivocally to Ted Koppel. This interview took place, in effect, not long before the earthquake that shook the financial markets and its institutions in 2009. In it, Warren Buffett warned of a new kind of investor, one that did not pay much attention to the fundamentals of the business, focussing instead on the short-term, thinking and acting speculatively, and with little sympathy for sustained growth or the long term.

A global world where information is easily propagated to every corner of the landscape has brought everyone closer together, impacting quotidian lives but also the lives of organizations, and the way business is conducted across the world. The geographical scope of information coverage can, in today's interconnected and web-like world of intricate economic relationships, be a much more important factor than factual content or rigour.

Following the crisis in the financial markets in 2008 there was in Great Britain and in most developed economies ample discussion about the role of the media and its contribution to the downturn in the economy. The media may indeed have a responsibility for what is the collective non-response to policy stimuli on social and economic issues and it does so by reinforcing negative perceptions and feelings about the economy and the lives of people.

The reinforcement of bad feelings among key stakeholders in the economy and society, namely investors and consumers, thus becomes a self-fulfilling prophecy.

Never before has information reached so many, unhindered and uncensored. The internet has, only in recent years, facilitated the democratization of access to information in revolutionary and unthinkable ways. Access to information by common people, otherwise destitute of any understanding of what goes on around them, is a radical departure from a status quo of information isolation or vetting depending on where one came from. In addition to that, the scrutiny of editorial guidelines and their inherent subjectivity along with the proliferation of a new breed of opinion-makers, who pass judgement on just about every contemporary issue, implies that analyses and opinion often replace factual content and this is also a relatively recent phenomenon. Ideological bias, personal agendas or economic interest, and often all of these simultaneously, act to make it difficult to separate fact from a constructed pseudo-reality.

Beyond the economic interests that frequently permeate these promiscuous relationships, a subjective and opinion-laden interpretation of reality replaces fact in the eyes of many. This has obvious consequences at a time of uncertainty when distinguishing what is real from what is merely subjective construction would be most welcome by many. It is clear that the financial crisis that has led to the worst economic crisis in decades is unfortunately a fact of contemporary times. However, its causes and societal ramifications and consequences are not unanimously and equitably understood.

In fact differing ideological filters will imply that the story be told differently, depending on where one comes from in the political and ideological spectrum. Not only is bias an issue here, but the effects of the financial crisis and their extrapolation to the real economy may be exacerbated, by a negativist and persistent reporting of the current situation as bad, thus reinforcing negative collective vibes.

The bankruptcy of the idea of self-regulation for the institutions of a financial system operating globally, that has introduced the world to a deep economic crisis the likes of which one struggles to find historical precedents in contemporary times, must objectively be unquestionable. This has meant that in its aftermath, societies and their elected governments must find it imperative to exercise a close monitoring of the institutions of the financial system and their activities in the coming decades. This has to be an overriding concern for policy-makers. In particular, mechanisms are needed that curtail speculative behaviour mitigating an undesirable distance between fictional and factual economies, between paper economies and economies of substance and production.

In this way, stock markets stand to play the role that is their raison d'être, that of being efficient and reliable barometers of real economic activity. The effective regulation, monitoring and enforcement by government of a set of principles that have been severely distorted in the past in the name of the free-market, constitute reasons for public concern. Also, and directly flowing from what has been described, is the malaise of contemporary economies, the nightmare of policy-makers in most developed economies worldwide, and that is an absolute ineptitude on the part of government institutions in restoring confidence in the system and devolving the initiative to economic agents.

Many, armed with solid academic credentials, experienced and versed on all matters economic have difficulty in understanding what is at issue here and in dealing individually in their daily lives with what is happening today. If this is the case for the apparently knowledgeable, for those that are not familiarized with economic theory, these problems manifest themselves as outright insuperable. In this context individuals react as expected, with extreme precaution, saving for a rainy day and focussing closely on their immediate survival. News of successive bankruptcies and groups of people protesting outside factories that shut down daily cannot fail to have a disproportionate and negative direct impact on the collective psyche, an impact that in absolute terms would never be as pronounced. But these are the costs of a state of immediate and global media scrutiny.

In contemporary societies, the role of the media has been much more than that of portraying facts objectively, and opinion and ideological bias as well as less honourable motives, including unreasonable economic interest and political manipulation, have become more prominent in the media agenda in western democracies. Fiction and opinion often exceed fact, and judgement and interpretation have come to replace objectivity of analyses to the point where both are undistinguishable to the common punter on the street. The role of the media should in essence be one of reporting fact, but at a time when all types of media avidly dispute the attention and the valuable and scarce time of the common person, its constituents individually need to do more and more to grab collective attention.

In a saturated, intensely fought and competitive environment, a kind of mass hysteria emerges, caused by the constant pursuit of audiences and ratings, an exacerbation of reality, post-rationalized and justified ad nauseum by what are perceived to be the interests of different audiences and stakeholder groups and the economic imperative of the organizations that sustain what is in effect a mega business. The gratuitous exposition of emotion must necessarily have an impact on the collective psyche conditioning the subsequent behaviour of those for whose benefit this is carefully orchestrated and manicured. If it attracts audiences, then it is all for the better.

The Vietnam War was broadcast daily into the living rooms of millions of American households, in the 1960s. This is widely acknowledged as one of the principal contributors to the withdrawal of the US from Vietnam in defeat, in what was undoubtedly the greatest humiliation ever inflicted on the American military structure in its 200-year history and beyond. The recurring and infamous vision of bags containing the bodies of young American soldiers being offloaded from Hercules C130s did more to end the war than the action of the Vietcong in the military theatre of operations. The protests that soon ensued in Washington DC were relentless, with Lyndon Johnson pressured into finding a compromise solution for an untenable and unwinnable war.

Many years later in Iraq, and in a context where technology allowed for real-time coverage of events and an exhaustive and detailed scrutiny of the situation on the terrain, the American Government, wisely advised by its military leadership, decided that the media coverage of the war would be different this time. The military hierarchy clearly saw that the coverage of events as they unfolded would have a decisive and detrimental impact on war objectives, and consequently on the national interest. With that in mind, the Government decided to censor any graphic exposure and reporting from the war theatre. The American Government was not about to make the same mistake of a few decades earlier in Vietnam.

Graphic images of dead American soldiers being carried away were rarely if ever seen by the masses back in America throughout the first Iraq war in 1991. This was true of regular broadcasting but of course cable channels were also inhibited from exhibiting and crucially obtaining this kind of footage. Today, and with the advent of YouTube, all of this would have been much more difficult to monitor, but at the time the images of crude realism that had emanated from Vietnam were replaced by a new concept of so-called surgical warfare in Iraq. Viewers could see from the comfort of their own homes, very much in the same way as could be found in any games arcade, a background of green, with a dot at the centre of a target, voices preceding a flash, followed by the clamour of enthusiasm for yet another job well done.

A sanitized version of violence, of course, impacts the collective psyche in a radically different manner from that which is suggested by the exposure to graphic images of dead soldiers in military body bags. We know rationally that the dot is indeed a human being, a person, but the internalization of that sentiment is strongly diminished by the absence of a visualization of the fact. It is a kind of diminished responsibility that we feel, and that in effect constitutes a dehumanization of the act.

Curiously, and in a cruel way, the dot on a screen, juxtaposed on a target, is not dissimilar from the screen of any computer game played by your average adolescent on a Saturday morning anywhere in the world. In an absolutely sinister way, our reaction does not differ much when watching a man being killed from hitting a dot on a computer screen. The crudeness of an image has powers that cannot be underestimated, and that is duly thought through by the military strategists and the warlords.

When Ben Shalom Bernanke, Chairman of the Federal Reserve Bank, hesitates in conceding an interview, he does it fully in the knowledge that just about everything he says will be deconstructed and subjected to interpretation by the economic stakeholders and, in reality, by virtually anyone who has a vested interest in the functioning of the markets. Not only will anything he says be deeply scrutinized, but newspaper editors and other media pundits, and the whole gamut of opinion-makers that proliferate in TV networks, radio and internet blogs, will seek to interpret his every word.

They can easily distort the true meaning and intentions of Bernanke's message for the benefit of audience ratings and often to the detriment of the interests of wider society. In a way, anything that Bernanke says is subject to a deep scrutiny, varying interpretations and alternative readings by whoever has potential access to mass communication, and if we are to include the internet that is virtually the whole planet.

When a few years ago, Steve Ballmer, President of Microsoft, and number two to Bill Gates at the helm of the organization, stated outside a hotel in Seattle that, 'There's such an overvaluation of tech stocks, it's absurd', the information quickly began to circulate on the internet and at the end of trading day the

NASDAQ had fallen to its fourth worst point ever. That afternoon, the personal wealth of one of the most important Microsoft shareholders had suffered a spectacular setback. That was Ballmer himself who had amassed a personal fortune of US$23 billion in Microsoft stock.

With the unprecedented fall of the NASDAQ, the net worth of Ballmer's Microsoft shareholdings was reduced by US$1 billion at close of trade. That afternoon he spoke to an attentive press. Few at the time felt sorry for Ballmer's loss as he was still worth a hefty fortune of around US$22 billion in Microsoft share value alone. Unfortunately, the same cannot be said of the thousands of other small Microsoft shareholders, who saw the value of their shareholdings in the organization come tumbling down in little over a few hours. This of course raises complex issues as to the legitimacy of what can be said and in which context it can be said. The borderline between one's personal freedom and that of others appears to be a complex affair in contemporary times. The role of mass communication in interpreting the cues and mannerisms of wheelers and dealers in contemporary societies has consequences that go beyond the mere reporting of fact. In effect they denounce an unambiguous shift away from reporting fact to fact-making and subjective interpretation.

The role of government is also being constantly redefined. This is an ongoing debate, one that has been fuelled by the considerable change pervading the world in contemporary times, largely induced by the recent turmoil in the global economy. The recurrent debate is over the superiority of the free-market model over the idea of state intervention and the close control by governments of economic systems and their constituent organizations and institutions.

The very notion of a paradigmatic clash with ideological antecedents manifested in political systems that were for decades mutually exclusive and antagonistic, seems to be a fundamental drawback to any attempt at reconciling the strengths of both models, with a view to attaining a sustainable and dynamic equilibrium. On the one hand, some justifiably construe the notion of excessive government intervention as akin to a civilizational backward leap, one that nullifies the many conquests of free-market economics, including the significant betterment of living conditions for just about everyone. On the other hand, if the current crises has illuminated the debate on the virtues and shortcomings of free-market economics vis-à-vis the role and scope of government intervention in any significant way, it is that the market is anything but regenerative in its capacity to restore equilibrium, at least in the way that Friedmanian neoclassics and the Chicago School monetarists had aspired and proposed.

Upon observation it is clear that the evidence grounded in reality strongly disputes a key tenet of free-market economics that, when in the pursuit of their well-being, individuals will inevitably contribute to the common good through the creation and subsequent distribution of wealth for everyone to enjoy. Although it is undisputed that the standards of living have risen sharply in virtually every economy under free-market philosophies, it is also unquestionable that in many cases the asymmetries between the haves and the have nots in societies are still very pronounced.

The idea that higher levels of individual wealth are strongly correlated with wealth distribution is strongly disputed, particularly by those who argue against unprecedented levels of income inequality throughout the world and often in developed economies. Nonetheless, few would argue against the fact that never like today has the population of many a place around the world attained standards of living of a calibre that is unmatched by anything witnessed at any time anywhere in the history of mankind. It is also true, however, that asymmetries in contemporary societies are vast and acute, and most tragically, conveyed for everyone to witness by means of a plethora of media who drastically exacerbate these differences.

Never like today have those asymmetries in living standards been so exposed for so many to see. The role of the media and also that of the new technologies in bringing information to people and shaping perceptions is unprecedented. The internet plays a critical role in the provision of information but also in the distortion of fact, and that cannot be underestimated. Watching on TV, often through vastly unrealistic lenses, many of the deprived witness in bewilderment and in anguish the portrayal of what passes for the quotidian everyday reality of common people who live in, what for the poor is, the inaccessible oasis of economically developed countries.

These portraits are most often than not sanitized and idealized versions of what life is supposed to be in the developed world. In surreal ways the anonymous masses of deprived cannot but feel an immense revolt, anguish and repugnance to what they see as conspicuous consumption, something that they cannot even begin to aspire, riddled as they are in the more mundane and immediate concerns of everyday human survival.

The last decade, if anything, has demonstrated that the developed world has not done well to underestimate and even to ignore the notion that permanent humiliation over a sufficient period of time will inevitably breed contempt.

If in addition to that the collective perception is such that social stratification and privilege are perpetuated by virtue of race, ethnic background, country of origin and difference in creed, it follows that much of the social unrest afflicting contemporary societies becomes easier to fathom.

The portrayal of a collective anguish euphemistically termed as animosity against the west (when more realistically it is just pure old fashioned hate) cooked in a cauldron of humiliation is one of the consequences of this. In the face of what are undignified living conditions, when contrasted against the utopian picture of an idealized western quotidian, the poor begin to express their disenchantment.

In a hotbed of religious fundamentalism, fringe elements in these societies find the ideal conditions for the manipulation of the millions of destitute. These, faced with dire economic conditions, uneducated and unskilled, do not possess the necessary educational and psychological filters to even begin to comprehend what is dawning on them. A failure to fully grasp reality and principally the underlying circumstances and conditions that have contributed to the abject poverty and inequality that pervades their existence and the absence of viable alternatives to an announced destiny of doom will inevitably breed the ground for manipulation, violence and religious fundamentalism. Education for all is of course the solution, but education provides exactly the kind of awareness that is the antithesis of totalitarianism and autocracy. In that way education is understandably undesirable for despots.

Deprived of even the most basic means of sustenance, offended in their dignity and watching others live with so much whilst they make do with nothing, it is no wonder that this growing army of the hungry has begun to revolt. One of the greatest challenges of the next decade is to reconcile this most crucial of dichotomies, the moral viability of a social model where the unconcerned wealthy live parallel, but not side by side, lives with the billions of destitute who barely struggle to survive. The have nots do not require much more in the way of evidence to conclude that all of this is no more than a well concocted, deliberate and sinister plan elaborated by those who control the world to exclude them from what they believe is rightfully theirs, the right to a dignified life. They may just be right on the last bit.

In this context, religious fundamentalism is the ideal catalyst for a dangerous chemistry of burning antagonism between the haves and the have nots. Religious fundamentalism is also often wrongly postulated as an indicator of a schism in civilizations. Economic asymmetries and social inequality would always constitute ample ground for acute protestation independently of culture or religious affiliation.

This is to do with a kind of economic asymmetry that is offensive to human dignity and that surpasses even religious belief as a trigger for social unrest. The have nots would still be protesting their exclusion from the rest of society if similar economic asymmetries were to prevail in more secular regimes. When people are not protesting that is normally because the wider the class and income asymmetries the more forceful the repression that is used to perpetuate them.

Switching gears, the reader will know of Michael Moore, political activist, cinematographer and social protestor with an acute distrust of anything corporate and a paladin of well-known causes against the large multinational conglomerates particularly if they are American. People probably know Michael best as a film-maker (*Roger & Me* and various others). He is, depending on where you stand in the ideological spectrum, a true Ralph Nader of contemporary times or a dangerous communist. He is also, more often than he would care, described as a dangerous anti-America protestor and worse of them all, a traitor.

The reason for introducing Moore at this point are the ideas behind a controversial book that he published a few years ago aptly entitled *Dude, Where's My Country* (2004), a follow-up to *Stupid White Men* (2002), where Moore takes a stab at the Bush (son) administration and particularly at Bush himself. All this is done with an explosive mix of comedic aggressiveness often bordering on serious character assassination.

In a judicial system that is well-known for its propensity for easy litigation, Moore had no qualms in directing extremely grave accusations at Bush when describing what, according to him, happened in America throughout the 1990s and 2000s. Moore alludes to the irreparable damage of the so-called War on Terror initiated by President Bush as a well-manicured distraction for a nation who turned a blind eye to the financial scandals that shook corporate America all through those decades.

Moore recalls the Horatio Alger complex, from which many Americans appear to suffer. Horatio Alger was a popular American author from the end of the nineteenth century. His books were mostly about those who came from the lower strata of society, who through hard work managed to reach the top, a kind of intellectual precursor to the American dream, a key cornerstone of twentieth-century capitalist philosophy. This thinking actualized to contemporary times means that the average American still believes that one of the perks of being American, and solidly inherent to that condition, is that the get rich quick theory of life will always be a possibility in America and for Americans.

Moore calls the reader's attention to this seductive myth of American capitalism to justify the behaviour of millions of American workers who began to invest in the stock market in the 1990s. In 1980, 20 per cent of the American people possessed some form of corporate stock. Back then the stock market was mostly a game for the wealthy. It was also a risky game.

The great economic boom of the 1990s could not have subsisted forever and it was therefore important that the middle classes were able to finance the growth of American multinationals. In that way workers were incentivized to buy shares in the companies that they worked for, investing in the stock market, thereby inflating the true market value of these companies' stock which often traded for ridiculously high prices. This was also the time when the wealthy decided to sell out and leave the stock market.

In September 2002, *Fortune* magazine presented a list of corporate crooks who had sold their holdings of company stock as the organizations they worked for sunk, their market valuation reduced by as much as 75 per cent between 1999 and 2002. Companies such as AOL Time Warner, Sun Microsystems or Qwest Communications saw their senior executives selling their stock at the high price point, whilst the average American merrily continued to buy stock from those companies, thus maintaining artificially high stock valuations. Did these senior executives know something that the common Joe or Jane did not? That they probably did is a very tempting answer, and perhaps one not far from the truth.

The American Treasury Secretary at the time, Paul H. O'Neill, would later concede that well before 11 September 2001 there had been plans to attack Iraq, thus defeating the fragile notion that there was indeed a link between the War on Terror and Iraqi terrorist activities, which supposedly was to cause the subsequent invasion of this country by the American military. Michael Moore also denounces the business relationships and interests between the Bush clan and several members of the Bin Laden family, dating back to the 1970s, with oil as the common denominator, and obscene profits being made in the process.

Coincidentally, or perhaps not, not one single Iraqi national played an active role in the 11 September tragedy. Effectively most terrorists were Saudi nationals, a country with whose royal family the Bush clan had very old and solid business connections.

Michael Moore's book was a success in the US and is frequently referenced particularly in ideological circles of a certain American left. His ideas are not taken as seriously as they should perhaps be, given Moore's own relaxed image and profile. However, equipped with the right dosage of irony and an acute spirit of scrutiny of the incumbent status quo, Moore keeps hammering away at corporate America and the Federal Government.

In a simple, humoured and razor-sharp way, he continues his crusade against what he sees as aberrations of the capitalist system. He deconstructs the contemporary reality of large American multinational organizations, approaching in singular fashion the issues currently afflicting American society. This was evident in Moore's film *Bowling for Columbine* where he denounced the gun problem in American high schools. Only recently the events in Newtown, Connecticut tragically brought the gun issue and the pervasive role of the National Rifle Association (NRA) back to the forefront. His work calls everyone's attention to the great conglomerate organizations, to white-collar crime, to nefarious and outrageous management and to unjustified and ostentatious greed.

Around that time, Bernie Ebbers, CEO of WorldCom, showed up on the front page of unsuspected titles, including *Time* magazine, alongside Bill Clinton, as the personification of what the modern entrepreneur in the new economic order should look like, the very embodiment of a macro-manager, a strategist of a large corporation, a visionary in the new economy. Everything he touched appeared to transform into gold, an alchemy where only a few seemed to be concerned about its details. The best business schools in the world lauded his iconic vision and his business model for WorldCom was the stuff of legend, with case studies written and lectures lauding his feats the world over, as many bright people attempted to explain Ebbers' secret to a few but well selected brilliant minds.

For US$60,000, these exceptional students would receive teachings in draconian forms of trimming down expenditure or streamlining cost structures, in what came to be euphemistically termed in the business school lexicon as cost rationalization. In the end, cutting excessive fat was what it was all about.

However, the reality underpinning all of this business wizardry, which many attempted to package in an attractive theoretical and conceptual body of knowledge, thus giving it the intellectual legitimacy that it sorely lacked, was much more sinister than that which words may hope to describe.

The whole thing, as it transpired later, constituted nothing less than deliberate criminal behaviour for the indulgence and benefit of Bernie himself, who ended up charged and convicted of several crimes and in 2006 was sent to jail to serve a prison sentence of 25 years. In order to clearly assess the promiscuity and cynicism entailed in all of this, it is worth mentioning that the Midas touch was given by Wall Street, for whom Bernie Ebbers epitomized anything and everything that was good about corporate America. Ebbers was seen by most as someone with a new business model who dared to defy the old boys in the telecommunications establishment, including the corporate likes of AT&T and Sprint.

The WorldCom case becomes even more sinister when it is known that seasoned individuals with many years of experience at the highest level of management in the telecommunications sector, for example the senior executives at Sprint and AT&T, WorldCom's direct competitors, and incumbents in the American telecommunications sector, were not able to comprehend how WorldCom was able to keep its cost structure so streamlined and controlled.

Nobody at AT&T or Sprint could figure out just how WorldCom could conceivably operate on such a low cost structure. In reality it did not. Once again, there occasionally are paradigm shifts in the world of business, either in a particular sector of economic activity or even globally, by virtue of someone emerging with new knowledge and technology or just a better business model.

The danger is in thinking that everything under the sun is a result of a radically new business model, or of improved management practices. The truth is that not many dared to question the raison d'être for Ebbers' success and the methods that anchored this success. There subsisted little doubt as to Bernie Ebbers' methods, but few cared to remember that the world had not borne witness to a miracle for a while.

As with the Barings Bank scenario, abnormal profitability, originating from speculative financial market activity, was never questioned. WorldCom's competitors should perhaps have had an inkling as to the real state of affairs in the Kingdom of Denmark. WorldCom, which started out as a small company operating out of an obscure town in Mississippi ironically called Clinton, couldn't have made all the right moves and walked all the right strategic paths whilst making a mockery of established companies like AT&T and Sprint and their lack of strategic acumen.

Instead of questioning the status quo, top executives in these companies engaged in intestine Board-level battles with members mutually apportioning blame on each other, exchanging accusations as they coped miserably with what they saw as their inability to compete with WorldCom. Those in charge of operations or new product development would blame marketing for not being able to sell AT&T services capably. Marketing in turn would blame production for not developing excellent products and services, at least good enough to compete with those of WorldCom's. That being the case they couldn't sell as well.

Amidst this pseudo-competitive environment, AT&T built thousands of miles of cable when the idea was put forward, and uncontrollably propagated that internet traffic would double every 100 days. Nobody ever knew the genesis of this story but it appears that a mere analyst working for WorldCom under the name of Tom Stluka conjured the idea that internet traffic would double every 100 days.

No one thought of asking him what the assumptions for building the forecasting model were but it soon became common knowledge that indeed internet traffic would double every 100 days. Not only did this prediction go beyond mere folklore, a pseudo-model of internet growth, built on falsehoods, soon became the centrepiece of WorldCom's strategy and amazingly also that of AT&T's and Sprint's. If all of this is beginning to resonate much like the key problems with macro-economic models and their surreal assumptions, then the outcome for both WorldCom as with macro-economic forecasting was not great.

In a subsequent interview to a national TV network, Stluka admitted to the projection on the growth of electronic traffic not exactly having been a forecast. In truth most of it was no more than sheer opinion. When queried on the working assumptions of the model he admitted in a rather candid and frank manner that there weren't any. Effectively the forecast of exponential internet traffic growth was not based on rigorous mathematical modelling. It was Tom Stluka's guess as to the future of internet traffic. As an opinion it was certainly as valuable as that of the reader's, or mine, only it came from inside WorldCom, making it perhaps an exercise in wishful thinking. Of course, it was an opinion that coincided with the strategic interests of WorldCom, but nevertheless, still an opinion.

However, this would constitute precisely the kind of pseudo-scientific knowledge that would justify WorldCom's leadership ideas and strategic thinking at the time. The cornerstone of WorldCom's strategy was focussed on a massive investment on cable technology, with the company using Stluka's findings to attract investors to the telecoms business. Incredibly long-established household names in the telecommunications industry, and foremost among which were AT&T and Sprint, also did not bother to question Stluka's internet traffic growth model, and they began to build cable as if there was no tomorrow.

The generalist press corroborated all of this and it didn't really matter that one or two voices, usually from academic circles, vociferously contested the validity of such a projection on electronic traffic growth. The message was not the one that everyone wished for and consequently, and as is the norm in these cases, the script dictates that the messenger is the one that needs riddance.

For WorldCom, however, the business model was simple and straightforward. From the moment that financial results began to dwindle it was never deemed important to change organizational strategy and the path where the company was heading. The most important thing for WorldCom executives was to hide the bad news. It was particularly important that Wall Street was not privy to any negativity emanating from the portrayal of a negative financial picture of the organization. From the moment that it began to transpire to the financial markets that not everything was running smoothly at WorldCom, investors would surely begin to lose interest and the chain of inward investment flows would be irreversibly broken.

In order for investors to keep an interest in the organization, financial results had to be consistently positive. Not only did current financial results have to be good, the viability of the company as a going concern had to be guaranteed. That also needed to be the perception of the financial markets. This is where an extremely favourable projected growth model in a crucial strategic business area for the organization, that of internet traffic, came in handy.

In this context does it really matter that there is no rationale or mathematical foundation underlying the model, or that in a strict sense one should not even be alluding to Stluka's endeavours as a forecasting model? As far as WorldCom was concerned there was a message of unfathomable corporate success that needed to be conveyed to the world. True or false, that was not deemed relevant. But it should have been.

WorldCom was rightfully expected to abide by the highest standards of pristine corporate ethical behaviour. The truth of the matter is that they did not. They did not in the case of WorldCom, but also in the cases of Barings Bank, Enron, Arthur Anderson, Madoff, AIG, the savings and loans debacle, and numerous others over little more than a decade. Perhaps a much more regulated environment with much tougher enforcement would have generated a different outcome.

In the case of WorldCom, in keeping a monster of this magnitude alive and well fed, something which in philosophy and procedure did not differ much from many of the euphemistically termed corporate mishaps of the 1990s and 2000s, that in a crescendo culminated in the financial debacle of 2008, one condition sufficed, and that was that the message conveyed to the market had to be positive. Good news attracted investors. The WorldComs of this world would continue to generate equity capital from avid investors looking for quick returns.

This was precisely the reason why WorldCom did not accurately report operational expenses that could have adversely impacted on their bottom-line picture, their income statements. Instead it treated these expenses as asset depreciations and reported them as such on the balance sheet. In reporting distorted and artificially high profits, WorldCom ensured a positive outlook which kept investors pouring in. The imperative here was to keep the show on the road by portraying as rosy a picture of the organization to Wall Street as was possible, and everything appeared to be possible in those times of relaxed regulation in the land of rampant capitalism. As WorldCom's reported company accounts had little adherence to any underlying reality, the company sought to manipulate reality in accordance with the interests of the stock market.

There had been ample precedent and a long-established tradition of creative accounting. Many authors had denounced dubious accounting practices over the years. In 1992, Terry Smith published *Accounting for Growth*. Having worked in the City, he decided to bring to the forefront what many knew was common practice in the field, the manipulation of accounting norms and principles in the often fraudulent portrayal of organizational reality. The book was not taken lightly by those with vested interests in perpetuating the status quo. It was clear even back in 1992 that the borderline between creative accounting and fraud was more tenuous than one would care to think.

The WorldCom debacle did not differ in essence from basic schemes of pyramid marketing. As long as more money was being pumped into the system than that which came out of it, the system worked. As soon as that ceased to be the case, problems arose. Whilst the message was positive, investors kept pumping money into the company. As soon as suspicion began to creep in, investors became concerned and almost immediately the organization and its viability as a going concern began to be seriously questioned. As the portrayal of the company became less positive, a sombre mood very soon began to characterize investor behaviour. Investors became suspicious and they began to divest from the organization. The process very quickly became a self-fulfilling prophecy in that a sufficiently significant group of people began to panic, making others run for cover and divest away from the company.

Just as in any middle of the road pyramid sales scheme, the moment of truth is at a key point when less money goes into the system than the payoffs that it needs to generate to pay avid investors who pump money into the system expecting abnormally high returns. Typically, in pyramid schemes, when there is a shortage of funds to pay interest on current deposits, or to reimburse those who decide to abandon the scheme on their capital outlays, the mere fact of this occurring triggers a whole snowball effect of depositors running for their lives and withdrawing capital invested. From then on there is no way back.

WorldCom and run-of-the-mill pyramid schemes share in essence a common denominator. The recipient of investment deposits has to go out and search for investment opportunities that offer higher rates of return than those he agreed to pay the depositor. If there is to be any idea of economic sustainability to the model and its viability in the long term, he also needs to do it legally, thus limiting the nature and scope of activities available for investment.

Of course all of this is of an extreme simplicity, but one should never underestimate the power of illusion. When buying a lottery ticket one never stops to calculate the statistical (im)probability of winning the top prize. Were we to do this we would never buy a lottery ticket or pick six numbers on the six/49 draw. However it is a fact of life that if there is one prosperous and lucrative industry, it is that of gambling. Even in times of economic crises, when other sectors of economic activity are depressed and superfluous expenditures in gambling would be expected to decline, the industry flourishes. It is often precisely in times of economic downturn that gambling prospers, anchored as the industry is on a collective psychology of hoping against hope.

In the case of WorldCom, not only were business and economics schools impressed by Bernie Ebbers' management style and WorldCom's revolutionary strategic business model, but AT&T, the American mammoth of the telecommunications industry, was incapable of understanding just how WorldCom was able to produce such spectacular financial results and, in particular, how it was able to streamline its cost structure and keep it a bare minimum.

WorldCom's cost rationalization strategy soon became a corporate obsession with WorldCom's competitors, and AT&T meetings of the Board often saw mutual accusations being thrown amongst its members, bewildered at WorldCom's cost-cutting prowess. AT&T meanwhile failed miserably in its attempt to bring their own cost structure down to comparable levels. CNBC was to document the cut-throat work environment at AT&T at the time as a climate of mutual accusation and apportioning of blame, with terrible consequences for the organization.

Top executives at AT&T, a long-established giant in the world of telecommunications, were simply unable to comprehend how a small-time hillbilly coming out of the backwater of Clinton, Mississippi could even begin to venture into the hi-tech world of telecommunications. For Ebbers to have entered that industry out of Clinton, Mississippi and to have done it successfully and in a way that he was able to outperform his competitors on every relevant business dimension defied logic. A company with no tradition or history in the market was able to outdo its competitors systematically.

WorldCom's tight control over its cost structure and the degree of effectiveness in bringing it down was unmatchable by its competitors, who simply failed to understand how this could be possible. As a sustainable business model it defied belief, or so one would assume that to be the case, but in effect few dared to question the ethics of the business and most preferred to embark on lauding the incredible management skills of Ebbers the alchemist, who could turn into gold everything he touched, from the motel business to the telecommunications industry.

Bernie Ebbers preached to whoever cared to listen to him that his management style had a lot to do with his past as a small hotelier or to be more precise a small-time motel chain owner. There, he alleged, no job was beneath management and everything had to be attended to. He would do a little bit of everything and that would have been where he had developed an uncanny ability for cost control. Every little thing counted. As an example he pointed out to some of the chores he had to undertake as owner/manager of a chain of motels, such as mowing the lawn, switching off the lights, as well other very mundane activities. A motel proprietor cannot afford to consider any task menial or too demeaning, he would vehemently argue, and if it was there to be done, he would do it. Bernie Ebbers often pointed to these anecdotes as allegories in the portrayal of a personality obsessed with cost control and a philosophy of rigour in running the business.

Many of these stories became folklore and they often surround Bernie Ebbers' mythology. Bernie, the infallible CEO, personified the draconian executive who optimized scarce corporate resources and soon became a larger than life character in the business world, and a symbol of the new economic order for the wider community. The media was instrumental in carrying all of this of course, as his pseudo-business model based on relentless cost-cutting was elevated to the pedestal of paradigm shift in business management thinking. This unusual competency was attributed precisely to Ebbers' past involvement in the motel business. As in many walks of life, myth replaces reality, and the media scrutiny is superficial and lightweight for as long as the message that is being conveyed coincides with what everyone wants to hear.

In effect, when things eventually took a turn for the worse, reports began to appear in the press that WorldCom employees were made to pay for their own coffee and that office lights had to be switched off when leaving a room, along with all kinds of draconian measures to ensure that superfluous costs were cut. Ebbers would allegedly monitor such mundane minutiae very closely. Bernie would later dispute all of these allegations and dismiss them as petty accusations, intentionally crafted to damage his reputation, but it soon became folklore that costs at WorldCom were maintained at such low levels precisely because Ebbers was effectively implacable in his control of the company and intolerant to any waste.

Much of this was of course in retrospect sheer perception as, in reality, Ebbers, as well as other members of the WorldCom Board of Administration, lived princely lives in the luxurious and elitist leafy suburbs of a regular city in the American south, in true 'Gone with the Wind' fashion. Here again there exists a world of distance between the myth of draconian cost-cutting at WorldCom and the reality of ostentatious living for its key figureheads.

AT&T, in a desperate move to catch up with WorldCom, also began to lower their cost structure. They did it by firing people, convinced that this was the only viable solution were they to stand a modicum of a chance of competing effectively against WorldCom's cost-cutting strategy. This was of course reflective of a deep-rooted sentiment of panic that pervaded the organization as it became clear that it was very difficult indeed to emulate WorldCom's cost containment achievements.

Thousands of employees were fired by AT&T. Other important market players, including Sprint, decided to let go of many more thousands, convinced as they were that this was the only way forward. If one stops for a moment and thinks that each of those workers was a breadwinner for an average family of four, it is safe to assume that tens of thousands of people were directly or indirectly affected by WorldCom's fraudulent behaviour. If we add to this the psychological impact of these practices on thousands of other companies in the same and other sectors of economic activity, the consequences of having a flagship company of the magnitude and structure of influence of AT&T, organizations who avidly watch for strategic hints from the big boys and see this particular brand of cost cutting as the way forward, and a good indicator as to what their own strategic path should be, then the total human and economic costs of WorldCom's corporate fraud are incalculable.

When finally the bomb went off, the administration at AT&T came to their senses and clearly understood the trap into which they had fallen. Purely and simply, for years they had been incapable of understanding how WorldCom could have been so competitive, thus maintaining their cost structure well below the industry average. It never crossed their minds that the magnitude and gravity of the scam was as cheeky and carefully crafted as it turned out to be. WorldCom's accounts were fraudulent and their reputable accountants validated and endorsed them.

Here again the power of illusion is immense and cannot be underestimated. The illusion always exists that someone, somewhere out there will always be capable of churning out a better business model, embodying a paradigm shift that occasionally revolutionizes the best practices in the sector. Even if the incumbents happen to be very senior executives with years of experience in a particular sector, and even if they are known to understand the business inside out and better than anybody else, there is always the possibility that someone, somewhere in the world, has indeed come up with a new business model, a better way of doing things.

In AT&T and Sprint's defence, it would not have been possible to suspect such audacious behaviour from Bernard Ebbers and WorldCom. Had they an inkling of suspicion, the word would have come out much sooner because all that the situation required was a trigger, which would have shied investors away from WorldCom for good as the true picture of the organization was divulged to the rest of the world. The trigger would of course have been any suspicion laid on WorldCom's accounts and their integrity.

When organizations abandon their core competencies, and that which they know how to do well, in the pursuit of activities whose essence and fundamentals are alien to them, the conditions for failure are effectively created. When companies go off the track, particularly to engage in speculative activities in the financial markets for which they have no vocation, they lose control over a fundamental aspect of their existence. To put it simply they lose their footing and know not where they are in the overall scheme of things.

They begin to worry less about building houses or plastic moulding machines, textiles or footwear or retail and enter into an obsession for closely monitoring the evolution of financial markets. They do so anxiously and so they should as under this new paradigm their financial success is linked to how the stock market progresses from one day to the next. Indeed their very success is only marginally attributable to their core business activity. At least that seems to be the case on the surface.

The volatility that is relevant to them ceases to derive from aesthetic, economic and socio-demographic changes in their target clientele and dangerously a new kind of volatility emerges, that of financial markets. However, when one looks at the genuine motivation behind starting a business, it rarely coincides with an exceptional interest or an uncanny ability to understand the world of the financial markets. Businesses arise out of a particular knowledge set of skills or interest of an individual(s) applied to a particular area or issue where there is a perceived market need that offers economic opportunity.

Contrary to this philosophy, the concerns of executives that head these organizations or of the individuals that founded them and had brilliant ideas and concepts that led to their creation were now centred in areas not related to the core business or central purpose that was the genesis and raison d'être behind the creation of these organizations. These financial areas, although important to the success of the organization, were in effect only peripheral to its competitive ability. In particular, speculative financial market activity did not intersect with the amassment of critical knowledge that contributed to an improved understanding of the dynamic determinants of competitiveness in a sector.

In so doing these executives were tragically taking their eye off the ball. They were withdrawing their focus from the fundamental and began to worry about the accessory. They became more complacent and ran risks that are inherent to this type of behaviour. Often they exposed their organizations to unbearable risk, in an environment where they knew little about its critical conditions of success or survival. They hired people that were experts but were then unable to monitor them as the nature of the business and the core competencies and knowledge required for its understanding suddenly became alien to them.

The other fundamental mistake is that, by taking their eye off the ball, they were in effect concentrating less and less on their core business, and that is an unbearable deviation from what they really know how to do. Their concerns ceased to be to understand the behaviour of market demand for the products they manufactured and the services that they provided. They began to pay less attention to new product and market development and they no longer focussed on innovative solutions to challenging threats and opportunities in their own backyard. They ceased to worry about increasing their presence in existing markets.

Instead of that, they allocated scarce resources into what they perceived to be investment opportunities of comparatively higher financial returns, at least when contrasted with the potential returns deriving from their core and original activities. The call was simply too appealing to reject, but it had a sizeable downside too. Often being completely illiterate on financial market matters, these people began to incur tremendous risks. These risks, more often than not caused irreparable damage to organizations.

What would happen if individuals with the strategic acumen and the leadership stature of Phil Knight of Nike, Fred Smith of FedEx, Akio Morita of Sony, Anita Roddick of Body Shop, or Bill Gates of Microsoft had been too busy playing around with futures or swaps and spending most of their days discussing these with their senior financial executives? They would have had very little time or energy indeed to develop all the wonderful products and ideas that they brought to the world and that were the fundamental reason for their immense personal and professional success, and of course for the success of all these incredible organizations that were created out of very little, and developed in the latter part of the past century into global conglomerates, with brands that are identifiable the world over.

Knight and Gates would have been too concerned with the volatility of the financial markets to have any time left to effectively create strategies or indeed focus on the vision for what their companies would later become. This is yet another consequence of a disproportionate importance paid to the financial markets rather than concentrating efforts, time and energy on the real economy. It is also reflective of a worrying trend as to the role played by the stock market, that of a transition from being an effective barometer of organizational performance in the economy to becoming itself the economy, an intangible and devoid of productive substance, a set of electronic transactions with no underlying real economy of production to back it up.

Obviously financial institutions and particularly investment banks are not the only ones to blame for this. Like in almost everything else in a complex system, such as today's global economy, the current state of affairs was arrived at through a multitude of wrongdoings and corporate and individual incompetence. This mostly derived from the evolving views of the role of government intervention in the economy over the last three decades, and critically its function and extent of regulatory influence in the shaping of economic activity. Top management in organizations are also to blame for the current state of affairs as they seem to have forgotten the fundamental aim, nature and scope of their activities, that of tending to shareholder value creation whilst ensuring the long-term viability of the organizations that they lead and manage.

The systemic nature of the problem suggests that, in being pressed to attain objectives of shareholder value maximization whilst harmoniously balancing the often conflicting interests of other stakeholders, top management in organizations are often tempted to adopt risky behaviour of the kind that would be avoided in other less pressured contexts and times. On the other hand, shareholders who look for quick capital returns on their stock investments are also to blame for not taking the long view. Shareholders exercise pressure on boards of administration with a view to obtaining quick financial results, but immediate financial results correlate with higher risks incurred and decision-makers need to tread these fine lines carefully and balance what are often mutually exclusive interests and objectives.

The economic and management sciences stand to learn a lot from what has happened to the world over the last ten years. In trailing the way for the future, it is crucial that the scientific building of the economic sciences draws on Popper's epistemology of falsification and the notion of paradigm shift as postulated by Kuhn (Fuller, 2003), as ways of revoking old truths that simply fail to meet the challenges of contemporary societies. In so doing they can perhaps contribute to the emergence of new solutions for fragile economic systems and institutions.

A paradigm shift means that a new way of thinking very naturally emerges to substitute the old and wasted ways, whose postulates and tried solutions no longer constitute valid answers to the challenges currently being posed by a new set of political, economic, sociological and technological realities characterizing the world. The world has changed, and governments and organizations have not been able to respond effectively to the new challenges that emerge in every domain, but in particular in the areas of ecology and the environment, corporate social responsibility, transparency, business ethics and corporate governance, and everything that touches upon the dynamic understanding of the needs of people in society.

A better fit has been attained in adjusting to technological shifts and their impact on economic systems and the quotidian lives of citizens, but this in turn poses other problems of human redundancy, namely unemployment and the questioning of individuals' contribution to society, how this is to take shape and in what form, eventually bringing to the forefront the need for new labour models and formats to emerge.

In this way, absolute truths, if there are any, are only awaiting falsification and to be replaced by new and better truths that possess improved explanatory power over the incumbent schemata. In so doing they become more effective responses to the contemporary challenges that face the world. This of course applies to society as it applies to organizations of any nature and in every sector of economic activity. These more recent truths have to suffer the scrutiny of extensive empirical evidence and need to adhere better to reality as well as predicting it more effectively than the old truths.

Explanatory systems resist to the point where it becomes impossible to continue to use them, due to an insurmountable distance that exists between the incumbent theoretical architecture and the underlying reality that it purports to explain. This is true for every science, but it is particularly true for the social sciences, given the volatility of its research object, people, expressed individually or collectively in societal systems.

The modelling of human behaviour in society, the attempt to find explanatory systems for understanding and forecasting social realities remain valid as long as they adhere closely to the underlying realities that they purport to explain but crucially also to predict. Explaining reality and not being able to predict it, due to the acknowledged limitations that are inherent to the social sciences, is a critical obstacle to the legitimacy of the social sciences and their credibility next to the wider community.

Reality Check...

Gerald Ratner and Keeping One's Mouth Shut

In the early 1990s, Gerald Ratner, CEO of then renowned jewellery retail chain Ratner, the largest retail group in the sector in the whole world was invited to speak at the Royal Albert Hall in London, where he was to receive an award, distinguishing him as executive of the year. In his carefully crafted speech, and having passed it around to his fellow directors at Ratner, he made a couple of remarks that to this day remain vivid in the memories of those who were present to honour such a distinguished guest.

Unfortunately, Ratner's remarks did not stay within the walls of the Royal Albert Hall and, tragically, and in a matter of hours, they were divulged to millions of readers, as his speech made the headlines of the tabloid press, and then to viewers who were to witness his comments in elaborate TV documentaries that exhausted the subject in the coming months.

At one point in his speech, Ratner, whose general comments on the Ratner organization had up until then been indeed very positive, made the following observation:

'We even sell a pair of earrings for under £1, and they are gold earrings too. That is cheaper than a prawn sandwich from M&S. Unfortunately, I have to say that the sandwich will probably last longer than the earrings, but then...'

Ratner went on to say '...Why are our products cheaper? Because they are total crap...' attempting to capture a raucous audience with a particular brand of humour which was to prove tragic. More to the point, the joke unequivocally led to the Ratner organization falling dramatically from grace in an epic stumble which went down in the annals of corporate disasters as the example of exactly what a leader should not do or say about his company.

As he hopelessly attempted to justify the lower quality of Ratner products, all that he was able to create was an unprecedented public animosity and backlash against an organization that people were familiar with, and to whom they had entrusted their custom for decades. The story would unfold in a dramatic way with dire consequences for the Ratner group and Gerald Ratner himself. The largest jewellery retail chain in the world, at one point totalling 2,500 stores, mainly in the UK, but also in the US, a group that united a number of very strong brands under one corporate umbrella soon dismembered and in a very short time-span the whole thing simply disintegrated.

The Ratner empire was made up of several prestigious brands, including the Ratner brand itself, catering to the low end of the market. It covered a whole spectrum of consumer choice from the lower segments in the market to the very top echelons, including the H. Samuel brand whose target market erred for merchandise of a much higher quality calibre.

What is factual in all of this is that Gerald Ratner's address to that avid audience in the Royal Albert Hall was destined to have damaging repercussions directly on the Ratner brand itself, and less to the whole universe of corporate brands over which Ratner exercised any ownership control or was in any way associated with. These brands had different names and somehow consumers were able to detach them from Ratner and his ways. There was a fear that some of these brands would subsequently be tainted by Ratner's statements and that the negativity implied in them would rub off on their reputation, but that was not to be the case.

Gerald Ratner had been a very successful entrepreneur up until then and at a very young age inherited the long-established Ratner group. He followed in the footsteps of his father who had founded the company 40 years earlier in the late 1940s. It didn't take Ratner long to make his mark. He embarked on what was to be a hallucinating acquisitions programme, a bold strategic move that included the takeover of several household names in British retail, including Zales, H. Samuel and others. Ratner built the world's largest jewellery retail empire in a short period of time, reaching at one point 2,500 stores in his endeavours.

Ratner was then justly nominated executive of the year, an accolade he was only too proud to be the recipient of. On the day of receiving his award in a formal ceremony held at the Royal Albert Hall in London he was asked to address the audience. Nervous and of a shy nature, Ratner was not accustomed to public speaking, a task that he did not particularly enjoy. He also felt the need to somehow justify what was widely perceived to be the lower quality of the products traded under the Ratner brand, and so he decided to consult his fellow directors at the Ratner organization to hear what they thought of the speech.

He circulated his speech around, and the story goes that one of the directors came back saying that this was a magnificent speech, perhaps the best that Ratner had ever written, but what was missing in it was a joke, and that he should build one into an otherwise inspired speech. Ratner rejected this at first on the grounds that this was a formal occasion, a very serious event, taking place at the Royal Albert Hall in front of the City, government officials and the attentive press, and therefore it would be wise to keep the speech a little bit more serious. The director finally convinced him to use one or two jokes that he had used in the past just to break the ice.

Ratner eventually gave in and decided that if he was to tell a joke he would use one that he had used before and had come out in *The Birmingham Post* a few years earlier. The jokes turned out to be of very bad taste indeed and the next day, the tabloid newspapers had headlines of the calibre of 'Rotners' and 'You 22 carat mugs' in *The Sun* and another unremarkable tabloid newspaper at that time.

There are various corporate lessons to be learnt from the Ratner tale. That one of his directors, upon reading the original speech, decided that it was indeed a great speech but all that was missing was a joke, only means that it is a lonely job up at the top and that in the final analysis it is up to the CEO to make a call on what to do and what not to do. Despite the mounting pressure, Ratner should have stuck with the power of his convictions.

Most of the speech was dead serious. He talked about the quality of his merchandise and how the Ratner brand took in more money per square foot than any other retailer in Europe, concluding that the reason why they were so successful was because they gave the customer what they wanted. All of this was great stuff. The director thought that all of this was great stuff too. Still a joke was missing. He approached Ratner with his suggestion but Ratner rejected the idea of a joke on the grounds that this was a serious occasion.

The director insisted and Ratner decided to use a joke that he had once made in an interview with a *Financial Times* journalist which had subsequently found its way into a local Birmingham newspaper. People laughed at it. It wasn't seen as demeaning and it fitted the self-deprecating, laugh at your own expense stereotype that is typically associated with the British public. It turned out to be a fatal mistake.

An unsuspecting Ratner initially began to talk about his organization, saying great things about what had been achieved in a relatively short period of time. He emphasized the organization's customer orientation, unparalleled in the British retail market. The joke came later as he rolled on undisturbed and fuelled by a very animated Royal Albert Hall. He culminated his speech with an astonishing question. 'Why are our products cheaper? ... (silent wait) ... because they are total crap!!!'

The following day Ratner would make the cover page of just about every newspaper in the country. It soon became common knowledge that everything Ratner sold was of very low quality. Media attention was rife and indiscriminate in its coverage, ranging from the tabloid crowd to the more serious mainstream titles. *The Mirror* and *The Sun* ran the story to its absolute exhaustion, calling the public's attention to the Ratner group's deliberate intention to ridicule customers and fool them with shoddy products.

People began to return the goods that they had bought a few days earlier. They came back the following day and the day after. They just kept coming back and store managers were in complete bewilderment at events as they unfolded in breath-taking succession and speed. Ratner thought the whole thing would die down but it never did. A few months later he resigned from his post as Chairman of the Board and the Ratner group filed for bankruptcy. The media who for years had been extremely supportive, hounded him down and the public never forgave him. A retail chain of more than 2,500 stores simply disintegrated in less than a year.

Gerald Ratner had been a true beacon of light and inspiration for the company's various stakeholders, although it is true that not all of them liked him. Many of his suppliers disliked the fact that he would sometimes return product without so much as a phone call to say that it was on its way back. He had lost the confidence of all of those with vested interests in the company, including clients, employees, suppliers, the media and others. What was initially thought of as an innocuous off-the-cuff remark became the genesis of his downfall and that of the organization tirelessly founded by his father and to which he had given his utmost best. Ratner never quite recovered from that personally.

10

The Competitiveness of Nations in the Twenty-first Century: The Links between Exports, FDI and National Competitiveness

The nature of competitive advantages in an economy and whether they are anchored in low costs of labour or alternatively on the sophistication of production processes, materialized in high-value products, is an important predictor of the competitiveness of nations. The empirical evidence suggests there to be a strong correlation between the nature of competitive advantages of firms in an economy and the economic competitiveness of nations.

This seems tautological, but the nature of a nation's competitive advantages will determine the long-term viability of a chosen model of national competitiveness. Whether these advantages are ephemeral in the sense that they can be easily replicated, or sustainable in that over and beyond the technological complexity and specific know-how upon which they are built they still benefit from an aura that comes from the possession of notorious and valuable brands, will be the make or break of any model of competitiveness for a national economy.

Table 10.1   Nature of competitive advantages of domestic companies in international markets (Top 20 ranking of the most competitive nations and EU economies under international intervention by the IMF, European Commission and European Central Bank)

Country	Sophistication of Products and Processes				
	2008	2009	2010	2011	2012
Switzerland	2nd	2nd	2nd	2nd	1st
Singapore	16th	13th	14th	15th	14th
Finland	6th	5th	4th	6th	5th
Sweden	5th	6th	5th	11th	12th
Netherlands	9th	9th	8th	10th	9th
Germany	1st	1st	3rd	4th	4th
USA	12th	16th	19th	20th	18th
United Kingdom	15th	15th	9th	5th	6th
Hong Kong SAR	22nd	19th	16th	21st	20th
Japan	4th	3rd	1st	1st	2nd
Qatar	36th	100th	58th	23rd	24th
Denmark	3rd	4th	6th	3rd	3rd
Taiwan, China	24th	21st	20th	18th	19th
Canada	40th	48th	56th	71st	83rd
Norway	20th	24th	25th	28th	25th
Austria	7th	8th	13th	12th	7th
Belgium	8th	10th	10th	9th	10th
Saudi Arabia	51st	39th	28th	27th	30th
Korea, Rep.	13th	17th	18th	17th	16th
Australia	37th	38th	59th	67th	62nd
Ireland	18th	18th	17th	16th	17th
Greece	34th	36th	50th	57th	57th
Portugal	55th	51st	45th	42nd	49th
Spain	27th	30th	32nd	31st	33rd

Source: World Economic Forum (2008–2012)

Whilst the competitiveness rankings of nations allow for a *snapshot* of an economy at any given point in time, the knowledge of how ephemeral or permanent competitive advantages are will indicate the degree of sustainability of the incumbent model of economic growth of a nation, or alternatively the need for its revoking by a new model whose characterization of competitive advantages is much more difficult to imitate by incoming players into the market. This occurs in the light of globally fiercely fought positions in export markets and competition for the attraction of FDI into national economies in a globally competitive environment.

In reality, competitive advantages that are based on the technological sophistication of production processes leading to products which incorporate high levels of technical knowledge are difficult to attain, and not easy to be usurped by newcomers, although technological gaps between the challenger and the incumbent players are easier to recoup than gaps in the understanding of markets, which require an all round notion of the outside world, cosmopolitism and an obsessed focus with the customer in all that it entails. In the absence of this, economies are insular and parochial, and will forever remain on the periphery of global economic activity, with all that this implies, in terms of limited wealth creation potential manifested in the degradation of indicators of human, social and economic development.

Nations that have acquired competitive advantages in their economies founded on technological virtuosity do not easily lose their grip on those factors which have conceded them with a source of competitive advantage. This is important in that there is a clear link between the degree of sophistication of production processes in industry and the relative position of nations in the competitiveness tables as is evidenced below.

Table 10.2 **Production process efficiency (Top 20 ranking of the most competitive nations and eu economies under international intervention by the IMF, European Commission and European Central Bank)**

Country	World's Best and Most Efficient Process Technology				
	2008	2009	2010	2011	2012
Switzerland	4th	3rd	3rd	2nd	2nd
Singapore	14th	13th	14th	13th	18th
Finland	6th	5th	5th	5th	4th
Sweden	2nd	4th	4th	4th	6th
Netherlands	8th	6th	6th	6th	5th
Germany	3rd	2nd	2nd	3rd	3rd
USA	11th	8th	11th	15th	11th

Table 10.2   Production process efficiency *continued*

Country	World's Best and Most Efficient Process Technology				
	2008	2009	2010	2011	2012
United Kingdom	20th	19th	17th	17th	17th
Hong Kong SAR	24th	26th	33rd	31st	31st
Japan	1st	1st	1st	1st	1st
Qatar	29th	16th	8th	20th	12th
Denmark	5th	7th	12th	9th	16th
Taiwan, China	13th	15th	16th	16th	20th
Canada	22nd	20th	15th	21st	23rd
Norway	12th	12th	10th	11th	13th
Austria	9th	9th	7th	8th	7th
Belgium	10th	10th	9th	7th	8th
Saudi Arabia	32nd	30th	25th	22nd	26th
Korea, Rep.	17th	21st	23rd	23rd	21st
Australia	23rd	23rd	24th	25th	24th
Ireland	18th	18th	21st	10th	9th
Greece	51st	63rd	70th	64th	69th
Portugal	37th	40th	36th	39th	41st
Spain	28th	32nd	40th	35th	35th

Source: World Economic Forum (2008–2012)

According to the Global Competitiveness Report of the WEF, the nations that have consistently shown up at the top of the global competitiveness league tables since 2008 have been all the ones that one would expect, including the Scandinavian nations, the USA, Germany, Singapore, Japan, and then not far below, the UK and France. Although these and a few other countries have here and there swapped positions in the competitiveness tables, the same nations have remained pretty much unchanged, as elite members of an exclusive list of the world's most competitive nations.

In attaining prominent positions in the competitiveness rankings, national economies take years to climb up the competitiveness ladder, as the variables that are conducive to higher national competitiveness levels are in good part behavioural in nature, and take time before the enactment of change produces tangible results. This is the case with such dimensions as the lower sophistication of domestic business environments or a corporate orientation whose philosophy is not geared towards the customer and his needs which take decades before substantive change is observable.

Due to the timeframes that are inherent to the manifestation of change in behavioural variables, the evolution of national competitiveness rankings over the years shows that it is not easy for a nation to emerge out of the blue and rise to the top 20 most competitive nations just like that. Losing competitiveness is another matter altogether and some nations lose competitiveness and abandon the upper echelons of these rankings quite quickly. Building national competitiveness is an arduous task that involves all stakeholders in society and certainly much more than economic agents in society, as it involves in a systemic way the government, the judiciary, the bureaucratic and administrative machine and many others.

Table 10.3   Global competitiveness trend (Top 20 ranking of the most competitive nations and eu economies under international intervention by the IMF, European Commission and European Central Bank)

Country	Competitiveness Ranking				
	2008	2009	2010	2011	2012
Switzerland	2nd	1st	1st	1st	1st
Singapore	5th	3rd	3rd	2nd	2nd
Finland	6th	6th	7th	4th	3rd
Sweden	4th	4th	2nd	3rd	4th
Netherlands	8th	10th	8th	7th	5th
Germany	7th	7th	5th	6th	6th
USA	1st	2nd	4th	5th	7th
United Kingdom	12th	13th	12th	10th	8th
Hong Kong SAR	11th	11th	11th	11th	9th
Japan	9th	8th	6th	9th	10th
Qatar	26th	22nd	17th	14th	11th
Denmark	3rd	5th	9th	8th	12th
Taiwan, China	17th	12th	13th	13th	13th
Canada	10th	9th	10th	12th	14th
Norway	15th	14th	14th	16th	15th
Austria	14th	17th	18th	19th	16th
Belgium	19th	18th	19th	15th	17th
Saudi Arabia	27th	28th	21st	17th	18th

Table 10.3   Global competitiveness trend *continued*

Country	Competitiveness Ranking				
	2008	2009	2010	2011	2012
Korea, Rep.	13th	19th	22nd	24th	19th
Australia	18th	15th	16th	20th	20th
Ireland	22nd	25th	29th	29th	27th
Greece	67th	71st	83rd	90th	96th
Portugal	43rd	43rd	46th	45th	49th
Spain	29th	33rd	42nd	36th	36th

Source: World Economic Forum (2008–2012)

Interestingly, nations that consistently show up at the top of the league tables in terms of the competitiveness of their economies tend to be the same nations that export more, that aggregate value to their exports of goods and services. When the analysis is on exports as a percentage of GDP rather than total exports, the association is not as strong, which suggests that although having a strong export sector is good for the vitality of an economy, a strong domestic consumer market as well as criterious public investment of reproductive potential are important contributors to the formation of GDP.

The nations that show up at the very top of the competitiveness rankings are also the same nations that are better at attracting FDI. These economies welcome more FDI than other nations, and not just any kind of FDI, but rather FDI into the capital-intensive sectors of cutting-edge innovation in sophisticated business sectors of high-value aggregation potential. There is an association between national competitiveness, exports and FDI. It is not always the case that nations will rank highly in all of these dimensions, but there is a strong correlation between the variables.

The competitiveness of a nation is therefore a barometer of its wealth creation potential and a strong predictor of indicators of human and social development, and crucially the sustainability of welfare systems, including health, education and social security. In acknowledging the link between national competitiveness and the welfare of populations, it is hoped that the primacy of micro-economics and firm competitiveness is established to the detriment of the dictatorship of macro-economics in governmental agendas.

A better balance between micro-economic and macro-economic policy needs to be attained, as well as a downplaying of the importance attributed to the economics of financial speculation whose scope of action is totally outside the realm of the economy of production of goods and services, and that serves no visible social or economic purpose. In justifying the critical role of a focus on micro-economics and the firm in wealth creation, it is important to emphasize the existence of a clear and positive relationship between competitiveness, exports and FDI.

Table 10.4   Top 20 ranking of national competitiveness, exports and FDI

Ranking	Competitiveness[1]	Exports[2]*	Exports (% GDP)[1]	FDI Atraction[3]	FDI Attraction (% GDP)[4]
1st	Switzerland	China	Hong Kong SAR	United States	Hong Kong
2nd	Singapore	USA	Singapore	France	Belgium
3rd	Finland	Germany	Luxembourg	China	Singapore
4th	Sweden	Japan	Belgium	United Kingdom	Luxembourg
5th	Netherlands	Netherlands	Ireland	Russian Fed.	Ireland
6th	Germany	France	Seychelles*	Spain	Chile
7th	USA	Korea, Rep.	Estonia	Hong Kong	Kazakhstan
8th	United Kingdom	Italy	Malta	Belgium	Mongolia
9th	Hong Kong SAR	Russian Federation	Hungary	Australia	Turkmenistan
10th	Japan	Belgium	Malaysia	Brazil	Lebanon
11th	Qatar	United Kingdom	Netherlands	Canada	Congo
12th	Denmark	Hong Kong SAR	Slovak Republic	Sweden	—
13th	Taiwan, China	Canada	Brunei	Germany	—
14th	Canada	Singapore	Vietnam	Japan	—
15th	Norway	Saudi Arabia	Czech Republic	Singapore	—
16th	Austria	Mexico	Bahrain*	—	—
17th	Belgium	Spain	Slovenia	—	—
18th	Saudi Arabia	Taiwan, China	Puerto Rico	—	—
19th	Korea, Rep.	India	Thailand	—	—
20th	Australia	United Arab Emirates	United Arab Emirates*	—	—

Sources:
[1]   World Economic Forum (2012)
[2]   World Trade Organization (2012)
[3]   World Investment Report (2012)
[4]   World Investment Report (2012)
*   2010 data: The obstacles to the attraction of FDI into any economy are shown in Figure 10.1

Obstacles to FDI according to the WEF:
- **Political and economic instability**
- **Bureaucracy**
- **Restrictive labour laws**
- **Instability in policy-making**
- **Fiscal burden**
- **Access to financing**
- **Fiscal legislation**
- **Unskilled labour**

Figure 10.1   Obstacles to FDI according to the WEF

It is worth mentioning that the nations that systematically show up at the top of the WEF global competitiveness ranking tables are in many cases but not in their totality those that show better performances in what concerns the sustainability of those competitive advantages. Those economies have built competitive advantages that are difficult to imitate and consequently present better economic growth perspectives in the future.

Nations that show good comparative performances on the solidity and sustainability of the competitive advantages of their economies are inherently less permissive to imitation by other economies who wish to copy that which leads to those advantages. There are cases of nations enjoying considerable competitive advantages that are based on unique products or processes, namely Italy (11th), Israel (8th) or Luxembourg (13th). None of these nations however, show up in the Top 20 most competitive economies in the world according to the Global Competitiveness Report of the WEF.

This shows in the case of the Italian economy that in spite of all the difficulties that are inherent to its huge public debt problem, Italy still benefits from a set of competitive advantages that are not easily usurped by low-cost economies. From this perspective this can only signify that there is hope for the Italian economy, which despite its historical political instability and at times ungovernability, together with its huge public debt burden, has still been able to maintain an economy of production of goods and services characterized by products of exceptional quality and design, anchored in extremely valuable brands of global notoriety.

Italy is not listed in the Top 20 ranking of the most competitive nations in the world. In fact, in 2012 it showed up 42nd in the WEF ranking of nations, but if it were to somehow manage a balanced budget in the foreseeable future and to control its enormous public debt, then Italy has a denominator of GDP that can potentially leverage its economy to the point of bringing the public debt/GDP ratio closer to the magic bullet of 60 per cent, which is widely acknowledged to be the bearable public debt level. As Stiglitz (2010) put it, it is not so much the size of the public debt that matters but rather the economy's capacity for absorbing it, in a clear allusion to the denominator of GDP in an economy and the inherent potential of economies to augment it. A public debt/ GDP target ratio of 60 per cent is very important but very difficult to attain as is evident in Table 10.5.

Table 10.5   If in 2015, countries balance the budgets they will achieve the public debt/GDP ratio of 60 percent in ...

Portugal	2037
France	2029
Germany	2028
Greece	2031
USA	2033
Belgium	2035

Source: IMD-World Competitiveness Centre (2010)

The Italian case and that of a few others illustrate that not all situations of excessive public debt are the same, and neither is the capacity of the real economies of production of goods and services in absorbing these high levels of public debt. Highly indebted nations that still manage to have a competitive economy have the potential to reach bearable public debt/GDP ratios by working on their real economies, and in this way augment the denominator of GDP in this ratio. Countries with low potential for economic growth because they are inherently uncompetitive, and who in addition to this are economies that have amassed insurmountable and fundamentally unpayable amounts of public and private debt, are nations that navigate in murky waters.

The vulnerability of an economy is a function of the degree of sustainability of its competitive model, and this is measured by whether the economy is anchored on ephemeral or more permanent competitive advantages. Less sustainable competitive models are a result of easy imitation of whatever gives them their competitive edge, be it technological, marketing advantages or branding differences or even the abnormal endowment of a pool of invaluable natural resources and raw materials. Unsustainable competitive advantages can be about an economic sector or a whole economy being outcompeted on price, or about short-lived technological advantages on products or production processes that, albeit more efficient, can be easily copied by interested and willing competitors.

In reality, although in many instances the focus of export strategies is on the diktat of price as an overriding and sometimes unique criterion for market competitiveness, in many export markets this is not the case and price is not exhaustive of the reasons why consumers buy product and prefer some products to the detriment of others. In particular, in the more sophisticated, discriminating markets where consumers have high levels of disposable income, price is not the most important purchasing criterion at all.

In this context what is important for export sectors in an open economy is that they are able to improve their relative position in the value chains of key export markets, by moving downstream in these value chains and controlling the elements that embody more value. This means that in export sectors, but also in the domestic market, firms need to be as close as possible to the consumer, as he who controls the brand and is closest to the customer controls the game.

The fundamental problem with the lack of competitiveness of nations is that, in key export sectors, firms in these economies tend to have a strong presence upstream in the value chains of these sectors but the same does not happen downstream for the consumer. Upstream in the value chain, in manufacturing, margins are low and increasingly squeezed. The level of competitiveness is high and the potential for imitation of whatever confers companies a competitive advantage also high. Advantages are thus not sustainable.

A strong presence upstream in value chains is not necessarily a good sign, as above average profitability only means that other players are attracted to those sectors which will ultimately drive profitability down. Incoming players can be a severe threat to incumbents in labour-intensive sectors of activity. The litmus test here is how vulnerable incumbents in these upstream sectors of economic activity are to competition and this is a function of the perennial or alternatively more permanent nature of competitive advantages. What ultimately defines the consistency and the holding of competitive advantages by incumbents are such factors as preferential access to raw materials and natural resources, if and when these play a key role in warranting incumbents with sustainable competitive advantages. In the absence of an abnormal endowment of immensely valuable natural resources and raw materials, what may work upstream in value chains are such technical protectionist measures as patents and licenses, and fundamentally the ability of a sector of economic activity in creating loyalty in their customer base throughout the lifetime of these patents and licenses. Technological protectionism rather than economic protectionism is the key in contemporary economies.

It follows from the previous point that the nations that rank higher in the global competitiveness league tables tend to be the ones that are better able to exercise control over crucial links of the global value chains of key export sectors. They do so by controlling the links in the value chain that are nearest to the consumer, where the margins are much higher and potential for imitation of competitive advantages low. There is therefore a link between the level of national competitiveness of an economy and the degree of control that it is able to exercise over the value chains of key economic sectors, as well as over international distribution and marketing.

Revoking of the Functionalist Product Paradigm and its Replacement with a Model of Value Aggregation:
- Rejection of a place upstream in value chains as it is downstream next to the consumer that the links in key value chains that effectively generate value are situated
- Finding a distinctive and valuable positioning in the global economy
- House of brands model (Japan, Germany and South Korea) as opposed to national communications campaigns, also called the branded house model
- Japan, Malaysia and South Korea with strategic directioning of government (MITI) may be good examples of the link between government and the economy

Figure 10.2   Revoking of the functionalist product paradigm and its
                replacement with a model of value aggregation

The link between value chain breadth, control of distribution and national competitiveness is shown in Table 10.6.

Table 10.6   **Value chain breadth by exporting companies (Top 20 ranking of the most competitive nations and EU economies under international intervention by the IMF, European Commission and European Central Bank)**

Country	Broad Presence Across the Entire Value Chain				
	2008	2009	2010	2011	2012
Switzerland	5th	3rd	4th	3rd	3rd
Singapore	14th	12th	10th	10th	10th
Finland	7th	9th	9th	7th	7th
Sweden	1st	4th	3rd	2nd	4th
Netherlands	9th	6th	7th	6th	6th
Germany	4th	1st	1st	4th	1st
USA	8th	11th	15th	14th	13th
United Kingdom	15th	15th	11th	9th	8th
Hong Kong SAR	11th	10th	13th	21st	17th
Japan	2nd	2nd	2nd	1st	2nd
Qatar	43rd	114th	85th	27th	23rd
Denmark	6th	8th	8th	12th	16th
Taiwan, China	17th	16th	16th	17th	19th
Canada	48th	38th	33rd	41st	51st
Norway	39th	40th	30th	34th	44th
Austria	10th	7th	6th	5th	5th
Belgium	16th	17th	18th	16th	11th
Saudi Arabia	33rd	29th	21st	22nd	24th
Korea, Rep.	12th	13th	14th	19th	22nd
Australia	72nd	78th	78th	75th	102nd
Ireland	19th	19th	19th	15th	14th
Greece	53rd	58th	75th	83rd	94th
Portugal	32nd	43rd	50th	44th	42nd
Spain	21st	24th	25th	24th	26th

Source: World Economic Forum (2008–2012)

Table 10.7   Control of international distribution and marketing by companies (Top 20 ranking of the most competitive nations and EU economies under international intervention by the IMF, European Commission and European Central Bank)

Country	Primarily Owned and Controlled by Domestic Companies				
	2008	2009	2010	2011	2012
Switzerland	3rd	3rd	6th	6th	4th
Singapore	57th	60th	58th	55th	42nd
Finland	14th	16th	25th	16th	17th
Sweden	17th	7th	3rd	8th	19th
Netherlands	9th	11th	11th	14th	15th
Germany	2nd	1st	2nd	4th	3rd
USA	4th	5th	8th	9th	10th
United Kingdom	13th	17th	19th	20th	14th
Hong Kong SAR	25th	21st	28th	18th	13th
Japan	8th	2nd	1st	1st	1st
Qatar	43rd	96th	50th	7th	2nd
Denmark	10th	13th	16th	10th	16th
Taiwan, China	11th	14th	14th	22nd	22nd
Canada	20th	33rd	36th	34th	34th
Norway	23rd	27th	20th	25th	28th
Austria	7th	6th	4th	3rd	8th
Belgium	28th	23rd	39th	39th	38th
Saudi Arabia	15th	9th	7th	2nd	7th
Korea, Rep.	12th	24th	24th	15th	11th
Australia	33rd	34th	31st	54th	75th
Ireland	52nd	53rd	70th	89th	88th
Greece	55th	55th	61st	61st	77th
Portugal	54th	57th	65th	69th	86th
Spain	32nd	46th	57th	44th	48th

Source: World Economic Forum (2008–2012)

There are sectors of activity in national economies that have no difficulty in manufacturing high-quality products that embody exceptional intrinsic technological competencies and design content, only to see others with strong presences down the value chain benefitting disproportionately from their work.

This means that great manufacturing is not enough and what is also required is the ability to bring product to market in difficult circumstances in open economic systems, in a context of intense competition which typifies most industrial and consumer markets. The analogy of the farmer that is able to grow excellent quality products from the ground and then sells them to intermediaries or directly to the large supermarket food chains, only to then see those very same products traded under a famous retail brand and being sold to consumers at infinitely superior prices than those he was paid for by the intermediary, is an excellent metaphor for an economy with low sustainability in its toolkit of competitive advantages.

In the less competitive economies, the overwhelming majority of stakeholders in the principal economic sectors, and in particular in key export sectors, do not understand the concept of management of key value chains, the importance of having important players in an economy being present in the principal stages of a chain that goes from production to consumption. In particular, they fail to understand the importance of controlling key links in these chains where value is concentrated and the difficult but very rewarding task of being close to the consumer.

A poorly sophisticated business environment does not offer a sufficient stimulus for organizations to seek a better understanding of the demands of heterogeneous markets. These have differentiated consumption patterns according to criteria whose comprehension would be of extreme importance to the sophistication of export sectors and their success in strongly discriminating markets. A low sophistication of the business environment and a low level of exigency in key stakeholder constituencies that characterizes many so-called developed economies, beyond traducing a low competitive intensity, also reflects a low orientation towards the customer on the part of organizations in domestic markets in these economies. The behaviour of firms in the domestic markets is naturally then perpetuated in export markets.

The low customer orientation that typifies key export sectors even in developed economies can be explained by a certain psychological insularity and the little if any pro-activity of domestic manufacturers, as well as a frightening myopia in what concerns the understanding of the role of effective control over worthwhile links in key value chains in export sectors and its critical contribution to the competitiveness of firms and nations in the global landscape.

Table 10.8   Degree of customer orientation by organizations (Top 20 ranking of the most competitive nations and EU economies under international intervention by the IMF, European Commission and European Central Bank)

Country	Degree of Customer Orientation and Retention				
	2008	2009	2010	2011	2012
Switzerland	3°	3°	3°	3°	2°
Singapore	10°	10°	18°	19°	12°
Finland	19°	27°	25°	15°	20°
Sweden	9°	5°	4°	2°	4°
Holland	12°	20°	28°	22°	24°
Germany	14°	11°	11°	18°	15°
United States of America	5°	9°	22°	24°	18°
United Kingdom	31°	40°	44°	34°	26°
Hong Kong	8°	4°	6°	11°	14°
Japan	1°	1°	1°	1°	1°
Qatar	67°	28°	12°	14°	5°
Denmark	6°	6°	7°	10°	8°
Taiwan, China	4°	7°	8°	9°	6°
Canada	15°	18°	13°	6°	13°
Norway	18°	14°	17°	31°	31°
Austria	2°	2°	2°	4°	3°
Belgium	11°	13°	10°	5°	10°
Saudi Arabia	51°	37°	31°	28°	36°
Korea	13°	15°	21°	16°	9°
Australia	17°	17°	20°	25°	25°
Ireland	20°	22°	19°	12°	11°
Greece	71°	75°	72°	88°	91°
Portugal	59°	65°	56°	54°	54°
Spain	43°	51°	66°	68°	66°

Source: World Economic Forum (2008–2012)

The existence of key industrial sectors in an economy that attribute a lesser importance to the critical notion of controlling valuable links in key supply chains is often reflective of a posture of apathy on the part of entrepreneurs, and a reluctance in going out of comfort zones of minimal risk assumption to adopt more pro-active stances and challenge the incumbent status quo. In reality when the prevailing culture in domestic markets is not one of systemic exigency, and when the business environment is not sophisticated and the pressure of stakeholders is inexistent, then it is not reasonable to expect companies to develop a customer-orientated philosophy. If companies are not pressured by the domestic business environment to be customer-orientated and to focus on the competencies that lead to customer satisfaction, then the same companies cannot be expected to behave differently in export markets.

The level of sophistication of consumer buying decision-making will shape the degree of responsiveness of the business environment to different levels of market exigency. Again the evidence shows that there is a correlation between national competitiveness and the sophistication of consumers in the context of buying decision-making, meaning that in contexts where consumers tend to be more sophisticated this coincides with economies that rank up higher in the competitiveness tables.

Table 10.9   Buyer sophistication in purchasing decisions (Top 20 ranking of the most competitive nations and EU economies under international intervention by the IMF, European Commission and European Central Bank)

Country	Degree of Buyer Sophistication				
	2008	2009	2010	2011	2012
Switzerland	1st	2nd	2nd	2nd	2nd
Singapore	9th	6th	10th	8th	8th
Finland	11th	18th	17th	9th	4th
Sweden	6th	3rd	3rd	4th	5th
Netherlands	13th	11th	9th	15th	14th
Germany	16th	22nd	18th	21st	15th
USA	5th	9th	13th	12th	10th
United Kingdom	22nd	10th	8th	13th	9th
Hong Kong SAR	4th	7th	14th	24th	7th
Japan	2nd	1st	1st	1st	1st
Qatar	39th	56th	39th	18th	19th
Denmark	8th	8th	21st	6th	31st
Taiwan, China	3rd	4th	5th	7th	6th
Canada	14th	14th	6th	11th	12th
Norway	15th	17th	12th	22nd	21st

Austria	7th	19th	25th	26th	27th
Belgium	17th	16th	15th	16th	13th
Saudi Arabia	58th	36th	20th	14th	29th
Korea, Rep.	10th	15th	11th	17th	22nd
Australia	19th	12th	16th	29th	33rd
Ireland	20th	24th	23rd	27th	23rd
Greece	51st	50th	58th	66th	80th
Portugal	57th	68th	56th	55th	67th
Spain	31st	35th	47th	44th	51st

Source: World Economic Forum (2008–2012)

On the other hand, economies where key stakeholders such as entrepreneurs and senior managers in firms are not cosmopolitan and customer-orientated, these are typically economies where the role and power of marketing and branding is not fully comprehended. By failing to create valuable brands of global notoriety, these firms are not tapping into critical sources of value generation in contemporary economics. Firms and entire economic sectors in nations that do not possess relevant emotional differentiation in key sectors of economic activity are left vulnerable to imitation by competitors in tough market environments. There is in this context a link between the position an economy occupies on national competitiveness rankings and the use that firms in that economy make of sophisticated marketing techniques and tools.

Table 10.10   Extent of use by companies of sophisticated marketing tools and techniques (Top 20 ranking of the most competitive nations and EU economies under international intervention by the IMF, European Commission and European Central Bank)

Country	Use of Marketing Instruments				
	2008	2009	2010	2011	2012
Switzerland	5th	2nd	3rd	5th	4th
Singapore	17th	14th	20th	17th	22nd
Finland	34th	31st	29th	26th	20th
Sweden	8th	4th	2nd	1st	5th
Netherlands	11th	7th	5th	4th	2nd
Germany	4th	6th	7th	10th	7th
USA	1st	1st	1st	3rd	3rd

Table 10.10   Extent of use by companies of sophisticated marketing tools and techniques *continued*

Country	Use of Marketing Instruments				
	2008	2009	2010	2011	2012
United Kingdom	3rd	3rd	4th	2nd	1st
Hong Kong SAR	12th	12th	13th	16th	13th
Japan	19th	11th	9th	9th	10th
Qatar	49th	22nd	6th	6th	8th
Denmark	6th	8th	11th	12th	18th
Taiwan, China	33rd	19th	18th	19th	21st
Canada	9th	10th	10th	11th	14th
Norway	24th	18th	15th	22nd	19th
Austria	7th	9th	12th	7th	6th
Belgium	16th	15th	14th	13th	15th
Saudi Arabia	50th	38th	26th	18th	31st
Korea, Rep.	20th	30th	32nd	32nd	27th
Australia	10th	13th	16th	21st	24th
Ireland	22nd	23rd	24th	23rd	16th
Greece	58th	54th	58th	67th	73rd
Portugal	36th	42nd	39th	39th	44th
Spain	14th	28th	38th	38th	36th

Source: World Economic Forum (2008–2012)

In the general area of retail, as an example, the competitive success of sectors of economic activity in key export markets depends on the effectiveness of differentiation strategies adopted by firms in those sectors operating in those markets. An economy's ability to export goods and services which are perceived by foreign constituencies as superior at some meaningful level to those of incumbent players in those markets and those originating from competitors in other nations is the litmus test of success for any national or sector export strategy and the key objective to be attained.

Often these goods and services are identical from the viewpoint of their functionality, the core functional benefit that they offer. Consumers in sophisticated markets tell products apart according to their subjective evaluation of a set of intangible cues incorporated into goods and services, and that go way beyond product functionality and transverse the whole spectrum of tangible characteristics in products to find its ultimate expression in brands of great notoriety and value.

Whether policy-makers and economic strategists like it or not, competitiveness cannot be cast in stone into the law of the country. It is more than a set of legislative procedures, a collective state of mind, a social awareness as to the need to develop individual and collective capabilities that allow societies to earn their keep and enjoy high standards of living, in the knowledge that others elsewhere in the world are in active pursuit of the very same desires and aspirations.

In European economies and in particular in the southern European nations this does not mean that just because of a privileged history and the occupation of a civilizational space where individuals have come to enjoy a social tradition of collective welfare that has been maintained for decades on the back of high levels of public debt, that this can go on for much longer. It simply cannot.

This is a fact in absolute terms due to the unsustainability of these national economic models, but it is also true in comparative terms as other nations are quickly catching up, the world is changing and the role of technology has meant that geo-political boundaries and economic ones do not coincide and the former are rendered irrelevant to the economic competitiveness equation. The global economy is not a zero sum game but the relative position that nations occupy in the competitiveness leagues will determine the sustainability of the collective lifestyles of their citizens and this includes the universal provision of health, education, as well as social welfare and generous pension benefit schemes that people have become accustomed to. Not everyone, surely, but certainly many and for far too long.

In affluent markets where consumers have discretionary income, the ability to surround one's product offering with a set of intangible cues makes the whole difference between first being able to penetrate these markets and second to be able to charge exorbitant prices for goods and services as a function of their perceived value.

Crucially, however, goods and services that are apparently identical are not that from the viewpoint of the consumer, and price premiums go to those companies whose products benefit from auras of higher perceived quality, cosmopolitism or reputational goodwill inscribed in well-recognized brands, that embody values that sufficient groups of people with disposable income subscribe and adhere to.

The country of origin of a product or service plays a critical part in the ascription of value to that good or service and this was approached in detail earlier. Country of origin stereotypes may ultimately determine the willingness of consumers in foreign constituencies to purchase products claiming a certain origin and crucially pay price premiums for goods and services that are otherwise identical and indifferentiable.

The strategic objective of national economies with strong export components to their GDP as well as those emerging economies that badly want to enter into key export markets is to get into the strict group of nations that benefit from positive country of origin auras and whose products are branded with positive images and reputations, allowing the economies of these nations and their export sectors to escape the perception of massification that characterizes other economies that are not able to differentiate their market offers.

These largely undifferentiated economies of mass production in nations that occupy civilizational spaces that, by virtue of history and culture, legitimately aspire to advanced indicators of social and economic development are faced with adverse demographic trends and these are unambiguous as to the unsustainability of those indicators of societal well-being. This happens because these nations are not competitive and their capacity for wealth creation is disproportionately inferior to the level of well-being expected in these societies, a condition that has been perpetuated by years of excessive spending and persistent living over budget.

These economies are stuck in the middle in the sense that they cannot sustain with any viability a cost-leadership model, nor can they aspire to have relevant differentiation strategies, particularly emotional differentiation anchored on reputed product, corporate and national brands. These nations or key economic sectors in them, whilst fighting it out in highly competitive export markets, simply find it impossible to compete effectively against the low-cost emerging economies as the pool of cheap undifferentiated labour is virtually limitless in the latter cases.

The typology of labour relations and the thresholds as to what is permissible in these emerging economies, the regulatory frameworks in which they operate, the standards of accepted behaviour, either explicit or principally implicit, are incompatible with the civilizational and cultural spaces of the developed nations against which they are competing for the same markets.

In an era of globalized economic activity these emerging economies are outcompeting the incumbent players on cost in labour-intensive market sectors by virtue of their incomparably lower labour cost structures. When the incumbents have not been able to find significant and valuable points of difference in their offer, when judged from the perspective of savvy global consumers, then they are in deep trouble.

If citizens in these nations have unduly gotten accustomed to a lifestyle and indicators of well-being that are incompatible with national levels of wealth creation, and in the absence of significant GDP growth if any, then the only way in which to circle the square is to incur debt and this is what has happened to many European economies.

The problem is that the civilizational space occupied by the incumbent nations has not been attributed to them by divine right. It derives instead from geographical privilege, historical tradition and past feats of glory. In the context of globalized economic relationships, and assuming the unequivocal correlation between the competitiveness of nations and fundamental indicators of human and social development, it becomes necessary to conquer the economic space that guarantees the rights of individuals and that perpetuates them in time in the light of a changing and increasingly adverse and highly-competitive global landscape. If this is not the case, these rights simply disappear and wither away as there is no underlying economic substance to guarantee them.

There exists generically a perceptual gap between that which economic agents and decision-makers in an economy understand to be the differentiating factors in key target markets and that which consumers and industrial buyers in these markets make of the critical success factors or buying determinants in these markets. In sophisticated markets where there exists disposable income, allowing for price discrimination between apparently identical offers, relevant differentiation is necessarily of the emotional and intangible kind, and is embodied in corporate and product brands that foreign constituencies aspire to and are willing to pay handsomely for.

The ability to attain sustainable differentiation is not necessarily grounded on technological superiority nor does its underlying philosophy need to be anchored on technocratic principles, meaning that this is not differentiation of a kind that is limited to technological content aggregated to the offer of an economy, or that it can be sustained by virtue of adding ever more complexity to a technological base. In the end technological superiority is always susceptible to imitation and low-cost economies quickly catch up in this cat and mouse game.

That said this seems to typify the logic and thought process of the more vulnerable economies and their competitive philosophies, the idea that constant innovation will in the end guarantee that we are always one step ahead of the game. Whilst innovation is key it is also clearly insufficient as it needs to be anchored in downstream activities that are high aggregators of value. In many situations there subsists a gap in competitive philosophy between what firms believe to be the make or break of industrial or consumer buying decision-making, its underlying criteria in global markets, what they effectively are, and in what measure they contribute to and shape buying decision-making, both at industry and at consumer levels.

The example of the German manufacturing model illustrates the adoption of effective technocratic differentiation solutions between competing offers, achieved through excellence in the provision of exceptional products that are technologically insuperable. The German model of industrial competitiveness means that manufactured German products are less susceptible to competition from foreign low-cost players. The German economy competes on capital-intensive sectors, with highly innovative products that incorporate cutting-edge technology.

The model is difficult to replicate, but in addition to this German manufacturing does not underplay the role of marketing in building exceptional brands of global notoriety that everyone wants to buy and for which they are willing to disburse large amounts of money. These product and corporate brands carry significant accounting goodwill that is reflected on the balance sheets of German organizations, but fundamentally these brands carry good stories among millions of consumers worldwide who will pay whatever is needed to have them, their tangible quality and aesthetic benefits, and fundamentally what they represent as metaphors for status quo, lifestyle and hedonism.

The German case however is not frequent in contemporary global economies, at least in a way that sees excellence in manufacturing and a concern for product and corporate brand-building cut across the entire manufacturing sector, occupying and exercising control over key links in important global value chains. The German model is also not easy to replicate and its complex set of competitive advantages not susceptible to imitation by competitors, as it integrates technological and marketing competencies that act systemically and that in the end traduce a market offer, that is at once highly innovative and technologically sophisticated but also understands the virtues of marketing and brand-building as well as refining the understanding of the customer to a fine art.

The German competitiveness model imposes incredible hurdles to potential new entrants who aspire to enter the German market due to the characteristics of insuperable quality and sophistication that are inherent to nearly everything that comes out of German manufacturing, and that seems to confer the German economy with competitive advantages that are apparently and upon observation unassailable.

The exceptionally high knowledge content thresholds, technical rigour, technological requirements and commercial acumen that German industry forces upon those who have any hope of breaking into its markets, makes it very difficult for new players to enter the German market or other capital-intensive markets where German industry has any vested interests. German industry imposes stringent quality parameters on potential suppliers to their key industrial sectors, in particular into capital-intensive, knowledge-based and innovation-driven sectors of economic activity. On the other hand, competitors to German industry have difficulties in imitating the competitive advantages of the German economy because over and above the obvious technological differential, the German model is also anchored on a fabulous stable of brands, both manufacturers' but also product brands.

That which appears to be dichotomous and mutually exclusive in other contexts does not seem to dissuade the German economic model of technocratic differentiation that is simultaneously anchored on extremely valuable brands of global notoriety next to average and affluent consumers alike. This is an excellent reconciliation between the tangible and intangible cues in market offers that are distinct and valuable. This combination of technocratic excellence, profound knowledge of the markets and technological acumen on the one hand, and the acknowledgement of the critical importance of branding in contemporary consumption on the other is rare in the history of the competitiveness of nations, but the German economy seems to have mastered what it entails to perfection.

Through a strict definition of exceptionally hard to attain parameters on standards of quality in the supply of intermediate goods into the German economy and its productive structure, and through the imposition of formidable technological barriers, German industry makes it very hard for others to break into market sectors where they are the incumbent and dominant players.

It is not all about technocracy or technological superiority however, and the notoriety achieved by strong and extremely valuable global brands emanating from the German economy adds to the excellent quality of innovative products that incorporate highly specialized knowledge. The German economy has thus been able to build a hybrid system in the acquisition of sustainable competitive advantages that are not easy to replicate, tending in this way to perpetuate their incumbent positions in highly competitive capital-intensive sectors of economic activity.

The German model associates the excellence of technocracy anchored in the state-of-the-art of technological innovation with a stable of brands of enormous reputation and accounting goodwill, and does this better than anyone else. This allows for the best firms in Germany to be insulated from low-cost competition from the emerging economies, either by virtue of technological supremacy or because they have exceptional brands to back up these excellent products.

The German economy thus obtains significant competitive differentials in relation to its competitors in the global scene, founded on technological excellence that has been built over decades, conquering an enviable reputation of rigour, discipline and competence which configure a technocratic philosophy of excellence that translates downstream into goods and services resulting from complex manufacturing processes, both not easily susceptible to replication by competitors in low-cost economies. An extremely high degree of exigency in the domestic market, as well as the prevalence of requisites of excellence in the parameters of quality that suppliers to the German manufacturing sector have to abide by, signifies quality thresholds of such an order that these constitute very effective barriers to the entry of new players into the German market.

Diffusion of technology and technical knowledge has become easier in the light of the globalization of business environments. Players in emerging low-cost economies are more than avid to gather knowledge, whether it is of a technical nature or market knowledge that will allow them to challenge incumbent players in sophisticated markets. Companies operating out of low-cost emerging economies, who challenge the incumbent players in cosmopolitan markets, often do so by imitating and improving on the set of competitive advantages that the incumbent was led to believe were sustainable, well-protected and not easily susceptible to imitation. In the end the relevant difference between competing offers in a certain market may consist of the hedonistic dimensions of consumption that are peculiar to that market, corporate reputation issues or the country of origin of the good or service in question.

The perceptions held by external stakeholders about a nation are summed up in its reputation. This goodwill towards a nation derives from country of origin perceptions related to tradition, perceived level of industrial development, politics, history and culture. Often these stereotypical notions are unfounded or based more on perception than fact, but the reality is that they transfer over from being a mere country stereotype to affecting buying decisions. These stereotypes also transfer over from product to product and across to unrelated products.

The reputation of a nation, and the way in which country of origin cues disseminate across sectors of economic activity and across products, is of extreme importance to the competitiveness of a nation and its relative position in the global economy. This being the case, any credible strategy to improve the competitiveness of a nation needs to be anchored on a deep understanding of whatever are deemed to be the competitive advantages of a particular sector of economic activity or even of an entire economy. This means understanding how competitive advantages can be built up, how ephemeral or how sustainable they may be, the viability of their maintenance in the foreseeable future and how to achieve all of this in the complex reality of organizations. The degree of sustainability of a particular model of national competitiveness is dependent upon the higher or lower degree of permeability of organizations in an economy to external competition, and this is in turn a function of how ephemeral the bases for differentiation that characterize its competitive model are.

Whilst acknowledging that the tendency in international trade is towards the free circulation of goods and services, and that artificial barriers to world trade are condemned to failure, the only credible way for an economy to survive and aspire to future economic growth has to be anchored on the obsessive pursuit of constant improvement in its domestic factors of competitiveness.

In this way companies, whilst operating in domestic contexts of extremely high exigency and competitive intensity, are forced to develop market competencies and skills that will enable them to compete effectively in foreign markets. By thriving in demanding and sophisticated domestic markets, organizations are better equipped to face distinct markets with differentiated purchasing requirements and differing degrees of stakeholder exigency.

In order for the competitive advantages in an economy to be durable and effective they have to constitute real obstacles to the ability of competitors to imitate that which makes the offer of goods and services from a particular economy different. In a globalized world and in open economic systems this means that the goods and services emanating from a sector of economic activity or from an entire economy have to be perceived as superior from the viewpoint of its principal stakeholder groups, and namely consumers in foreign markets. The competitiveness of an economy is thus dependent upon its structural capacity to consistently show superior comparative performances on critical factors of competitiveness, in comparison to that of competing economies pursuing the same customers in the same export markets.

The scrutiny of external stakeholders, namely that of consumers, is crucial for the evaluation of the competitive capacity of an economy and the sustainability of its competitive advantages. In any given economy, the preferences of discerning consumers in foreign markets for products emanating from that economy to the detriment of competitors' products is the best possible sign of the sustainability of a competitiveness model. In order for this to happen, incumbent players in economic sectors of activity need to focus on the dynamic and on real-time understanding of the set of reasons underlying consumption decisions in sophisticated foreign markets.

Consumption decisions that consistently favour national organizations and their products constitute the necessary validation as to the quality and sustainability of competitive advantages in key export sectors for an economic sector or indeed for a national economy. The domestic economy needs to abide by exactly the same principles. It is not reasonable, as is evident from the empirical evidence, to have a sector of economic activity or important players in an economy that are not competitive in the domestic market for varying reasons, related to the predominance of virtual monopolies or less competitive and intense domestic markets, and then expect these same firms to be able to deal with cut-throat foreign markets, higher levels of exigency and consumer sophistication. National competitiveness, the intensity of local competition and the effectiveness of anti-monopolistic policies are thus positively related.

Table 10.11   Intensity of local competition (Top 20 ranking of the most competitive nations and EU economies under international intervention by the IMF, European Commission and European Central Bank)

Country	Intense in Most Industries				
	2008	2009	2010	2011	2012
Switzerland	20th	27th	36th	24th	20th
Singapore	30th	21st	28th	33rd	21st
Finland	16th	31st	52nd	71st	68th
Sweden	14th	20th	5th	10th	22nd
Netherlands	3rd	4th	10th	6th	1st
Germany	1st	1st	2nd	9th	8th
USA	4th	5th	16th	18th	18th
United Kingdom	10th	6th	8th	3rd	5th
Hong Kong SAR	7th	35th	32nd	14th	9th
Japan	9th	8th	7th	4th	2nd
Qatar	53rd	14th	3rd	5th	12th
Denmark	25th	11th	23rd	46th	29th
Taiwan, China	5th	2nd	1st	1st	3rd
Canada	23rd	24th	20th	21st	19th
Norway	21st	19th	27th	32nd	32nd
Austria	2nd	3rd	6th	8th	7th
Belgium	6th	7th	4th	2nd	4th
Saudi Arabia	50th	37th	24th	17th	14th
Korea, Rep.	49th	39th	14th	15th	11th
Australia	18th	17th	11th	7th	6th
Ireland	39th	49th	51st	59th	40th
Greece	52nd	68th	77th	82nd	95th
Portugal	41st	46th	45th	56th	62nd
Spain	15th	22nd	26th	23rd	23rd

Source: World Economic Forum (2008–2012)

Normally the work begins at home, with the acquisition of strong domestic market competencies, only for firms to expand progressively according to criteria of risk minimization. Strong market competencies are therefore dependent upon the competitive intensity of the domestic market and other variables including consumer sophistication, cosmopolitism and degree of customer orientation.

Table 10.12   Effectiveness of anti-monopoly policy (Top 20 ranking
of the most competitive nations and EU economies under
international intervention by the IMF, European Commission
and European Central Bank)

Country	Policies that Effectively Promote Competition				
	2008	2009	2010	2011	2012
Switzerland	19th	21st	23rd	21st	16th
Singapore	20th	8th	9th	11th	5th
Finland	6th	6th	4th	4th	4th
Sweden	4th	2nd	1st	1st	3rd
Netherlands	1st	1st	2nd	2nd	1st
Germany	2nd	3rd	3rd	23rd	24th
USA	8th	11th	17th	17th	17th
United Kingdom	15th	17th	8th	3rd	9th
Hong Kong SAR	53rd	84th	63rd	55th	55th
Japan	21st	13th	7th	9th	15th
Qatar	47th	39th	30th	27th	8th
Denmark	3rd	5th	6th	5th	10th
Taiwan, China	26th	22nd	21st	24th	19th
Canada	16th	19th	14th	12th	21st
Norway	9th	9th	11th	16th	11th
Austria	7th	12th	16th	13th	29th
Belgium	12th	14th	13th	18th	30th
Saudi Arabia	42nd	41st	28 th	15th	12th
Korea, Rep.	23rd	31st	43rd	41st	38th
Australia	5th	7th	15th	22nd	18th
Ireland	18th	20th	25th	26th	22nd
Greece	50th	59th	72nd	83rd	91st
Portugal	30th	43rd	49th	58th	68th
Spain	33rd	32nd	33rd	36th	49th

Source: World Economic Forum (2008–2012)

A sophisticated and intensely demanding domestic market creates the heightened competitiveness that allows organizations to thrive abroad. In this context the variables to consider in expansion strategies relate at least in an initial phase to geographic, cultural and psychological proximity as ways of minimizing business risk. As a way of example the first Zara store outside Spain was opened in Oporto and both geographical and cultural proximity were important for Zara in its strategic delving into the internationalization of its retail operations. It is then important to reiterate at this juncture the idea that the competitiveness of nations is not something that results from legislative procedure per se, although legislation may potentially induce behavioural change in economies and societies that lead to marked improvements in the competitiveness of nations.

In that way, the deterministic imperative of the consumer dictates that in order for the economy to acquire and maintain sustainable competitive advantages, firms in key sectors with export potential have to meet the stringent requirements of differentiated groups of consumers abroad in an effective manner and better than other competitors for the same markets. These key export sectors have to maximize their chances of success next to foreign consumers by adjusting to each export market, and treating it in accordance with its specific requirements, idiosyncrasies and specificities.

National competitive advantages are not a set of competencies that derive from any legislative package, no matter how good and comprehensive this may turn out to be. Government legislation may favour or run counter to a philosophy of national competitiveness, and it may potentially play an important role in inducing behavioural change leading to higher competitiveness levels, but per se it means nothing as a predictor of whether a nation will be competitive in the global stage. Like everything else in the competitiveness equation, legislation is but a part of a comprehensive package that includes a number of other variables acting systemically.

More than the outcome of legislation, the competitiveness of a nation is a state of mind, a collective heightened alertness that allow for the pre-empting of market requirements and responding to them effectively and expeditiously. It is about an awareness that every stakeholder in the economy has to have that comes from a history of permanent exposure to markets, understanding their demands, adjusting to their volatility and preferring a pro-active posture to the detriment of reactivity and late change.

It also helps if the country in question has a long-standing industrial and manufacturing tradition, not so much because of the technological implications inherent to that, or the implied level of knowledge, innovation or know-how that it may suggest, but because of the behavioural inferences that are part and parcel of organizational cultures that have long been accustomed to timekeeping and work ethic, as well as rigour and discipline.

The relative position of nations in the rankings of country competitiveness depends as we saw earlier on the nature of competitive advantages in an economy and how susceptible firms in that economy are to the potential imitation of their production processes and products by other firms in other economies. The singularity of the market offer of key export sectors in an economy determines the difficulty or even the impossibility of its replication by firms in competing economies. This is probably the single most important and deterministic factor in the perpetuation of competitive advantages in important sectors of economic activity, and perhaps the safest indicator as to the growth potential of an economy in the medium to long-terms, with all the repercussions that this has on the competitiveness of nations and the sustainability of key indicators of human and socio-economic development. The reason is simple. If the specific set of competitive advantages in question confer abnormal profitability to a firm or group of firms in a particular sector of economic activity, this will attract new players to this market, thus reducing overall average profitability for the sector. If the competitive advantage is easily replicable there will be a very quick erosion of whatever it is that confers a firm or an economic sector with a temporary competitive advantage.

A nation with a model of economic competitiveness that allows for an easy imitation of whatever it is that constitutes a set of momentary competitive advantages cannot be a competitive nation, at least in a sustainable way, given that competition for just about every economic sector that is not natural resource-based is intense. If the competitive advantages of capital-intensive key export sectors are easily susceptible of imitation, and if profitability is consistently above average for the sector, then it is safe to assume that new players will quickly enter into the market. If, on the other hand, the differentiating factors in that economy are true aggregators of value, unique and not easily susceptible to replication, then one can speak with propriety of a truly competitive economy.

The idea is that more than the specific competencies that confer competitive advantages upon an economic sector, more than a set of ephemeral technical and knowledge competencies, this is a philosophical question of the fundamental orientation of organizations, of the economy and the choice of a model of economic development for the domestic market, that transverses all sectors of economic activity, in particular those who have vested interests in playing a part in key export markets. The prevailing paradigm needs to be one of careful management of global value chains to ensure presence in key positions within those chains, and to exercise control over the links in these chains that effectively generate value.

There does not appear to be sufficient recognition paid to this and the real dimension of the problem that this presents to most European economies, nor a clear conscience as to its consequences on the viability of the incumbent economic models. In the light of current levels of consumption, and in a context of a collective culture of acquired rights which is perhaps a good characterization of some European economies, it is crucial that wider society acknowledges that the viability of those acquired rights is completely dependent upon the ability of a nation to create wealth consistently. The importance of an archetype of national competitiveness that is based on the acquisition and maintenance of sustainable competitive advantages in the real economy is in this way something absolutely critical for the future of Europe in the coming decades.

The smaller economies in the EU, particularly in the south, are open economies that have borrowed excessively over the last decade or so and are now strongly dependent upon the exterior for the financing of their economies. In some cases, for cultural and historical reasons, these economies are in many ways collectively unprepared to understand the elementary rules of the competitiveness game. Many in these nations legitimately reject the diktat of competitiveness and claim that competitiveness should not be the be all and end all of the life of a nation.

These people are becoming ever more vocal all over Europe, and in particular in the nations that have been the subject of severe austerity measures, including Spain, Portugal and Greece, but not only, as the problem appears to all too quickly be spreading to the rest of Europe. However, and in accepting that peoples' concerns are legitimate in the sense that no one wants to abdicate from their acquired rights, the key question here is whether these economies are formatted to be competitive in the global arena, in the light of contemporary determinants of modern competitiveness. It is understandable that people will reject giving up on the standards of living that they have grown accustomed to, including the provision of high-quality, universal, free for all health, education and an all encompassing and very generous welfare state, but the question is whether they can sustain this state of affairs.

Policy-makers, independently of the ideological spectrum and the party political quadrant where they originate, seem on the other hand to be formatted to devise sophisticated legal frameworks that are politically and ideologically laden, and whose apparent complexity traduces a bureaucratic philosophy, which is precisely the antithesis of the pragmatism required by modern competitiveness of the real economies of production of goods and services. This is particularly true for some southern European economies that lack sophisticated business environments.

As much of this is very foreign to decision-makers who are still very much embedded in the idea of the primate of macro-economic thinking and financial economics, as opposed to micro-economics and the competitiveness of firms in the real economy, then it is all still not very intuitive to policy-makers. Given the urgency of nations in switching paradigms and to shift radically towards a philosophy of competitiveness, anchored on value aggregation to highly innovative and creatively crafted goods and services, this collective bureaucratic mentality, which is the antithesis of effective entrepreneurship, is all the more pernicious and worrying and its eradication from societies and economies paramount.

Building competitiveness in national economies has to be the overriding objective of European nations in the light of an increasingly globalized world. It constitutes the only guarantee of national independence in the long term for the smaller European nations, but is also critical for the UK, particularly in the light of its historical role in Europe and its dependency upon key export markets in this continent.

It is very possible, and this is certainly the case with some southern European economies, but not only, that even if some of them saw their external debt pardoned it would not take long, and extrapolating from the current levels of spending in these countries, before they would again reach a situation equivalent to what they are experiencing today, due to the chronic budget imbalances and uncontrollable public spending that still prevail in these nations and their structural incompetence in creating wealth.

Of particular concern is the public debt over GDP ratio of these economies and their implied incapability in sustaining levels of wealth creation that are compatible with historical and current levels of public spending. What this means is that, as things stand, even if these economies were to run budget surpluses in the near future, albeit hell freezing is a more likely scenario, for current GDP levels and principally in the light of frail prospects of the emergence of a real economy of production of goods and services, there is little hope that this ratio will be reduced for these economies, and the possibility of public debt/GDP rations in the 60 per cent range are a mirage in a desert of economic despair. This only reinforces the imperative of micro-economic competitiveness and a stronger focus on firms and their critical role in economic recovery.

The problem with these economies is structural, not only to do with excessive spending but also related to their inability to generate sufficient wealth to justify the standards of living that citizens enjoy. The levels of GDP in these economies, and in particular their GDP per capita, do not warrant the levels of consumption and the social welfare enjoyed by their respective societies. By standards of living we refer not only to consumption levels but also to universal health coverage and education and a generous welfare system, as the provision of these is also a function of an economy's capacity for wealth creation. This seems to be controversial but there is nothing wrong in the idea of a nation and indeed individuals living within their means. For people this means their income, and for nations it is GDP.

What should be highly questionable is for national economies to consistently live beyond their means and for governments to make critical mistakes on dubious public investment decisions outside any strategic framework, or comprehensible economic intent, as constituted the sheer throwing away of a crucial window of opportunity that was the European structural aid that was pumped into the smaller European economies throughout the 1980s and 1990s with the ultimate purpose of bringing these economies to European standards, a pre-condition of a truly harmonious European economic geography.

The analogy between individuals and nations makes sense and is not out of order here. If one overspends and resorts to borrowing because he is investing in personal education that will ultimately lead to the betterment of his income earning potential that is one thing. If the individual makes some disastrous investment decisions along the way then friends, if and when they can, should come to the person's aid, however they cannot be held responsible for wrong decision-making. Worse still, why should others pay for conspicuous and irresponsible consumption?

The analogy of the individual living within his or her means fits perfectly the context of a national economy. Nations need to live within their means and excessive debt only makes sense in the context of it being incurred for the purposes of strategically planned reproductive investments with a strong likelihood of future returns. Education as a way of example would show up at the top, in the priority list of investment for any economy.

The comparative capacity for adjustment of a sector of economic activity, or of an entire economy of a nation to the determinants of global competitiveness, will determine its comparative economic performance vis-à-vis that of other nations competing for the same export markets and FDI. The performance of key sectors of an economy on relevant competitiveness criteria in key export markets is an indicator as to the comparative ability of a nation to compete in the global stage. The structural inadequacy of a nation's economy is on the other hand directly linked to its inability to guarantee the levels of human and social development that society collectively aspires to.

The problem with many of these economies is that their most important players have negligible presences in foreign markets and absolutely no expression next to sophisticated and cosmopolitan segments in the more affluent markets. Consumers in these markets avidly seek branded goods and services and a symbolism of the kind that coincides with, and is adjusted to, the reigning values in these societies.

Entrepreneurs have in this context to understand what the cues and manifestations of cosmopolitism are in foreign markets, in the sense that their foremost task is to interpret what the key determinants of consumption in each market are, reflecting market differences in the supply of differentiated market offers, tailored in accordance with the specific requests of different customer groups.

All of this has to be reflected in the building of market offers in such a way as to constitute a significant improvement on that which the competition has to offer. Crucially this superiority in relation to the competition has to be factual but it also needs to be perceptual, in the sense that discerning consumers in foreign markets will need to perceive offers as superior in relevant dimensions of consumption.

In assessing the competitiveness of a nation, or that of companies in key economic sectors, country size isn't necessarily a limiting factor. There are cases of small nations, territorially or in terms of their population, whose economies are nonetheless competitive in the global stage. This is the case of the

Scandinavian economies, and in particular Finland, which with a population of about five million manages to have a very competitive economy, with notable worldwide renowned brands of exceptional goodwill and accounting value. Nokia is the best example of a great Finnish corporate brand. Switzerland and Singapore are also examples of competitive economies that have clear geographical and territorial limitations.

More than country size, what seems to matter and affect negatively the competitiveness of a nation however is the absence of a critical mass of firms in key sectors of economic activity, the excessive fragmentation of the structure of property in key manufacturing sectors, or also the opposite of this, a prevalence of monopolistic models that do not favour intensity of competition and rivalry in domestic markets, promoting instead a sterile and stagnant business environment.

Countries that err on labour-intensive economic models instead of capital-intensive models of competitiveness tend in the light of global competition to be much more susceptible to low-cost players, and their economies are therefore more vulnerable and consequently in deeper trouble. European economies that are not technologically comparatively advanced, and that have not made it a focus of their strategic outlook to invest in knowledge-based competencies, are already facing insurmountable obstacles and will continue to do so as these things do not go away easily.

This is particularly evident when these economies are geographically located and occupy civilizational spaces, where their citizens aspire to and have come to expect high levels of state protection and welfare, as well as top-notch indicators of human and social development, expressed in universal coverage for health and education as well as handsome unemployment and pension schemes.

More than the impact of country size, national competitiveness is about a set of societal behaviours and a philosophy whose overriding obsession is the notion of aggregation of value to exported goods and services. National competitiveness is also about the creation of systemic conditions that are conducive to the attraction of inflows of FDI, in the knowledge that global investors have a plethora of investment opportunities and alternatives to choose from, that these are not geographically bound and reside all over the world.

Global Brands

- Holland and Britain with Shell, Holland with Phillips, ABN Amro, and the connection with KPMG (Peat Marwick and Klynfeld), Endemol, DAF (trucks), Heineken, Ahold.
- Product and corporate brands and country brands are very difficult to imitate.
- Many British brands of global notoriety
- Finland with Nokia, Sweden with Ericsson, IKEA and Volvo, Tetra Pak, Astra Zeneca (Sweden and Great Britain), Asea Brown Bovery (Sweden and Switzerland)

Figure 10.3   Global brands

In what concerns the aggregation of value to goods and services, the creation and nurturing of corporate and product brands, their development and the subsequent acquisition of global notoriety is of the utmost importance to the competitiveness of nations. Nations which consistently rank up there alongside the most competitive economies in the world are also the nations that possess the most valuable corporate and product brands according to credible barometers, including the WEF and its rankings of national competitiveness and Interbrand and its work on brand valuation.

Table 10.13   Top 20 most valuable global brands (2012)

Ranking	Brand	Variation %	Value USD Millions	Country
1st	Coca-Cola	+8%	77 839	USA
2nd	Apple	+129%	76 568	USA
3rd	IBM	+8%	75 532	USA
4th	Google	+26%	69 726	USA
5th	Microsoft	-2%	57 853	USA
6th	General Electric	+2%	43 682	USA
7th	McDonalds	+13%	40 062	USA
8th	Intel	+12%	39 385	USA
9th	Samsung	+40%	32 893	Korea, Rep.

10th	Toyota	+9%	30 280	Japan
11th	Marcedes Benz	+10%	30 097	Germany
12th	BMW	+18%	29 052	Germany
13th	Disney	-5%	27 438	USA
14th	Cisco	+7%	27 197	USA
15th	Hp	-8%	26 087	USA
16th	Gilette	+4%	24 898	USA
17th	Louis Vuitton	+2%	23 577	France
18th	Oracle	+28%	22 126	USA
19th	Nokia	-16%	21 009	Finland
20th	Amazon	+46%	18 625	USA

Source: Interbrand (2012)

There are therefore sociological traits and characteristics of the collective psychology of a nation that hinge on the willingness of entrepreneurs to take risks on the creation of brands, risks inherent to going downstream in key supply chains and sticking close to consumers in sophisticated retail markets. The propensity to take risks by key economic agents far outweighs issues of territorial size and population density when it comes to assessing the competitive potential of a nation.

Again, some European economies appear to be stuck in the middle between a strategic choice for labour-intensive economic models that are simply not viable in the light of emerging low-cost economies, and an inability to master cutting-edge technology that is inherent to capital-intensive, knowledge-based models of economic competitiveness. In addition to this, these economies are not brand savvy or cosmopolitan, their business environments are not sophisticated and therefore do not exercise adequate competitive pressure over incumbent players in their domestic markets, so that when going abroad firms in these economies are not at all prepared for the level of competitive intensity that they find.

The degree of customer-orientation of firms in these economies is consequently minimal, and the collective grasp of marketing issues negligible. These are also not knowledge-based societies, and they are also not known for the quality of their education, or of the research that comes out of their better institutions of higher learning. The links between national competitiveness and the quality of scientific research institutions and that of educational systems is shown in Table 10.14.

Table 10.14   Quality of scientific research institutions (Top 20 ranking
of the most competitive nations and EU economies under
international intervention by the IMF, European Commission
and European Central Bank)

Country	The Best in their Field Internationally				
	2008	2009	2010	2011	2012
Switzerland	2nd	1st	2nd	2nd	2nd
Singapore	13th	12th	11th	12th	12th
Finland	9th	13th	13th	18th	13th
Sweden	11th	6th	5th	4th	9th
Netherlands	10th	7th	9th	8th	8th
Germany	6th	5th	6th	10th	10th
USA	1st	2nd	4th	7th	6th
United Kingdom	7th	4th	3rd	3rd	3rd
Hong Kong SAR	29th	34th	35th	32nd	31st
Japan	15th	15th	15th	11th	11th
Qatar	30th	32nd	22nd	6th	5th
Denmark	12th	9th	12th	14th	18th
Taiwan, China	21st	18th	17th	19th	19th
Canada	4th	11th	8th	9th	16th
Norway	22nd	20th	23rd	28th	27th
Austria	18th	21st	20th	21st	21st
Belgium	5th	8th	7th	5th	4th
Saudi Arabia	47th	38th	37th	36th	37th
Korea, Rep.	14th	22nd	25th	25th	24th
Australia	8th	10th	10th	13th	7th
Ireland	17th	16th	16th	16th	14th
Greece	73rd	77th	88th	90th	93rd
Portugal	33rd	31st	28th	23rd	22nd
Spain	55th	44th	43rd	39th	36th

Source: World Economic Forum (2008–2012)

Table 10.15   Quality of the educational system and its link to national competitiveness (Top 20 ranking of the most competitive nations and EU economies under international intervention by the IMF, European Commission and European Central Bank)

Country	2008	2009	2010	2011	2012
Switzerland	3rd	2nd	2nd	1st	1st
Singapore	2nd	1st	1st	2nd	3rd
Finland	1st	4th	6th	3rd	2nd
Sweden	12th	12th	8th	8th	12th
Netherlands	13th	15th	14th	10th	13th
Germany	23rd	27th	18th	17th	20th
USA	19th	22nd	26th	26th	28th
United Kingdom	28th	30th	28th	20th	27th
Hong Kong SAR	22nd	28th	25th	21st	23rd
Japan	31st	31st	35th	36th	43rd
Qatar	16th	10th	4th	4th	4th
Denmark	6th	6th	10th	16th	19th
Taiwan, China	25th	17th	17th	19th	24th
Canada	8th	5th	5th	7th	6th
Norway	11th	16th	19th	22nd	18th
Austria	14th	18th	24th	24th	26th
Belgium	4th	7th	7th	6th	5th
Saudi Arabia	70th	60th	41st	25th	32nd
Korea, Rep.	29th	47th	57th	55th	44th
Australia	9th	14th	12th	13th	15th
Ireland	7th	8th	11th	11th	9th
Greece	82nd	90th	118th	120th	115th
Portugal	73rd	68th	76th	76th	61st
Spain	52nd	78th	107th	98th	81st

Source: World Economic Forum (2008–2012)

The link between national competitiveness and organizational staff training and employee development is shown in Table 10.16.

Table 10.16 **Extent of staff training and employee development (Top 20 ranking of the most competitive nations and EU economies under international intervention by the IMF, European Commission and European Central Bank)**

Country	Extent of Investment in Staff Training and Employee Development				
	2008	2009	2010	2011	2012
Switzerland	2nd	3rd	2nd	1st	1st
Singapore	3rd	2nd	4th	4th	3rd
Finland	11th	9th	9th	8th	2nd
Sweden	4th	1st	1st	2nd	6th
Netherlands	8th	10th	11th	10th	8th
Germany	12th	11th	8th	16th	13th
USA	6th	8th	10th	12th	15th
United Kingdom	22nd	26th	28th	15th	14th
Hong Kong SAR	29th	25th	27th	26th	24th
Japan	5th	5th	6th	6 th	5th
Qatar	33rd	23rd	19th	24th	11th
Denmark	1st	4th	7th	3rd	10th
Taiwan, China	16th	19th	31st	30th	31st
Canada	19th	12th	12th	18th	23rd
Norway	7th	7th	3rd	5th	9th
Austria	18th	24th	14th	14th	12th
Belgium	13th	13th	15th	13th	20th
Saudi Arabia	52nd	45th	34th	28th	35th
Korea, Rep.	10th	29th	42nd	41st	42nd
Australia	17th	18th	20th	17th	28th
Ireland	21st	15th	23rd	22nd	16th
Greece	81st	101st	105th	114th	115th
Portugal	70th	79th	73rd	72nd	73rd
Spain	63rd	73rd	89th	90th	105th

Source: World Economic Forum (2008–2012)

To top this off, citizens in these economies have been treated to standards of living that are incompatible with current and historical levels of national wealth creation. They are accustomed to enjoying social welfare rights which were largely the result of a miscalculation at best, and most likely attributable to politically irresponsible mismanagement of collective expectations, in the light of what these economies could realistically provide. Of particular concern, and as a footnote to this picture of irresponsible expenditure that still goes on unhindered in these economies, are the extraordinary incomes earned by fat cats in the utilities sectors, holding key positions in public and private administration in politically motivated rotative executive appointments.

Most of this happened over the last two decades, and to be fair these economies had been able to sustain reasonably good social welfare policies, and in some cases, exceptional national health services without losing their grip on the public debt variable. However, and over the last couple of decades, governments have just lost touch with reality, and this is one that dictates a deterministic relationship between a nation's capacity for wealth creation and the level of welfare that it can bestow upon its citizens.

The wealthier nations in the EU, and in particular Germany, are also to be held responsible for this as they created a state of perceived collective laissez faire in the whole process by virtue of their large subsidization of this state of affairs, mainly as part of the financial packages to recoup the structural backwardness of these economies. Exorbitant external public debt was accrued as dubious and essentially non-reproductive public investments were made largely in the areas of civil construction and useless infrastructure, whilst insufficient attention was given to education, the micro-economics of the firm and its key role in wealth creation.

What is happening now is that this insatiable appetite for foreign products has had to be curtailed as much of it rode on the back of massive public and private debt incurred over years of careless over-expenditure and unrealistic perspectives on the economy and life in general. This is well expressed in the consumption boom that these economies witnessed in the 1990s. The tragedy with these economies is that the private sector has failed to develop any worthwhile competencies, entrepreneurial initiative or business acumen, nor does it have the cosmopolitanism to understand foreign markets.

Without a market-savvy, knowledgeable and sophisticated entrepreneurial class that understands the world, an economy simply cannot establish a platform for preference for its products in global markets. This is reinforced by the fact that just about every export sector is characterized by cut-throat globally competitive business environments. In addition to all of this, businesses, particularly small businesses, are finding it difficult to obtain credit financing in the light of the credit crunch, partly because of the economic crisis but also because these are nations that suffer from bad credit ratings, resulting from negative investor perceptions as to their default-risk. These are economies that have had to be intervened in order to ensure their solvency.

Table 10.17   Country rating by credit rating agencies (EU countries under international intervention by the IMF, European Commission and European Central Bank)

Country	Moody's			Standard & Poor's			Fitch		
	2010	2011	2012	2010	2011	2012	2010	2011	2012
Ireland	Aa2	Ba1	—	A	BBB+	BBB+	A+	BBB+	BBB+
Greece	Ba1	Ca	C	BB+	CCC	CCC	BBB-	B+	CCC
Portugal	A1	Ba2	Ba3	A-	BBB	BB	A+	BB+	BB
Spain	Aa1	Aa2	Baa3	AA	AA-	BBB-	AA+	AA-	BBB

Source: Various (2012)

The truth of the matter however is that even during the more affluent times of credit abundance, small and medium-sized firms, with much in the way of disposable credit, were still not able to build up sustainable competitive advantages or even enhance their knowledge and understanding of the imperatives of competitiveness in sophisticated markets. Instead they were insular and reactive, and now they are paying the price for that collective posture. The failure of a whole class of entrepreneurs in creating the appetite for national products next to sophisticated consumers in foreign markets, in ways that fit well with the buyer decision-making criteria of the more affluent buyers in consumer-savvy markets, explains the lack of competitiveness of these economies.

The total absence of a collective entrepreneurial spirit illuminating dynamic individuals which could potentially set the course for key sectors of economic activity with export potential is unfortunately the norm with these national economies. There are of course exceptions to the rule, but their very mentioning and immense success at times only corroborates the notion that, along with undisciplined public overspending, one of the crucial problems with national competitiveness in any economy is the absence of a truly dynamic entrepreneurial class. The need to enumerate examples of best practice and excellence in an economy is ample evidence that these cases do not exist in sufficient numbers, to the point where they are the norm and not remarkable exceptions.

Under current conditions and with this state of affairs, fiscal discipline, and strict budget deficit and public debt control objectives are crucial to the creation of macro-economic conditions that facilitate the micro-economics component of the competitiveness equation. Macro-economic stability however is far from sufficing as a condition for economic growth and development.

What truly matters for national competitiveness are the leveraging effects on GDP that result from an economy possessing the right fundamentals in terms of its structure and composition, as well as micro-economic dynamics, including its standing on the critical dimensions of innovation and the sophistication of its business environment. Failing this, to expect austerity measures to have an immediate impact on national competitiveness is unrealistic and fundamentally wrong.

The degree of effectiveness in the application of austerity measures in an economy depends upon the performance of the economy on a set of structural factors, its dynamism, innovative capabilities and market sophistication. An economic structure that is unadjusted in relation to the determinants of global competitiveness in modern economies is in dire need of profound structural reformation in key areas that directly or indirectly impinge on the nation's ability to compete globally.

This reformist imperative is all encompassing and cuts across various areas of the lives of societies. It refers to the minimization of obstacles that impede the functioning of a dynamic economy such as a stagnant bureaucracy or a morose and inefficient legal justice system and the judiciary, but relates fundamentally to a much needed emphasis and obsession with investment in a society of knowledge leading to a knowledge-based economy embedded in a sophisticated business environment.

The sedimentation of a nationwide philosophy of competitiveness takes time to implement. It requires perseverance, constancy of effort and may take generations before the philosophy is deeply entrenched into a society and an economy as there are cultural imperatives that play a critical role in augmenting or alternatively hindering the outcome of all of this. The added difficulty here is that in these situations the management of political cycles tragically takes precedent over the strategic interests of nations, and they are often irreconcilable with the imperative of reformation.

Stiglitz has stated that it is not so much the size of public debt that matters, but it is more the capacity for its absorption by the real economy of the production of goods and services. This should bring to the forefront the critical importance of economic growth as a condition for the attainment of public debt/GDP ratios in the order of 60 per cent. This is what is called the bearable public debt level, a level of public debt that allows for macro-economic stability and creates the conditions for micro-economic competitiveness, thus ensuring real economic growth. In effect this is about the transformation of a vicious circle into a virtuous one.

It is not possible to solve the problem of a rampant and out of control public debt/GDP ratio only via the attainment of a tighter budget discipline by simultaneously curtailing public expenditure and increasing taxation. It is an imperative of policy that a stronger focus on GDP growth is achieved, leading to the improvement of the balance of trade of nations and the potential for attracting FDI into economies.

On the micro-economic side of the equation, the focus needs to be on the aggregation of value to transactionable goods, importation substitution for domestic production wherever possible and the general reduction of the consumption of imported goods, as well as making economies more attractive to potential FDI inflows. Given current forecasts of economic growth, it is very unlikely that many European economies are able to achieve bearable public debt levels of around 60 per cent in the coming decades.

This shows yet again that budgetary discipline is crucial, yes, but it will be economic growth that will save the day. By acknowledging that and understanding that national competitiveness, value aggregation to exports and attraction of FDI are imperatives of economic growth, it stands to reason that it is crucial to understand the determinants of these variables in modern economies.

The German economy, as any other economy that produces exceptional quality products based on state-of-the-art knowledge and technology, still needs foreign consumers to purchase its exported goods and services.

Germany needs its foreign markets to remain dynamic and preferably with acquisitive power in order for consumers in these markets to continuously purchase German exported goods.

However, even if Germany or any of the more developed economies were to lose their traditional export markets in Europe, it would still be possible to adopt a geographic diversification strategy for its exported goods with a view to entering into other markets. In particular, Germany or any other economy that produces exceptional quality products would be able to target the large groups of affluent consumers in emerging economies or search for alternative markets for its high-quality products.

There are economies in Europe, however, that manufacture undifferentiated goods that nobody recognizes and that compete in restricted markets solely on the basis of price. These economies have a much more poignant problem than that of the German economy or of the other nations that have real economies of production of goods and services and that export to demanding and sophisticated markets.

The problem with these economies is that if they lose their core export markets, because all of a sudden they have become uncompetitive on price, then there is no plan B. They have not developed a stable of corporate or product brands that are appealing to discerning, sophisticated and affluent consumers the world over, and so and in the absence of exceptional educational levels of their populations, or other knowledge-based competencies that they may have, there is not much left to do unless that is they start tapping into their endowment of natural resources in a radically different manner from what they have done in the past.

The Germans and the other economically developed nations can always come up with a diversification strategy for their exports by searching for consumers in other geographies. It may take them a while before acquiring positions of dominance in emerging markets, but there is one crucial element in all of this, and that is that consumers want their products, they recognize their brands and they aspire to the values that these brands stand for. This goes for both product as well as corporate brands, and it applies to both products and services.

It may take them a while to do it, but they have what it takes, a real economy that offers that perspective in very realistic terms. The same happens perhaps and to a lesser extent with the British, the French or the Italian economies, albeit in different ways, as all of these nations have different characterizations of their economies and their structure and composition of exports of transactionable goods.

The German economy and the economies of the countries whose emphasis is on the production of goods and services that consumers from all over the world want, and for which they are willing to pay price premiums can, in the event of demand for their goods in their traditional markets melting down, search for the more elitist segments in emerging economies, such as China or Brazil. They can also tap into other segments in these economies.

This is based on the simple assertion that the German real economy of production of high-quality goods and services is able to place products of excellence in consumer markets with disposable income anywhere in the world, next to consumers that are more than willing to pay price premiums for these products. These companies and their goods are perceived as superior by prospective consumers not only in terms of their quality, but also in terms of their reputation, both corporate and product.

If there is a problem with the German micro-economy, it will be one whose solution will have to be found on a strategic realignment of the economy into other geographies, as this is an economy that is based on the provision of goods and services that people want and ascribe value to, as opposed to an economy of undifferentiated goods that anybody can replicate cheaper, or even worse an economy of financial speculation with no underlying substance.

On the other hand, nations whose deliberate historical focus has not been on the real economy, or that have deviated intentionally or not from a strategic paradigm characterized by the production of goods of high knowledge content and incorporated technology, will find it hard to survive. Unless production processes and products result from technology and knowledge that are difficult to imitate, these economies will not stand a chance of survival in the light of the current dynamics of the global economy and the relative easiness with which anyone can replicate labour-intensive competitive models in much cheaper ways.

These unbranded economies have no particular significance on the world stage and they have a fundamental problem, even when discounting for relative size. These are economies that, by not having corporate or product brand that appeals to the curiosity and interests of sophisticated consumers in high disposable income markets, have more to worry about than losing their core markets. The problem that they have is that they have no products that consumers want. Better put, they may have the products but they do not have the brands.

The branded house model of communicating the country brand has been adopted by such nations as Australia, with the objective of creating notoriety for the country and enhancing its profile, emphasizing certain dimensions of economic potential for the benefit of foreign constituencies, thus promoting key export sectors, attracting tourism revenue and making the country more palatable to foreign direct investors. The branded house model of country brand communication may not be the most effective way of improving country image with foreign stakeholder constituencies, but it is one that is used mostly by countries that do not possess strong corporate or product brands of a global notoriety.

There is an alternative to the branded house model and this is the house of brands model. In all probability, a house of brands model where the quotidian of our daily lives is filled with positive experiences with exceptional branded goods of great value and notoriety is more effective for the objective of augmenting value to these goods, as a function of their known origin, than massive paid campaigns to communicate the image of a country. It is also more credible as consumers are inherently suspicious of institutional advertising.

These economies need to have a detailed understanding of the buying decision-making process in every export market in B2B as well as B2C contexts, and to acknowledge that the relevant consumption criteria in sophisticated markets do not consist entirely of the attributes that are visible in products. It is not only about the attributes that can be easily experienced in the consumption process, including product quality or design, but it is about other criteria that are much more important, external to the product, intangible and difficult to reproduce and replicate by competing players in the market.

These criteria act together to insulate the nation's offer of goods and services from that of competitors, differentiating it in a way that is perceived as being superior by consumers. In the end the ultimate aim is for consumers in foreign markets to establish preference, loyalty and pay premium prices for our products to the detriment of alternative offers.

Some European economies need to be able to tell good stories around their exports, to build excellent reputations for their corporate and product brands. The aura of goodwill that gets transferred from a country's reputation onto to its products as a result of accumulated reputation constitutes much more than mere positive externalities for an economy. On the contrary, in the context of contemporary global economic contexts that are characterized by highly intensive competitive environments in global markets, reputational goodwill is an essential pillar of the competitiveness of those nations, a differentiating and lasting mark that is transferred over to the goods and services that emanate from key economic sectors.

The British economy, by way of example, has to be able to differentiate itself clearly and effectively in key export sectors of national economic activity otherwise it will remain vulnerable to direct competition from players in countries that have incomparably lower labour cost structures and that reflect these downstream in low retail prices next to discriminating consumers, as are the cases of the emerging economies, including China and India.

In this scenario, any European economy that follows a competitive model based on labour-intensive economic activities will not stand a chance in the light of current competitive dynamics. With respect to that there cannot subsist any doubts. Whilst acknowledging that the British economy is historically capable of placing into the market highly innovative and good-quality products, in order to command premium prices for these products it has to gain the legitimacy to do that, and this can only be achieved by positioning these products distinctively in the minds of very demanding consumers in foreign markets. Any economy in the developed world which fails to do this will simply not be able to compete on the world stage on anything where labour costs are an important component of cost structures in manufacturing processes. If Britain is not competitive in the global market, it will not be capable of maintaining the standards of living of the British population at the levels that it is accustomed to.

Excessive public spending and private consumption, as well as non-productive public investments and the absolute waste of scarce resources, have contributed to the accumulation of public and private debt, both at worrying current levels across Europe. Negligible growth in GDP over the last decade or so has caused a worsening of the public debt/GDP ratio to dangerous levels, which is ample demonstration, if one was needed, of unsustainable levels of government debt incurred.

The notion of sustainability here refers to the capacity for absorption of current public debt levels in the light of projected GDP growth estimates. The perspectives for growth in GDP for the coming years are also not enthusiastic given the political lack of definition as to Britain's role in Europe, the state of a political Europe, the European economy and the importance of European markets for British exports. This being the case, it is difficult to understand the economic rationale that may justify any significant improvement on the current outlook of the economy and any prospects of a recovery given the systemic and integrated nature of the British economy vis-à-vis the economies of European countries.

For the smaller and more vulnerable European economies, all of this is a clear indication of a reformist imperative that, whilst acknowledging the macro-economics of the problem, looks with a sharper focus at the micro-economics of firms and industry as a proxy to national competitiveness, which is in turn linked to the sustainability of current indicators of social and economic development in these nations.

What remains is about reiterating the overriding principles of budgetary discipline and living within the limits of a nation's resources and capacity to generate wealth. Nations have to live within their means but also expand their wealth creation capabilities to accommodate the indicators of social and human development that they have grown accustomed to, particularly in the light of growing demographic pressures that run counter to the maintenance of those acquired rights in societies.

Problems with Public Debt/GDP above 60 per cent:

- Credit restrictions and credit worthiness
- Strongly restricted commercial and investment flows
- Negative economic growth
- Unemployment
- Significant losses in competitiveness
- Substantial lowering of the standards of living
- Severe austerity measures
- High market volatility

Figure 10.4   Problems with public debt/GDP above 60 per cent

The structural problems that need a reformist agenda towards finding a systemic solution for improving the competitiveness of the British economy relate to the enhancement of its comparative performance vis-à-vis that of competing economies on key criteria that constitute the determinants of national competitiveness. Many of these economies that are now completely riddled with debt are nations where debt was incurred not for public investment of a kind that would translate into more competitive and innovative economies, or more sophisticated business environments somewhere down the line.

Many of these nations have been amassing debt but their economies have still lost ground in the structural variables that characterize competitive modern economies, that is, in the factors that correspond to the pillars of innovation and the sophistication of the business environment in the competitiveness of nations. In this context, there are European economies with unbearable public debt/GDP ratios, well above 60 per cent, and in some cases in the order of 130 per cent and 140 per cent. If in addition to their inability to curtail spending levels they are also incapable of growing their economies under the incumbent economic growth models that they subscribed to, then there does not appear to be a quick fix solution looming on the horizon for any of them.

Table 10.18 shows the link between national competitiveness and government debt as a percentage of GDP.

Table 10.18   Government debt as a percentage of GDP (Top 20 ranking of the most competitive nations and EU economies under international intervention by the IMF, European Commission and European Central Bank)

Country	Government Debt/GDP (%)				
	2008	2009	2010	2011	2012
Switzerland	56.8	45.6	41.6	55.0	48.6
Singapore	96.3	99.2	113.1	97.2	100.8
Finland	41.0	40.6	52.6	48.4	48.6
Sweden	46.9	47.4	51.8	39.6	37.4
Netherlands	51.4	64.6	68.6	63.7	66.2

Germany	63.2	67.2	72.5	80.0	81.5
USA	60.8	70.5	83.2	91.6	102.9
United Kingdom	43.0	51.9	68.2	77.2	82.5
Hong Kong SAR	1.2	16.9	33.4	4.8	33.9
Japan	195.5	196.3	217.6	220.3	229.8
Qatar	11.7	4.8	15.7	17.8	31.5
Denmark	31.8	40.1	51.8	44.3	46.4
Taiwan, China	34.2	43.2	38.0	39.7	40.8
Canada	68.5	63.6	81.6	84.0	85.0
Norway	82.7	55.7	49.2	54.3	49.6
Austria	61.3	65.7	70.3	69.9	72.2
Belgium	88.3	93.2	101.0	97.1	98.5
Saudi Arabia	23.3	18.9	22.9	10.8	7.5
Korea, Rep.	24.6	25.2	34.9	30.9	34.1
Australia	15.4	14.2	19.2	22.3	22.9
Ireland	29.9	47.5	70.3	96.1	105.0
Greece	102.4	101.1	119.0	142.0	160.8
Portugal	71.8	75.3	87.0	83.3	106.8
Spain	42.6	46.8	62.6	60.1	68.5

Source: World Economic Forum (2008–2012)

The debt incurred by these economies also did not seem to benefit the collective wealth of these societies as is clearly evidenced when we look at the evolution of GDP per capita. Unless this debt was used for public investment, whose return will turn out to be visible at some point in the future, which does not seem reasonable, then and to the exclusion of any other variable or event, including the occurrence of natural disasters, what appears to be a certainty is that much of this debt was incurred for the purposes of conspicuous consumption as is also evidenced below.

Table 10.19   GDP per capita (Top 20 ranking of the most competitive nations and EU economies under international intervention by the IMF, European Commission and European Central Bank)

Country	Gross Domestic Product per Capita in Current US Dollars				
	2007	2008	2009	2010	2011
Switzerland	58,084	67,385	67,650	67,246	81,161
Singapore	35,163	38,972	37,293	43,117	49,271
Finland	46,602	51,989	44,492	44,489	49,350
Sweden	49,655	52,790	43,986	48,875	56,956
Netherlands	46,261	52,019	48,223	47,172	50,355
Germany	40,415	44,660	40,875	40,631	43,742
USA	45,846	46,859	46,381	47,284	48,387
United Kingdom	45,575	43,785	35,334	36,120	38,592
Hong Kong SAR	29,650	30,755	29,826	31,591	34,049
Japan	34,312	38,559	39,731	42,820	45,920
Qatar	72,849	93,204	68,872	76,168	98,329
Denmark	57,260	62,626	56,115	56,147	59,928
Taiwan, China	16,606	17,040	16,392	18,458	20,101
Canada	43,485	45,428	39,669	46,215	50,436
Norway	83,923	95,062	79,085	84,444	97,255
Austria	45,181	50,098	45,989	44,987	49,809
Belgium	42,557	47,108	43,533	42,630	46,878
Saudi Arabia	15,481	19,345	14,486	16,996	20,504
Korea, Rep.	19,751	19,505	17,074	20,591	22,778
Australia	43,312	47,400	45,589	55,590	65,477
Ireland	59,924	61,810	51,356	45,689	47,513
Greece	28,273	32,005	29,635	27,302	27,073
Portugal	21,019	22,997	21,408	21,559	22,413
Spain	32,067	35,332	31,946	30,639	32,360

Source: World Economic Forum (2008–2012)

Some of these nations have the same public debt problem that other economies also have, but their tragedy is that they are not structurally formatted to grow. What this means is that the pillars of competitiveness upon which these economies have been built, and where strategic investments have been made in the past, are not the ones that in the end will traduce an above average national competitive ability in the light of contemporary global competitive dynamics.

In other words, other economies who have had a much more strict scrutiny of their public and private investments, including reproductive investments on innovation, the sophistication of the business environment, and above all education, will tend to do much better when the returns on these investments become visible, and in many ways, even in aspects like education these are not long-term returns, as educated citizens exercise pressure over other stakeholders in the economy by virtue of their sheer conscience of their rights and duties.

Public debt levels measured in absolute terms in these economies are often lower than those of other nations, but the perceived and de facto ability of these nations to repay the incurred debt, reflected in public debt/GDP ratios, shows that the outlook is bleak for those nations as the growth prospects in these economies are slim at best. So it is not in fact the size of debt that matters, but the perceived capacity of economies in repaying it, and this is measured by potential GDP. Wealth creation in turn is a function of the behaviour and performance of these economies on critical pillars of competitiveness, namely those of innovation and the sophistication of the business environment.

The debt problems of these economies are therefore not only budgetary problems to do with a lack of fiscal discipline and overspending. All of these are factual but the danger for these nations is that their economies are not structurally ready to grow in the light of the determinants of contemporary global competitiveness. The political challenge is to engage in structural reforms that are independent of the management of political cycles and this is very difficult to achieve.

These reforms are about creating the conditions that lead to value aggregation in exports and the attraction of FDI inflows into an economy. By making economies structurally competitive, and working on the key determinants of exports and FDI, the performance of economies on these two crucial variables will naturally improve, not because of a pseudo-sophisticated macro-economic agenda, but for the simple fact that key stakeholders eventually come to the realization that it is in the micro-economy of the firm that true competitive advantage resides.

The work of government is to revoke structural obsolescence where it exists, resorting to criterious public investment and pursuing a sense of adequacy between the resources and capabilities in an economy and the global determinants of national competitiveness, the requirements of export markets and the criteria that make or break FDI inflows into an economy, and to be able to express all of this this through a clear national competitive strategic intent. The problem with these economies is that, in some cases, even if their external debt was to be pardoned, given their structural budgetary imbalances it would not take long before they would be once again highly indebted nations as these are economies that are simply not structured so as to excel on the determinants of competitiveness in a global context. This profound sense of adequacy between a nation's resources, skills and capabilities and the determinants of global competitiveness is, in the light of interdependent and systemic economic relations, what is required. It is not about great macro-economic tales and formulae. It is instead about the micro-economics of the firm in getting economies kick-started and back on track.

Only a favourable comparative performance of national economies on the determinants of competitiveness will allow for the generation of a level of wealth that is compatible with the indicators of human and social development that are expected by individuals in these societies. In order to maintain these indicators of welfare, in the light of adverse demographic indicators and the impossibility of economic growth under the incumbent competitive models, the only way in which these economies will be able to square the circle is by continuing to accumulate debt. This means the perpetuation of a very dangerous and negative downward spiral dynamic, probably spinning out of control.

The structural obsolescence of these nations is not so much of a technocratic or infrastructural nature as these economies are, by and large, up to date when it comes to technological innovation. They have the technology and the infrastructure. Where these economies present significant gaps in relation to the more competitive economies is in the factors that are the real determinants of competitiveness in the context of the global economy, namely the reduced comparative efficiency of both the labour and the goods and services markets, as well as the lower sophistication of their business environments. Even when they are on a par with the most competitive nations on innovation for example, other factors kick in to dilute these capabilities, as is the case of the morose functioning of the judicial system or the failure to enforce intellectual property rights. The table below shows the link between national competitiveness and the availability of latest technologies in the economy as well as the same link this time with the protection of intellectual property rights.

Table 10.20   Availability of latest technologies (Top 20 ranking of the most competitive nations and EU economies under international intervention by the IMF, European Commission and European Central Bank)

Country	Widely Available Technologies				
	2008	2009	2010	2011	2012
Switzerland	7th	6th	5th	2nd	2nd
Singapore	14th	14th	20th	17th	12th
Finland	3rd	3rd	4th	5th	3rd
Sweden	2nd	2nd	1st	1st	1st
Netherlands	15th	10th	9th	6th	4th
Germany	8th	16th	17th	20th	17th
USA	5th	5th	7th	18th	14th
United Kingdom	10th	18th	15th	7th	6th
Hong Kong SAR	19th	11th	10th	12th	8th
Japan	13th	12th	18th	15th	11th
Qatar	32nd	25th	25th	31st	25th
Denmark	4th	7th	13th	9th	20th
Taiwan, China	23rd	33rd	33rd	37th	40th
Canada	9th	9th	14th	14th	18th
Norway	6th	4th	3rd	3rd	5th
Austria	12th	13th	8th	10th	13th
Belgium	18th	19th	12th	8th	9th
Saudi Arabia	41st	43rd	39th	36th	34th
Korea, Rep.	22nd	24th	23rd	24th	26th
Australia	20th	21st	22nd	23rd	19th
Ireland	33rd	34th	34th	32nd	29th
Greece	62nd	64th	59th	56th	58th
Portugal	28th	23rd	19th	16th	15th
Spain	40th	41st	32nd	33rd	33rd

Source: World Economic Forum (2008–2012)

Table 10.21　Intellectual property protection including anti-counterfeiting measures (Top 20 ranking of the most competitive nations and EU economies under international intervention by the IMF, European Commission and European Central Bank)

Country	Very Effective				
	2008	2009	2010	2011	2012
Switzerland	1st	4th	4th	3rd	4th
Singapore	2nd	1st	3rd	2nd	2nd
Finland	4th	3rd	2nd	1st	1st
Sweden	9th	2nd	1st	4th	12th
Netherlands	11th	9th	10th	9th	5th
Germany	6th	13th	9th	13th	10th
USA	18th	19th	24th	28th	29th
United Kingdom	22nd	21st	17th	11th	6th
Hong Kong SAR	21st	23rd	18th	14th	11th
Japan	14th	20th	21st	22nd	18th
Qatar	25th	36th	28th	15th	8th
Denmark	3rd	6th	12th	6th	21st
Taiwan, China	28th	27th	26th	29th	22nd
Canada	19th	18th	13th	18th	17th
Norway	12th	14th	16th	12th	14th
Austria	5th	5th	11th	16th	16th
Belgium	20th	22nd	23rd	26th	24th
Saudi Arabia	38th	31st	30th	25th	27th
Korea, Rep.	26th	41st	44th	46th	40th
Australia	10th	12th	14th	19th	19th
Ireland	16th	16th	15th	10th	15th
Greece	44th	42nd	50th	52nd	64th
Portugal	29th	33rd	40th	42nd	42nd
Spain	34th	40th	42nd	43rd	50th

Source: World Economic Forum (2008–2012)

The less developed economies also fall short of the more competitive economies on their relative performance on key drivers of national competitiveness, namely the less sophisticated business environment that characterizes these economies, as well as their low innovation capabilities and the way these economies fail to assimilate innovative processes and incorporate innovation into their market offer, thus missing out on significant value augmentation possibilities. The table below shows the association between national competitiveness and firm-level technology absorption.

Table 10.22   Firm-level technology absorption (Top 20 ranking of the most competitive nations and EU economies under international intervention by the IMF, European Commission and European Central Bank)

Country	Aggressive Absorption of Technology by Firms				
	2008	2009	2010	2011	2012
Switzerland	5th	3rd	4th	4th	3rd
Singapore	13th	13th	15th	10th	8th
Finland	8th	9th	12th	11th	6th
Sweden	4th	6th	2nd	1st	1st
Netherlands	27th	25th	25th	21st	22nd
Germany	12th	14th	14th	14th	16th
USA	3rd	5th	11th	18th	14th
United Kingdom	20th	22nd	21st	22nd	23rd
Hong Kong SAR	16th	17th	18th	15th	7th
Japan	2nd	2nd	3rd	3rd	4th
Qatar	40th	19th	8th	7th	9th
Denmark	6th	7th	13th	9th	18th
Taiwan, China	10th	12th	10th	13th	19th
Canada	18th	21st	22nd	29th	30th
Norway	9th	8th	5th	5th	10th
Austria	7th	10th	16th	12th	13th
Belgium	25th	27th	28th	26th	31st
Saudi Arabia	44th	40th	26th	23rd	20th
Korea, Rep.	15th	15th	9th	8th	11th
Australia	17th	16th	19th	19th	15th
Ireland	29th	32nd	32nd	35th	33rd
Greece	90th	98th	91st	89th	94th
Portugal	39th	34th	27th	27th	27th
Spain	57th	49th	49th	46th	48th

Source: World Economic Forum (2008–2012)

In the light of a generalized absence of a strategic orientation for the development of the economies of nations in these circumstances, what subsists are disconnected sectors of economic activity, churning out goods and services of low aggregated value, firms and output that are scarcely orientated towards the stringent requirements of international markets. In this context, firms attempt to survive rather than having concerted and systematic strategies for key sectors of economic activity in approaching promising export sectors. What typically happens is that in one or two sectors, key players acquire a relative prominence at a regional level, not as a result of deliberate policy formulation but due to the ingenuity, will and initiative of founders, owners, managers and workers of companies that dare to think differently and take risks. These are the exception rather than the rule though.

The fundamental question that needs to be put forth to individuals in these societies is one of the unsustainability of their lifestyles, including the quality and universality in the provision of healthcare and education on the basis of current GDP levels in these economies. The same thinking goes for social welfare in general, including pension schemes that are unadjusted to the economic realities of these nations. This does not apply only to the poorer nations of the EU but increasingly to the wealthier nations that are also struggling.

This has all the indicators of becoming a huge social crisis, as in the case of government pension schemes these result from contractual obligations assumed by the state, involving the acquired rights of individuals, as well as expectations that were legitimately held by citizens who upheld their part of the contract. All of this however hits a brick wall, which is that of the inability of nations to grow their economies and their limited capacity for wealth creation, at least to the level where these acquired rights can be economically legitimated.

The capacity for wealth creation of these nations is simply insufficient to justify the magnitude and breadth of coverage of social welfare schemes that most European citizens have come to expect, albeit to different degrees of generosity across the different member states. If economies do not grow then the welfare state unequivocally needs to be reformulated. In this context, what appears to be critical is a perception of fairness in the distribution of effort to transpire. The perception of free-riding and exception makes it much more difficult to implement the political reforms that are necessary across Europe.

Any other justification for excessive private and public spending, and unsustainable social welfare schemes, measured by the quality in the provision of healthcare, education and social security, outside the framework of wealth generation for a nation can only mean borrowing. Accumulation of even more debt is of course untenable in the light of current circumstances and given the absolute dependency of these economies on external institutions for the financing of their economies. This calls into serious doubt not only the economic but also the political sovereignty of these nations.

In the case of many of these nations loss of sovereignty is not a farfetched deviation from their current condition, or one that is too dissimilar from what they already experience today. However a more prominent focus needs to be put on refining the balance between the objectives of public debt reduction through working on chronic structural budget deficits and the strategic work that needs to ensue on the structural determinants of competitiveness that lead to economic growth.

Nations should search for an improvement in the variables of GDP over which it is reasonable and possible to intervene and work strategically on, and those are the items of exports and imports in the balance of trade and FDI, as well as reproductive public investment that is underpinned by sound national strategic criteria. Public investment should be in innovation, in the knowledge economy and in the dimensions that induce behavioural change in society, that act as drivers of national competitiveness by favouring the occurrence of a greater sophistication in the business environment, but this will only work if the efficiency enhancers of the labour and goods and services markets also work.

Without sustained economic growth it is impossible to guarantee the social welfare state as we know it. People may call these their acquired rights or inscribe them into the law of the land, but if there is no economic substantiation to those rights, now or in the foreseeable future, then, in the light of adverse demographics and a global economic crisis, no matter how sophisticated the legislation is uncompetitive economies render these laws toothless. The only way, outside the scope of wealth creation and economic growth, to maintain the status quo on some viable form of a European welfare state, over and above getting the social systems to work better and more efficiently, is by incurring more public debt. It is as simple as that. Debt however is no longer a viable option.

If the relevant stakeholders in an economy, including policy-makers and entrepreneurs, are not able to understand clearly what underlies consumption decisions in the various export markets, and if they cannot figure out for key economic sectors, for which there are legitimate strategic aspirations, export strategies, that meet the specific requirements of these markets, then these national economies will not be able to overcome crucial inhibiting factors for their competitiveness in the global economy.

These economies will very quickly find it impossible to justify current levels and indicators of human and social development as well as the degree of state protection and welfare warranted to their citizens, no matter how vocal the respective populations are in venting their anger and grief at respective governments. Over and above the efficiency in the running of social systems, it is an economic question.

Economies that are not able to compete in the global market through the pursuit of distinction and perceived difference – accommodating the needs of every market, capturing their idiosyncrasies and specificities – will not be able to sustain the standards of living that their citizens have been accustomed to. This is the result of decades of overspending, excessive private consumption and generally the provision of very generous government-sponsored welfare systems, including the universal provision of health, education and social security.

European economies with abysmal economic growth records, which have fallen dramatically in global competitiveness rankings as well as in other credible indicators, are economies that are now finally confronted with the cruel reality of their condition, and this means that they are faced with huge and urgent cuts in social programmes, as well as needing to come up with economic growth agendas fast.

Competitiveness rankings, with all their subjectivity, are important in that they shed light on what is permissible for a given level of wealth in an economy. Admitting conditions of comparative government efficiency in the running of the welfare state, including the provision of health, education and social security, a nation's relative position on the global competitiveness tables allows for countrywide comparisons as to what the state can cover, as competitiveness is directly correlated with the capacity for wealth creation and consequently to indicators of human and social development.

This means that nations that have low economic growth potential cannot *ceteris paribus* and in a sustainable way guarantee a social welfare state on a par with that of wealthier nations and nations that show stronger potential for the growth of their economies. There is therefore a positive correlation between the relative position of nations in competitiveness rankings and the degree of legitimacy with which the populations of these nations may aspire to better standards of living, and possibly to what their national governments can do for them. In other words, there is a strong link between national competitiveness and indicators of social and human development. It is therefore important for policy-makers to determine the viability of a population's standards of living and what the state can realistically provide for, in the context of the economic reality of the nations concerned.

Under conditions of comparative efficiency in the running of social systems, it is then the actual and potential competitiveness of a nation, and therefore its capacity for wealth creation in the foreseeable future, that will determine the sustainability of social welfare systems. Competitiveness rankings are thus more than barometers of the economic status of nations. They are a good proxy to the realistic attainment of indicators of human and social development of a society and its members.

National competitiveness today transcends the economic dimensions of the life of a nation. It is a philosophy that should be embraced by every stakeholder in an economy. It reports above everything else to a set of conditions inherent to the characterization of a nation, whose nature and scope extend well beyond the economic, but which will impact on the competitive ability of that nation and its economic performance.

Over and beyond the imperative of an economy having to spend within its current budget constraints, it is about economies that produce goods and services of high quality and sell them in foreign markets to whoever avidly seeks to buy them and what they stand for. This constitutes the principal guarantor of the sustainability of competitive advantages at firm level for an economic sector or even for the entire economy of a nation. However, and in the light of global competitive dynamics, even the accomplishment of all of that may not be enough. Beyond fiscal discipline and the proliferation of innovative and creative manufacturing sectors in the economy, something else needs to happen. If nobody knows that we exist, the whole exercise is pointless and this is where marketing and branding come in.

It is important to look at the best practices of others, what the more competitive nations do with products that are functionally similar to ours, and in particular how they augment value to these products. The same goes for comparable sectors of economic activity or analogous manufacturing processes. How are other players in the global market, companies originating from other countries, able to aggregate value to goods and services in a way that we are not? What are their particular circumstances, and what do they do better?

These are products that comply with the same functional requirements and provide the same benefits as ours, yet they are able to command premium prices in sophisticated markets and we are not. In particular, these are products that sophisticated consumers that have money and that are smart enough to discern between competing offers prefer to the detriment of our products. Why?

It is also about time that we collectively arrive at the conclusion that economic agents and in particular consumers are not as rational as they were thought to be and as economic theory had postulated and has had us believe for decades. In fact, consumers may be too gullible for their own good as some of the work coming out of behavioural economics, including the research of people like Dan Ariely at Duke University and others, have concluded. Not only are consumers not rational, other stakeholders in the economy are not rational either and this should urgently inform the thinking of policy-makers when it comes to matters of macro-economic policy formulation, including the very difficult and crucial task of instilling confidence in economic agents and the economy.

In aiming to aggregate value to exported goods in stringent and sophisticated markets, it is important that both entrepreneurs and workers understand the nature and characteristics of demand in each market, at each point in time, as well as the decision-making processes in industrial and consumer markets and the buying determinant criteria in these markets.

It is therefore crucial that an understanding of the drivers of competitiveness in modern economies is attained, diagnosing where an economy is situated compared to the performance of other economies that compete with it for the same markets, with a view to improving its relative global position. This is achieved by focussing on the improvement of the dimensions of competitiveness that matter, and it can be done by looking into industry best practices, and the economic sectors of nations that attain better performances in global competitiveness rankings.

A strict focus on price in export markets as a result of labour-intensive models of economic development, anchored on low costs of labour, is utterly inappropriate for European players and will inevitably lead to failure as a competitive strategy for a sector or for an entire national economy. Price as a unique criterion for competitiveness has been inculcated in the minds of entrepreneurs through successive currency devaluations in certain European economies.

The lever of exchange rate policy was in the past used irresponsibly by pressured national governments who were actively lobbied by key export sectors to devalue national currencies for the purposes of cheapening exports in foreign denominations, thus artificially making these goods more competitive in foreign markets. The devaluation mechanism of exchange rate policy used over decades in these economies has contributed to the breeding of a class of complacent domestic entrepreneurs. These were lured into a false sense of security, into thinking that low price and competitiveness are interchangeable terms. This is not true at all.

In key sectors of economic activity, the focus has long shifted to criteria other than price that have come to play a much more important role in buying decision-making by virtue of societal changes in the dynamics and psychology of consumption as well as by rising disposable income levels. This is true in decision-making processes both in B2B but also in B2C contexts. In many buying situations, and not only in the cases of the purchase of luxury brands, criteria other than price have become important determinants of buying decision-making for informed consumers.

An excessive focus on price by firms operating in key export markets, which comes from the implementation of successive currency devaluation policy measures, leaves export sectors too vulnerable to price competition. This is dangerous in the light of global competitive dynamics, with players originating from emerging economies with much lower labour cost structures, in labour-intensive sectors acquiring relative competitive advantages, through what are unbeatable cost structures that are reflected downstream in low retail consumer prices.

Many European economies are stuck in the middle, a terminology that Harvard economics Professor Michael Porter coined for industry competitiveness, but one that aptly applies in the present context. These economies are unable to follow a cost-leadership strategy and they can't differentiate their offer in such a way for it to be perceived as superior and worth paying a price premium for by foreign constituencies.

Only by understanding each market in depth – not only in relation to its traditional typology, its demographic and economic characterizations, but by going well beyond that and searching for the determinants of success in each market, its specificity and potential – can a company, a group of companies, an economic sector or even an entire economy have success in the formulation of export strategies in demanding and sophisticated business and consumer markets alike.

For just about every export market the level of competition is very intense. This is particularly evident with respect to price competition in labour-intensive sectors, but competition is also cut-throat in capital-intensive sectors of economic activity. In the knowledge economy, such criteria as the ability to innovate and widespread access as well as use of technology are key sources of competitive advantage. In addition to this, sectors of economic activity that for some reason show abnormal profitability levels attract new players and intense competition, resulting in decreased average profitability.

In order for this systematic scrutiny of the markets to be effective, it should be complete and exhaustive of the psychological, cultural and historical aspects which extend beyond the more obvious characterizations of demographic trends or disposable income. This is a critical condition in finding a sense of adequacy between supply and demand with consumers of high acquisitive power that can always choose amongst competing offers.

Anything outside this thinking means that companies limit themselves to bringing undifferentiated goods to markets. These goods are easy to imitate by firms in emerging economies which have much lower labour cost structures and steep learning curves for whatever it may be that constitutes a competitive advantage for incumbent players in a market. This is quickly learnt and replicated.

A bias for price as the overriding competitive criterion in key export sectors of economic activity can potentially taint the whole economy as a price-taker. This occurs as it is not common for an economy to have a reputation for the exceptional quality of its products in a particular segment, trading goods at high prices in sophisticated market segments, and to have simultaneously and coexisting with that, an image of low cost for other sectors, competing strictly on the basis of price in the same markets. There is normally a congruence of image and reputation that transverse across sectors to make a wholistic and unified country image, that is, positive country of origin effects for a particular economic sector or for a set of products are transferred over and benefit other sectors and products, while its opposite is also valid, that is, negative stereotypes are projected across sectors.

National reputation tends to transverse sectors of economic activity. Country images are transferrable from sector to sector and it is difficult for the foreign consumer, armed with scarce information about the country of origin of the products that are purchased, to mentally reconcile images that are not congruent, that is for example, images of a certain elitism and sophistication for a certain type of product, that coexist with images of low cost in products coming out of other sectors of economic activity. These are critical issues in modern economies and do not seem to deserve the proper attention from policy-makers.

In summary, these economies are structurally unadjusted to the determinants of global competitiveness and consequently more vulnerable to competition from players in other economies. It follows that even in the event of a sustained balanced budget in these economies and an improvement in what concerns the compliance with objectives of public debt reduction, it is very improbable that these nations are able to attain a bearable public debt level in the order of the targeted 60 per cent of GDP.

In most developed economies that are afflicted by debt, a bearable public debt/GDP ratio can only be achieved through a significant improvement in the denominator of GDP. This objective is unattainable in the short and medium terms for the debt-ridden economies and in particular for those whose growth prospects are abysmal. An acceptable ratio is also only achievable in the long term if there is an all encompassing reformist strategic agenda that improves the performance of these economies on key dimensions of competitiveness. It does not suffice however that an improvement of the magnitude that is necessary in the performance of the national economies happens only in absolute terms, but also comparatively in relation to the performance of other competing economies on the same dimensions of competitiveness.

According to the Global Competitiveness Report of the WEF, European economies in general and in particular the economies of southern European nations have been losing ground on the competitiveness rankings tables over the last decade or so. It appears from this evidence alone that Europe has progressively been losing ground in terms of its global competitive position. This seems to corroborate the notion that there appears to be an adjustment between the relative rankings of European economies in these competitiveness tables and the structural realities of nations as well as their flimsy hopes of economic growth in the foreseeable future.

On the other hand, this abrupt fall in competitiveness of some economies in Europe in a short period of time, at least in the context of the economic history of nations, traduces something a lot more sinister and worrying. Some European economies appear to be signaling that they have definitely lost the global competitiveness train.

Although European economies in general tend to score well on institutional and infrastructural items and on the critical dimensions of innovation in the economy, the less competitive economies continue to suffer from grave problems when it comes to the efficiency of their labour markets, as well as the efficiency of the goods and services markets. In particular, these economies show very negative performances when it comes to the sophistication of their business environments.

If the pillars of the efficiency of labour and goods and services markets are susceptible to change and can be improved through the enactment of policy in order for this to happen, a profoundly reformist agenda is required. The same happens with changes in the judicial systems, and their inefficiency and inadequacy in the smooth running of contemporary societies and the economy. However in order for change to work it will take time and a collective will to change. This does not seem to be the case, certainly in the southern European nations.

These issues as well as matters of institutional transparency are also susceptible to change through legislation that induces behavioural modifications. However a change in the collective behaviour of societies on items that make up for the pillar of the sophistication of the business environment is something much more complex and difficult to effect. Both will take generations before any change is felt as these matters are largely behavioural in nature and scope.

The sophistication of the business environment is a crucial dimension of modern economic competitiveness and a strong predictor of the sustained economic growth of nations and it cannot be changed from one day to the next. On the contrary, it implies profound change in the behaviours of every stakeholder that is involved at all stages of every value chain in the domestic market, but also critically in export sectors. Embedded in this thinking and critical to its outcome are the absolute importance of the domestic market and consumers in it, and the creation of an internal culture of profound and stringent exigency. This is something that cannot be attained from one day to the next.

The problem with inducing behavioural change in stakeholders in an economy, leading to a more sophisticated business environment, is that it entails the revoking of old paradigms governing the functioning of stagnant and inadequate structures, of deep-rooted behaviours and attitudes of entrepreneurs, workers and consumers in every sector of economic activity, in short everyone. Behavioural change is much more complex and difficult to effect, as the problem is not so much legal or judicial but has instead an educational and cultural genesis.

The relative performance of an economy on the pillar of sophistication of the business environment traduces a higher or lower capacity of a nation for the development of an economic model of competitiveness that is based on the fundamental notion of value aggregation at each stage of each productive process, from logistics to distribution and consumption, for every key link in every value chain. It does so by instilling a philosophy of excellence that has to cut across an economy and in reality an entire society.

All of this implies a coordinated strategic approach to the competitiveness of a nation that requires time and commitment from its principal stakeholders and, foremost amongst these, policy-makers and entrepreneurs. Policy-makers are responsible for the definition of strategic guidelines and general orientations for the competitiveness of an economy, and should work to reduce ambiguity in policy and bureaucracy as well as ensuring a permanent scrutiny of the deviant elements to the intended trajectory and that these are removed from the path of firms.

The strategic purpose and intent have to be materialized in the constant improvement of the critical competitiveness factors identified herein, not only in absolute terms but also comparatively when contrasted with the performance of other nations on the same dimensions of competitiveness. This is the work of government, but fundamentally the role of firms in the economy.

Summing it all up, occasional lip service has been paid to much of this and when reference is made to it this is done in an unsubstantiated way, ideologically biased and party political in its approach, when the evidence is not ambiguous on this matter. The road to national competitiveness should also be straightforward, and that is excellent comparative performances on the pillars of innovation and sophistication of the business environment anchored on a culture of facilitation of economic activity that comes from efficient labour and goods and services markets.

The more competitive nations in the world are not those that export low value-added products, or that base their export strategies on low price competition, although there are emerging economies including China that adopt this model with much success. However, the demographic specificity of China, the never-ending pool of resources, cheap labour and feudal systems make it a unique case, to which no other nation, with perhaps the exception of India, can aspire to emulate.

Models of competitiveness that are anchored on low labour costs are simply not viable for the competitiveness of European economies. If these sectors deliver above average profitability they are sustainable until such a time as someone finds out, which, in this day and age means now. This is the corroboration of the vulnerability of an economic model based on labour-intensive sectors of economic activity to the low-cost emerging economies. Further evidence suggests that the nature of competitive advantage in contemporary economies and the choice of successful models of competitiveness clearly points the other way, to knowledge-based, innovation-driven economies.

Models of national competitiveness that are intended to be sustainable, anchored on labour-intensive, low costs of labour that typify the emerging economies, where favourable demographic factors guarantee uninterrupted flows of almost free labour, cannot and should not be sustained by European economies that occupy civilizational spaces that are in the antipodes of these nations, their labour relations traditions and cultural idiosyncrasies. These are not comparable and a low labour cost model is thus unattainable which leaves a model of national economic competitiveness based on knowledge, innovation and the constant pursuit of sophisticated business environments in capital-intensive sectors of economic activity as the only way forward.

In general, competitive economies are precisely those where the labour force is well remunerated for their efforts in adding rare and valuable knowledge to complex production processes. This is not coincidental. It means that *ceteris paribus*, what these economies have done better than others is to work on the critical pillars of competitiveness, namely the factors of innovation and sophistication in the business environment. In this way they have been able to aggregate value to goods and services in such a way as to more than compensate for these differentials in the costs of highly specialized labour. They can do this because they are able to enforce premium prices for their goods and services in export markets through exceptional brands of global notoriety.

We conclude therefore that a model of competitiveness based on low-cost production will never be viable for any European nation, as it would be subjected to intense competition coming out of the Far East and other emerging economies. A context of unhindered international trade and a continuous flow of goods and people render the notion of a national economy, confined to a limited geography or territory, as inappropriate and most likely redundant.

The mobility of capital, organizations and increasingly of people makes it difficult to determine the origin of firms and of the products that emanate from them. National competitiveness therefore, and the ability of an economy to aggregate value to exported goods or to attract FDI, is more and more a function of its singularity and its capacity for insulating its offer, and the set of characteristics that confer it a competitive advantage and distinguish it from others. These traits may be technical in nature or be traced back to a knowledge base, a tradition, or a way of doing things, but together they constitute the overall country offer.

The potential for the replication of the unique features that derive from complex manufacturing processes may be low, when and if these processes and their resultant products have been patented and licensed. But even more difficult to imitate are brands that have acquired strong and favourable reputations with sophisticated consumers in foreign markets, and which can be traced back to manufacturing sectors in economies that benefit from positive country of origin cues. In the same way, savvy and rational investors that can opt to invest wherever they want to will want to look for something unique and different from all the other alternative investment options in other geographies and economic realities.

In a truly global economy, and given the description above, any idea of competition based on low labour costs for a European economy, no matter what the average wages are in that country, will be nothing but a colossal strategic mistake. This is of particular relevance to European economies in that it is simply impossible to fight competition from the emerging economies in an effective manner with a low labour cost model. Whether wages are high or low has to be analysed in the context of the productivity levels associated with those wages. Low wages may occur in contexts of abysmal productivity levels, and on the contrary high wages may be paid in contexts where the very high productivity levels in these economies would justify even higher wages.

The main symptom that something is structurally imbalanced in some European economies is the acknowledgement that the low salaries paid in some countries go hand in hand with the even poorer productivity levels in these economies. This means that low wage economies are precisely those that rank lower in the correlation tables linking productivity and salaries. In other words, the wages in these economies are low but they are still higher than what their productivity levels justify. This appears to be the case in the poorer economies in Europe, particularly those who still possess significant labour-intensive sectors of economic activity. This is a huge problem in that citizens in these nations share a common geography in the EU and they have been wrongly led to believe that they should expect a similar treatment to that of other Europeans, as if wage levels were a political question and not a sheer consequence of what the economy can take. Although the citizens of some European economies believe that their wages are low, they are still too high when contrasted against the productivity levels that are generated. The productivity levels in these economies are too low for the salaries that are paid.

The empirical evidence suggests that national competitiveness is correlated with productivity and salaries. This is true of Switzerland and Singapore and less true of Germany and the Scandinavian nations as we saw. It further indicates that the workers in the more competitive nations have higher average wages than those of workers in other nations whose competitive performance is more modest. Workers are thus paid higher wages in the more competitive economies to reflect their skills and competencies. The uniqueness of these knowledge-based skills is in turn associated with higher productivity levels in the economy. The mechanism here relates to the singularity of competencies that are offered by skilled labour and that cannot be easily found anywhere else, and what they add to manufacturing processes and to their resultant output.

A knowledgeable worker is capable of offering the kinds of unique competencies that better reflect the exigencies of a global economy. An undifferentiated labour force on the other hand has nothing special to offer to production processes and products, and this means that these are easily susceptible of imitation and hence cannot possibly command value next to discerning industrial buyers or consumers in the global markets. Productivity levels are necessarily low in these cases.

Skilled workers, on the other hand, operate in capital-intensive, knowledge-laden manufacturing and business environments, in economies that are precisely the ones that show up at the top of the competitiveness rankings. These are also the economies where the highest positive correlations between productivity and salaries can be found, meaning that wages have to reflect worker productivities and not the other way around.

This shows unequivocally that the labour productivity problem is not to be attributable first and foremost to the worker, but it is rather about a much more complex problem that involves every stakeholder in a modern economy, and in particular entrepreneurs, who need to be dynamic and pro-active in understanding and anticipating markets as well as management, that need to endow workers with the necessary skills that will make the output of their work more valuable and more productive.

The correlation between salaries and productivity is relevant because it shows that in the final analysis, in capital-intensive sectors that are characterized by strong technological content and high levels of applied knowledge, what matters is not so much the remuneration of the labour force, it is instead whether wages are reflective of the value added to processes and products by skilled workers with unique and inimitable knowledge resources. Wages have to reflect productivity levels then, and as a corollary to this thought, wage increases with a view to increasing productivity are inadmissible policy mistakes. It is not whether workers are paid handsome salaries. It is more about those salaries being or not being accurate reflections of the complexity and sophistication of labour skills and their contribution to high value-added goods and services. This is the only economic rationale and relevant scrutiny that should be used here, and it should not be underpinned by subjective moral or ethical judgment.

What is also of relevance is the assessment of the singularity of what these individuals are able to offer to production processes and products, and the acknowledgement that the uniqueness of a labour force results from systematic investments in the acquisition of specialist skills. If on the other hand these skills can be easily found anywhere in the world, in that they require minimal effort in their attainment, then the labour force that is required by an economy is undifferentiated and massified and wages will have to be low enough to reflect that.

This means that often even when wages are considered to be low they are too high for the corresponding productivities that the economic activities that they remunerate are able to generate. What ultimately makes salaries be judged to be high or low in relation to corresponding productivities is how labour skills and competencies translate into the aggregation of value to goods and services that avid consumers want to buy and pay premium prices for.

The salaries of workers are also higher in economies with strong export sectors that possess excellent brands of global notoriety and enormous accounting goodwill. This once again brings to the forefront the issue of workers' wages, and the imperative of paying more to those who, by virtue of the rarity and exclusivity of their skills, competencies and inimitable knowledge applied to processes and products, are able to aggregate value to resultant goods and services. This constitutes a decisive contribution to the numerator of output in the productivity ratio of an economy.

We can therefore conclude that it is precisely the more competitive economies, where the best companies coexist, aggregating value to goods and services in key export sectors, controlling the links that generate more value in international value chains, that are able to attract more and better FDI and can, by virtue of this, pay their workers higher wages. Crucially, these economies also possess very dynamic domestic markets. All of this corroborates the systemic and integrated nature of modern economies where performance on the drivers of national competitiveness needs to be looked at in comparative and dynamic terms.

The problem with economies that have low labour productivities may be linked to other issues related to the characterization of the labour force, such as worker training deficiencies, its intellectual and technical unpreparedness to acquire specific competencies, difficulty in applying complex knowledge skills to good use in highly sophisticated production processes and in augmenting benefits to core product functionality. All of this is the responsibility of workers in that they are direct intervenients in manufacturing processes, however it is nevertheless a much more fundamental task of pro-active entrepreneurship and senior management as well as that of strategic policy-makers operating at a macro-level of the economy.

The ability to develop a unique set of labour skills will therefore determine the higher or lower ability of workers in an economy in aggregating value to the output of that economy. In that way, the determination of wage levels needs to be linked to the value that is generated by the unique set of skills that are contributed to complex production processes, and that are not susceptible of easy replication from competitors elsewhere. The productivity levels of workers are therefore not about the quantity of output generated for a specific allocation of productive inputs in an economy, but rather, ceteris paribus and given an optimal allocation of production inputs about the market value of that output.

The solution to low national productivity levels is not necessarily about the lowering of workers' wages and in many aspects what needs to be done is precisely the opposite of this. Workers need to acquire the best possible competencies and knowledge-based skills to then transfer these to production processes and products, and only then justify higher wages.

If, however, the economy is fundamentally labour-intensive, then in keeping up with competitor's low labour costs, wages need to be reduced in order for an economy to remain competitive. Of course in reality and in the light of the civilizational space occupied by nations where these workers apply their trade, it is impossible to compete with the very low wages of competing emerging economies. Failing that, the only way out of this is to focus on innovation, education and worker training in capital-intensive sectors, with a view to escape the determinism of low-cost labour from these less developed nations.

In so doing, workers are able to interact with technology in sophisticated production processes and augment value to products. Workers deal with technological complexity better as they are more skilled, making both processes and products much more sophisticated and appealing to discerning consumers and much more difficult to imitate. Thus economies benefitting from specialized labour are better equipped to supply goods and services that are more in tune with the requirements of external markets.

Workers that are equipped with complex knowledge in capital-intensive and technology-based sectors of economic activity, whose set of competitive advantages are difficult to replicate, will naturally contribute to products and services by aggregating immense value to them. It is not only about the potential for replication of technology but fundamentally about the applied knowledge base that is needed to extract value from the combination of technology and labour expertise in complex production processes.

In addition to knowledge of a technical nature and the technological requirements imposed by capital-intensive sectors of economic activity, there is also the imperative of market knowledge and the creation, nurturing and management of product and corporate brands. Only this way can an economy aggregate value to its exports and facilitate the attraction of FDI into its shores. Aggregation of value to exports and higher FDI are important contributors to GDP growth and national productivity. Productivity and wages are in this way strongly correlated.

In the light of the current global economic context, characterized as one of extreme competitive intensity, in almost every sector of economic activity, there are important questions that need to be asked. Is there a typology of national competitiveness that unites innate sociological characteristics as well as other acquired traits of the collective character of nations? Is there an archetype of competitiveness that is adequate for certain nations, but not for others? If a society does not possess this important set of characteristics collectively, does this mean that its economy is simply incapable of being competitive?

If a nation follows a particular path to competitiveness that is not in accordance with its cultural idiosyncrasies and identity, societal characteristics and specificities, can it effectively pursue a sustainable competitive strategy? In the light of substantive differences in culture, can the economy of a nation not pursue a different model of competitiveness that fits better with its cultural identity, its peoples, tradition and history? How does this happen and how can it be effected in concrete action? How can a nation play the global competitiveness game with any degree of success, improve its indicators of social and economic development, and do this in accordance with the specificity of its peoples and its cultural idiosyncrasy?

A strong competitive intensity in the domestic market, and its characterization as dynamic and sophisticated, are determinant factors of the competitiveness of a nation. This means that firms in key export sectors that are accustomed to a strongly contested domestic market will be better prepared to face the demands of the more sophisticated external markets, as any organization that is able to handle key domestic value chains successfully, will know how to cater to stringent buying requisites abroad. Learning with the state of the art of competition in economic sectors worldwide is compulsory as competitiveness is not about waking up one day and deciding that we are all of a sudden going to be competitive. It is a state of mind that should pervade people in organizations, economic sectors and entire national economies.

Competitiveness has to be both a philosophy and a systemic process, entailing the collective behaviours of stakeholders in an economy, working towards the same end, in the knowledge that in the light of global economic dynamics, to be competitive is not an option. It is instead critical to the survival of firms operating in cut-throat business environments and crucially to the survival of the lifestyles of individuals, at least to the standards that they have been accustomed to.

In the light of intensely disputed markets and the volatility of the world economy, competition for consumer preference is simply an inevitability of life. If we don't do it, someone else will, and they will do it cheaper too. A nation's ability to be more or less competitive has a direct bearing on indicators of human and social development for the society in question. A competitive nation is one with huge potential for wealth creation and thus competitiveness is a good barometer of socio-economic development.

With time, and with the constant challenges that come from the business environment, individuals and organizations, economic sectors and whole economies become very good at what they do. If whatever they do, they do better than the competition, consistently and systematically, then it stands to reason that they are able to improve their competitive position vis-à-vis that of other nations, who contest the same consumer markets and attract the same sources of FDI.

It is about submerging into a globally competitive context in a particular sector of economic activity, and to acknowledge that success, however it is measured, from survival, to commercial success, to consistently achieving above average returns on investment and profitability is not independent of the actual and potential competitive context in that sector of economic activity, and the capacity of organizations in excelling in difficult contexts.

This has to be put into perspective in a global context, as with falling barriers to the movement of capital, people and firms, abnormal profitability levels in a certain sector attract global players to that sector of economic activity, thus increasing competition and reducing average profitability levels to what the competitive environment allows. When this happens a condition for survival is to work on criteria of competitiveness that ensure distinctiveness and perceived superior value, both of which are not easy to achieve in strongly competed business environments.

Being competitive in the global market is also a complex process that cannot be sorted from one day to the next, no matter how good one's strategic idea is for the competitiveness of a nation. The strategic success of an economy in a global setting is not independent of the competitive characterization of domestic markets, the capital of goodwill accumulated by brands that organizations in those economies embody (both product and corporate) and the values that they personify and represent to their principal stakeholders in sophisticated markets.

These target markets consist of affluent consumers that have disposable income, and are more in tune with the permanent search for the satisfaction of hedonistic needs, adopting buying criteria that go well beyond price, design or technical content, to include aesthetic expressions of their individualized preferences or the societal values of the places where they belong. The most competitive economies in the world are those that are able to understand the rules and complexity of this game, and the most competitive firms in those economies are those that adopt these principles as their unequivocal and unambiguous philosophy. In this context, the history of these product and corporate brands is a guarantor of quality in the consumption experience and the satisfaction of hedonistic dimensions of consumption, that go well beyond the functional needs of consumers, and that characterize contemporary consumer markets, should be the overriding objective of firms operating in any modern economy.

This is a radical shift from yesteryear, not because the luxury ends of most markets were not there before, on the contrary there have always been higher ends within every market segment, but with disposable income and rising brand awareness, people are willing to pay price premiums for what are functionally the same products. What used to happen though was that the mass market was a huge chunk of the totality of consumer expenditure in most markets, and now just about every consumer market has its own little niches and specificities that require different value propositions and clever responses on the part of suppliers. Every consumer market and perhaps every industrial market are susceptible to segmentation of one kind or another.

Product or corporate brands achieve that which suppliers with no track record, history or presence in the imagination and minds of sophisticated consumers abroad cannot hope to achieve, or at least find it much more difficult to do, and that is for these products to be in some way distinguishable, valued and preferred by consumers who know them and what they stand for.

From that we can conclude that those organizations and their products are able to command a capital of reputational *goodwill* that makes their business clients (B2B) or customers (B2C) prefer them and their brands to others in the buying decision-making process whilst, crucially, also being willing to pay more for them. It is possible to conclude then that the idea of being competitive at an international and even global scale does not happen overnight. It is worth acknowledging that this is a morose process, variable from sector to sector, expensive and requiring of persistence in the management of stakeholders and their expectations.

There are examples, including that of post-war Japan, where change in external stakeholder perceptions had to be managed in line with the objectives of internationalization of the Japanese economy. This took decades to be effected with a degree of success. What is implied here is that positive country of origin effects are linked with national competitiveness, but changing national stereotype cannot be done overnight.

There are organizational examples of successful change in external stakeholder perceptions about organizations emanating from certain countries. The aforementioned case of Spanish group Inditex, owners of remarkable retail brands including the likes of Zara, Massimo Dutti and others, is an example of an organization that in a little over two decades went from zero to global notoriety and incredible commercial success. In reality, the Spanish retail fashion industry and the Spanish economy has been anything but a contributor to the competitiveness of the Inditex group and its flagship corporate brand Zara, both from the viewpoint of the little intensity of competitiveness in the domestic market or the sophistication of its business environment. The perceptions held by foreign stakeholders of Spain and Spanish fashion has never been one of trendy cosmopolitanism and vanguard values. On the contrary, Spain insofar as fashion retailing is concerned, has always been regarded as parochial and peripheral, at least in the Anglo-Saxon world.

There is then no alternative for European economies other than to learn to compete globally through constant exposure to demanding market situations that will sharpen their competitive abilities. Firms and economic sectors need to compete through the real determinants of competitiveness in the light of current macro-economic settings and scenarios and the global business environment that characterizes most contemporary markets and economic relations between nations.

All of this is of course not independent from a greater or lesser sustainability of a federalist European political model, but any future path for Europe does not preclude individual economies from seeking to acquire the competitive conditions that are required from them in the global economy. The problem is that in this as in all other matters there is no such thing as a homogeneous and balanced Europe.

The EU has amongst its constituent member nations countries that rank very highly in the global competitiveness tables living alongside others that are totally unprepared for the exigencies of modern economic competitiveness, as these nations have not been able to take full advantage of the investments made in bringing them up to scratch when it comes to the acquisition of the competencies that traduce the real determinants of competition in a globalized world.

The very idea of a European super state should mean for the smaller nations precisely the antithesis of a posture of abdication of responsibility and a downplaying of the importance of these smaller economies seeking to be truly competitive in their own right. The worst possible outcome for all is the free-riding of the smaller nations on the back of the more competitive and wealthier nations, as this will generate inevitable and understandable animosity.

A loss of political sovereignty, in a context where these nations have long lost their ability to exercise any control over macro-economic policy, have no monetary or exchange rate levers and are only left with stringent guidelines on taxation and spending policy, should only force the governments of these nations to procure and instill a philosophy of competitiveness in firms, sectors of economic activity and entire economies – a focus on micro-economics that allows for the safeguarding of these nations as politically independent entities, thus ensuring their economic viability. If the less economically developed member states in Europe lose political sovereignty, in the name of a united and federalist Europe, and on top of that their national economies are also uncompetitive in the global arena, then these nations lose their sovereignty and autonomy altogether.

There is a widely held view in the more vulnerable economies in Europe that, whenever needed, the wealthier nations will come to their aid. There is of course a risk of moral hazard in this, in that much like the psychological effect of currency devaluation on national competitiveness, the perception that there is always a cop out, an easy solution, an abdication of responsibility that results from not needing to be competitive via the real determinants of competitiveness, is an awful legacy to leave, one that perpetuates a state of dependency and which of course translates into a complete abdication of national sovereignty and the moral and ethical stigma that comes with free-riding.

This is endemic to the collective psyche of the smaller European economies and may induce a much unwanted relaxation over fundamental matters, notably the effective reduction in public expenditure and fiscal discipline as well as, crucially, the imperative of a reformist agenda, both pre-conditions to the creation of a macro-environment that allows for a leap forward in national competitiveness. More than anything, the reformist agenda that leads to the revoking of incumbent models of national competitiveness is absolutely critical for the future economic growth of European nations in the light of a globalized economy.

As can be easily inferred from the abrupt falls in the competitiveness rankings of these smaller European economies over the last few years, and faced with the scenario that characterizes the world economy today, the paradigm shift that needs to occur in national competitiveness models cannot be delayed. A reformist agenda that leads to the improvement of national competitiveness needs to be implemented and, if it is not, there are serious risks of a strong civilizational retrocess with a tremendous negative impact on short-term indicators of the quality of life of individuals, as is already the case in countries like Greece, Spain, Ireland and Portugal, with others swiftly and surely following suit.

Nobody will come to save the day and financial aid will always have corresponding trade-offs as there is no such thing as a free lunch. Any notion of a spirit of European cooperation will never replace the imperative of these smaller nations in taking good care over their own destinies. It is simply not possible to waste an historical reformist opportunity that leads to a paradigm shift in the competitive models of the economies of the less competitive nations.

It is thus crucial that any financial aid package is not misconstrued as the perpetuation of the European federalist myth that leads to the abdication of collective national responsibility and crucially nullifies the so-called feeling of urgency, of being between a rock and a hard place, which inevitably leads to paradigm shifts and to civilizational leaps forward as societies are confronted with the inevitable. Amidst all of this it is crucial that the people are not forgotten, which calls for an equitable distribution of the collective effort and a true and healthy spirit of compassion for the more vulnerable, both marks of great civilizations.

Over and beyond the aspects of financing of small and medium-sized firms and the credit crunch that businesses have been feeling for half a decade now, which are in themselves crucial and need urgent addressing, it is critical that the conditions are created for organizations to finally resort to their reserves of competency and creativity, and to compete openly in markets, not expecting the protectionist hand of government to be there whenever market conditions take a turn for the worse.

In the cases of the smaller European economies their governments cannot help them, and in the cases of the wealthier nations they have their own problems to attend to. Organizations that do not possess their own in-house competencies will have to acquire them in order to be competitive in domestic markets first and in foreign ones subsequently. Those who fail to do this are doomed in the light of current competitive dynamics.

The state has the role of acting as a facilitator in the simplification of bureaucracy, and in making institutions function, ensuring transparency and justice. The state also has a role as instigator of a strategic path for the nation, defining general strategic orientations for the competitiveness of the economy, coordinating, monitoring and correcting the strategic trajectory through legislative action or through stimuli that lead to more competitive economic sectors.

The state also has as its function – the definition of a roadmap of competitiveness, articulating the nation's resources with implicit market requirements – but it is not up to the state to replace the fundamental task of firms, that of doing their homework, which consists of the characterization of market demand dynamically and preferably in real time and subsequently responding to it effectively.

The market, for better and for worse, will eliminate those players that do not show any competitive viability. This Darwinistic-like natural selection of organizations will mean the prevalence of firms in economic sectors operating in clusters, localized pockets of integrated specialist knowledge and technical know-how, history and tradition, catering to foreign markets who avidly dispute the goods that emanate from them.

A market logic that imposes clever links and interconnections between industry and universities and centres of excellence in research in particular areas of high potential economic value is what is sought, as is the interface between the economics of value chains and knowledge applied in them, including both technical and market knowledge. In order for any of this to materialize or have any significant expression or relevance downstream for sophisticated consumers, products of excellence that eventually come out of manufacturing processes still have only achieved part of the objective. They still need to be packaged under a brand mantra of values that coincide with those that are sought by consumers in key target markets and commercialized under brand names of great notoriety and value, reflected into significant increments of accounting goodwill in the balance sheets of organizations.

The latter part of the statement above is crucial in that even if all of the technical criteria for success are verified, many firms will never be viable in a global competitive context, as those who are simply unable to work on the soft skills of their market offer will not be successful. These soft skills are erroneously called soft in that, in effect, they are critical determinants of firm competitiveness in foreign markets. In other words, without the soft dimensions of supply, firms are not ready to face a world that looks for the full monty of technological prowess, expressed in quality excellence as well as exquisite brands that people recognize and ascribe immense value to.

Organizations which have the know-how and technical knowledge in sectors with some tradition and history, but that have not worked well in translating the determinants of foreign market demand into brands that respond to them effectively, or which have not thought these issues through in pro-active and strategic ways, are not formatted for success in markets of intense competition and exigency.

Organizations are often not orientated towards an idea that stands above all others, that more than an idea is a philosophy of the critical importance of aggregating value to goods and services at all stages, from production to distribution and consumption. This needs to pervade each task, each stage of the productive process, each link in each value chain, beginning with the search for the optimal combination of inputs in the production process and ending with after-sales service and a constant scrutiny and monitoring of consumer satisfaction.

There is often in many organizations a psychological gap between what is an entrenched domestic philosophy, an all pervasive orientation towards the attainment of production efficiencies, a focus on excellence in the pursuit of the tangible dimensions of supply on the one hand, and the external competitive imperative of having to exceed the expectations of ever more demanding consumers on the other.

The model of national competitiveness suggested below is based on the idea of a dynamic adequacy between a set of interdependent domestic factors and volatile external determinants. The level of adequacy that is permanently sought between domestic and external factors will determine the ability of a nation to be consistently competitive. It is in the systematic search for the minimization of this gap in performance between actionable domestic factors and dynamic external determinants that a nation's ability to compete globally, its capacity for value aggregation to exports of transactionable goods, as well as the improvement in its appeal for much desired FDI inflows resides.

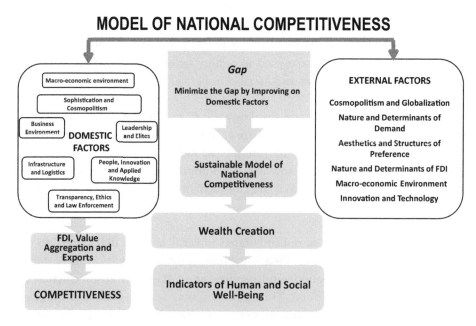

Figure 10.5   Model of national competitiveness

It follows that an overriding national policy objective for the competitiveness of nations has to be one of a persistent and systemic improvement on the performance of domestic factors in a balanced and harmonious way, with a particular focus on the removal of obstacles that constitute true bottlenecks to competitiveness.

In presenting a general model of competitiveness for nations in the twenty-first century, the empirical evidence has allowed for the identification of the real determinants of national competitiveness, and in particular the criteria that uniformly characterize the most competitive economies, those that export more, that are more capable of aggregating value to their exports and those nations which are best at attracting FDI.

More often than not these are the same nations. The ones that are competitive are the ones that export more, and not just any kind of exports, but rather goods of higher aggregated value. These nations are also the best at attracting FDI into their shores. Nations that outperform their competitors on the true determinants of global competitiveness are well on their way to overcoming the challenges that are posed to them by the global modern economy of the twenty-first century.

References

Ariely, D. (2008): *Predictably Irrational*, Harper Perennial.

Barro, R. J. (2003): *Nothing is Sacred: Economic Ideas for the New Millennium*, The MIT Press.

Becker, D., Hill, S. (2010): *The Coaches*, Sports Wisdom.

Deming, W. E. (2000): *Out of the Crisis*, The MIT Press.

Doyle, P. (1992): *Marketing Management and Strategy*, Prentice Hall.

Doyle, P. (1999): *Value-based Marketing: Marketing Strategies for Corporate Growth and Shareholder Value*, Wiley.

Espejo, R., Harnden, R. (1989): *Viable System Model: Interpretations and Applications of Staffford Beer's VSM*, John Wiley & Sons Ltd.

Friedman, M., Friedman, R. (1979): *Free to Choose*, Down Jones & Co., Inc.

Fuller, S. (2003): *Kuhn vs. Popper: The Struggle for the Soul of Science (Revolutions in Science)*, Icon Books Ltd.

Galbraith, J. K. (1967): *The New Industrial State*, Princeton University Press.

Galbraith, J. K. (1958): *The Affluent Society*, Houghton Mifflin.

Han, C. and Terpstra, V. (1988): 'Country of Origin Effects for Uni-National and Bi-National Products'. *Journal of International Business Studies*, Vol. 19, No. 2, summer, pp. 235–55.

Interbrand (2012): 'Best Global Brands – 2012'.

IMD World Competitiveness Center (2010): 'World Competitiveness Yearbook'.

Krefetz, G., Gittelman (1982): *The Book of Incomes*, Holt, Rinehart, and Winston.

Moore, M. (2004): *Dude, Where's My Country?*, Warner Books.

Moore, M. (2002): *Stupid White Men*, HarperCollins

Morello, G. (1984): 'The "Made In" Issue: A Comparative Research on the Image of Domestic and Foreign Products'. *European Research*, Vol. 12, No. 1, January, pp. 4–21.

Peters, T. J. and Waterman, R. H. (1982): *In Search of Excellence: Lessons from America's Best-Run Companies*, Harper Paperbacks.

Samuelson, P. A. and Nordhaus, W. D. (1999): *Economics*, 16th Edition, McGraw-Hill Companies.

Schooler, R. D., Wildt, A. R. and Jones, J. M. (1987): 'Strategy Development for Manufactured Exports of Third World Countries to Developed Countries'. *Journal of Global Marketing*, Vol. 1, No. 1–2, fall–winter, pp. 53–68.

Senge, P. (1990): *The Fifth Discipline: The Art and Practice of the Learning Organization*, Doubleday.

Smith, T. (1992): *Accounting for Growth: Stripping the Camouflage from Company Accounts*, Random House.

Soros, G. (2009): *The Crash of 2008 and What it Means: The New Paradigm for Financial Markets*, Public Affairs.

Soros, G. (1998): *The Crisis of Global Capitalism: Open Society Endangered'*, Public Affairs.

Stiglitz, J. (2010): *Freefall: Free Markets and the Sinking of the Global Economy*, W. W: Norton & Company. Inc.

UNCTAD (2008): 'World Investment Report'.

UNCTAD (2012): 'World Investment Report'.

Webster's English Dictionary: Canadian Edition (2002): Strathearn.

World Economic Forum (2000 to 2012): 'Global Competitiveness Report'.

World Trade Organization (2012): 'Annual Report 2012'.

Web References

www.fitchratings.com
www.moodys.com
www.standardandpoors.com

Index

For Product Safety Concerns and Information please contact our EU
representative GPSR@taylorandfrancis.com Taylor & Francis Verlag GmbH,
Kaufingerstraße 24, 80331 München, Germany

Printed and bound by CPI Group (UK) Ltd, Croydon, CR0 4YY

01/05/2025

01858368-0007